MAY 2009

DATE DUE

ation:

Guide

Virtualization:
A Beginner's Guide

DANIELLE **RUEST**
NELSON **RUEST**

New York   Chicago   San Francisco
Lisbon   London   Madrid   Mexico City   Milan
New Delhi   San Juan   Seoul   Singapore   Sydney   Toronto

The McGraw·Hill Companies

Library of Congress Cataloging-in-Publication Data

Ruest, Danielle.
 Virtualization: a beginner's guide/Danielle Ruest, Nelson Ruest.
    p. cm.
 Includes index.
 ISBN 978-0-07-161401-6 (alk. paper)
 1. Virtual computer systems. I. Ruest, Nelson. II. Title.
 QA76.9.V5R88 2009
 005.4'3–dc22

                                         2008055751

McGraw-Hill books are available at special quantity discounts to use as premiums and sales pro-motions, or for use in corporate training programs. To contact a special sales representative, please visit the Contact Us page at www.mhprofessional.com.

Virtualization: A Beginner's Guide

1234567890   DOC DOC   019

ISBN   978-0-07-161401-6
MHID   0-07-161401-X

Sponsoring Editor Jane K. Brownlow	**Copy Editor** Lisa McCoy	**Illustration** International Typesetting and Composition Danielle Ruest, Resolutions Enterprises Ltd.
Editorial Supervisor Patty Mon	**Proofreader** Bev Weiler	
Project Manager Madhu Bhardwaj (International Typesetting and Composition)	**Indexer** Steve Ingle	**Art Director, Cover** Jeff Weeks
	Production Supervisor Jean Bodeaux	
Technical Editors Chris Wolfe Ruben Spruijt Duncan Epping	**Composition** International Typesetting and Composition	

This book is dedicated to everyone who wants to move to a virtual infrastructure. There's a lot of hype in the hypervisor market, and we hope this book will help you wade through it. Good luck with your projects!

ABOUT THE AUTHORS

Danielle Ruest and **Nelson Ruest** are IT futurists specializing in IT infrastructure optimization and efficiency. They are authors of multiple books, including *Microsoft Windows Server 2008: The Complete Reference* (McGraw-Hill), the *MCITP Self-Paced Training Kit (Exam 70-238): Deploying Messaging Solutions with Microsoft Exchange Server 2007* and the *MCITP Self-Paced Training Kit (Exam 70-640): Configuring Windows Server 2008 Active Directory* (Microsoft Press), as well as the *Vista Deployment and Administration Bible* (Wiley and Sons). Their next book is *MCITP Self-Paced Training Kit (Exam 70-652): Configuring Windows Server Virtualization*.

Danielle and Nelson have been touring the United States for two years, delivering a multicity tour on "Virtualization: Five Steps from Pilot to Production" (http://events .techtarget.com/virtualization2008), which is designed to help organizations move to a virtual infrastructure. They have also delivered several full-day courses on virtualization, mostly at Interop in Las Vegas (www.interop.com). Both are involved as freelance writers for several IT publications, as well as producing white papers for various vendors (www.reso-net.com/articles.asp?m=8) and delivering webcasts and conferences (www.reso-net.com/presentation.asp?m=7).

Nelson and Danielle work for Resolutions Enterprises, a consulting firm focused on IT infrastructure optimization. Resolutions Enterprises has been in business for more than 20 years and can be found at www.Reso-Net.com.

About the Technical Editors

Chris Wolfe is a senior analyst for Burton Group Data Center Strategies. He covers server virtualization and data center consolidation, data protection, management and classification, disaster recovery, and business continuity. Prior to joining Burton Group, Chris was a nationally recognized independent consultant, the CIS department head at the ECPI College of Technology, and consultant with CommVault Systems. With 14 years of experience in virtualization, data protection and recovery, high availability, and enterprise storage management, Chris is an industry leader in virtualization coverage. Chris also authored *Virtualization: From the Desktop to the Enterprise*, the first book published on the topic. His virtualization presentations and workshops are consistently amongst the highest rated sessions at conferences in both the United States and Europe.

Ruben Spruijt works as Solutions Architect at PQR, a major IT company that designs, implements, and migrates advanced IT infrastructure, and is a Microsoft Gold Certified Partner, Citrix Platinum Solution Advisor, VMware Premier and Consultancy Partner in the Netherlands. In his job, Ruben is primarily focused on Application and Desktop Delivery, hardware and software virtualization. He is a Citrix Certified Integration Architect (CCIA), Citrix Certified Enterprise Administrator (CCEA), and Microsoft Certified Systems Engineer (MCSE+S). Ruben has been awarded the Microsoft Most Value Professional (MVP), Citrix Technology Professional (CTP), and RES Software Value Professional (RSVP). He has written several articles that can be downloaded from www.virtuall.eu.

Duncan Epping is a senior consultant for VMware's Professional Services Organization (PSO) in the Netherlands. His main focus is Server Virtualization. He also runs a blog on Yellow-Bricks.com that mainly deals with virtualization topics. He has extensive experience with virtualization projects of all sizes and is passionate about the technology.

AT A GLANCE

CONTENTS

Part I
Architect for Virtualization

Part III

Consolidate the Benefits

FOREWORD

Virtualization is a technology with a lengthy history, dating back to work by IBM in the late 1960s and early 1970s. That being said, it's easy to find a little irony in the fact that you're standing here holding a copy of *Virtualization: A Beginner's Guide*. If virtualization has been around for so long, why on earth would you need a *beginner's guide*? The answer to that question is probably the reason why you're reading this in the first place.

What has changed about a technology that has existed for 40 years? Virtualization's intent and core concepts aren't much different, but as it reaches the age of 40, one could say that virtualization is having a bit of a midlife crisis. If virtualization could go back and change anything about its life, it turns out that it would change a lot. Virtualization never really wanted to be a proprietary technology, limited to select vendors and very expensive hardware. Instead what virtualization really wanted was to be free and open to anyone who wanted to use it, and to be able to run on commodity x86 hardware.

So if you're just getting to meet virtualization, you've met it at the right time. Virtualization is no longer a fringe technology for IT's rich and famous, but it is a technology for everyone. Practically all IT shops use virtualization technology in one form or another today, and virtualization is emerging as a core building block for most IT infrastructures. For many organizations, x86 server virtualization is a way of life. All new applications are deployed as virtual machines (VMs) unless the application owner can justify why a physical resource is needed.

Virtualization removes the physical hardware dependencies from server operating systems, allowing them to be moved and recovered like never before. Instead of having to perform scheduled hardware maintenance at some obscure hour over the weekend, server administrators can now live migrate a VM to another physical resource and perform physical server hardware maintenance in the middle of the business day. This level of flexibility has allowed many of us in the IT community to find something that has been missing for a very long time—predictable time off and a personal life to go along with it! In addition, I've worked with several organizations that had abandoned disaster recovery (DR) tests because "they were bad for morale." Discrepancies in physical resources between production and DR sites would make disaster recovery testing extremely complex and a massive strain to IT resources. As you can imagine, the hardware independence brought about by virtualization has removed the traditional complexities associated with DR and has allowed many organizations to reliably test DR much more frequently than they ever had. In fact, I've found that organizations using virtualization as a core element in their DR strategy became fully confident in the execution of their DR recovery plan for the very first time.

Virtualization is changing almost every aspect of how we manage systems, storage, networks, security, operating systems, and applications. Making matters worse, you now have countless virtualization alternatives at your disposal. Weighing the pros and cons of each choice as well as successfully implementing and managing them is no easy task. That is why I personally have found the content of this book so valuable. I first started working with x86 virtualization technologies in 2000. Back then some of my colleagues were calling VMware "VM Scare." It's safe to say that no one is scared or laughing now. Still, while I've had the benefit of watching x86 virtualization mature, I've also witnessed the extensive growth of complexity associated with correctly deploying, securing, and managing virtual infrastructures. Understanding the nuances associated with each virtualization platform is essential for successfully deploying virtualization solutions and avoiding the hazards that a particular solution may present.

If you've made it this far, I really hope you continue reading. Nelson Ruest and Danielle Ruest are IT and virtualization experts who share their immense knowledge in this book. I have long been a fan of both Nelson and Danielle because of their methodical easy-to-digest writing style and the relevance to real-world problems contained within their work. If you're looking to hit the ground running with any virtualization project, large or small, this book is going to give you the start you need, and along the way will offer you some cautionary tales that will even take some seasoned virtualization veterans by surprise.

—Chris Wolf, Senior Analyst, Burton Group

ACKNOWLEDGMENTS

Thank you to all of our course and session attendees for helping us make this book as complete as possible. Your questions have greatly helped flesh out the issues that most anyone moving to a virtual infrastructure will be concerned about. Also, thank you to the vendors included in this book for being so candid with information on their products.

Thank you to our multiple technical reviewers for their diligent efforts in reviewing the book and making sure that its technical content was as correct as it could be.

Thank you to McGraw-Hill for giving us the opportunity to help IT professionals everywhere by writing this book. Also, thank you to the production team for making this one of the easiest book productions we have ever participated in. Keep up the good work!

INTRODUCTION

There's a new wind of change in the IT industry today. It's called virtualization. Virtualization in the datacenter can occur at several levels, but the type of virtualization that has created this wind of change is guest operating system (OS) or server virtualization. Guest OS virtualization is a software layer that provides the ability to expose physical resources to make them available to several different virtual machines at the same time. Guest OS virtualization technologies come in two flavors. The first is a software layer that is used to simulate a physical machine on top of an existing operating system running on a hardware host. The second is a hypervisor—a software engine that runs directly on top of the hardware, eliminating the overhead of a secondary operating system.

Whichever version of server virtualization you use, it is this ability to run one or more virtual machines on top of one physical host that has opened up all sorts of possibilities in the datacenter. With this technology, it is now much easier to create testing, training, or development, and even production environments, and turn them into malleable entities that respond to business needs when they appear. For training, development, and testing environments, this technology is especially useful because you can easily reset them to original settings whenever a session has been completed. It is also easier to create secure virtual desktop environments as well as rely on virtualization to reduce the total number of physical boxes to manage. In addition, virtualization solves most, if not all, of the problems organizations have always had with application management. Finally, virtualization opens up vast possibilities in terms of business continuity.

However, bringing all of these technologies together into a single clear architecture can be an unruly task at best. This is what this book attempts to do. And to make it easier for everyone to understand, it has been divided into three parts which together, form the **ABCs of Virtualization**.

The ABCs of Virtualization is based on three key tasks:

▼ Part I: Architect for Virtualization begins the exploration of all of the different virtualization layers and how they fit together in the modern datacenter. It is composed of three chapters, each of which outlines a part of the five-step program Resolutions has been touting for more than two years for the implementation of a virtual infrastructure.

■ Part II: Build Your Virtualization Infrastructure begins the build process and moves you through each of the detailed steps you need to perform to transform your existing datacenter into a dynamic datacenter, one that will respond dynamically to each of your business needs. Chapters 4 and 5 help you look at what needs to change at the physical layer. Chapter 6 helps you get started by outlining how to transform your existing training, testing, and development environments into virtual infrastructures. Chapters 7, 8, and 9 help you implement server virtualization and move your current workloads into virtual machines. Chapter 10 details how you can profit from desktop virtualization, both at the local and at the central level. Chapters 11 and 12 complete this section by looking at how you can take advantage of application virtualization to resolve all of your application management issues. Chapter 12 finishes off with a look at how you blend server, desktop, and application virtualization together to create volatile virtual desktops that help reduce many of the desktop management woes most organizations face on an ongoing basis.

▲ Part III: Consolidate the Benefits completes the move to virtualization by looking at how your datacenter habits change once you are running a virtual infrastructure. Chapters 13 and 14 look at the security and the protection of your newly updated infrastructure. Chapter 15 lets you examine how you can finally resolve business continuity issues with virtual infrastructures, and Chapter 16 closes off the discussion with a look at how management approaches must change now that you are running virtual workloads instead of physical machines.

Together, these three parts attempt to present a coherent view of virtualization. This will help you move forward with one of the most exciting technologies to appear in the IT world. Virtualization will have several impacts on your existing datacenter, including:

▼ The impact on your network

■ The impact on your operations

■ The impact on your business processes

▲ The impact on your bottom line

The last impact will be the best. Virtualization projects are a rare breed in IT because they actually pay for themselves in a short time. Nevertheless, they are projects and should be managed as such if you want to get it right the first time.

PART I

Architect for Virtualization

CHAPTER 1

The Move to Virtualization

Datacenters around the world are looking to virtualization technologies to reduce their carbon footprint. They are tired of running server systems at 10 percent or less utilization ratios, yet having these systems continue to draw power and require space and cooling just like any other machine. Virtualization promises server hardware usage ratios of 80 percent or more while delivering the same workloads on a much smaller hardware, and therefore carbon, footprint.

Once again, Microsoft is to blame for the situation most datacenter managers find themselves in. Well, it's not really Microsoft's fault—the fault lies in how people have come to use the software Microsoft produces, especially their operating systems. Microsoft Windows became popular in the datacenter with the release of Windows NT Server in the 1990s. At that time, Microsoft was the underdog and competed heavily to make its server operating system (OS) accepted in enterprise datacenters. This is no joke. Some governmental jurisdictions even went as far as implementing binding rulings, stating that Microsoft Windows was not to be used for server or networking workloads at any time. The same occurred in many corporations. Penetrating the datacenter was an uphill battle for Microsoft all the way, but Windows' ability to deliver networked services at the same time as it supported application execution was a compelling offering that no one could resist. The rest is history. Today, most datacenters run some version of Windows on their servers.

But how did these servers get to a 10 percent or less utilization ratio? Well, mostly it was Windows NT's fault. As they deployed this server OS, administrators discovered that Windows NT was a monolithic operating system. Since many operations, especially application operations, were performed at the kernel level of the OS, administrators quickly discovered that when an application froze, it would often freeze the entire OS and cause a Blue Screen of Death (BSOD) for the server as a whole. As a consequence, people started creating single-purpose servers when they deployed workloads on Windows NT. As the name implies, a single-purpose server will only run a single application. If the application fails and causes the server to fail, it will not disrupt any other application that may be co-hosted on the server. This approach quickly trickled down to end-user customers. If a business customer wanted to introduce a new technology to meet a new business need, one of the first things they would state is that they did not want to share workloads with anyone else just to make sure their application was not impacted by any other. This quickly led to massive server proliferation, with projects often introducing several production servers when implementing new technologies, as well as introducing additional servers in support of test and development environments. Based on these approaches, datacenters everywhere quickly saw Windows and other servers proliferate.

Over time, Microsoft solved the monolithic OS problem as they delivered ever-increasingly powerful versions of Windows Server, but people's habits didn't change along with the OS. Still today, end-user customers refuse to have their application hosted on the same server as another, stating that they cannot trust the stability of the other application, or even that they do not want to lose service because another application will have a different update schedule than theirs. Because of this, administrators are often forced to deploy additional physical servers, even if they know better.

Habits aren't the only reason why there is so much server sprawl. Application vendors often require their applications to be isolated in order to support them. In addition, security and new compliance requirements are also causes for application isolation. The more applications you find on a server, the larger the attack surface on that server. In this case, administrators don't have a choice; they must isolate systems and create more servers.

Windows is no longer the problem; it is people's perceptions and long-term habits that need to change. And they need to change fast, with space quickly becoming a premium in the datacenter, cooling systems being overrun by the sheer number of physical servers, and power costs soaring through the roof because of the rising cost of non-renewable resources.

While many people run mixed operating systems in their datacenters, it is mostly because they run Windows servers that they need to consider some form of consolidation, often through virtualization. It is not because of UNIX or Linux, even though the single-purpose server scenario has often spilled over onto these operating systems as well. More than 76 percent of servers being virtualized today run some form of Microsoft Windows (source: Enterprise Strategy Group Brief, Microsoft Will Turn Up the Server Virtualization Volume in 2008, January 2008). You can expect this number to grow as virtualization becomes mainstream this year and the next. Virtualization is a powerful solution for supporting any x86 server transformation, including Windows, UNIX, and Linux.

IN COMES VIRTUALIZATION

Analysts can say what they want, but providing information technology (IT) services is a big job. According to the analyst firm Gartner, more than 70 percent of IT budgets are spent on infrastructure, and in many cases, the numbers can be even worse, especially before consolidation and/or optimization projects.

This is where virtualization can help. Most administrators will look to server virtualization to help reduce the physical footprint of their datacenter. But moving to a virtualized datacenter, whatever its size, is more than just deploying a virtualization engine and converting some physical servers. Like any new technology, virtualization requires serious thought and considerable planning before it can deliver the benefits administrators have come to expect from it. In fact, when you plan for virtualization, you should answer the following questions:

▼　What is virtualization?

■　Why would we need it?

■　How can it improve my business?

■　What types of virtualization technologies exist?

■　Which terms should I be familiar with?

■　What is the cost/benefit ratio of virtualization?

■　What new challenges will it bring to the datacenter?

■　How should I structure my virtualization solution?

- ■ Which applications or services are good virtualization candidates?
- ■ Which server platforms or form factors are best suited to support virtualization?
- ▲ Am I missing anything else?

This is the focus of this book: to help you answer these questions as you ponder virtualization and the potential benefits it can offer your organization.

According to Ziff-Davis Research, February 18, 2008, there are several common virtualization drivers (see Figure 1-1), with the most common being the lowering of hardware costs and an improvement in server utilization ratios. There is no doubt that the major factor driving the move to virtualization is server virtualization, yet it isn't the only datacenter layer that can be virtualized.

In a survey released in January 2008, the Enterprise Strategy Group found that of 341 respondents, all of them intended to deploy virtualization solutions in the future (see Figure 1-2), and more than 70 percent of them intended to do it within the next 12 months. In another survey released in December 2007, the same research firm found that of all of the respondents (365) already running a virtual solution, more than 70 percent of them were relying on VMware (see Figure 1-3). Of course, this second survey was released well before Microsoft entered the fray with its built-in virtualization solution with Windows Server 2008 Hyper-V. Today, these results may be different, but one thing is certain: Every datacenter in the world will make some use of virtualization solutions in the next five years. If you're using some form of x86 or x64 technology, virtualization is definitely in your future.

The first place to start is to gain a full understanding of the concepts inherent in datacenter virtualization and what they may mean to you from now on.

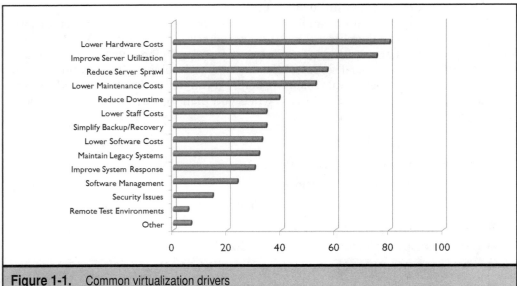

Figure 1-1.   Common virtualization drivers

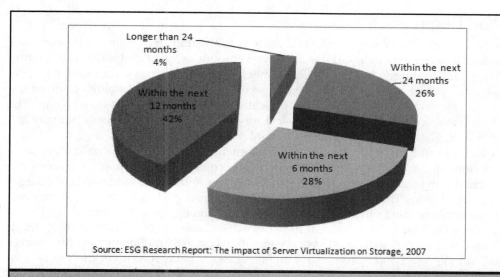

Figure 1-2.   Server virtualization planned adoption

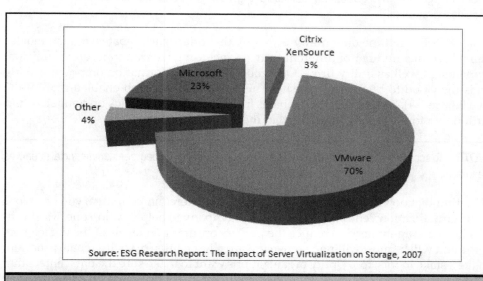

Figure 1-3.   Primary server virtualization solutions

Before You Begin

With the rising cost of energy, more and more organizations feel the need to move to a greener datacenter, one that will use a reduced amount of space and a reduced amount of energy and cooling to host a smaller number of physical servers. As mentioned previously, this can be achieved through the use of virtualization technologies within the datacenter at server, workstation, and application levels. The benefits far outweigh the disadvantages since the only good physical server operating at 10 percent capacity is a server that has been transformed into a virtual machine.

Power and utility companies also see the benefit from machine virtualization, since their customers can greatly reduce their power and cooling consumption ratios, ensuring that current power generation facilities can last longer and address the needs of a larger community of users. This is why many of them have developed rebate programs for organizations implementing virtualization projects and removing physical servers from their datacenters. The first to do so was California's Pacific Gas & Electric (PG&E), which developed a rebate program that could save organizations up to $4 million per site for a server virtualization project and introduced it on November 8, 2006. Incentives can range from $150 to $300 per server, with the program being capped at 50 percent of total project costs. PG&E pioneered this effort with virtualization manufacturer VMware Corporation.

NOTE For the PG&E Rebate Program announcement, go to www.pge.com/about/news/ediarelations/newsreleases/q4_2006/061108.shtml. For more information on the PG&E Rebate Program, go to www.ge.com/mybusiness/energysavingsrebates/incentivesbyindustry/hightech/hteeincentives.shtml.

Today, PG&E is not the only utility company that offers such rebates. In fact, rebates are available from a number of different sources, including federal, state, and municipal governments, as well as utility firms. One good source of information on power-saving rebates is the Good to Be Green Web site. This site includes a Web-enabled map of the U.S. (see Figure 1-4). To find potential rebates in your area, simply click on your state and then drill down to the rebate programs that may apply to you.

NOTE To access the Good to Be Green USA map, go to www.goodtobegreen.com/financialincentives.aspx#nc.

If you find that no virtualization rebate program is offered in your area, you can work with your virtualization vendor and your utility company to help develop one. Most utility firms have an urgent need to reduce the power consumption levels of the datacenters they serve and will be most willing to move towards the creation of such a rebate program. They have a stake in this, too. Utility organizations want to make sure the datacenters that are housed in their grid remain in their grid and remain as customers. In addition, they want to make the most efficient use of the energy they provide and manage. So to them, it makes economic sense to have organizations both stay in their grid and consume energy more efficiently.

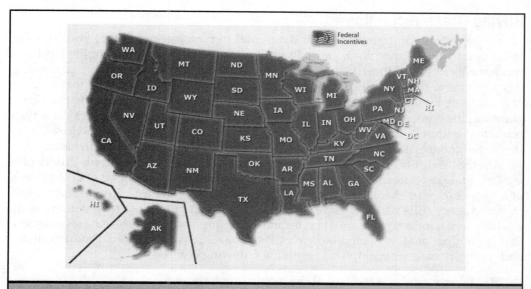

Figure 1-4.   The Good to Be Green Web-enabled USA map of rebate programs

However, whether you work with the utility firm to create a program or you rely on an existing program, you will find that you must apply for this program before you begin the virtualization project. Here's why:

▼   The utility firm must perform a power consumption analysis before the virtualization project begins. This will identify how power is being used in the datacenter through traditional consumption methods.

■   The utility firm will perform an initial analysis on potential power consumption reductions through virtualization and use this as the baseline for the project go-ahead.

■   You perform your virtualization project and transform physical servers into virtual machines, reducing the power consumption levels.

■   A post-project assessment is performed.

▲   The post-project assessment is compared to the initial baseline, and new power consumption levels are identified. Any discrepancies between the original baseline and the final results will be adjusted, and final monies will be provided to the project.

For this reason, you must contact your utility firm *before* you begin your project; otherwise, they will be unable to determine previous consumption rates and determine the potential savings in energy you could benefit from.

Buying Green Technologies

Of course, when you transform your datacenter to turn the majority of your physical systems into virtual machines, you will most likely be replacing some of the hardware components in your infrastructure. Since one of the major reasons you are performing this project is to reduce the carbon footprint of your datacenter, you should make a point of continuing in this vein and making it one of your datacenter's underlying principles. Greening the datacenter means more than just reducing the number of physical servers contained within it. It means moving forward with green policies and practices. One of the best of these is the acquisition practices in support of new machine purchases.

Another Web site with a focus on green IT technologies is the Electronic Product Environmental Assessment Tool (www.EPEAT.net), which was developed over the course of a two-year effort thanks to an initial grant provided by the U.S. Environmental Protection Agency (EPA). EPEAT developed a set of criteria in order to help determine the environmental impact of information technology equipment. It produced a set of criteria that is divided into three compliance models: Bronze, Silver, and Gold. Products fit into each category based on compliance with the following criteria:

▼ Bronze products meet all of the required criteria.

■ Silver meets all of the required criteria and meets 50 percent of the optional criteria.

▲ Gold meets all of the required criteria and all of the optional criteria.

EPEAT maintains a list of approved equipment (see Figure 1-5) on their Web site in addition to providing a series of resources for equipment buyers—resources such as support for request for proposal (RFP) criterion creation, model RFPs to use, and help during acquisition processes.

EPEAT Registered Products Search Tool			
Product	**BRONZE**	**SILVER**	**GOLD**	**Total**
Desktops	4	54	54	112
Integrated Systems	0	20	0	20
Monitors	19	299	14	332
Notebooks	0	239	14	253
Totals	23	612	82	717

Figure 1-5.   The EPEAT Registered Products Search Tool is constantly updated as new products qualify in either the Bronze, Silver, or Gold categories.

NOTE For more information on the required and optional EPEAT criteria, go to www.epeat.net/Criteria.aspx.

Relying on EPEAT to buy green complements the virtualization project because it furthers your efforts to reduce long-term power consumption ratios.

Green Asset Disposal

Another "green" aspect of your virtualization project will be the disposal of superfluous equipment. As you move through your project and replace existing physical systems with virtual machines, you will need to find ways to dispose of the machines you no longer need. In many cases, you'll find that you can reuse much of the hardware you are reducing. But if the purpose of your virtualization project is to reduce your carbon footprint, it doesn't make sense for you to reuse all of the equipment you are replacing. In addition, you must find ways to securely wipe information and intellectual property from the systems you will get rid of. Most organizations already have secure information protection plans for obsolete hardware, but few have a green asset disposal program.

As a consequence of the new move towards green technologies, new services have been developed to help organizations achieve both goals: secure asset disposal while reducing the carbon footprint of the disposal process itself. A simple search on the Internet will locate several services that offer both green and secure disposal, but one of the most popular services is Green Asset Disposal (www.greenassetdisposal.com), which specializes in this type of system disposal. Green Asset Disposal will recycle, remarket, and even purchase the assets you need to pass on. They offer a pickup service to facilitate your disposal, and will also provide you with information on how to properly dispose of technologies ranging from servers, PCs, and other obsolete IT equipment.

If you're going green, make sure you rely on green disposal procedures to get the most green for your buck.

USE A FIVE-STEP PROCESS

Like any other IT project, virtualization projects must be structured. Over the course of the last ten years, Resolutions Enterprises and the authors of this book have developed a strategy for the move to virtualization. This strategy has been tested through a multitude of delivery projects, as well as through a series of presentations throughout the U.S. and Canada. The presentations were delivered through two multicity tours, one on server consolidation in 2007 and one on virtualization in 2008, as well as several full-day courses on the topic. In each case, attendees and client organizations found this strategy to be sound and direct, as well as a valuable aid in their own move to virtualization.

According to Resolutions, the move to virtualization relies on five key steps:

1. **Discovery**   The first step begins with datacenter inventories and the identification of potential virtualization candidates.

2. **Virtualization**   The second step focuses on gaining a complete understanding of the value choices that virtualization can offer.

3. **Hardware maximization**   The third step focuses on hardware recovery and how you can make judicial investments when adding new hardware or replacing older systems.

4. **Architecture**   The fourth step looks to the architecture you must prepare to properly introduce virtualization technologies into your datacenter practices.

5. **Management**   The last step focuses on the update of the management tools you use to maintain complete virtualization scenarios in your new dynamic datacenter.

Each of these building blocks brings you one step closer to a complete virtualization solution.

Virtualization is much more than simply loading a virtualization technology on a server and transforming one or two workloads into virtual machines. In order to make the most of your virtualization project, you must learn how different virtualization solutions fit together, what each vendor offers, and what you actually need to implement to make the most of virtualization technologies in your datacenter while addressing your business needs. The Resolutions Five-Step Process will greatly assist you in this endeavor.

CHAPTER 2

Begin the Five-Step Process

Chapter 1 introduced the Resolutions Five-Step Process. This process helps you begin to understand the value proposition virtualization can offer to your organization. The first step, Discovery, lets you identify what is in your organization's network and gives you a view of how it could be transformed. Step two, Virtualization, begins the introduction of the various virtualization technologies and leads you through an understanding of how they integrate together to create the dynamic datacenter.

STEP ONE: DISCOVERY

One of the elements we have been able to confirm throughout our multicity tours is that IT administrators do not like inventories. That's right. On average, about 15 percent of the thousands of people involved in our tours actually had an up-to-date inventory in hand, yet the inventory is an absolute must when you're dealing with IT. How can you manage what you don't know you have? How can you move to virtualization if you don't know how many servers you are running and what their purpose in your network is?

We all know that the reason most IT administrators are looking to server virtualization is because of the datacenter crunch. There is no more room in today's datacenters. Adding more servers always requires more power input as well as more cooling. Datacenter upgrades are expensive. Why move forward with them if you don't actually need them?

In addition, physical servers are hard to provision. People using Windows servers run all sorts of technologies, from disk imaging to Windows Deployment Services (WDS), to try to reduce the overhead of preparing a physical server. And when the server is finally provisioned, you'll find out that the acquisition cost was high only to run the entire hardware collection at less than 15 percent utilization. What's worse, when it comes time to protect the system and the applications it runs from disaster recovery, you'll have to get involved in an expensive business continuity solution—replicating the data contained within this server to a mirror installation in a remote site. Who can afford this? Yet we know that more than 80 percent of organizations that suffer a total IT failure will not recover and will go under. This is a significant risk to run.

PCs are also a problem. Few organizations want to take the time to upgrade their systems to new versions of the operating system. Just look at what happened to Vista. More than 90 percent of all the attendees of our tour did not move to Vista and have no intention of doing so. Everyone is waiting for the next version of the operating system (OS). In addition, more than 75 percent of our attendees are letting their users run PCs with administrative rights. No wonder they have no end of issues with their workstations and mobile systems. The issues are compounded with PCs because of their very nature. PCs are distributed throughout the entire organization, in every site, in every location, on the road, and even in employees' homes. This makes them even harder to manage and repair.

Applications also have their fair share of issues. Application conflicts constantly arise no matter what IT administrators or application developers do to avoid them. Microsoft has released the Windows Installer service to protect systems from application changes, but creating Windows Installer files is a complex process that takes time and costs money. But the worst is the deployment model everyone relies on: Pushing thousands of bits to all of the endpoints in the organization is definitely not the best practice when it comes to system repair or even license management. There has to be a better way. And there is.

Inventory, Inventory, Inventory

It's amazing just how many organizations do not know what the content of their infrastructure is. Yet, this is the most important step to any virtualization project. Knowing the content of your network can help you maintain it as well as control its growth. If you don't know what you have, how can you make sure you can protect it and administer it, or, even worse, transform it into a dynamic datacenter?

Can't be bothered to go out to buy an inventory product and then deploy it? Don't have the time to prepare an inventory? Don't worry. One of the easiest ways to generate an inventory of your network is to work with free tools. For example, many people use the Microsoft Baseline Security Analyzer (MBSA) to scan their networks for vulnerabilities and required updates. MBSA is easy to set up and run against all of the systems in your infrastructure. Once a scan is complete, MBSA provides you with information on each system it scanned, including Internet Protocol (IP) address, operating system, installed applications, and, of course, vulnerabilities. You can easily turn this valuable data into an inventory by linking the results of any MBSA scan with Microsoft Visio through the Microsoft Visio Connector for MBSA. Visio will automatically generate a graphical image of your network and display detailed information on each device when you click on it (see Figure 2-1). With these tools in hand, you could generate your first inventory in a few seconds! You'll be amazed at what you'll find.

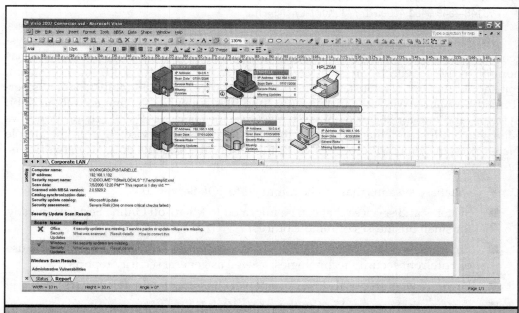

Figure 2-1.   Using the Visio Connector for MBSA

NOTE For more information on MBSA, go to http://technet.microsoft.com/en-us/security/cc184925 .aspx.aspx. To download the Visio Connector for MBSA, go to www.microsoft.com/downloads/details .aspx?FamilyID=8EA27D78-32B5-4F37-A7FD-99EE2AA76C62&displaylang=en.

NOTE Microsoft also offers a Visio Connector for System Center Operations Manager (SCOM). You can use SCOM to create a visual representation of your network. To download the SCOM Visio Connector, go to http://technet.microsoft.com/en-us/security/cc184925.aspx.

Scan for Potential Virtualization Candidates

MBSA is not the only free tool you can use to perform your initial analysis. Microsoft also provides the Microsoft Assessment and Planning (MAP) Toolkit Solution Accelerator. MAP is a tool that can be used to scan your entire network for assessments. It was formerly released as the Windows Vista Hardware Assessment Tool and was designed to allow organizations to scan their existing PCs to determine their potential for hosting the Vista OS. Microsoft soon realized two things. First, no one was moving to Vista. And second, if the tool could scan for Vista hardware requirements, it could also scan for a wide variety of assessments. Therefore, Microsoft changed and adapted the tool to support a whole series of other operations.

NOTE For access to MAP, go to www.microsoft.com/downloads/details.aspx?FamilyID=67240b76-3148-4e49-943d-4d9ea7f77730&displaylang=en.

MAP is an agentless analyzer that collects information on all of the identified systems. It works mostly on Windows systems and requires the use of an account that has administrative privileges on each target computer. MAP can be run from any system, but should preferably be installed on an administrative workstation. Installation is performed through a Windows Installer file. Two files are available: one for x86 or 32-bit systems, and one for x64 or 64-bit systems. Once installed, MAP will rely on Windows Management Instrumentation (WMI), the Remote Registry Service, or even the Simple Network Management Protocol (SNMP) to identify the systems on your network. Assessments included in MAP include (see Figure 2-2):

▼ Database systems that can be migrated to SQL Server 2008

■ Systems and services that can be migrated to Microsoft Online Services (mostly for small businesses or remote offices)

■ Environments that can profit from Network Access Protection (NAP) or the use of Forefront security technologies, as well as general security reports

■ Power-saving proposals to reduce power consumption in datacenters

■ Systems that can run Vista with Service Pack 1

- Systems that can run Microsoft Office 2007

- Systems that can run Windows Server 2008

- Server roles that can be migrated to corresponding Windows Server 2008 roles

- Performance reports from servers or workstations

- Server consolidation through virtualization with Microsoft Hyper-V and Windows Server 2008

- Applications that can be virtualized through Microsoft Application Virtualization

▲ Potential optimized desktop scenarios

Each assessment provides a comprehensive series of reports based on the purpose of the assessment.

Default reports are in English, but can be localized in French, German, Japanese, Korean, Spanish, and Brazilian Portuguese. Report details will depend on the type of report you use MAP to run. For example, running a MAP report for Windows Server 2008 readiness will include details about approved drivers and required hardware updates. Reports on server virtualization will identify current workloads and potential candidates for virtualization (see Figure 2-3).

NOTE Microsoft is constantly improving MAP. There may be many more reports available through it by the time you read this.

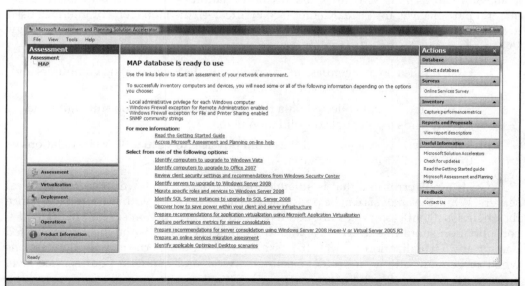

Figure 2-2. Using MAP to perform system assessments

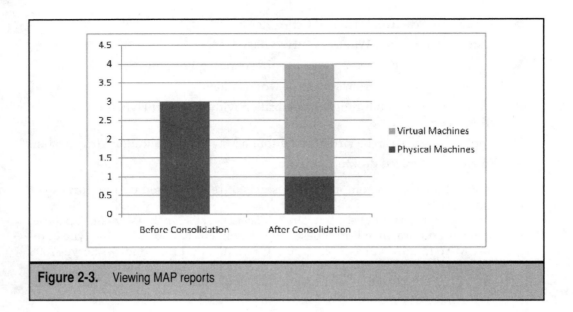

Figure 2-3. Viewing MAP reports

Microsoft is not the only vendor to offer solutions for system assessment. VMware, the founder of x86 virtualization, also offers two tools that can be used for an assessment of the servers that could be transformed into virtual machines. The first and most readily available to all users is VMware Guided Consolidation (VGC). VGC is available as an integral part of VMware VirtualCenter (see Figure 2-4), the management interface used to control both physical hardware and virtual machines running on VMware technology. VGC performs its analysis through three key steps:

1. First, it relies on an agentless infrastructure to discover existing computers and collect performance information from them.

2. Second, it analyzes collected data for hardware consolidation suitability and recommends a potential consolidation plan.

3. It allows you to convert machines from physical to virtual (P2V) installations through the VMware Converter.

VGC is a powerful tool that is suitable for networks with fewer than 100 physical servers. While the analysis can be performed on a live network with little impact—since the engine is agentless, it does not add overhead to a production server's workload—consolidation should be tested in a laboratory first because it is the most complicated part of any virtualization project. If possible, you should perform your conversions when servers are offline to protect existing services and maintain your service level agreements (SLAs) with end users.

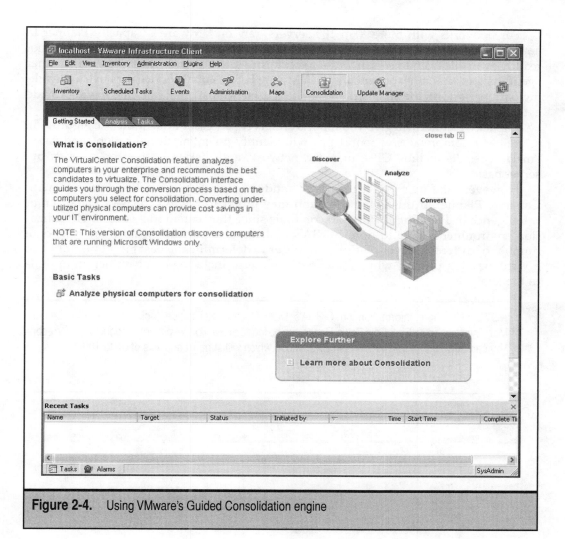

Figure 2-4. Using VMware's Guided Consolidation engine

Obtain the VMware Guided Consolidation by downloading an evaluation version of VMware's VirtualCenter. Evaluations last 60 days, which is appropriate since it will give you enough time to properly analyze your network.

NOTE   VMware VirtualCenter is included as part of VMware Infrastructure. To obtain an evaluation copy of VirtualCenter, go to www.vmware.com/download/. An evaluation serial number will be required to run the tool. You will receive it once you register on the Web site.

For networks with more than 100 servers, rely on VMware's Capacity Planner to analyze your server resources. Unfortunately, Capacity Planner, while free to use, is not readily available to end users. In order to perform a scan using Capacity Planner, another agentless tool, you must either contract VMware Professional Services or have a consulting partner perform the analysis. The analysis itself is most often free, and it will provide extensive information about the servers you can consolidate.

Capacity Planner will give you reports on server processor utilization (see Figure 2-5), as well as a comprehensive report that will identify potential virtualization candidates. Analysis results include CPU, memory, network, and disk utilization on a server-by-server basis.

However, like many, you may fear vendor bias when a reseller comes in with Capacity Planner. If this is the case, you may prefer to rely on CiRBA's Data Center Intelligence or PlateSpin's PowerRecon tools since they can model several virtualization environments. In addition, CiRBA's tool can also perform what-if analysis on a number of different server platforms in order to determine the best target platform for a virtualization project, while PlateSpin's will also include power reduction options in the analysis.

NOTE For more information on CiRBA's Data Center Intelligence tool, go to www.cirba.com. More information on PlateSpin PowerRecon can be found at www.platespin.com/products/powerrecon/. You can download a free version of PowerRecon which will support analysis of up to 100 servers.

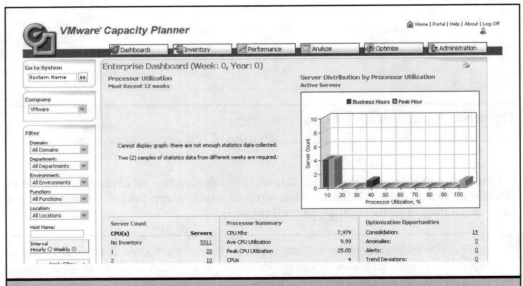

Figure 2-5. Using VMware's Capacity Planner tool

Unlike the other tools mentioned here, CiRBA's tool can also take into account non-technical factors that impact the consolidation. For example, site, department, security zone restrictions, maintenance windows, and service-level requirements all play a role in determining the eventual consolidation plan. However, the tools that only collect performance data cannot account for any of the non-technical elements in the consolidation project. Without this information included in the analysis, you have to account for it manually. Using a tool like CiRBA's will let you factor these elements into your computations and provide a better overall view of where you need to be.

PowerRecon on the other hand will monitor up to 2,000 servers at once and if you combine the commercial version of this tool with PlateSpin PowerConvert, you will be able to automate the conversion process once your analysis is complete.

Other tools are available, but the most common are MAP, VGC, VMware Capacity Planner, CiRBA's, and PlateSpin's. Keep in mind that whichever tool you use, you must run the analysis over time. Your intent is to identify which systems are running, when they need resources, how many resources they require, when resources are at a low threshold, and when they peak. For this reason, you should run the analysis for at least one month. Running it for this period of time will at least give you the high and low utilization ratios for each server during a monthly cycle. The analysis will not identify peaks and lows for longer periods, for example, for applications that peak on a quarterly or semi-annual basis. Keep this in mind when you review the results of your analysis.

NOTE   Be very careful during this analysis because it will form the basis of your future infrastructure. Properly identifying the required resources for each server workload will allow you to properly size the hardware you will move these workloads to once you virtualize them. You can never be too careful when you perform a virtualization candidate analysis because once you virtualize your systems, information on physical resource requirements for these workloads will no longer be available.

You also want to time your analysis as closely as possible to the implementation. It's always a good practice to reanalyze an environment a few weeks before the implementation. If there is a significant gap between the time you perform the analysis and the time you move forward with the project, you may find that new application requirements that were not captured in the earlier analysis will be missed altogether.

Categorize Server Resources

Once you have the results of your analysis, you can categorize each machine role into groups. For example, you can identify the server roles or functions in the following service types:

▼   **Network infrastructure and physical servers**   These servers provide core networking functions, such as IP addressing or name resolution, including support for legacy systems. They also provide virtual private networks (VPNs) and routing and remote access services. And, because they are a base-level service, they run the virtualization role on physical machines.

- **Identity management servers**   These servers are the core identity managers for the network. They contain and maintain the entire corporate identity database for all users and user access through Lightweight Directory Access Protocol (LDAP) services. For Windows Server 2008, these would be servers running Active Directory Domain Services. This function should not be shared with any other as much as possible, unless it is a core networking function, such as name resolution through the Domain Name System (DNS).

- **File and print servers**   These servers focus on the provision of storage and structured document services to the network. These functions form the basis of information sharing within productivity networks.

- **Application servers**   These servers provide application services to the user community. Some examples would be Exchange Server, SQL Server, and so on—in fact, any service running within productivity networks.

- **Terminal servers**   These servers provide a central application execution environment to users. Users need only have a minimal infrastructure to access these servers because their entire execution environment resides on the server itself.

- **Dedicated web servers**   These servers focus on the provision of Web services to user communities. For example, in Windows Server, the Web Edition is specifically designed to meet these needs.

- **Collaboration servers**   These servers provide the infrastructure for collaboration within the enterprise. Examples of these services include Windows SharePoint Services, streaming media services, and unified communications.

Servers can be further categorized according to their location and server type. For example, the servers you use in the headquarters datacenter will not be the same type as those you use in remote offices. Also, if you use tower, rack-mounted, or blade servers, you should identify this in your analysis. Applications or workloads can be further categorized into the following groups:

- Commercial versus in-house or custom applications
- Legacy versus updated
- Infrastructure applications
- Support to the business
- Line of business (LOB)
- Mission-critical applications

Each of these application categories will be useful when you move to virtualization.

Rationalize Everything

After you complete the evaluation of the systems you have in place, you will be ready to move on towards virtualization. However, it is important that you distinguish between server and physical consolidation. Server consolidation means reducing the number of servers in your datacenter, creating larger servers that host multiple workloads. Yet in most cases, organizations that perform a virtualization project will not perform server consolidation; they will perform physical consolidation. Take the following example.

Organization A has 100 physical servers. After performing an extensive analysis and selecting the virtualization engine to use, Organization A determines that they can transform each and every existing workload into a virtual machine. To do so, they must use 10 physical machines to run the 100 virtualized workloads. The result? One hundred ten servers. This is not a server consolidation project. It is a physical consolidation project. Of course, Organization A will profit from the move to virtualization because they will have 90 fewer machines to manage, but their administrators will not have less work since they now have to manage 10 more machines than before.

This is why rationalization is the most important aspect of any virtualization project. Your goal should be to have fewer servers when you finish the virtualization project than when you began, and this should include the physical servers you will need to run the virtual machines you create. There is no better time to perform a service or workload consolidation or rationalization than when you are migrating to a new virtualized infrastructure. Keep the following questions in mind as you scan through the results of your analysis:

▼ What is the utilization ratio for each machine?

■ Are there any "parked" machines—machines that belong to specific user groups but that are not constantly used?

■ Are there any obsolete machines?

■ Is there any way to combine workloads?

▲ Is there any other way to reduce the machine footprint?

How well you address these questions and apply their answers will determine just how many machines you will be left with once you complete your project.

STEP 2: VIRTUALIZATION

As you gather information about your systems, you can move on to step 2 and begin to learn about the different virtualization technologies and how they can help solve specific business issues in your organization. Possibly the best place to start is with virtualization itself. According to Merriam-Webster's online dictionary (www.merriam-webster .com/home.htm), virtual reality is "an artificial environment which is experienced through sensory stimuli (as sights and sounds) provided by a computer and in which one's actions partially determine what happens in the environment." This is exactly what happens with virtualization: Virtual machine software creates one or more virtual workstations or servers on a real, physical system (see Figure 2-6). Everything depends on what is available on the real machine: hard disk space, processor capability, network interface cards, and amount of random access memory (RAM). The virtual machines you create with virtualization software can support the installation and operation of any number of operating systems, including all versions of Microsoft Windows, MS-DOS, Linux, some forms of UNIX, and so on—basically any x86-based operating system, even those running on the x64 extension of this platform. They can communicate with the physical host and other machines on the network just as if they were real machines in their own sense.

Physical machine partitioning has been around since the 1960s when IBM began partitioning their mainframe servers to host multiple instances of their operating system. In this case, the partitioning technology was used to run multiple, or rather parallel, instances of the same operating system. While IBM invented system partitioning, it wasn't until the 1990s that this type of partitioning was introduced to the x86 processor architecture. It was also at this time that physical system partitioning was renamed virtualization. This type of virtualization was first introduced to let end users run operating systems such as Windows on other platforms, such as the Apple Macintosh. In fact, in 2003, Microsoft acquired French company Connectix, which specialized in designing "virtual machine" software to run Windows operating systems on Macintosh computers, giving Macintosh users access to the thousands of applications available on the Windows platform. This began Microsoft's fray into the world of machine virtualization.

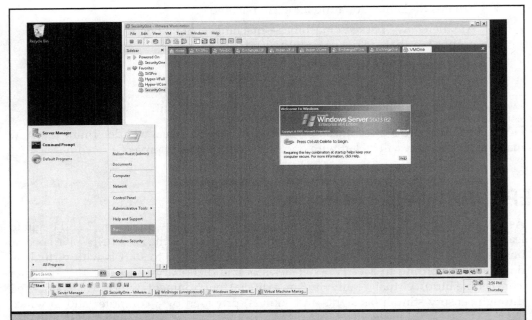

Figure 2-6.   Using a virtual machine in VMware Workstation

Microsoft was late, of course, because VMware Corporation had been working with machine virtualization since the late 1990s through the introduction of VMware Workstation, an end-user–oriented product that was designed to let you run any number of additional instances of an x86 operating system. VMware then realized the power of virtualization and moved it to the server level, beginning the massive boom in machine virtualization we see today. Now VMware is the market leader in virtualization and offers the broadest spectrum of solutions for datacenter virtualization.

In the end, IBM's machine partitioning was much like Xerox's invention of the mouse and the graphical interface. Xerox invented these technologies in their Palo Alto Research Center (PARC) many years before they became popularized, but it was Apple, not Xerox, that gained notoriety for the two tools. Today, many people think both inventions originated with Apple, but in fact, Apple only borrowed from existing innovations and repackaged them into a format that would have broad appeal. The same occurred with VMware and IBM's original system-partitioning technology. While IBM had the original idea, it was VMware that put the idea into practice in such a way that it quickly became popular and is now a billion-dollar industry of its own. The key to VMware's success is that unlike IBM, VMware's virtualization technology lets you run a variety of different operating systems. In addition, it lets you run them on inexpensive commodity hardware, which puts the technology within the reach of any IT department.

The ability to run multiple virtual machines on top of a single physical machine makes this technology exciting indeed for anyone who needs to create, set up, and reuse machines running almost any operating system. This is what gives VMware-like virtualization its best value.

Defining Virtualization

Today, virtualization technology has evolved and can now apply to multiple layers within the datacenter. This is why it is important to fully understand which types of virtualization are available. In a dynamic datacenter—one that takes full advantage of the value propositions of virtualization—there will be at least seven layers of virtualization (see Figure 2-7).

▼   **Server Virtualization (SerV)** is focused on partitioning a physical instance of an operating system into a virtual instance or virtual machine. True server virtualization products will let you virtualize any x86 or x64 operating system, such as Windows, Linux, and some forms of UNIX. There are two aspects of server virtualization:

■   **Software Virtualization (SoftV)** runs the virtualized operating system on top of a software virtualization platform running on an existing operating system.

■   **Hardware Virtualization (HardV)** runs the virtualized operating system on top of a software platform running directly on top of the hardware without an existing operating system. The engine used to run hardware virtualization is usually referred to as a *hypervisor*. The purpose of this engine is to expose hardware resources to the virtualized operating systems.

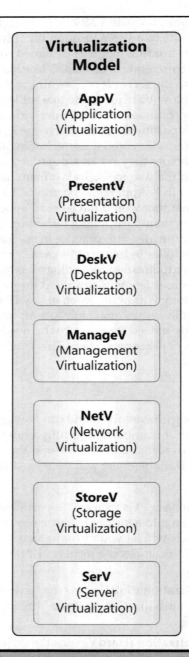

Figure 2-7.   The seven aspects of virtualization

When working with server virtualization, the physical server becomes a host for all of the virtual operating systems or virtual machines (VMs), which become workloads running on top of this host.

■ **Storage Virtualization (StoreV)** is used to merge physical storage from multiple devices so that they appear as one single storage pool. The storage in this pool can take several forms: direct attached storage (DAS), network attached storage (NAS), or storage area networks (SANs); and it can be linked to through several protocols: Fibre Channel, Internet SCSI (iSCSI), Fibre Channel on Ethernet, or even the Network File System (NFS). Though storage virtualization is not a requirement for server virtualization, one of the key strengths you will be able to obtain from storage virtualization is the ability to rely on thin provisioning or the assignation of a logical unit (LUN) of storage of a given size, but provisioning it only on an as-needed basis. For example, if you create a LUN of 100 gigabytes (GB) and you are only using 12GB, only 12GB of actual storage is provisioned. This significantly reduces the cost of storage since you only pay as you go (see Figure 2-8).

■ **Network Virtualization (NetV)** lets you control available bandwidth by splitting it into independent channels that can be assigned to specific resources. For example, the simplest form of network virtualization is the virtual local area network (VLAN), which creates a logical segregation of a physical network. In addition, server virtualization products support the creation of virtual network layers within the product itself. For example, using this virtual network layer would let you place a perimeter network on the same host as other production virtual workloads without impacting either of the networks or letting the virtual machines access each other.

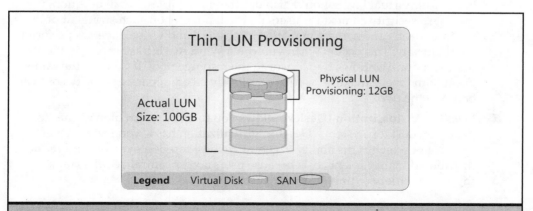

Figure 2-8.   Using thin provisioning through Storage Virtualization can significantly reduce storage costs.

■ **Management Virtualization (ManageV)** is focused on the technologies that manage the entire datacenter, both physical and virtual, to present one single unified infrastructure for the provision of services. ManageV is not necessarily performed through a single interface. For example, in large datacenters, you will want to divide different service deliveries into layers and separate operations between them. In smaller datacenters, you may not have the staff to divide the responsibilities, but you should at least ensure that administrators wear different "hats" when they work with the various layers of your architecture. In fact, you should make sure that two key layers are segregated at all times:

  ■ **Resource Pools (RP)**, which includes the collection of hardware resources—host servers, racks, enclosures, storage, and network hardware—that makes up the datacenter infrastructure

  ■ **Virtual Services Offerings (VSO)**, or workloads that are made up of the virtual machines—servers and/or desktops—that are client-facing and offer services to end users

  One key factor in this segregation is the creation of different security contexts between resource pools and VSOs. Since your administrative teams are not the same and do not have the same responsibilities—resource pool administrators must ensure that proper resources are available for VSOs, and VSO administrators must ensure that proper services are delivered to end users—you limit the possibility of contamination from the virtual to the physical world by using completely different security contexts between the two.

  For example, your physical layer should use strong passwords and ensure that all communications between management consoles and physical hosts are encrypted at all times because passwords are communicated over these links. Your virtual layer should also use these principles, but in addition, it will provide a security context for users that will not rely on such stringent policies.

  In some instances, the segregation of physical and virtual layers is performed automatically. This occurs when you run a Windows infrastructure in the VSO but use a non-Windows hypervisor in the resource pool. If you use the same OS at both layers, make sure you consciously create separate security contexts between the two.

■ **Desktop Virtualization (DeskV)** allows you to rely on virtual machines to provision desktop systems. Desktop virtualization has several advantages, the least of which is the ability to centralize desktop deployments and reduce distributed management costs because users access centralized desktops through a variety of thin or unmanaged devices.

NOTE   In the end of 2008, VMware acquired technology from a company called Trango Virtual Processors in order to move virtualization beyond the desktop to mobile handsets. VMware's Mobile Virtualization Platform (MVP) is designed to create a virtual layer on mobile handsets to allow you to run multiple mobile systems on the same handset. For example, you could run one platform for work and another for personal use. In addition, by virtualizing the mobile handset, VMware's MVP will make it easier for you to move your personal settings from phone to phone. Watch for more on MVP in 2009 and beyond.

■   **Presentation Virtualization (PresentV)**, until recently called Terminal Services, provides only the presentation layer from a central location to users. While the need for PresentV is diminishing because of the introduction of technologies such as Application Virtualization, the protocols used for PresentV are at the forefront of both DeskV and SerV technologies since they are the protocols used to access, use, and manage virtual workloads.

▲   **Application Virtualization (AppV)** uses the same principles as software-based SerV, but instead of providing an engine to run an entire operating system, AppV decouples productivity applications from the operating system. AppV transforms the distributed application management model because you only need to virtualize an application once. From then on, the application virtualization engine will make the virtualized application run on any version of Windows. What's even better is that products such as Acresso Software's AdminStudio (www.acresso.com/products/licensing/adminstudio.htm) will take all of the applications you have already packaged to run with the Windows Installer Service in MSI format and convert them to AppV formats overnight in a batch process. AdminStudio supports both the Citrix and the VMware AppV formats. Transform your applications into AppV format, and you'll never have to touch them again! Work is also being done by major AppV vendors such as Microsoft, Citrix, InstallFree, Symantec, and VMware to apply AppV to server applications. While AppV only works on the 32-bit platform right now, work is also being done to make it work on 64-bit or x64 platforms. Both server-based AppV and x64 AppV may be available by the time this book gets into print.

NOTE   You can also create successful application virtualization deployments with some Solaris and Linux applications. Vendors such as Data Synapse, Trigence, and Transitive have had some success leveraging application virtualization on Linux and Solaris applications, especially in the financial sector.

While there are seven layers of virtualization, there are other key terms that make up the language of virtualization in the datacenter. These include:

▼   **Host server**   The physical server running virtual machine workloads.

■   **Guest operation system**   A virtualized operating system running as a workload on a host server.

- ■ **Resource Pool** The collection of hardware resources, including host servers that make up the datacenter infrastructure.

- ■ **Virtual Service Offerings** The virtual machines that are client-facing and offer services to end users. They are also often referred to as *virtual workloads.*

- ■ **Virtual Appliances (VAPs)** Pre-packaged VSOs that run a specific application or workload.

- ■ **Policy-based workloads** VSOs that are powered up on an as-needed basis through automated policies.

- ▲ **Operating system virtualization** Often misconstrued as guest OS virtualization, this is nothing more than OS partitioning because it can only run one single OS type in parallel instances. The value of this type of "virtualization" is limited because you must have a need to run the particular OS. Products of this type include Solaris Containers and Parallels Virtuozzo Containers, which runs the Virtuozzo OS—a version of Linux—in parallel.

Now that you understand most of the key terms, let's delve into what each of the three core virtualization technologies—SerV, DeskV, and AppV—can bring to the datacenter.

What Is a Virtual Machine?

As you now know, virtualization is a technology that partitions a computer into several independent machines that can support different operating systems and applications running concurrently. The great advantage of this is that you can take a physical server that is running at 10 percent utilization and transform it into one running at 60 to 80 percent utilization by loading it up with multiple virtual machines. The underlying hypervisor software will run directly on the hardware and act as a coordinator to manage multiple operating systems in VMs. In this situation, each instance of an operating system running in a virtual machine becomes a self-contained operating environment that runs on top of the hypervisor and behaves as if it is a separate computer.

VMs are then made up of several different components (see Figure 2-9):

- ▼ **Configuration file** A file that contains the settings information—amount of RAM, number of processors, number and type of network interface cards (NICs), number and type of virtual disks—for the virtual machine. Each time you create a new virtual machine, you create a virtual machine configuration file, that is, a file that tells the virtualization software how to allocate physical resources from the host to the virtual machine. This file indicates where the hard disk file or files are located, how much RAM to use, how to interact with the network adapter cards, and which processor or processors to use. Because it only contains settings, this file is usually small and is either in pure text or Extended Markup Language (XML) format.

Folders				
☐ ExchangeVMs	ExchangeLCR.vmx.lck	7/9/2008 9:06 AM	File Folder	
ExchangeETOne	ExchangeDiskF.vmdk	1/7/2008 2:46 PM	VMware virtual dis...	314,752 KB
ExchangeLCR	ExchangeLCR.vmdk	1/7/2008 2:46 PM	VMware virtual dis...	5,518,208 KB
ExchangeOne	exchangelcr.vmem	12/24/2007 8:59 AM	VMEM File	393,216 KB
	ExchangeLCR.vmsd	12/19/2007 5:47 PM	VMSD File	0 KB
	exchangelcr.vmss	1/7/2008 2:47 PM	VMware suspende...	17,457 KB
	ExchangeLCR.vmx	1/7/2008 2:47 PM	VMX File	2 KB
	ExchangeLCRDiskD.vmdk	1/7/2008 2:46 PM	VMware virtual dis...	62,336 KB
	ExchangeLCRDiskE.vmdk	1/7/2008 2:46 PM	VMware virtual dis...	288,896 KB
	ExchangeLCRDiskG.vmdk	1/7/2008 2:46 PM	VMware virtual dis...	24,384 KB
	nvram	1/7/2008 2:47 PM	File	9 KB
	vmware.log	1/7/2008 2:47 PM	Text Document	38 KB
	vmware-0.log	12/24/2007 8:58 AM	Text Document	130 KB
	vmware-1.log	12/21/2007 11:29 A...	Text Document	52 KB
	vmware-2.log	12/20/2007 2:54 PM	Text Document	40 KB

Figure 2-9.   The different files included in a VMware VM

■ **Hard disk file(s)**   Files that contain any information which would normally be contained within a physical hard disk. Each time you create a virtual machine, the virtualization software will create a virtual hard disk, that is, a file that acts like a typical sector-based disk. When you install the operating system on the virtual machine, it will be contained in this file. Like a physical system, each virtual machine can have several disk files. Because it simulates a hard disk, this file is usually significant in size, though all virtualization engines support automatic growth, letting the system start with a smaller file size and scale it as new content is added to the virtual machine. There are two main types: virtual machine disks (VMDK) from VMware and virtual hard disks (VHD) from Microsoft. Both use a flat file format and, like databases, will continually grow each time information is added. Once again, like database files, virtual disk drive files can be compacted to recover unused space within the file.

NOTE   Virtual hard disk files will not necessarily grow as data is added; ESX server, by default, leverages fixed-size virtual hard disk files, so a new 16-GB virtual disk will consume 16GB from the beginning. The only exception to this is if you use the `-thin` switch when you create a new VMware virtual disk from the command line. One other exception is with back-end arrays that support thin provisioning, where a default VMware 16-GB virtual disk may only consume 4GB, for example.

■ **In-memory file**   A file that contains information that is in memory for the running VM and that will be committed to the hard disk files when the virtual machine is shut down.

- ■ **Virtual machine state file**   Like real machines, virtual machines support operational modes similar to Standby or Hibernation. In virtualization terms, this means pausing or suspending as well as saving the state of the machine. When a machine is suspended, its suspended state is saved to a file. Because it only includes the machine state, this file is usually smaller than a hard disk file.

- ▲ **Other file(s)**   Files that contain logs and other virtual machine-related information.

There are other file formats that support the most advanced features virtualization offers, but the file types discussed previously are the most common forms. In addition, each virtualization product supports "undoable" disks. This means that the product provides a means to return the virtual machine to a previous state by discarding changes that may have been made to the machine. This is a powerful feature that is extremely useful in testing and development scenarios, and can even be useful in production. For example, if a virus infects a virtual machine but you have a previous snapshot of the files that make it up, you can shut down the infected VM and return to a previously uninfected copy. Of course, you would be careful about doing this since you may lose data, but it is a level of flexibility that is simply unavailable on physical machines.

The major advantage of this is that the physical disks that normally make up a machine running an operating system are "liberated" from their physical constraints by being transformed into files in a folder. This means that since a machine is now completely contained within a single folder, it becomes mobile and transportable. The same machine can run on a workstation, on a server, on a cluster, or even in a remote location. If you want to protect the VM, simply copy the files that make it up to another location. This is why server virtualization technologies are so revolutionary. Try doing any of this with a physical machine!

Because all virtual machines are composed of a series of files, it is easy to duplicate them and repurpose them at any time—providing, of course, you have the appropriate physical disk space. Also, because virtual machines are always made up of at least two files, it is a good practice to place each machine into a folder of its own on the host hard disk. Then, if you need to make a copy, you simply copy the whole folder.

Virtual machines are also easy to back up and restore. Because backing up involves only copying a set of files, you can make regular backups at critical phases of any project. If anything goes wrong, it is easy to return to a previous version of the machine. No special backup agent is required because as far as the backup tool is concerned, virtual machines are stored on a file server.

Server Virtualization Models

As mentioned earlier, there are two virtualization models for SerV (see Figure 2-10). The first, software virtualization or SoftV, is often used to begin virtualization projects because it relies on simpler and often free technologies, but is less efficient because it requires an underlying host operating system (OS). This underlying host operating system also requires resources and, because of this, will impact the operation of the virtual machines running on top of it. For this reason, organizations will not use this model unless it is for testing or development. Because it runs on top of an existing operating system, it is often simpler to rely on SoftV to learn how server virtualization technologies work.

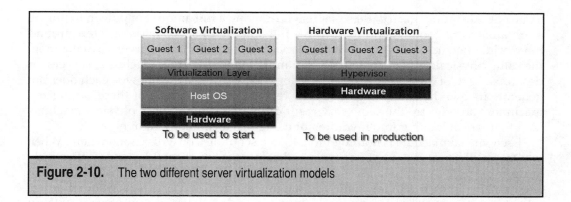

Figure 2-10.   The two different server virtualization models

However, SoftV should never be used in production unless you have low service level agreements and you can afford to have the services made available within the virtual machines taken offline for longer periods of time without negatively impacting users. Few organizations have this level of flexibility with their networked services. In addition, running a virtualization product on top of an existing OS makes all of the virtual machines subject to the update process for the host OS. If reboots are required, all of the VMs will be rebooted as well. Not the best of scenarios.

For this reason, you must use the second model when you move to production, the hardware virtualization layer, or HardV. In this case, the hypervisor code will be integrated directly into the hardware and will simply expose the host server's hardware to the VMs that are running on top of it and take very little away from the physical resources of the host, letting as many virtual machines as possible run on it. In addition, since the host does not actually include a normal OS, it does not require patching, or at least does not require patching and updates at the same rate as the operating systems running in the VMs. This minimizes the impact the hypervisor has on the machines it hosts. Because of this, HardV is, by far, the best model to use for serious server virtualization.

For example, VMware ESXi is a 32-megabyte (MB) hypervisor that does not require an OS and can run directly from firmware or an internal universal serial bus (USB) key. VMware is not the only vendor that offers a hypervisor that is integrated with the host server hardware. This level of integration gives you the opportunity to create a new diskless host server model using nothing but RAM, processor, and network resources to host virtual machines.

NOTE   VMware ESXi is also a free technology. You can download a fully functional version from www.vmware.com/go/getesxi. Microsoft also offers a free version of its hypervisor, Windows Hyper-V Server, but it has limited functionality and does not provide all of the features you obtain from the version found in the Windows Server 2008 code. You can download it from www.microsoft.com/windowsserver2008/en/us/hyperv.aspx.

Server virtualization is still the most popular of the different virtualization technologies, and rightly so. Just think of all of the thousands of servers today running at less than 10 percent utilization—and that is generous, as many are running at less than

5 percent utilization. Each of these servers is drawing a full amount of power, requiring a full amount of cooling, and requiring a full amount of space in datacenters around the world. Then imagine that when properly configured to run in server virtualization, the same physical server can actually run more than ten virtual machines, servers, or desktops. Each of these virtual machines does not require its own power, each does not generate its own heat, and each does not require space, yet each of these virtualized machines can offer up the same services it did while running on a physical machine. Isn't that worth looking into if you're not using this technology right now?

Each virtual machine is nothing more than a set of files on a disk somewhere. When you take a physical instance of a server and convert it to a virtual instance—effectively performing a P2V conversion—you transform the physical machine into a set of files in a folder. Then once it is in this state, you can move it from server to server, shut it down, reboot it, hibernate it, and basically do anything with it that you could before without any significant performance degradation.

Major Server Virtualization Vendors

Guest OS virtualization vendors abound, but three main vendors have taken the market by storm:

▼   Citrix offers a host of different virtualization technologies (www.citrix.com/ xenserver) and is aiming to expand its offerings into all of the virtualization realms. XenServer comes in four flavors. Express Edition is a free starter version of the product. Standard Edition is the basic version, which supports two VSOs at once. Enterprise adds the ability to pool hardware resources and run unlimited VSOs. Platinum Edition adds dynamic provisioning of both hosts and VSOs. Citrix offers an original equipment manufacturer (OEM) version of their hypervisor, which comes built into server hardware. Citrix also offers XenDesktop for DeskV and XenApps for AppV.

■   Microsoft offers a host of virtualization technologies in each of the virtualization realms, with additional products in the pipeline (www.microsoft.com/ virtualization). Microsoft currently offers Virtual Server 2005 R2 SP1 and Virtual PC 2007, which are both free but are SoftV products. Its enterprise-class hypervisor, Hyper-V, is part of the Windows Server 2008 OS and will only run on x64 hardware. Microsoft also offers Microsoft Application Virtualization for AppV, Terminal Services for PresentV, and has made some acquisitions to get into DeskV.

▲   VMware offers the most mature products, with a full range of server and desktop virtualization tools (www.vmware.com). It offers VMware Server, which is another free SoftV product; VMware Workstation; and Virtual Infrastructure, which is a complete platform based on its ESX Server hypervisor. VMware was the first to offer a hypervisor baked into the server hardware with ESXi and to make it a free add-on to a host server. VMware also offers the Virtual Desktop Infrastructure (VDI) for DeskV and ThinApp for AppV.

Running any of these vendor products will let you virtualize any environment, whether it is training, testing, development, or even production. And what's even better is that each of these vendors offers a free version of their tools to let you begin your virtualization project without having to break the bank.

NOTE Microsoft Hyper-V will run on any system that is able to run Windows Server. This means it will run on thousands of server configurations. Look up the Windows Hardware Compatibility List for more information at www.microsoft.com/whdc/hcl/default.mspx. VMware ESX and Citrix XenServer will run on select configurations only. For information on the systems supported for VMware, look up the VMware Systems Compatibility Guide for ESX Server 3.5 and 3i at www.vmware.com/pdf/vi35_systems_guide.pdf, and the I/O Compatibility Guide for ESX Server 3.5 and 3i at www.vmware.com/pdf/vi35_io_guide.pdf. For system configurations for Citrix XenServer, look up the XenServer Compatibility list at www.citrix.com/English/ps2/products/feature.asp?contentID=1453254.

Oracle (Oracle VM), Novell (Xen), Red Hat (Xen), IBM, Sun (xVM), Virtual Iron, and others also all offer their own hypervisors, which can and will become confusing if you're trying to figure out which tool to use. Keep to the three main vendors if at all possible. It may not be possible, as some vendors will not support their applications if they are running in a competitor's hypervisor. For example, Oracle will only support its applications if they run on Oracle VM (www.oracle.com/technologies/virtualization/docs/ovm-faq.pdf). Microsoft, however, has a "best effort" support policy for their products running in any version of a hypervisor, whether it is theirs or not (see Knowledge Base Article number 897615 at http://support.microsoft.com/kb/897615).

Keep this in mind when you choose your virtualization platform and management products. Management products, especially, should be hypervisor-agnostic to ensure that you can continue to manage your infrastructure if you do end up running more than one hypervisor. Table 2-1 outlines the various products available from different manufacturers.

Vendor Product	Description
Citrix XenExpress Edition www.citrix.com/ English/ps2/products/ subfeature.asp?contentID=683152	A free edition that is a production-ready virtualization platform and supports dual socket servers with up to 4GB of RAM. XenExpress can host up to four virtual machines on each system and can be upgraded to Standard or Enterprise Edition.
Citrix XenServer Standard Edition www.citrix.com/ English/ps2/products/ subfeature.asp?contentID=683151	XenServer is a virtualization platform for Windows and Linux guest operating systems, and is a native 64-bit Xen hypervisor. XenCenter administrator console supports multiserver management.

Table 2-1. Major Virtualization Solutions (*continued*)

Vendor Product	Description
Citrix XenServer Enterprise Edition or OEM www.citrix.com/English/ps2/ products/subfeature.asp?contentID=683150	In addition to the base features of the Standard Edition, the Enterprise Edition offers XenMotion Live Migration and the ability to manage hardware resource pools.
Citrix XenServer Platinum Edition www.citrix.com/English/ps2/ products/subfeature.asp?contentID=1297952	In addition to the base features of the Enterprise Edition, the Platinum Edition lets you unify virtual and physical server provisioning.
Citrix XenDesktop www.citrix.com/ English/ps2/products/ product.asp?contentID=163057	XenDesktop includes several editions as well. The Express Edition is free and supports up to ten users. The Standard Edition is an entry-level desktop virtualization platform. The Advanced Edition supports virtual desktops but does not include application delivery. The Enterprise Edition adds virtual application delivery. And the Platinum Edition offers an end-to-end desktop delivery solution with virtual application delivery, complete performance monitoring, and Quality of Service (QoS) capabilities, as well as remote virtual desktop support.
Microsoft Virtual Server 2005 Release 2 Service Pack 1 Enterprise Edition http://technet2.microsoft.com/ windowsserver/en/library/ bcc5e200-88af-4a64-963b-55f1efb251d11033 .mspx?mfr=true	Microsoft Virtual Server is a free tool available in both 32-bit and 64-bit versions; however, it only supports 32-bit virtual machines.
Microsoft Virtual PC 2007 www.microsoft.com/ windows/products/winfamily/ virtualpc/overview.mspx? wt_svl=20323a&mg_id=20323b	Virtual PC is also a free tool that can run multiple PC-based operating systems simultaneously on one workstation.
Windows Server 2008 Hyper-V http://technet2.microsoft.com/ windowsserver2008/en/library/ c513e254-adf1-400e-8fcb-c1aec8a029311033 .mspx?mfr=true	Hyper-V is an integrated server role within Windows Server 2008. It is a native 64-bit hypervisor that can run 32-bit and 64-bit VMs concurrently.

Table 2-1. Major Virtualization Solutions (*continued*)

Vendor Product	Description
VMware Server Virtualization www.vmware.com/products	VMware offers several versions of its virtualization products. VMware Server is a free SoftV product. VMware ESX 3i is a free hardware-integrated hypervisor. VMware ESX Server can also be installed on non-hardware–integrated systems. VMware Virtual Infrastructure is a comprehensive set of tools for virtualization management and deployment, and comes in several different editions.
VMware Desktop Virtualization Tools www.vmware.com/products	Virtual Desktop Infrastructure (VDI) is designed to host desktop environments inside VMs running in the datacenter. VMware ThinApp is an AppV solution that supports almost any application. VMware Workstation is a flagship desktop virtualization tool that can run the widest variety of operating systems. VMware Fusion is another desktop virtualization tool, but is designed to run on the Macintosh.

Table 2-1.   Major Virtualization Solutions (*continued*)

There are several benefits to server virtualization:

▼   The first one is certainly at the deployment level. A virtual machine can often be built and customized in less than 20 minutes. You can deliver a virtual machine that is ready to work right away in considerably less time than with a physical machine. But you will have to be careful not to introduce VM proliferation into your infrastructure. You need to continue to control machine requests, whether they are physical or virtual. You don't want to end up with a whole series of virtual machines just because you can create them easily.

■   Another benefit is virtual machine mobility. You can move a VM from one host to another at any time. In some cases, you can move it while it is running. This is a great advantage and will help reduce downtime in your network.

■   Virtual machines are just easy to use. Once it is built and configured, you just start the machine and it is immediately ready to deliver services to users.

■ Virtual machines support standard configurations. You can control the way VMs are built: Just create a standard VM and copy the source files for this VM each time you need a new machine. This way, you will always have standard configurations for any VM.

■ Virtual machines also support the concept of volatile services. If a tester or developer needs a virtual machine to perform a given series of tests, you can fire up a new VM, provide it to them in minutes, and then, when they are done with it, you simply delete it. Try doing that with a physical machine!

■ VMs can be certified by the virtualization vendor, ensuring you are using the best of their technology's capabilities with your VMs.

■ VMs are also secure because they can be completely isolated at any time; just cut off their communications through the host's virtualization technology.

■ VMs can be scaled out or scaled up. To scale out, simply create more VMs with the same services. To scale up, shut down the VM and assign more resources, such as RAM, processor cores, disks, and NICs to it.

▲ VMs are also ideal for disaster recovery, since all you need to do is copy their files to another location, either within your datacenter or to another site entirely.

Because of these core benefits, it is difficult to imagine why anyone would not want to use server virtualization. Server virtualization lets you map computing resources to business requirements in a one-to-one relationship. It allows you to lower IT costs through increased efficiency and resource allocation. You can provision the resources you require on an as-needed basis. Virtualization lets you treat your datacenter as a single pool of resources, blending server hardware with all of the other hardware in the datacenter (see Figure 2-11). With server virtualization, you can turn all end-user service offerings into virtual workloads and turn all hardware resources into resource pools, creating a new datacenter, one that divides all workloads into virtual and physical representations.

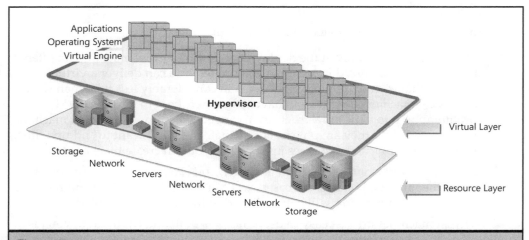

Figure 2-11. Working with resource and virtual layers in the datacenter

Desktop Virtualization

The same technology that powers server virtualization can also power desktop virtualization. Desktop virtualization centralizes desktop deployments so that you can gain complete control over them, letting users rely on a variety of endpoints—thin computing devices, unmanaged PCs, home PCs, or public PCs—to access your corporate desktop infrastructure, once again through the Remote Desktop Connection (RDC). The main difference between DeskV and PresentV, or presentation virtualization, often called Terminal Services or server-based computing, is that in PresentV, users must share the desktop environment with all of the other users connecting to the server. In DeskV, each user gets access to their own desktop, limiting the potential impact of the applications they need on other desktop sessions. By containing applications within virtual desktops, you can guarantee that if something untoward occurs in one virtual desktop, it will not affect any of the others running on the same server.

Just think of what you can do with virtualized desktops by placing them in virtual instances on a server and giving users remote access to the enclosed and controlled environment a virtual desktop provides. As administrators, you can use them to test patch and service pack deployment, provide support in multisystem environments, provide training to end users and technicians alike, or simply provide controlled environments. When your test or training is done, just reset the virtual machine back to its original state and you're back in business. DeskV can be quite a time-saver compared to the cost of managing distributed systems throughout your infrastructure. If you have existing desktops, you can turn them into unmanaged devices because all you need from the physical workstation are three things:

▼ A base operating system, which can be anything from Windows XP to Vista or beyond. This base operating system must be patched and updated, which is something you must do anyway.

■ Proper virus protection, another item you must manage anyway if you have physical desktops.

▲ A Remote Desktop Connection client.

That's it. You don't need additional applications or any other overhead on the system. Managing these endpoints is much more cost-effective than when you have to deploy and update hundreds of applications on them.

If your organization can afford it, transform all of your physical desktops into thin clients. Thin clients update themselves, don't really have any internal software, and are much easier to manage than actual desktops. Each single desktop system you remove from your environment will reduce your power consumption by 650,000 kilowatt-hours per year.

There are several other reasons for moving to virtual desktops. Here are a few:

▼ You can create enterprise-standard lock-down PCs on unmanaged remote PCs. By centralizing the desktop through server virtualization, you can lock down the corporate PC image while letting users run free on the unmanaged physical desktops. This gives you standard, centralized configurations and users are still happy because they can do whatever they feel they need to on the unmanaged PC.

- You can create time-controlled PC images. If your organization is in the habit of hiring temporary or seasonal employees, you can generate time-controlled virtual PC images, which will disappear once the need for them is over. Temporary employees can even work from home using their own PCs, since all they need to access your corporate image is an RDC client, which is part of every Windows installation by default.

- You can also secure information by keeping desktops in the datacenter. By controlling how remote connections are enabled for the virtual PC, you can ensure that any data generated through the PC image is kept within the datacenter and cannot leave the premises. This gives you complete control over corporate intellectual property.

- You can encapsulate complex or sensitive applications, isolating them from any others. For example, employees that must use several different levels of security to access corporate data often had to use several different physical PCs to properly access this data. Now, you can provide them with several different virtual PC images, each configured to support the appropriate level of security.

- DeskV can provide a new migration path to new operating systems. Many people do not move to newer operating systems such as Vista because they must upgrade all of their endpoints to do so, but when you run the new OS in a virtual environment, no endpoints need change since they only require an RDC client to access the updated desktops. This greatly facilitates desktop migrations.

- ▲ DeskV is also a great model for testing and development since like any server virtualization machine, they support undoable disks and can easily be spawned when needed.

To move to a centralized desktop environment, all you need to do is generate a core virtual image and then spawn all other images from this first and standard configuration. From then on, users can rely on any endpoint to access their own personal virtual PC image, even through the firewall (see Figure 2-12).

Application Virtualization

The last key virtualization layer that most closely resembles server virtualization is application virtualization. Application virtualization, or AppV, creates software or service isolation on top of the OS through a special virtualization layer. In this regard, AppV most closely resembles software server virtualization, or SoftV, because it requires an underlying operating system to function. The advantage AppV offers, however, is that it completely protects the OS from any changes applications can make during installation. That's because when you prepare an application for AppV, you don't capture the installation process as organizations did traditionally; instead, you capture the running state of the application or whatever is required to make the application functional on an OS. Because of this, AppV-enabled applications can simply be Xcopied to endpoints since no installation is required. This provides a powerful model for distributed application management. AppV also provides support for application consolidation.

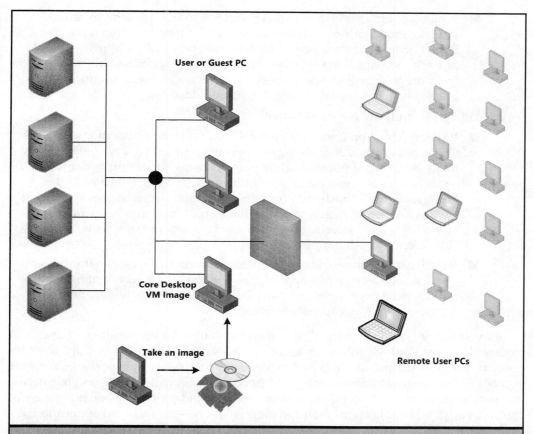

Figure 2-12.   Relying on DeskV lets you maintain standard central images, which users can access from any endpoint.

There are several vendor solutions for AppV:

▼   Application virtualization through streaming technologies:

■   Microsoft Application Virtualization (MAV, formerly SoftGrid) allows you to deliver applications that are never installed and are dynamically delivered on demand. MAV can be deployed on desktops, laptops, or terminal servers. MAV is a core component of the Desktop Optimization Pack for Software Assurance. For more information, see http://technet .microsoft.com/en-us/appvirtualization/default.aspx.

■   Citrix XenApp (formerly Citrix Presentation Server) is an end-to-end Windows application delivery system that offers client-side and server-side application virtualization, as well as presentation virtualization. For more information, see www.citrix.com/english/ps2/products/product .asp?contentid=186.

- ■ Symantec Software Virtualization Solution Pro (SVS) is an application virtualization platform that works through local system filters. The Pro Edition includes a streaming component formerly called Appstream and provides perhaps the most advanced streaming platform on the market. For more information, see www.symantec.com/business/products/overview.jsp?pcid=pcat_infrastruct_op&pvid=sv_sol_pro_1.

- ▲ Agentless application virtualization:

  - ■ VMware ThinApp (formerly Thinstall) encapsulates applications from the OS and each other, eliminating costly regression testing and conflicts from badly behaving applications. Just plug in an .msi or .exe file to deploy a virtual system environment, including registry keys, Dynamic Link Libraries (DLLs), third-party libraries, and frameworks, without requiring any installation of agents or applications on the underlying operating system. For more information, see www.vmware.com/products/thinapp/?hl=en&rlz=&q=thinapp&meta.

  - ■ InstallFree Bridge provides a clientless platform that creates a transparent "bridge" between virtual applications and the OS, protecting the OS from any application changes. For more information, see www.installfree.com/pageload.aspx?page=products_bridge.html.

As you can see, two vendors, VMware and InstallFree, offer solutions that do not require the prior deployment of an agent on the target desktop. This truly liberates applications from any ties or binds and makes them completely transportable. Whether you opt for an agentless or an agent-based AppV solution will depend on your needs, but in most cases, agent deployment is rarely an issue and provides a better measure of control over virtual applications than agentless solutions—no agent, no application; it's as simple as that.

There are several advantages in virtualizing applications. Traditional application installations penetrate the operating system and change its configuration. Eventually, managed or unmanaged systems become completely transformed and unrecognizable. For this reason, many organizations continually reimage their desktops over time to reset them to a known configuration. Instead, application virtualization protects the operating system from any modifications and supports completely secure environments (see Figure 2-13).

And, most importantly, any application that has been virtualized can run on any version of Windows. That's because the AppV layer manages all interactions between a virtual application and Windows. Once an application has been virtualized, it no longer needs to be repackaged each time you need to change the OS. For this reason alone, AppV is one of the most powerful new technologies IT can adopt.

As you can see, virtualization has a significant impact on servers, desktops, and applications. For the servers, virtualization supports hardware consolidation, increases the green footprint of the servers, and provides the best model for business continuity. For the desktops, virtualization supports desktop centralization, information protection, and can provide a secure desktop environment. Finally, virtualization provides

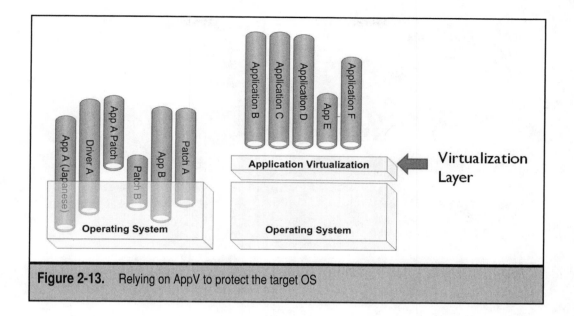

Figure 2-13. Relying on AppV to protect the target OS

the only model organizations should use for distributed system management of applications. The challenge for organizations is knowing how to bring these three layers of virtualization together in a coherent implementation in order to make the most of each technology.

WORK WITH THE FIRST TWO STEPS

The first two steps of the Resolutions Five-Step Process focus on the discovery of new technologies and how they can help your organization move towards a whole new datacenter. Virtualization technologies offer a new paradigm for IT in the datacenter, turning the static environments we have worked with in the past into dynamic environments that can offer services on demand. However, this transformation does not occur on its own; it must be tempered with new ways of doing things. This is what the next three steps will help provide.

CHAPTER 3

Complete the Five-Step Process

Chapter 2 began the Resolutions Five-Step Process. While the first two steps were focused on the discovery of both what is in your network and what virtualization actually is, the remainder of the five steps focus on how you need to adapt your environment to make it all work. Step three outlines how your view of hardware needs to change. Step four looks at how each of the layers—hardware and software—work together to form a cohesive architecture. And step five looks at how your management needs to change to adapt to the dynamic datacenter.

STEP 3: HARDWARE MAXIMIZATION

Now that you understand the different levels at which you can apply virtualization, you can begin to think of how virtualization technologies, especially server virtualization, will change the hardware you run your workloads on. The datacenters of most organizations have evolved into server rooms replete with small, single-purpose servers running from direct-attached storage. While this works in a world rich with resources and where no one needs to worry about space, it no longer works in the dynamic datacenter.

When you move your servers and desktops to virtual workloads, you must consider changing the nature of the hardware you rely on to ensure that the systems you run your virtual workloads on are always highly available. In addition, since the transformation of the datacenter relies on moving low-use workloads onto fewer hardware systems, it is important to make sure that each of the systems you run offers the widest amount of resources to these workloads. For this reason, you must rethink the datacenter and most likely transform it into a leaner and meaner resource pool.

Move to 64-Bit

Since your hardware servers are now going to run multiple virtual workloads, you must consider hardware that can deliver the best price/performance. One of the first places to start is with potential bottlenecks. One of the most important bottlenecks is random access memory (RAM). Since each virtual machine must address its own memory, your server configurations must be designed with the utmost in memory configurations. In addition, the system must use the best resources to make this memory available to each virtual machine. For this reason, it is important to consider 64-bit processor architectures.

In this case, you must look to x64 processors, not Itanium or IA64. x64 processors are an extension of 32-bit x86 architectures and, because of this, can run much of the same code x86 systems can. But, because the x64 architecture is a 64-bit architecture, it can address a lot more memory than x86 systems can. Memory has always been the problem with computing systems. Many years ago, Apple Chairman Steve Jobs was quoted as saying that "developers would just have to learn to program tightly" when referring to the memory limitations of the original Macintosh, which was shipped with only 128 kilobytes (KB) of RAM. It only took Apple eight months before they produced the Fat Mac, a version running with a full 512KB of RAM. The rest is history.

Computers have always needed access to a lot of memory. In fact, memory has been touted as the single most significant limitation for application operation. We're a long way from the kilobytes of the original Macintoshes or IBM PCs, but even when computers are running with true 32-bit processor architectures and the corresponding operating systems, it is possible to run into memory bottlenecks. That's because the 32-bit processor is designed to address no more than 4 gigabytes (GB) of RAM (see Figure 3-1).

In default configurations, the base 4GB of a 32-bit system is divided into two sections. The first 2GB is reserved for kernel processes. This space is allocated to the core operating system (OS). The second 2GB of RAM is assigned to application virtual memory. This is the space where applications can execute. Stopgap measures can change these configurations. For example, if you assign the /3GB switch to the boot process, the kernel process space will be reduced to 1GB and 3GB will be reserved for applications. In this situation, applications have access to more physical memory, but then the core OS becomes a bottleneck because it cannot address its full complement of memory. You can also use the Physical Address Extension, or /PAE switch, at startup. This changes the memory management space from 32 to 36 bits and allows the operating system to swap application memory into the Address Windowing Extensions, providing more physical memory to the system beyond the base 4GB. But when applications need to execute code, they must be swapped back into the base 2GB of application virtual memory (see Figure 3-2). This means that even if a system "sees" more than 4GB of RAM, applications are still bottlenecked by having to fit into the base 2GB to execute.

The only way to move beyond these limitations and access more memory while still executing the same application code is through x64 processor architectures. By default, x64 processor architectures can address more memory, much more memory than their x86 counterparts. The maximum amount of physical memory that will be accessible to your applications depends on the operating system you choose to run. Table 3-1 outlines the various memory limits available based on the version of Windows you run on your x64 machine.

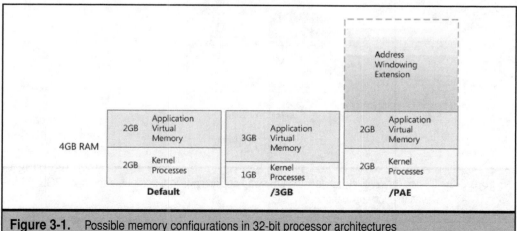

Figure 3-1.   Possible memory configurations in 32-bit processor architectures

Windows Version	Physical Memory Support
Windows XP Professional x64	128GB
Windows Server 2003 Standard x64 Edition	32GB
Windows Server 2003 Enterprise x64 Edition	2 terabytes (TB)
Windows Server 2003 Datacenter x64 Edition	2TB
Windows Vista Home Basic x64	8GB
Windows Vista Home Premium x64	16GB
Windows Vista Business, Enterprise or Ultimate x64	128+GB
Windows Server 2008 Web or Standard x64 Edition	32GB
Windows Server 2008 Enterprise x64 Edition	2TB
Windows Server 2008 Datacenter x64 Edition	2TB

Table 3-1. Memory Support for Windows x64 Editions

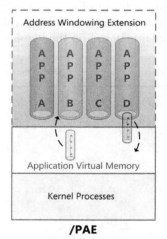

Figure 3-2. Using the /PAE switch lets the OS swap applications into and out of the base 2GB available for applications.

For example, if you are running the x64 Web or Standard Edition of Windows Server 2008, your systems will be able to access up to 32GB of physical RAM. If you are running the x64 Enterprise or Datacenter Edition, your systems will be able to access up to 2TB of RAM. That is significantly more than what is available on a 32-bit system. In addition, each OS can access more than 16TB of virtual memory. Of course, no one has a server configuration that is available with support for 2TB of RAM or a workstation configuration with access to 128GB of RAM, but they can't be that far away.

For Windows Server 2003 systems to access the full RAM capabilities of the x64 platform, they must be running Service Pack 2 or later. In addition, Microsoft claims the x64 versions of Vista Ultimate, Enterprise, and Business Editions can ultimately access more than 128GB of RAM, but the Microsoft Developer Network Web site claims that applications will only have access to 128GB even if more can be found on the system hardware.

One thing is sure: Each and every Windows or Linux OS based on x64 code can access more memory by default than any x86 or 32-bit OS. Accessing this much RAM means applications can now fully execute as intended. Microsoft's Windows Server operating systems can assign a full 8TB of virtual memory to any application. And applications don't have to be written in native x64 code to take advantage of this change; even 32-bit applications will see a performance gain when running on an x64 OS because for the first time in their history, these applications can gain access to a full 4GB of RAM without having to share the base memory blocks with the OS. No more switches are required, and application performance improves in every single instance. The application, however, must be able to support the /LARGEADDRESSAWARE option within its code to profit from the full 4GB of RAM.

If you want to remove the single most constricting bottleneck from your systems, look to x64 operating systems. Few vendors, if any, now sell x86 processors, and all organizations who own them should be running x64 operating systems on x64 hardware, even though the x86 OS is compatible. Best of all, you don't even need to change your applications to access this feature. Every x86 application is x64-compatible by default.

In addition, the current price of 32- and 64-bit server-class machines is nearly identical. Both AMD and Intel offer x64 processors. Many hypervisors are also 64-bit–only hypervisors. While not all hypervisors are 64-bit, all of them at least use 64-bit memory managers. This is one more reason why 64-bit hardware is a must. If you're going to take the time to move to a virtual infrastructure, you should make sure that the systems you use to host virtual workloads are the best and are ready to perform this task for the long term.

Rely on Shared Storage

In addition to removing resource bottlenecks in your server configurations, you must remove potential single points of failure. When you place 10, 20, or even 30 virtual machines on a single host server, you must make sure that there is no way for this host server to fail; otherwise, all of the virtual workloads will also fail, causing some irate end users. For this reason, you must configure hardware with high availability in mind.

In most cases, this means using some form of clustering. While vendors like Microsoft and Citrix actually rely on clustering services to protect the virtual workloads running on their systems, VMware uses a custom configuration called High Availability (HA).

In the end, each configuration is the same: Several computer nodes are linked together to protect the workloads they run. Should one machine fail, the workloads are automatically transferred to another available node.

What makes these configurations work is shared storage. Each node is linked to the same storage container. This means that when a workload needs to fail over, the files that make it up do not need to be moved or copied to the next available computer node. In addition, virtualization technologies support the ability to dynamically move workloads from one system to another when the virtual workload needs more resources than are currently available on the node it resides on at the time. The workload is automatically moved to another node that has available resources without administrative interaction. Once again, this can only be made possible when the virtual workload is located on shared storage of some sort. This is why the best way to store virtual machines is to rely on shared storage (see Figure 3-3). You can store all virtual machines on a shared storage subsystem. In addition, because the systems attached to a shared storage infrastructure are located in the same site, they are considered to provide site-level redundancy. And, since the virtual machine is the point of failure, every application you run inside of them is automatically highly available.

Be careful that your shared storage subsystem does not become a single point of failure of its own. Always think redundancy when planning for hardware components that will support virtual workloads.

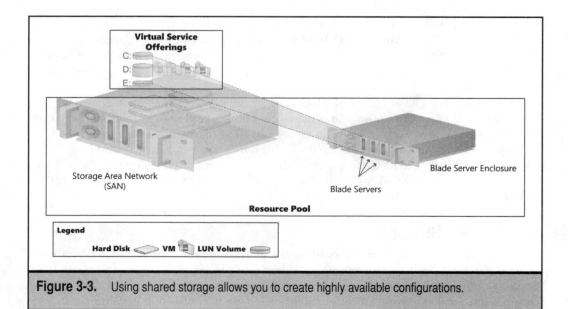

Figure 3-3. Using shared storage allows you to create highly available configurations.

Be Aware of Licensing Costs

The monetary savings of virtualization are incredible and make for an easy business case. First, you save on all of the hardware you no longer need to buy. Second, software manufacturers such as Microsoft have changed their software licensing models to support virtualization ever since the release of Windows Server 2003 R2 (WS03R2) and continuing on with Windows Server 2008 (WS08). Buying a license of Windows Server 2003 R2 or Windows Server 2008 Enterprise Edition now grants you up to four free virtual instances of the OS, as well as providing a license for the host server if you choose to run Windows Server on it. Each additional license gives you up to four more guests. Buying a license of Windows Server 2003 R2 or Windows Server 2008 Datacenter Edition gives you the right to run an unlimited number of virtualized instances of any Windows Server OS. Table 3-2 outlines some of the savings involved in virtualization. Of course, if you run Linux workloads, the licensing issue might be moot.

To help you discover the benefits of virtualization and its impact on operating system licensing, Microsoft has developed a Virtualization Calculator, which can be found at www.microsoft.com/windowsserver2003/howtobuy/licensing/calculator.mspx. The two calculators provide two ways to estimate the number and cost of Windows Server Standard, Enterprise, or Datacenter licenses for virtualization scenarios. The first calculator is designed to estimate the licenses and cost of Windows Server by edition, as well as numerous Microsoft Server products on a single, physical server (see Figure 3-4). The second calculator helps you estimate the licenses and costs of only the Windows

Category	Potential Saving
Hardware	Each server or desktop you do not purchase puts money in your pocket.
OS Licensing	Using Windows Server 2003 R2 or 2008 Enterprise Edition saves 75 percent on license costs if you intend to virtualize a Server OS.
	Using Windows Server 2003 R2 or 2008 Datacenter Edition provides unlimited virtual machine licenses.
Power	Each machine (server or desktop) you virtualize does not draw any more power than its host.
Cooling	Each machine you virtualize does not require any more cooling than its host.
Datacenter Space	Each machine you virtualize does not require any more space than its host.

Table 3-2.   Potential Savings Due to Virtualization

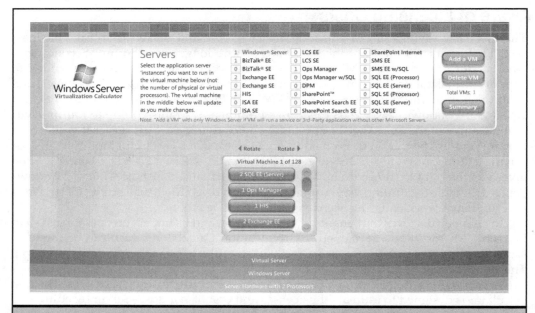

Figure 3-4.   Microsoft Virtualization Licensing Calculator Number 1

Server OS by edition for one or more physical servers (see Figure 3-5). Rely on these tools to determine just what the potential savings of virtualizing Windows Server operating systems can be. Finally, you can rely on Microsoft's return on investment (ROI) calculator to determine the benefits you'll obtain from moving to virtualization.

NOTE   For more information on the Microsoft ROI calculator, go to www.microsoft.com/virtualization/ ROItool/default.mspx.

In addition, Microsoft has modified the licensing model of the Windows Vista desktop. The new Windows Vista Enterprise Centralized Desktop (VECD) license allows you to run up to four virtual desktops per user at one time with one single Windows license. It also lets you run any version of the Windows desktop. For example, you could run two copies of Vista, one copy of XP, and one copy of Windows 2000 per user with the same license. This model lets you manage and maintain applications that do not run on newer versions of the OS by placing them into virtual machines that run older versions. You can learn more about VECD at www.microsoft.com/virtualization/solution-product-vecd .mspx.

In all, even vendors of proprietary code such as Windows understand the value of virtualization and the need organizations have of reducing their carbon footprint by moving to a dynamic datacenter model.

Windows Server Virtualization Calculator

Price per License for Each Edition

Standard*	$ 719
Enterprise*	$ 2334
Datacenter	$ 2381

Please use model A or B

A. Group servers by # of processors and average number of VMs

B. List each server individually

Print   Reset   Need Help?

* Standard and Enterprise editions include CALs. A single Standard Edition license does not grant rights to run both a host OS and guest OS, so an additional license is required for the host OS. Standard Edition is able to run on 1-4 processor servers and Enterprise Edition is able to run on 1-8 processor servers.

Disclaimer

A.

Processor	# of Servers	Avg # of VMs per Server	Number of Licenses Needed			Price for Each Edition		
			Standard	Enterprise	Datacenter	Standard*	Enterprise*	Datacenter
1	10	20	200	50	10	$ 143800	$ 116700	$ 23810
2	5	30	150	40	10	$ 107850	$ 93360	$ 23810
4	0	0	0	0	0	$ 0	$ 0	$ 0
8	0	0		0	0		$ 0	$ 0
16	0	0			0			$ 0
32	0	0			0			$ 0
64	0	0			0			$ 0
			350	90	20	$ 251650	$ 210060	$ 47620

B.

Server	# of Processors	# of VMs on Server	Number of Licenses Needed			Price for Each Edition		
			Standard	Enterprise	Datacenter	Standard*	Enterprise*	Datacenter
1	2	20	20	5	2	$ 14380	$ 11670	$ 4762
2	2	20	20	5	2	$ 14380	$ 11670	$ 4762
3	2	20	20	5	2	$ 14380	$ 11670	$ 4762
4	2	20	20	5	2	$ 14380	$ 11670	$ 4762
5	2	20	20	5	2	$ 14380	$ 11670	$ 4762
6	2	20	20	5	2	$ 14380	$ 11670	$ 4762
7	2	20	20	5	2	$ 14380	$ 11670	$ 4762
8	2	20	20	5	2	$ 14380	$ 11670	$ 4762
9	2	20	20	5	2	$ 14380	$ 11670	$ 4762
10	2	20	20	5	2	$ 14380	$ 11670	$ 4762
11	4	30	30	8	4	$ 21570	$ 18672	$ 9524
12	4	30	30	8	4	$ 21570	$ 18672	$ 9524
13	4	30	30	8	4	$ 21570	$ 18672	$ 9524
14	4	30	30	8	4	$ 21570	$ 18672	$ 9524
15	4	30	30	8	4	$ 21570	$ 18672	$ 9524
			350	90	40	$ 251650	$ 210060	$ 95240

Figure 3-5.   Microsoft Virtualization Licensing Calculator Number 2

Rely on New Server Form Factors

Because you need x64 servers linked to shared storage, you can begin to consider different server form factors. Today, organizations build complex multipurpose servers for remote offices or small organizations. With virtualization, you no longer need to do this. For example, you might build a remote office server to include several roles—domain controller, file server, print server, management server, database server, and so on. Building such a server requires many compromises. Domain controllers should always be protected at all times. Having users access file or print services through a domain controller forces you to either reduce the security of the server or make file access more complex than it needs to be. With the advent of virtual machines, you can now separate all of these roles without having to pay extra licenses. But this means looking to new server types. All-in-one-servers or server pods, which include two physical servers, network switches, and shared storage (see Figure 3-6), are ideal for this scenario, whether it is for a remote or small office.

HP, for example, now offers blade enclosures that can host both server and storage blades in the same enclosure. In addition these enclosures can run on normal, 110-volt power outlets, no longer requiring special power installations to operate. Right now,

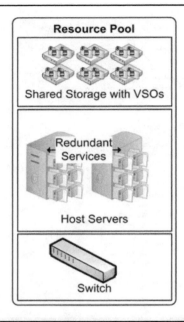

Figure 3-6. Using a server pod to host VMs in small or remote offices

HP offers two different types of such enclosures: the c3000 (see Figure 3-7), which is a half-height enclosure that is good for a small office, and the c7000, which is a normal, full-height enclosure. To learn more about these enclosures, go to http://h20384.www2 .hp.com/serverstorage/cache/536425-0-0-0-121.html.

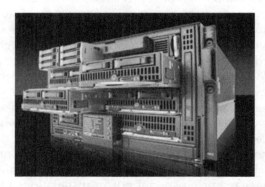

Figure 3-7. The HP BladeSystem c3000 half-height enclosure, commonly called "shorty"

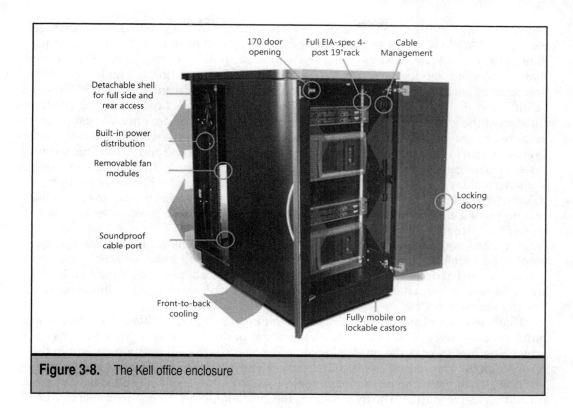

Figure 3-8. The Kell office enclosure

Finally, if you need to place new enclosures in locations that do not have datacenters, you should look to new enclosure models. Another vendor, Kell Systems, sells new smart enclosures that fit in any office (see Figure 3-8). These enclosures look just like standard office furniture, but provide cooling, power, and space in a soundproof casing for either blade or rack-mounted servers. This makes a lot of sense if you want to secure your host systems but virtualize all of your workloads, even in remote offices. For more information on Kell Systems, see www.kellsystems.com.

There is no doubt that as you move forward with your virtualization project, looking to new hardware, or at least repurposing existing hardware, will be something that you must include in the various phases of your project.

STEP 4: ARCHITECTURES

The next step in the process is to update and revise your datacenter architectures. Working with multiple virtualization layers can become quite confusing if they aren't structured properly. You've already seen that there are quite a few elements to a virtualized infrastructure. For example, to protect your virtual workloads, you'll want to use x64 systems linked to shared storage and arranged into some form of high-availability cluster.

But you can also cluster in the virtual layer. For example, when you build an Exchange Server 2007 Mailbox server to store user mailboxes, you'll most likely want to take advantage of the failover clustering and replication capabilities of this product to ensure that the Mailbox service provided by the Virtual Service Offering is highly available. The same might apply to a SQL Server database server. If you want your Web servers to be highly available, you'll probably build them into a Network Load Balancing cluster. Clusters at the virtual layer are not only good practice, but they are often a must. That's because any machine that is clustered is much easier to maintain—offload the workload to another machine in the cluster so you can patch the current one and so on. This means systems management has little impact, if any, on end-user productivity. And clustering in the virtual layer is practically free since you don't need custom hardware to support it. Keep in mind that clustered virtual machines must use non-affinity rules to ensure the two nodes of a cluster do not reside on the same host; otherwise, it would be useless to cluster the virtual machines (VMs) in the first place.

But when you build clusters within a cluster, it can become confusing. Another example of a possible source of confusion is when you create virtual servers to provide services to virtual desktops that are running virtual applications inside virtual networks while relying on virtual storage. Quick. Which layer isn't virtualized in this scenario? Tough to answer, isn't it?

That's where a visual architecture can help (see Figure 3-9). In this architecture, you build seven different layers of virtualization and address each with a particular construct. The first layer is the physical layer and will include each component within the resource pool. The second is the storage layer and will rely on storage virtualization technologies to provision just as many logical units (LUNs) as you need for both physical and virtual resources. The third layer is the allocation layer. Since Virtual Service Offerings (VSOs) are nothing more than a set of files in a folder somewhere, they can and should be moved dynamically from one physical host to another as additional resources are required or when management operations are required on a specific host. It is this allocation layer, or the tracking of VSO positioning, that transforms the datacenter from static to dynamic. It is also within this layer that you create and assign virtual networks based on your hypervisor's capabilities.

The fourth layer is the virtual layer; it is where you determine what will be virtualized and will eventually come to include server and workstation workloads. The fifth layer addresses both physical and virtual resource management. Keep in mind that both resource levels rely on a different security context. In addition, you may use different tools to manage the two infrastructure levels. The sixth layer is the PC layer. While many will move to virtual desktop infrastructures to reduce the cost of managing distributed systems, others will find that by moving to virtualized applications, the entire business model of distributed desktop management is positively transformed—so much, in fact, that they will never go back to application installations.

The last and final layer is the business continuity layer. Since Virtual Service Offerings are nothing more than files in a folder somewhere, business continuity practices become much simpler: Just replicate the make-up of every virtual machine to an off-site location and you'll have a duplicate of your entire datacenter available at all times. In addition, the physical resources in the remote datacenter need not be the same as

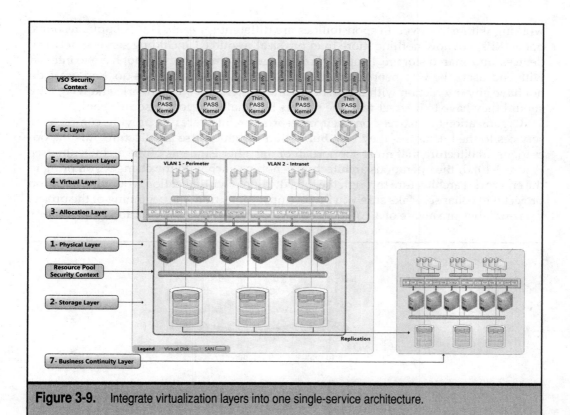

Figure 3-9. Integrate virtualization layers into one single-service architecture.

those in the production datacenter. After all, in a disaster, you only need to start and run critical services. This should take considerably fewer resources than running the entire production system.

There you have it. A seven-layer virtualization architecture with each layer building upon the other to support the new, dynamic datacenter. Now that you understand each layer and what goes into it, you can start building the infrastructure that will run it. And, when you feel ready, you can convert your physical workloads into Virtual Service Offerings and completely transform your datacenter once and for all. Of course, the best place to start will always be in the laboratory. Test everything fully before you move to production systems.

STEP 5: MANAGE VIRTUALIZATION

The dynamic datacenter is now divided into two layers: resource pools and Virtual Service Offerings. Because of this, operations should be divided into two segments as well. If you have the staff, you should dedicate separate staff to manage each layer. If not, you should ensure administrators and technicians learn to wear different "hats" when working with each layer. Responsibilities are different for each. For example, resource pools (RPs) are now nothing more than physical resources, including servers, network devices, and shared storage. People who manage these resources do not have to interact with end users the way people who manage your virtual workloads do. End users do not have any interaction with the switches and routers in your network, and if so, why should they have to interact with the servers that make up your resource pools?

Organizations must rely on their enterprise architectures to provide complete IT services to the businesses they run. But within the enterprise architecture, it is the operations architecture that must support all of the other elements of the architecture (see Figure 3-10). If the operations architecture is not in synch with the changes you bring to the enterprise architecture through the introduction of virtualization, your virtualization project will collapse. Make sure you involve operations from the beginning of the project to ensure they are aware of all of the facets of IT affected by virtualization.

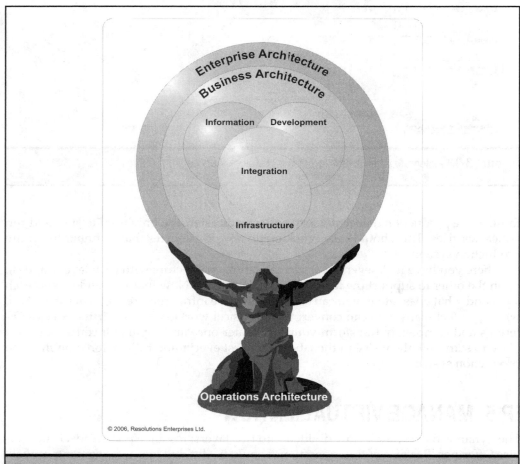

© 2006, Resolutions Enterprises Ltd.

Figure 3-10.   The Operations architecture provides support for all other architectures.

NOTE For more information on enterprise architectures and how they interact with operations, see www.reso-net.com/articles.asp?m=8#f under "Architectures."

The changes introduced by virtualization are far-reaching. The activities related to VSOs entail several different tasks. Security contexts are also different. Your host servers can be part of a highly secure infrastructure since only administrators need to interact with them. Your VSOs must be more relaxed since both end users and administrators must interact with them.

NOTE For a list of more than 150 administration tasks for RPs and VSOs, see *Windows Server 2008: The Complete Reference* by Ruest & Ruest (McGraw-Hill, 2008).

Focus on VM Management

In addition, virtual machine management brings issues of its own to the fore. Because of this, you will need to review your management structure, and in doing so, you will need to ask the right questions when you are looking for new management tools. For example, consider the following questions:

▼ How are VM source images tracked and updated?

■ How are VM snapshots tracked? Each virtual machine can include up to 512 snapshots of previous states. If you have 1,000 virtual machines, this can add up to a considerable amount of snapshots.

■ How are move, adds, and changes (MACs) tracked, especially when machines are dynamically moved from one host to another?

■ How are virtual workload policies prepared and deployed? Policies can include the types of resources assigned to a virtual machine, the priority one VM is given over another, the times of day when the VM must have access to core resources, and so on.

■ Are there special dependencies between applications and VMs? If you have a multi-tier application running in a virtual environment, linking front-end Web servers to back-end databases, you must be aware of virtual machine dependencies and so must your management tools.

■ How is security managed between resource pools and Virtual Service Offerings? What kind of segregation is in place? Are all communications to resource servers encrypted to protect passwords?

■ What kind of troubleshooting support does the tool provide when VMs or hosts go down? Can the tool identify root causes—physical or virtual or both—of the problems you face?

■ Is the tool fully functional and does it provide a one-stop shop? Can it manage every aspect of virtualization?

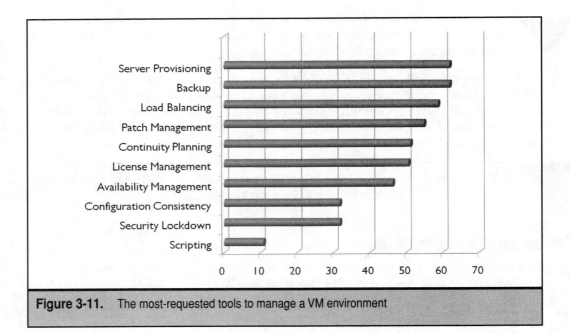

Figure 3-11.   The most-requested tools to manage a VM environment

■   Should you use the same tools for the resource pool and the VSOs? Perhaps a segregation of tools would help in securing the two infrastructures separately.

▲   Is the tool hypervisor-agnostic? Will it grow with your needs? What if you need to implement new hypervisors due to application support policies? Can your tool accommodate these changes?

You're not alone in looking for the right tools. Most administrators and managers moving to virtualization are also preoccupied with systems management and support for both the physical and the virtual world. According to a survey performed by Ziff-Davis Research on February 18, 2008, administrators look for tools to solve specific management issues (see Figure 3-11).

RELY ON THE VIRTUALIZATION DECISION FLOWCHART

Now you're ready to begin the project. You have just enough understanding to know where virtualization can help and how you should proceed. Each level of virtualization will bring specific benefits with its introduction into your datacenter. However, you need a structured approach for the implementation of the three core aspects of virtualization: server, desktop, and application virtualization. For this, you need a specific decision process (see Figure 3-12). This flowchart addresses each implementation aspect and ties it to

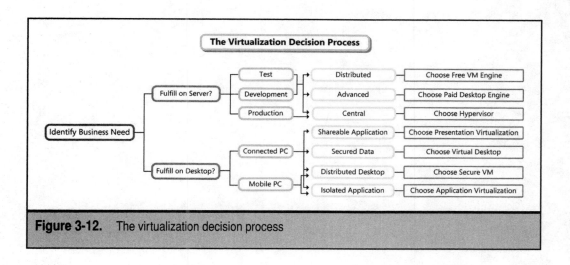

Figure 3-12. The virtualization decision process

the business need you wish to fulfill. As you can see, it outlines whether the fulfillment of the business need will be on the server back-end or the desktop front-end and then proceeds from there based on how you want to address the need.

The remainder of this book will move through this flowchart to help you understand how each aspect is addressed. First, you'll need to prepare your physical infrastructure. This is addressed in Chapters 4, 5, and 6. Then you'll need to implement server virtualization in order to support both physical server consolidation and desktop centralization. This is addressed in Chapters 7 and 8. Then, once your server infrastructure is in place, you can move to desktop virtualization through the instructions in Chapter 10. Finally, application virtualization and the concept of the volatile virtual desktop are addressed in Chapters 11 and 12. The remaining chapters address security and business continuity to round out your virtual infrastructure and dynamic datacenter.

PART II

Build Your Virtualization Infrastructure

CHAPTER 4

Perform a Comprehensive Analysis

A s you have seen in Chapter 1, there are a lot of reasons for moving from a physical to a virtual infrastructure for service delivery. Traditional datacenters are facing similar issues on a worldwide basis. According to a Network World analysis performed on January 7, 2008, power and cooling costs in the datacenter are skyrocketing and need to be controlled (see Figure 4-1). In addition, all datacenter managers agree that:

▼ Physical servers are taking up too much room

■ Physical servers are underused, sometimes from 5 to 15 percent

■ Physical servers generate too much heat

■ Physical servers need more and more power

■ Physical datacenters need complex business continuity solutions

■ Downtime is a constant issue that must be eliminated

▲ Hardware management is complex and must be simplified

The answer to all of these woes is, of course, virtualization. Virtualization transforms the physical server by increasing its workload up to 80 percent while delivering the same services organizations have come to expect from IT infrastructures.

Because of this, virtualization has a direct impact on server sales. Research firm IDC predicts that the three-year sales forecast of servers will be cut by $4.5 million. Originally, IDC projected that the sale of servers would increase by 61 percent by 2010, but now its forecast is down by 31 percent.

Organizations are discovering that the break-even point is three virtual machines per host server, and a minimum of 15 servers need to be physically consolidated to cover the implementation costs of virtualization. While many are using rack-mounted servers for this consolidation, blade servers are also a viable option since they are far easier

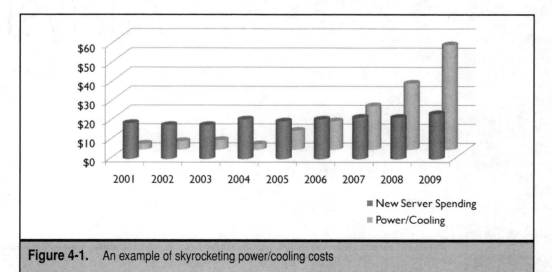

Figure 4-1.   An example of skyrocketing power/cooling costs

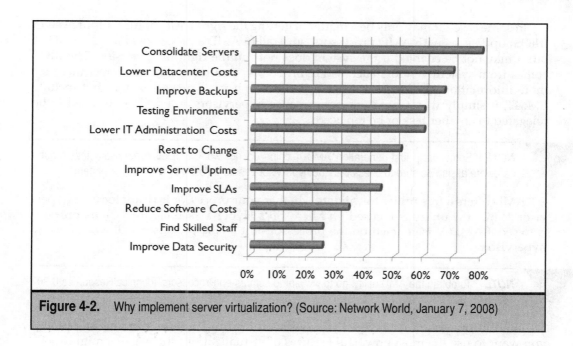

Figure 4-2.   Why implement server virtualization? (Source: Network World, January 7, 2008)

to implement once the blade enclosure is set up. Organizations moving forward with virtualization projects reap several benefits (see Figure 4-2).

But moving to virtualization is not a simple project and must be approached with care. Chapters 2 and 3 highlighted the importance of two aspects of the Five-Step Process for virtualization: the first, Discovery, and the third, Hardware Maximization. Both are extremely important to the success of the project. Discovery fuels the planning process by providing the input for the change, and Hardware Maximization lets you create the hardware foundation that will support your new virtualized service offerings. Both are addressed in this chapter and the next.

BEGIN THE ANALYSIS

The first thing you should do to prepare your physical servers is analyze your IT environment to identify if areas need improvement before you move on to virtualization. Ideally, all of your physical servers are newer and include the right processors—those with hardware virtualization capabilities. For Intel, this means a Virtual Technology (VT)–enabled processor or a processor that includes the Extended Memory 64 Technology (EM64T). With AMD, this means an AMD-V–enabled processor. Be very careful when evaluating your servers because if they do not include these features, you will not be able to run some hypervisors. For example, you will not be able to run hypervisors such as Microsoft Hyper-V or Citrix XenServer on it; the virtualization engines from Citrix or Microsoft simply won't load if your processors are not VT-enabled. No hypervisor, no virtual machines.

In some cases, it may only be a matter of getting the right Basic Input/Output System (BIOS) update, as with AMD processors, since all of AMD's processors include AMD-V, but it may not be enabled if the system does not run the right BIOS version. The BIOS comes from system vendors such as HP or Dell, so you may have to contact them for more information. As for Intel, it's much simpler; if your processor does not include EM64T, it simply won't run high-performance hypervisors and will either need to be relegated to another task or be replaced.

NOTE Some early first-generation AMD-V chips do not work with all hypervisors that require hardware assist. Be sure to check with the hypervisor vendor before you purchase a system.

AMD offers a free utility to validate whether your processor is ready to run a hypervisor. While the utility is focused on Microsoft's Hyper-V (see Figure 4-3), its purpose is to see if AMD-V is enabled on the processor; if it is, the processor will work for any hypervisor.

NOTE To obtain the AMD utility, go to www.amd.com/us-en/Processors/TechnicalResources/0,30_ 182_871_9033,00.html.

In addition, you must ensure that your server processors use the same stepping if you want to use the most powerful features of virtualization, such as live migration—moving a virtual machine from one host to another while the virtual machine is still running and delivering services to end users. For VMware, this feature is called VMotion; for Citrix XenServer, it is called XenMotion. This process basically copies all of the in-memory processes from one physical server to another. Since the contents of memory include processor instruction sets, the process of moving those contents from one machine to another will only work if the two processors can handle the same instruction set. For this reason, this process will not work between Intel and AMD processors, and in many cases, will not work between two Intel processors unless they have the same stepping. The CPUID development site includes a utility that you can

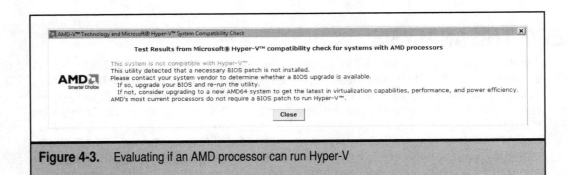

Figure 4-3. Evaluating if an AMD processor can run Hyper-V

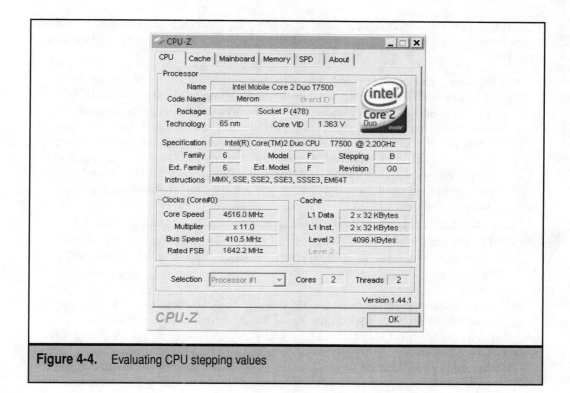

Figure 4-4. Evaluating CPU stepping values

use to evaluate CPU stepping values, CPU-Z.exe (see Figure 4-4). Run this utility on any servers you want to retain as hosting equipment to make sure you can match processor families into groups of host systems.

NOTE   Intel "flex migration" solves the Intel-to-Intel migration issues. AMD has a similar feature. Both rely on the hypervisors to support "feature disable bits," which turns off more advanced hardware-assisted virtualization features that are not supported by all nodes in the cluster. The hypervisor you use will let you configure this feature. If this is important to you, make sure you check the hypervisor support for this feature before you choose it. For example, the first version of Microsoft Hyper-V does not include this feature. However, VMware does it through a feature called CPU Masking which is part of its Enhanced VMotion Compatibility (EVC) setting. In fact, you can use this feature to support the live migration of VMs from an Intel to an AMD processor and back.

NOTE   To obtain the CPU-Z utility, go to www.cpuid.com/cpuz.php.

But server validation is not the only activity your planning process needs to include. In addition, you must evaluate each of the hardware layers that will affect virtualization, including:

▼ **Storage**   You must perform two activities at the storage level. First, you can use tools such as the Windows File System Resource Manager—available in Windows Server 2003 R2 and 2008—to identify the status of the content of your storage containers: direct attached, networked attached, and storage area networks, if you have them. Then you should rely on this analysis to determine which files could be archived. The second activity is to look for storage that can be reused as virtual machine containers. Ideally, storage will be shared when hosting virtual machines. For this, you must use tools that come from your storage vendors.

NOTE   For more information on Windows File System Resource Manager, see http://technet2 .microsoft.com/windowsserver2008/en/library/d6d480ca-18ec-4dee-aafc-a9e7971038cf1033 .mspx?mfr=true.

■ **Network bandwidth**   You should identify the current network bandwidth usage. Rely on tools such as the Windows Network Monitor, Windows Performance Monitor at the network interface card utilization level, or tools from third parties. You want to be able to identify if the available bandwidth can support additional workloads, such as live virtual machine migrations, or even if it can support storage traffic through protocols such as Internet Small Computer Systems Interface (iSCSI).

■ **Power and cooling**   You should perform a power and cooling audit to ensure your datacenter infrastructure can handle a move to a virtual infrastructure. The audit will serve two purposes. First, it will act as a starting point for a potential rebate from utility companies for moving to a virtual infrastructure. Second, it will identify any issues with your current infrastructure. You can use tools from American Power Conversion at www.APC.com to identify possible issues in the datacenter infrastructure.

▲ **Hardware consolidation**   You should scan your network to identify potential hardware consolidation candidates. For this, you can use the tools from VMware, Microsoft, or others as described in step one of the Five-Step Process.

NOTE   Enterprise-class consolidation tools can do all of these things. However, tools such as CiRBA's Placement Intelligence Technology tool (www.cirba.com), while they can support all of these functions, are available only on a subscription basis, with a specific cost attached to each physical server you run in your network.

Put as much emphasis as possible into these four studies. The value of each study will depend on the size of your infrastructure. For example, if you only have 25 physical servers, a power and cooling audit may not reap as many benefits as if you have 2,000 physical servers, but it is still important to know that your current systems can handle the change you are planning for.

Remember, if you are not starting off on the right foot with your virtualization project, you will run into issues further down the road when your physical systems cannot handle the load your virtual machines place on them. Avoid this pitfall and perform in-depth analyses now.

CAUTION   Too many organizations focus solely on performance when conducting a consolidation analysis and don't consider non-technical limitations until late into the consolidation project. Items such as security subzone, site location, department ownership, service level agreements (SLAs), and even product licensing can all impact the eventual consolidation plan. Make sure you include them in your initial analysis.

PERFORM A STORAGE CONSOLIDATION STUDY

As mentioned earlier, there are two steps to any storage validation for virtualization. First, you want to scan all storage to identify what can be removed from the infrastructure. Too many IT shops simply continue to add storage whenever space issues arise without analyzing what it is they are storing. For example, when a user sends out a 5-megabyte (MB) Microsoft PowerPoint slide deck to ten others through e-mail, you often end up with multiple copies of the presentation in your storage systems. If all of the users are on the same Microsoft Exchange mailbox server, at least Exchange will deduplicate the ten copies within the e-mail system, but as soon as users are on other mailbox servers, you get more copies. In addition, some users will copy the presentation to the file system, which creates even more duplicates. In the end, the 5-MB presentation can easily take up to 100MB of space.

When you move to virtualization, you will want to obtain storage technologies that can support deduplication, not at the backup level, but at the storage level. Virtual machine files often range into multiple gigabytes in size and can take up enormous amounts of space, but if your storage engine can deduplicate their contents as they are stored, you will save a lot on your disk substructure.

This is why file server analysis is so important. If you can recover this space, deduplicate items, and otherwise archive unused data, you can release the storage spindles to other purposes. Once again, there are several tools that can help you perform this task. Windows Server has included a File System Resource Manager (FSRM) since the 2003 R2 version. This engine can scan all file servers and classify storage in a number of different ways. For this tool to work, each file server must be running either Windows Server

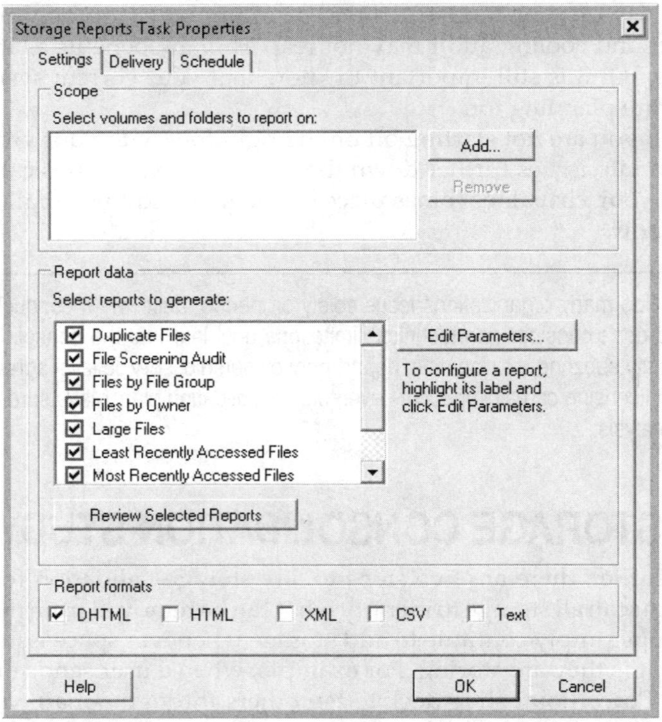

Figure 4-5. Preparing storage reports with FSRM

2003 R2 or 2008 and have the FSRM engine loaded on it. Storage reports can be run from any server in the group and can provide comprehensive information on a variety of data storage aspects (see Figure 4-5).

Several other tools are available for the generation of storage reports. For example, storage provider EMC offers the File System Assessment tool, which is most commonly used by consulting firms to help you determine just how much of your storage—direct attached (DAS), network attached (NAS), or storage area networks (SAN)—is being wasted by storing the same information more than once or, even worse, storing unused information.

The second part of your assessment identifies storage types. As mentioned in Chapter 3, you most often need to consider shared storage in some way in order to support the most advanced features of the virtualization engines available today and provide high availability for your virtual workloads. However, not all virtual workloads will require shared storage. For example, you may determine that some outages are acceptable on certain types of environments. Testing and development environments will often run on DAS for smaller networks because the cost of shared storage for these workloads is simply not justifiable. In addition, smaller offices may opt to create virtual infrastructures based on DAS. This is possible if each of the direct attached containers is replicated to the other to make sure virtual machine content is in sync between the hosts that share a high-availability configuration. Products such as LeftHand Virtual SAN Appliance (VSA) will let you replicate contents from one DAS container to another. VSA supports VMware now, and will probably support the other major hypervisors by the time you read this book. Find it at www.lefthandnetworks.com.

NOTE   HP acquired LeftHand Networks in October 2008.

Medium offices may opt for NAS devices, as they provide file sharing services and can be linked to more than one host. Large datacenters will most certainly opt for SANs since they will require top-level performance from the storage arrays.

Knowing what type of storage is in use, how much storage is available, and how systems are connected to storage will greatly assist in the preparation of the host server infrastructure. Virtual machine files tend to be large and will require fast and efficient storage to run at their best.

REVIEW EXISTING NETWORK BANDWIDTH

With virtualization, network usage will also change. In many cases, organizations will opt to move to iSCSI to connect to shared storage containers instead of using the more traditional Fibre Channel connections through host bus adapters (HBAs). In this case, all storage traffic runs over the network and requires significantly more throughput than network resources alone.

In addition, each virtual machine running on a system must have network connections of some type. Virtualization technologies support virtual machine isolation, virtual machine connections to the host server only, or full connectivity for the virtual machine. The latter requires additional network interface cards on the host server. If a host is running 30 or more virtual machines at the same time, you will have to ensure it has enough network interface cards (NICs) to support these workloads. But you also have to make sure your current infrastructure—switches, routers, hubs—support the additional workload at the network layer. In some cases, you may have to upgrade some of the networking components in your datacenter. Once again, it will depend on the workload you plan to run at the virtual layer, but this analysis is also just as important as any of the others.

Therefore, when you scan your current network status, you should try to answer the following questions.

▼   Which services are running and what bandwidth do they require? For example, if you are currently running technologies such as Microsoft Exchange Server 2007 or SQL Server 2008, you may already have set up replication partners in remote sites. Adding to this workload may put the workload at risk.

■   Moving memory contents from one host server to another puts a strain on your physical servers as well as the network. Technologies such as VMotion or XenMotion often require network paths of their own to function adequately. Is your infrastructure ready to support this additional traffic?

■   If you choose to rely on shared storage and access it through iSCSI, will your networking equipment support the additional load?

▲   How old are your switches and routers? Are any upgrades required? Are any ports left?

The answers to these questions will help you assess what you will require at the networking level when you prepare the host environment.

PERFORM A POWER AND COOLING AUDIT

One of the most attractive aspects of virtualization and physical server consolidation is the potential power savings. Power savings are calculated on a per-server basis. Utility companies have devised an equation to calculate your potential power savings:

$$\text{Savings}_{\text{Power}} = E_{\$}[(S_{\text{TTLPWR}})_{\text{Before}} - (S_{\text{TLLPWR}})_{\text{After}}]$$

Table 4-1 explains the values used in the equation.

NOTE   For more information on calculating potential power savings, look up *Virtualization: The Most Impactful Solution to the Data Center Power Crisis* by VMware at www.vmware.com/files/pdf/ Energy_Efficiency_WP.pdf.

According to IDC professional John Humphries (data released in 2007), the state of the datacenter infrastructure is such that there is now $140 billion in excess server capacity, which is comparable to a three-year supply of servers. Power expenditures are an average of $0.50 for every $1 dollar spent on server acquisitions. More than $29 billion is spent on power and cooling industry-wide. Space is also at a premium. Server space in the datacenter costs $1,000 per square foot, $2,400 per server, and $40,000 per rack. Operating costs range up to $8 in maintenance for every $1 spent on new infrastructure components. The current server administration ratio is 20 or 30 servers per administrator.

Input	Description	Default Value	Source
S_{TTLPWR}	Standard power ratings for servers	Before/After 1 CPU: 475W/550W 2 CPU: 550W/675W 4 CPU: 950W/1150W 8 CPU: 1600W/1900W 16 CPU: 4400W/5200W 32 CPU: 9200W/11000W	From manufacturer's Web sites in server specifications. Can also use a tool like Dell's Data Center Capacity Planner.
$E_\$$	Price per hour of 1 kW of electricity	$.0813 (average in U.S. in 2005)	Energy information administration
λ	Constant	.67 (delta between, before and after)	APC estimate

Table 4-1. Calculating Potential Power Savings

Reducing this footprint and increasing the value derived from hardware is a must. This is why power and cooling assessments are important. They help in two ways.

▼   First, they give you an idea of how your infrastructure can handle the move to virtualization.

▲   Second, they provide the potential for rebates from your utility company.

Many organizations have never performed a power and cooling assessment, and may be at a loss as to how it should be approached. Fortunately, APC offers several free tools to help out in this case (see Table 4-2). These tools fall into three categories. The first are calculators, which, once you provide them with input, will provide estimates of costs. The second are selectors, which help you choose how to organize datacenter contents. The third are illustrators, which provide graphical outlines of your choices and calculations. Each has value.

NOTE For more information on APC TradeOff Tools, see www.apc.com/prod_docs/results .cfm?DocType=TradeOff%20Tool&Query_Type=10.

The Data Center Carbon Calculator is used to identify your current carbon footprint (see Figure 4-6). It relies on the inputs you provide based on potential scenarios to outline just how much carbon dioxide (CO_2) your datacenter produces and what its equivalent in automobile output is.

APC Product	Description
Data Center Carbon Calculator	Identify the impact of changes in datacenter efficiency on energy cost and carbon footprint
Data Center Efficiency Calculator	Identify the impact of alternative power and cooling approaches on energy costs
Data Center Capital Cost Calculator	Identify the impact of physical infrastructure design changes on capital costs
Virtualization Energy Cost Calculator	Identify the impact of server virtualization and datacenter design choices on energy and space savings
Data Center Power Sizing Calculator	Identify the impact of server and storage configurations on IT load capacity and required utility input power
Data Center InRow Containment Selector	Identify the impact of preferences and constraints on the recommended containment approach

Table 4-2. APC TradeOff Tools for the Datacenter Infrastructure

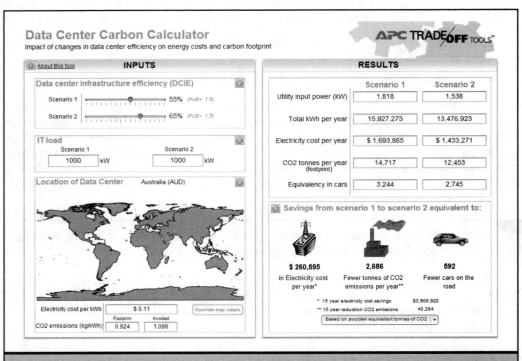

Figure 4-6. Data Center Carbon Calculator (Courtesy of APC)

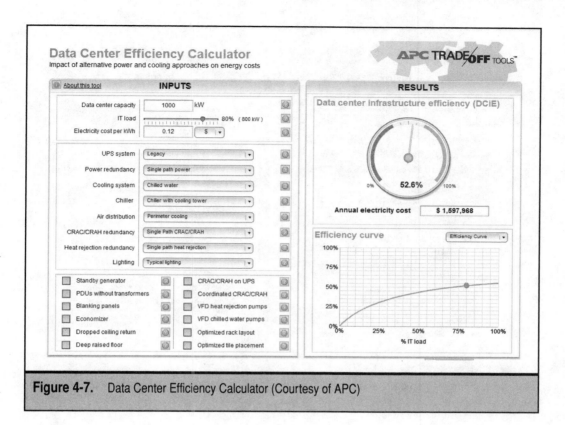

Figure 4-7. Data Center Efficiency Calculator (Courtesy of APC)

The Data Center Efficiency Calculator also relies on input you provide about your datacenter configuration to help determine where you stand in overall design and utilization efficiency (see Figure 4-7). This calculator is used to validate that your current datacenter configuration is as efficient as possible.

The Data Center Capital Cost Calculator helps you when you plan infrastructure changes to your datacenter (see Figure 4-8). If you determine that your datacenter design is not as efficient as it could be, you can rely on this calculator to help determine which changes offer the best value for the cost.

The Virtualization Energy Cost Calculator is probably the most valuable calculator in this grouping, since it outlines just how much power and cooling you will save

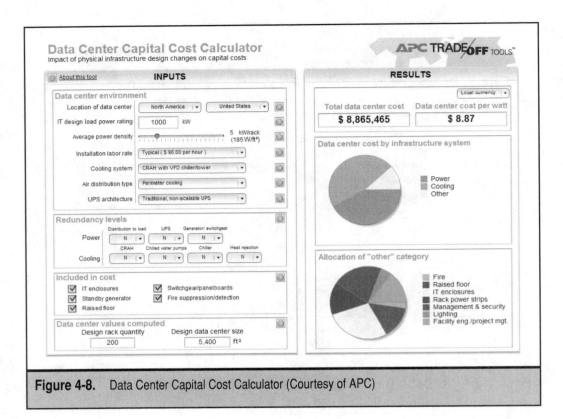

Figure 4-8.   Data Center Capital Cost Calculator (Courtesy of APC)

based on virtualization technology (see Figure 4-9). Its most valuable component is the graphics outlining the impact on your virtualization bill. Note that you must rely on the information outlined in Chapter 7 to properly determine your server consolidation ratio, since not all hypervisors are created equal and will not support as many virtual machines per host.

Since you will be changing server and storage configurations in support of virtualization, the Data Center Power Sizing Calculator will help determine what impact these new configurations will have on your datacenter (see Figure 4-10). Rely on this calculator to help determine the best configurations that suit your environment.

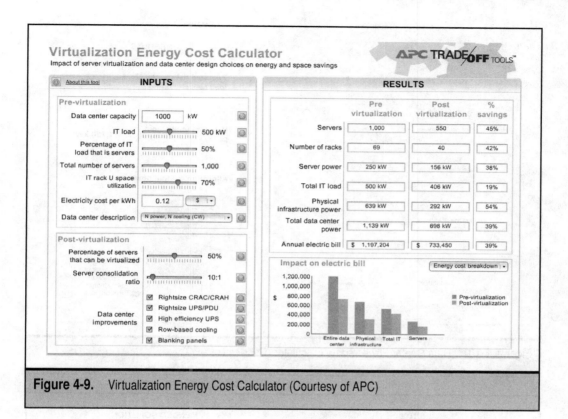

Figure 4-9.   Virtualization Energy Cost Calculator (Courtesy of APC)

Finally, the Data Center InRow Containment Selector will help you determine the best containment approach for your server racks as you prepare them to host virtualization infrastructures (see Figure 4-11). Use it in conjunction with the Data Center Power Sizing Calculator to help determine your best and most efficient rack configurations.

While you may not be used to datacenter analytics, these free tools make them easy and straightforward. At the very least, you should determine the carbon footprint, the efficiency of your datacenter, and the potential savings virtualization will bring.

NOTE   Remember that you can also rely on Microsoft Assessment and Planning Toolkit (MAP) to perform power assessments.

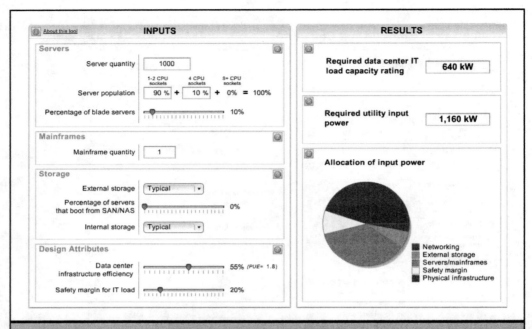

Figure 4-10.   Data Center Power Sizing Calculator (Courtesy of APC)

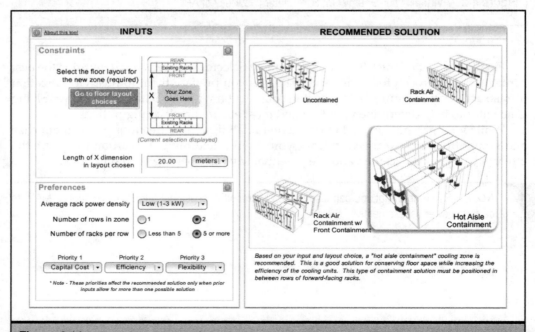

Figure 4-11.   Data Center InRow Containment Selector (Courtesy of APC)

RELY ON OTHER TOOLS

There are also other tools you can rely on to obtain more information. For example, VMware offers a free online Total Cost of Ownership (TCO) / Return on Investment (ROI) Calculator, which will take you through a series of questions about your environment to help you determine the payback for a virtualization project (see Figure 4-12). This calculator is useful because it helps you budget your project and identify potential project timelines.

NOTE   For more information on the VMware TCO/ROI Calculator, see www.vmware.com/products/vi/calculator.html.

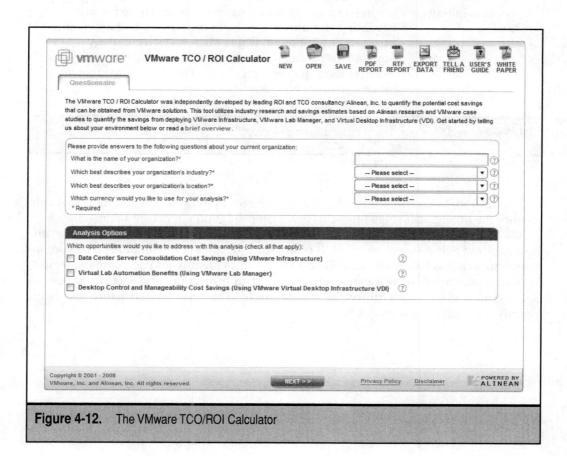

Figure 4-12.   The VMware TCO/ROI Calculator

Tools	Description
Optimization Self-Assessment Tool	Tool that analyzes your infrastructure and platform. It provides a report that includes a personalized and private optimization score, peer comparison, and value assessment for your organization. Find out more at www.microsoft.com/optimization/tools/overview.mspx.
Infrastructure Optimization (IO)	IO is the customer execution path Microsoft offers to help businesses drive towards dynamic systems capability. Find out more at www.microsoft.com/io.
The Dynamic Systems Initiative (DSI)	Dynamic Systems is Microsoft's vision for what an agile business looks like and what you should drive towards becoming as a business to meet the demands of a dynamic business environment. DSI is Microsoft's technology strategy for products and solutions that help businesses increase their dynamic capability. Find out more at www.microsoft.com/business/dsi/default.mspx.

Table 4-3.   Additional Sources of Information from Microsoft

In addition, Microsoft offers several other sources of information and tools that help identify the potential savings physical server consolidation offers (see Table 4-3).

Of the three sources of information, the most useful for data collection is the Optimization Self-Assessment Tool. It offers three options for evaluation. The core infrastructure option focuses on base IT services, such as identity and access management, device management, security and networking, data protection, and security processes (see Figure 4-13). It is useful for the evaluation of your base infrastructure and helps identify any missing components.

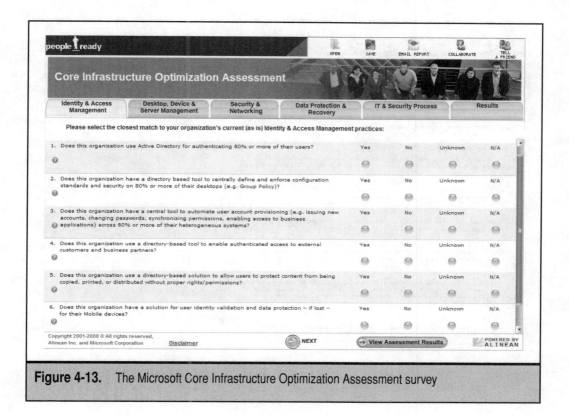

Figure 4-13. The Microsoft Core Infrastructure Optimization Assessment survey

The Business Productivity Infrastructure Assessment focuses on productivity services, such as collaboration, unified communications, content management, business intelligence, and search services (see Figure 4-14). It is useful to identify how your IT services support your business processes.

Finally, the Application Platform Assessment helps you focus on future growth and customization through development, Service-Oriented Architectures (SOA),

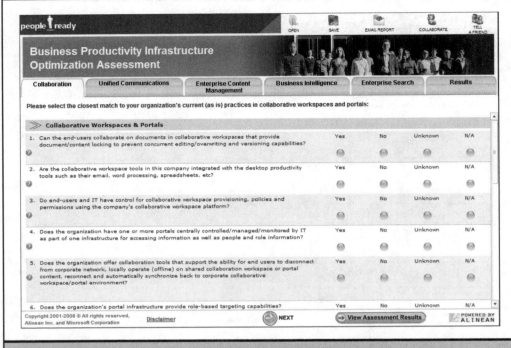

Figure 4-14.   The Microsoft Business Productivity Infrastructure Optimization Assessment

data management, user experience evaluations and, once again, business intelligence (see Figure 4-15). This assessment provides value for organizations that have custom requirements.

Each of these tools provides additional insight into your existing infrastructure and services and the potential change you can implement when you move to a virtual infrastructure.

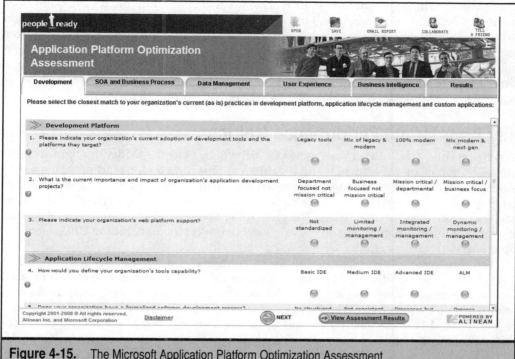

Figure 4-15. The Microsoft Application Platform Optimization Assessment

PERFORM A SERVER CONSOLIDATION STUDY

Another vital step to the project is the server consolidation study. As pointed out in Chapter 2, you must have a thorough understanding of your current service infrastructure to move to virtualization. You must identify the following components in this study:

▼ Categories of servers providing specific services

■ Links between applications and dependencies

■ Workload types, with a specific focus on the resources required to support a specific workload, be it memory, CPU, disk access, or network access

■ Workload peak hours, as well as duration of the peaks

■ Workload schedules, be they daily, weekly, monthly, or even semi-annual

▲ Special workload requirements, such as custom hardware, dongles for application activation, and so on

These values will help plan how your workloads will be migrated to a virtual environment and where they can reside. One of the most important aspects of virtualization planning is virtual workload positioning—making sure that the host server's resources are used appropriately by the varying workloads it runs and manages. For example, if one of the workloads requires network resources early in the morning, you need to make sure the other workloads do not contend for the same resources. You can only plan this when you have identified workload characteristics, as outlined previously.

Identify Appropriate Performance Metrics

When you collect data about your workloads, it will be essential to identify the appropriate performance metrics if you want to gain an appropriate understanding of the workloads you will be transforming. If your workloads are running on Windows, you can rely on tools such as the Performance console. It allows you to capture data on how your servers perform on a regular basis. The great thing about the Performance console is that it supports the evaluation of every single facet of a workload, including CPU, memory, disk, and network resources.

You can create a Performance Monitoring console that automatically tracks resource usage on all servers. This console will need access rights to performance counters on each server you monitor, so it is best to use administrative privileges to launch the Performance Monitor console (on Windows Server 2008, go to Server Manager | Diagnostics | Reliability and Performance | Monitoring Tools | Performance Monitor) and then proceed as follows:

1. Use the plus sign in the toolbar to add a counter.

2. In the Select Counters From Computer field, type the name of the server you want to view. Remember to use the Universal Naming Convention (UNC) name, for example, *ComputerName*.

3. Select the performance object and the counter (click the down arrow to view counters), and click Add.

4. Repeat for any other server you want to include. Click OK when done.

5. Now that all the servers are added, use More Actions | New | Data Collector Set from the action pane.

6. Name the collector set "Server Monitoring," click Next, save it in the default location, and click Next again.

7. In the next dialog box, click Change under Run As to add appropriate credentials to this collector set. Click OK.

8. Click Save, click Close, and click Finish.

9. To run the collector, move to Server Manager | Diagnostics Reliability And Performance | Data Collector Sets | User Defined. Right-click your collector set, and select Start.

10. Run it on a regular schedule to review resource usage on your servers.

The items you include in your monitoring should contain the following elements for each server in your network:

▼   Logical disk, Free disk space (% free logical disk space)

■   Logical disk, Disk time (% logical disk time)

■   Logical disk, Disk reads and writes

■   Logical disk, Disk queuing (average disk queue length)—*active by default*

■   Memory usage (available memory bytes)

■   Memory paging (memory pages per second)—*active by default*

■   Network interface (current bandwidth)

■   Network interface (output queue length)

■   Network interface (packets/sec)

■   Paging file activity (% paging file usage)

■   Physical disk, Disk queuing (average disk queue length)

■   Physical disk (split IO/sec)

■   Processor usage (% processor time)—*active by default*

■   Processor interrupts (processor interrupts per second)

■   Server paged pool (server pool paged peak)

■   Server service (total server bytes per second)

■   Server work items (server work item shortages)

▲   Server work queues (server work queue length)

Use the Explain button to learn what each setting refers to. Monitor these settings over time to identify how your servers and their workloads perform. An appropriate schedule would include the following:

▼   Weekdays at peak times, such as 7:00 A.M. to 9:00 A.M., 11:00 A.M. to 2:00 P.M., and 3:30 P.M. to 6:00 P.M.

■   Weekdays at non-peak times

■   Weekends at various times, such as Saturday afternoon, Sunday morning, and Sunday afternoon

▲   Weeknights at the times your batch jobs run

Run the schedule over the course of at least one month. The schedule should also include your business cycles. If you have special business peaks, you should take them into account in your evaluation. Combine the data from this analysis with the data from other analysis tools, as discussed in Chapter 2.

Interpret the Results

The data you collect will include several different types of output. Interpreting this data will depend on the source of the data itself, for example:

▼ Data you collect from Microsoft MAP can be interpreted directly, since it provides charts and reports that are specifically designed for the purpose of physical server consolidation.

■ Data you collect from either of the VMware tools—Guided Consolidation or Capacity Planner—can also be interpreted directly, since they are also created for the purpose of physical server consolidation.

▲ Data you collect from the Windows Performance console often requires additional processing in order to provide appropriate results. Note the following items:

   ■ If your Average Disk Queue Length is three or greater, your disks are overworked, unless you do not have enough memory in the server and disk thrashing is caused by virtual memory swapping.

   ■ If the % Processor Time is consistently low and there are a lot of idle times, the processor is underused, unless there are other bottlenecks causing the processor to wait for instructions.

   ■ If Memory Usage is high and Page File Swapping is consistent, your server does not have enough memory and more will be required when it is virtualized.

   ■ If your Network Interface is consistently busy, the workload is network-intensive and will require more than one virtual NIC once it is transformed. Note, however, that this value depends on the source physical NIC speed. If you move the physical machine to a virtual machine that resides on a host using 10-gigabyte (GB) Ethernet NICs, and the original machine ran on a 100MB NIC, the problem may go away on its own.

Bring all of the data together to attempt to create a global picture of your workloads. Also make sure you add your own understanding of your business processes to the overall report. Finally, pay attention to custom hardware components because they will require special approaches during the transformation of the workloads.

Your aim is to create a Basic Consolidation Estimate (BCE), which categorizes all of your workloads and identifies how and when they will be transformed.

RATIONALIZE EVERYTHING AGAIN

Now that you have your evaluation information in hand, you can rely on your server inventory in order to identify which servers can be rationalized, which can be retired, and which need to be replaced. That's right; the first step to start with once the inventory is collected should be rationalization. You should use your analysis to identify

▼   Servers with poor CPU utilization. These are all candidates for virtualization.

■   The servers that are "at rest." These may be candidates for removal.

■   The servers that can be simply shut down. These are additional candidates for removal.

■   The servers that are the best candidates for virtualization and whose hardware will not be reusable as a host server. This should include most workloads. Only unique workloads cannot benefit from virtualization today.

▲   The servers that are candidates as potential hosts. This should include the newest servers with similar processor capabilities.

This will help you categorize all servers. You should create batches of servers and from those batches identify the best virtualization candidates based on the complexity of transformation, from easy to moderate to difficult. Finally, rationalize everything by getting rid of anything you can. Don't forget the easiest server to manage is the one that is not there. Also, remember that while you keep servers on hand in the physical world because of their complexity of preparation, in the virtual world, you'll be able to create volatile servers much more easily. Volatile servers are servers that have a short duration period and are created for specific time-based purposes. Once the purpose is done, the server can simply disappear. While you can't do this in the physical world, it is definitely possible in the virtual world. For this reason, you may be able to remove some of the physical servers that were being kept around "just in case."

TIP Since you will be moving to a virtual or dynamic datacenter, you will most likely take advantage of the possibilities of physical-to-virtual (P2V) migrations. For example, Microsoft System Center Virtual Machine Manager (SCVMM), located at www.microsoft.com/systemcenter/scvmm/default .mspx, has the ability to capture physical machine images and convert them to virtual machines. This is quite useful for both testing and preparing for your new Virtual Service Offerings (VSO) environment. If you rely on a non-Microsoft hypervisor, such as that provided by VMware or Citrix, you can use other migration tools. VMware offers the free VMware Converter (www.vmware.com/products/converter); Citrix also includes a conversion capability within the XenCenter console, but it can also rely on SCVMM, since it supports the same virtual machine format as Microsoft does.

A server today provides a function. It is not a product. Many organizations have taken to single-instance servers when working with older versions of Windows. This approach started with Windows NT. Though NT itself was a solid product, many of the operations or applications organizations performed with it made it unstable. Often, the best way to deal with this instability was to dedicate the server to one specific role. Another reason for this approach was project-based hardware acquisitions—each time a new project required a server, it would acquire its own and add one or more new single-purpose servers into the production network, as well as creating test and development environments of its own. Unfortunately, the single-purpose-server approach works to increase the number of servers in the organization to the point of proliferation. Many existing servers are never used to their full capacity.

Consolidation involves fewer, fatter servers. Fewer servers mean simpler management. You can improve service levels because it is easier to maintain the operation of a few centralized servers than it is for several distributed servers. There is less downtime, since servers tend to be centralized and provide easier physical access. Applications can be deployed more rapidly because most of the code resides on the server itself. It is easier to standardize because fewer physical elements are involved. And, with virtual servers, you can easily move one virtual instance of a server from one physical host to another, providing dynamic responses to increased business needs.

There are four justifications for consolidation.

▼ **Centralization**   Relocating existing servers to fewer sites.

■ **Physical consolidation**   Many smaller servers are replaced with fewer, more powerful servers.

■ **Data integration**   Several distributed databases are consolidated into a single data repository.

▲ **Application integration**   Multiple applications are migrated to fewer, more powerful servers. Applications must have a certain degree of affinity before this integration can occur.

Through the use of virtualization technologies, you will be able to take better advantage of a single server's hardware by installing multiple instances of operating systems inside virtual machines. On average, you will be able to run between 10 to 20 virtual machines per physical host, depending, of course, on the configuration of the physical host and on the hypervisor you choose.

Keep in mind that a virtualization project is, by default, a physical server consolidation project. But you can, through diligence and effort, turn it into a server consolidation project through rationalization. Get rid of anything you can. This makes a lot of sense when you think of some of the workloads you run. Try to rationalize the number of servers you virtualize, especially multiple development and test environments, as well as servers that run single workloads, if you can.

CHAPTER 5

Build the Resource Pool

Once you've completed your analysis and you're ready to proceed, you can look to the conception and building of your resource pool. You'll need to plan carefully in terms of what you will actually virtualize, what you'll need in place to begin, and where you'll start virtualizing. To do so, you'll most likely need to update your networking, storage, and perhaps server infrastructure. Then, when you feel you're ready, you'll want to put a laboratory in place and get set to actually virtualize your infrastructures, after, of course, intensive testing.

The components of your resource pool will vary greatly, depending on several factors. Small organizations with fewer than 50 servers will want to put less expensive infrastructures in place and will probably not need the levels of high availability that larger organizations will look for. Medium organizations will want to look to more robust infrastructures, and large organizations will want to put in place the very best there is. Everything depends on business need and budget. Those with low budgets can still move forward and achieve amazing results. Those with appropriate budgets will be able to move to the latest technologies and create very resilient infrastructures.

In addition, the hypervisor you choose will have an impact on how you will proceed. Not all hypervisors are created equal and, therefore, have significantly different characteristics. This topic is examined in depth in Chapter 7, and you will want to examine this chapter in detail before making your final choices for the configuration of your resource pool. As stated in Chapter 1, you will most likely end up using more than one hypervisor, unless you are a small shop or you have complete control over your technological choices. The latter is seldom seen, as political pressures from others often tend to influence technological choices even though their arguments leave a lot to be desired. Because of this, many end up running hybrid infrastructures that don't really mesh well together, but they have no choice. Political pressure or not, make the most of your choices and validate them as much as possible. Homogeneous infrastructures are always the easiest to manage and protect, but if you find you have to build a heterogeneous environment, focus on the management tools you choose. Chapter 16 will be of great help to you in this task.

PLANNING AND PREPARATION

One of the most important tasks you'll perform once you have the inventory is determining how to approach your virtualization project. This involves identifying what to virtualize and in what order. This will form the structure of your virtualization project. Start small and build up until everything you want to virtualize is virtualized.

What to Virtualize

When you are planning for virtualization, one of the first questions to ask is which servers can I virtualize? It's easy. Most server workloads, even those that require custom hardware, can be virtualized. However, there are exceptions.

▼ Servers utilizing more than eight CPU cores may pose a challenge. If you have physical workloads that are running on more than eight CPU cores, you will not be able to virtualize them as-is because the maximum number of processor cores addressed by virtual machines is eight. However, you can circumvent this limitation in one of two ways.

- If your physical server demonstrates that it does not actually rely on more than eight cores, you can easily virtualize it.

- If your physical workload uses all of the cores it currently has, there may be a way to split up the functions it runs into more than one virtual machine, letting you virtualize the workload anyway. For example, a server running Microsoft Exchange 2007 may run with more than eight cores, but since Exchange is designed to run up to four different workloads, either together or apart, you may be able to split workloads onto more than one virtual machine, letting you virtualize the system.

- Servers utilizing more than 85 percent of their physical resources may pose a challenge. Once again, Exchange Server provides an excellent example. If your Exchange server is running with most of the resources on the physical system, you may opt to keep it as-is. However, virtualizing it will give you several advantages—liberation from physical constraints, possible replication for system protection, easy business continuity—and for this reason, you may want to virtualize the system anyway even if it turns out to be the only virtual machine running on a host.

▲ Servers that require custom hardware, such as Universal Serial Bus (USB) dongles or modems may be hard to virtualize. However, there are technologies that support the virtualization of these devices.

- USB ports can be virtualized because most modern hypervisors will support virtual USB ports. If your application requires a USB port to appear as a local device so that it can recognize the dongle it requires for licensing purposes, you can turn to custom hardware, such as Digi's AnywhereUSB, to create dedicated USB ports over Internet Protocol (IP) connections for virtual machines (VMs) that require them. Find out more at www.digi.com/products/usb/anywhereusb.jsp.

- Call center servers, fax servers, and routing and remote access servers can also be a challenge because they all require access to multiple modems. While hypervisors can virtualize serial ports, you still need to attach them to the modems. You can rely on two products for this. Virtual Modem Pro will create virtualized IP modems. Find out more at www.eltima.com/products/virtual-modem-pro. Digi also offers serial cards that can be used to create multiple modem entry points. Find out more at www.digi.com/products/serialcards.

As you can see, there are challenges to virtualizing 100 percent of your workloads, but they can be overcome. Remember that if you need special hardware, you will need to create at least two host servers to support this role to provide high availability for the services that depend on them.

Replace Anything Beige

When you pose the question of what should you virtualize, the answer is still easy: everything you can. However, you'll want to start with specific steps.

▼ Consider starting with servers that are chronically reconfigured. These are often test or development environments, because they are regularly reconfigured or even reprovisioned. While these tasks are arduous in the physical world, they become a snap in the virtual world since you can easily duplicate virtual machines and you have access to undoable disks, which makes reconfigurations a snap. Consider using some of your existing hardware as hosts for these workloads since they will not need the high-availability levels that production systems will.

■ Then move on to low-hanging fruit. This includes anything "beige," anything without blinking lights, or anything with low utilization ratios. This often includes workloads such as file or print servers, Web servers, and small departmental applications. Even home-grown applications are excellent candidates for the first phase of virtualization. In addition, domain controllers or identity servers are ideal candidates for virtualization since their operational model is many small servers that provide built-in redundancy services.

■ Next, look to high-risk legacy servers—any servers that run applications that, for some reason, cannot be upgraded and must run on older operating systems. Hopefully, you're not still running archaic operating systems such as Windows NT, but if you are, there is no better Windows NT than a virtualized Windows NT. Once you create a virtualized NT, it is much, much easier to duplicate it on an as-needed basis. Try doing that on a physical basis. Legacy applications often tend to be essential to the business, but also tend to have low utilization workloads because of their very nature. They are excellent candidates for virtualization.

▲ Keep complex workloads for last. Workloads that are more resource-intensive, such as e-mail servers, database servers, or even clustered servers, are more difficult to convert since they require more advanced knowledge of the virtualization platform and they often offer mission-critical services. Practice with the smaller workloads first and then move to the more complex workloads when you have mastered the hypervisor you're using. These workloads will also usually include servers that have custom hardware requirements.

Make sure you understand the input and output per second (IOPS) requirements for each of the workloads you are virtualizing. This will let you create proper virtual machine configurations in support of the applications as you transform them.

Choose the Implementation Method

You can choose among several different implementation methods. At first, when organizations were pioneering virtualization, they required a lot of external help. Many organizations opted to implement virtualization through partners because it was an untested field and little knowledge about the different products was available. Today, the story is different. Just the fact that you have this book in hand demonstrates that knowledge about virtualization is significantly easier to access.

There are still three different implementation scenarios, however.

▼   You can do everything on your own, learning about the different virtualization technologies, choosing a platform, and then moving forward through a phased approach.

■   You can hire a partner to give you a jump start. Jump start programs are useful since they give you a head start by beginning the project for you and then making the different phases of the project easier to access. At the end of the jump start, you have configured host systems, a sample of virtualized servers, and some basic training for your personnel.

▲   You can outsource the entire project. This model uses outside resources to perform each phase of the project. Many organizations feel more comfortable with this approach, but keep in mind that if you are one of them, your choice of partners must be careful indeed because only partners with the right experience will perform well in this project. Once again, this book can help by giving you guidance and identifying where you need to watch for pitfalls.

Which you choose will once again depend on who you are, the size of your organization, the business need driving the virtualization project, and your budget. There is nothing wrong with doing it yourself, just as there is nothing wrong with outsourcing. However, we cannot stress how important your choice of partner will be if you choose to go down this path. Only partners with demonstrated skill in virtualization will be able to provide the help you need.

PREPARE THE NETWORK LAYER

Now that you have decided how to proceed, you can identify just how your infrastructure needs to change. The first place to start is by looking at the network layer. As mentioned earlier, you'll need to determine if your networking equipment is up to the task of handling the added bandwidth virtualization requires. If anything seems amiss, replace it.

Then you'll need to look to your network infrastructure. Virtualization often requires several virtual local area networks (VLANs). A VLAN is a logical grouping of network nodes that behave as if they were connected to a single wire even though they are located on different physical LAN segments. If you opted to use Internet Small Computer Systems Interface (iSCSI) for shared storage access, you'll need to create different

VLANs for the traffic that will move from your host servers to each shared storage container. Keeping each storage container on a separate VLAN will improve performance and simplify traffic management. VLANs are also useful for network segregation—for example, separating production networks from perimeter networks, separating server workloads from end-user traffic, and so on. Finally, if you plan to use live VM migration, you should dedicate a VLAN for this traffic alone, making sure your systems have a high-priority bandwidth when they need it most. In fact, you may even choose to dedicate a switch to this traffic to ensure even higher priority and security because live data is being transfered.

You also need to consider the physical network identification card (NIC) configuration in your servers. Host servers often have a minimum of four NICs, as follows:

▼ Two NICs are reserved for service consoles or virtual machine management traffic. Service consoles are used to manage the virtual environment and, as such, need high-priority traffic for management purposes. This traffic should be encrypted at all times because it often contains administrative passwords and other sensitive information. Using Internet Protocol Security (IPSec) or the Secure Sockets Layer (SSL) protocol to secure this traffic is a best practice. You use at least one separate NIC for this process because it separates management traffic from virtual machine traffic and can provide additional security. For example, if you have a VM web server that is located in a perimeter network and you share both web server and management traffic on the same NIC, it is possible that the NIC could be compromised and then malicious users would have access to management traffic. You use two NICs for this purpose to provide redundancy and further isolation of the management traffic.

■ One NIC is reserved for live virtual machine migrations. Dedicating a NIC to this traffic will provide it with the high priority it needs. This NIC should not be shared with any of the virtual machine traffic and should be at least a 1-gigabyte (GB) NIC to provide the required throughput. This NIC should be assigned to the live migration VLAN.

▲ One or often more NICs are reserved for virtual machine workloads through the VM kernel. These NICs are shared between the physical host and virtual machines. Like all other physical devices, network interface cards are often underutilized by physical workloads. This means that several virtual machines can share the same NIC. However, you should assign at least one host NIC for every four virtual machines you run on the host. This may mean you will need more than four NICs per host.

In addition, you should assign static IP addresses to both hosts and virtual machines as much as possible. In IP version 4 (IPv4), this means using one of the private address pools. In IPv6, this means using either globally unique addresses for each server or site-local addresses, which are similar to the private address pools available in IPv4. Ensure that your Domain Name System (DNS) is properly configured for all IP addressing, both virtual and physical. This means both forward and reserve lookups.

In fact, you may determine that it is best to use two DNS infrastructures: a physical one that includes only resource pool addresses and a virtual one that includes all of the Virtual Service Offerings (VSO) addresses.

If virtual machines need access to or need to be accessed from remote locations, you will need to make sure your firewalls are properly configured to allow this traffic. In most cases, when organizations start moving towards virtualization, they often use physical workstations to access Virtual Service Offerings. Make sure the firewalls on all devices, physical and virtual, allow traffic in appropriate patterns.

NIC teaming—or the aggregation of multiple NICs to provide fault tolerance, added bandwidth, and high availability—should also be considered if possible. As discussed earlier, you should always avoid single points of failure in your system configurations. If you have several VMs sharing a single physical NIC and this NIC breaks for any reason, you will have a failure in several workloads. Using NIC teaming prevents this from happening since it provides device redundancy should any mishap occur.

Networking in Virtual Layers

Virtual machine technology is designed to support multiple virtual networks within the same physical host. For this reason, you can actually host virtual machines from different network zones within the same host. Hypervisors manage this process by using and creating virtual switches for each network. For example, in Microsoft Hyper-V, the physical NICs on a host server are transformed into virtual network switches (VNS), which can then be assigned to several different networking modes in the virtual layer (see Figure 5-1).

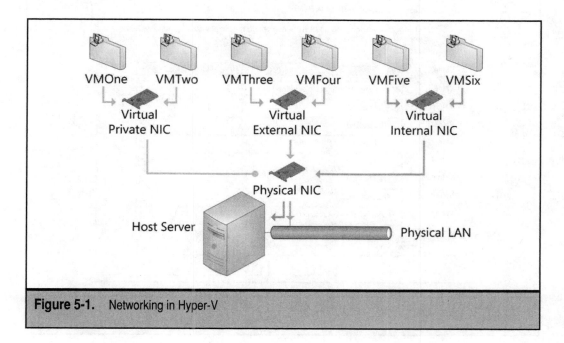

Figure 5-1.   Networking in Hyper-V

Then, you can assign virtual network interfaces to one of three connection types:

▼ An External Virtual NIC will be linked to the VNS to gain access both to the host and to the external network.

■ An Internal Virtual NIC will be linked to the host and will also allow each of the virtual machines tied to this NIC to communicate with each other. No external communications are supported.

▲ A Private Virtual NIC will link virtual machines to themselves only and will not provide any communications to the host system.

The VNS process removes all settings from the physical NIC except for the Microsoft Virtual Switch. For this reason alone, you should have more than one NIC in a physical host. Many administrators perform host server configurations remotely through Terminal Services. When you do this and there is only one NIC on the system, all Terminal Services communications are lost and there is no longer any means of communicating with the host remotely. You must then sit at the server to complete its configuration. Using at least two NICs in the host avoids this issue.

VMware also supports virtual network switches. For example, VMware Workstation, a SerV product, will support ten virtual network switches by default (see Figure 5-2). Each VNS can be configured independently to provide complete VM isolation, if required.

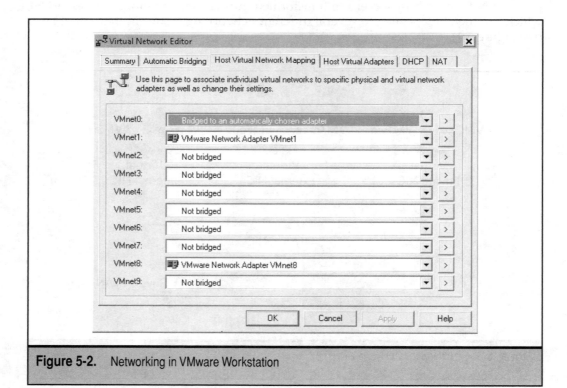

Figure 5-2.　Networking in VMware Workstation

When working with hypervisors, you'll find that you can create as many virtual NICs as are required by your VMs. In addition, services such as Network Load Balancing (NLB), which balances a workload between several machines by redirecting traffic at the network layer, work perfectly well within the virtualization layer so you can create highly available VM configurations by working with the virtual networking capabilities of the host server. Most virtualization engines also support Network Address Translation (NAT) to provide access to multiple VMs through one single physical IP address. For this reason, these virtualization engines often include the ability to provide Dynamic Host Configuration Protocol (DHCP) services to VMs.

You should make a point of carefully documenting the virtual networks you create through the use of virtual network switches on your host servers.

PREPARE STORAGE

Storage configurations should be shared among the host systems as much as possible. If this is not possible—for example, if you opt to create a low-cost host configuration relying on direct attached storage—you must implement a replication service between hosts in order to support high availability of the virtual machines. This configuration is often best for small shops that will only run a few hosts. Windows Server 2008 Hyper-V, for example, because it is part of Windows Server, supports this type of highly available configuration through failover clustering, using a majority node set to create a cluster that does not share data. It must, however, also rely on a replication system in order to ensure that the contents of each node in the cluster be identical. While technologies such as Exchange Server 2007 and SQL Server 2008 offer this replication mechanism through log shipping—the generation of a copy of each database transaction log on local as well as remote systems, keeping databases in sync—Hyper-V does not; at least not yet. Microsoft, however, does provide a list of replication partners that are supported in these configurations at www.microsoft.com/windowsserver2008/en/us/clustering-multisite.aspx. This strategy is based on the multisite clustering capabilities of Windows Server, but in this case, each node can either be in the same or different sites, depending on your requirement.

The multisite clustering configuration is one that will be used either by small shops or by large shops requiring multisite redundancy for their VMs. Most other organizations will rely on shared storage—either network attached storage (NAS) or storage area networks (SAN)—to configure high availability for their host servers. In this configuration, each host server is attached to one or more shared logical units (LUN) of storage (see Figure 5-3). By providing connections to multiple hosts, the shared storage container can support high availability because a host does not need to copy the contents of the storage container to gain access to it. Instead, the high-availability technology simply disconnects the failing host and enables the connection to the failover host, providing service continuity. In these configurations, all hosts in a server pool must be connected to the same storage container.

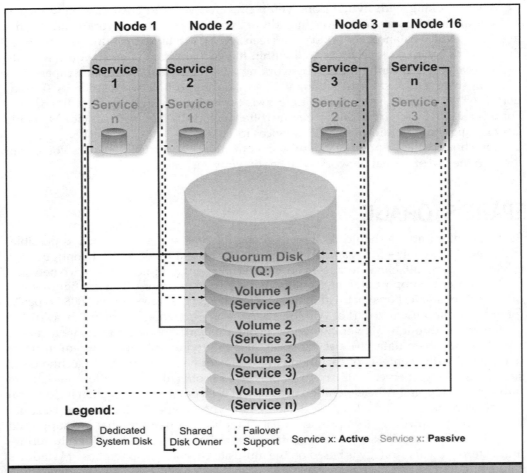

Figure 5-3. Highly available configurations require multiple connections to the same storage container.

NOTE High availability does not work the same way as live machine migration. Live migration copies the in-memory contents of a VM from one host to another and then activates it, causing no break in service. This technology is used to move machines to new hosts in order to provide a maximum number of resources to the VM. High availability, on the other hand, is used when a host server fails. Because there is a failure, there is a slight interruption of service between the failure and the failover.

While high availability is provided through clustering services in Windows Server 2008 Hyper-V and other hypervisors based on the Linux Xen code, it is provided through two technologies in VMware: the High Availability (HA) component and the Virtual Machine File System (VMFS). VMFS, especially, is used to manage any container that will host virtual machine files. One of the features of VMFS is to be able to share container connections with multiple host servers in an HA pool. This means that any system tied to a shared storage container can be the host of another host's virtual machines in case of a hardware failure of some kind (see Figure 5-4). HA works in conjunction with VMFS to provide virtual machine failover from one host to another in the event of a hardware failure (see Figure 5-5). VMFS is a true cluster file system, which makes it an essential part of the HA configuration in an ESX Server implementation.

Also, while other virtualization technologies rely on the features of their host operating system (OS) to create memory swap files, it is VMFS that creates and manages these files for VMware host servers. VMFS also stores all undo, redo, log, and configuration files for the VMs.

Another component requirement for virtual machine storage is the requirement for other media type files. While host servers can share their physical drives, such as DVD or floppy drives, through Raw Device Mapping (RDM), running multiple VMs on a host often means having to access multiple copies of these devices at the same time.

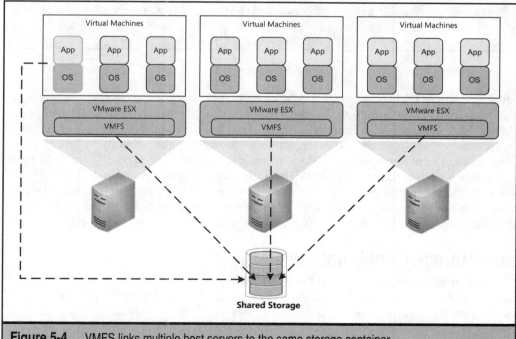

Figure 5-4. VMFS links multiple host servers to the same storage container.

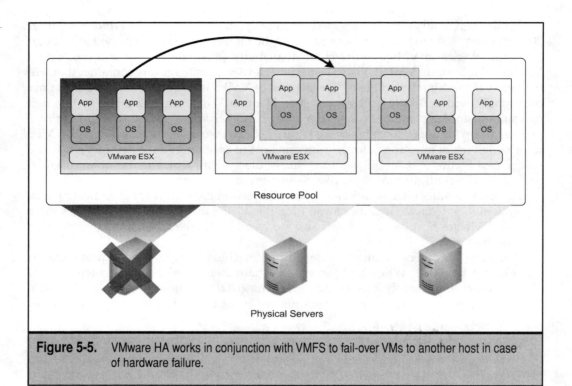

Figure 5-5. VMware HA works in conjunction with VMFS to fail-over VMs to another host in case of hardware failure.

Sharing a single DVD drive with 20 VMs won't work. In order to circumvent this issue, hypervisors have the ability to create virtual drives that emulate both DVD and floppy drives. Each is stored in an image file of some kind. For example, DVDs are often stored in ISO file format (with an .iso extension) and can be targeted directly to link to a VM. Your storage containers will also have to make space for this type of media. In many cases, this is performed on a Network File System (NFS) storage container. This NFS container is shared among multiple VMs through simple file sharing services, which means that it can easily be centralized so that only one such container need to be managed in the entire datacenter. In Windows, this would be a standard Windows File Server.

Prepare Storage Configurations

Shared storage must be connected to the host server in some fashion. If your shared storage is a NAS device, your connection to this device will be through network interface cards since the NAS device is a file sharing unit that will provide file services in either NFS or standard Windows file sharing format. However, if your device is a SAN, you must determine how to connect to the device.

SANs are usually connected to host servers through either iSCSI or Fibre Channel. iSCSI relies on network interface cards to transform storage traffic into network traffic. While iSCSI does not offer the same performance on its own as Fibre Channel does, it can approximate these performance levels through network card aggregation—adding multiple NICs to the iSCSI load to increase data throughputs. Today, SANs are being configured about evenly through both methods. Fibre Channel does provide better throughput and does not add any load to the network, but the number of host bus adapters (HBA) that are supported by the virtualization manufacturers is far less than the number of NICs they support. For this reason, many opt for iSCSI so they have better choices when it comes to system configurations. Note, however, that iSCSI may be a better choice for small to medium organizations because of the cost. Large organizations will often opt for Fibre Channel HBAs since they can provide better performance in the long run even though they cost more at first.

In addition, many organizations configure host servers to have direct attached storage for the hypervisor partition as well as the host console, and then use shared storage to store and maintain all of the virtual machine files. This configuration varies, since today, several manufacturers offer host server configurations that already include the hypervisor on an internal USB drive, making the direct attached storage (DAS) configuration unnecessary. However, if you find you must use DAS in host servers, use solid state drives as much as possible to obtain the very best IOPS speeds.

You will also want to be wary of the number of VMs each storage container hosts. While a LUN can host up to 100 VMs, it might be best to maintain no more than 32 VMs per LUN to improve performance. Performance will vary with the Random Array of Inexpensive Disks (RAID) configuration of the drives. RAID 5 is often the most used RAID type because it protects data while providing acceptable performance. But today, RAID 10 may provide the best performance because it both mirrors and stripes the disks, getting the best read/write performance while protecting all drive contents. RAID 10 is more costly in the number of disk drives needed to complete the configuration, but in the long run, it may provide the best structure for your shared storage containers (see Figure 5-6).

Virtualize Storage

When you work with shared storage, you will also be working with shared storage management technologies. These technologies have the ability to virtualize storage, making it easier to access storage containers wherever they are located. Basically, virtual storage technologies transform physical storage into logical views. In some cases, this software can scan all storage, DAS, NAS, and SAN, and aggregate it to provide one unified logical view of all storage in an organization.

Virtual storage focuses on the volume, not the actual disks. It is hardware-agnostic so that it can work with storage containers from many vendors at once, letting you choose best-of-breed products. It provides a central console for all storage management.

Virtual storage technologies can be a combination of hardware and software or they can be software-only, which provides the most flexibility. Storage containers are policy-based and can be turned on as needed. But the best feature of virtual storage is "thin provisioning."

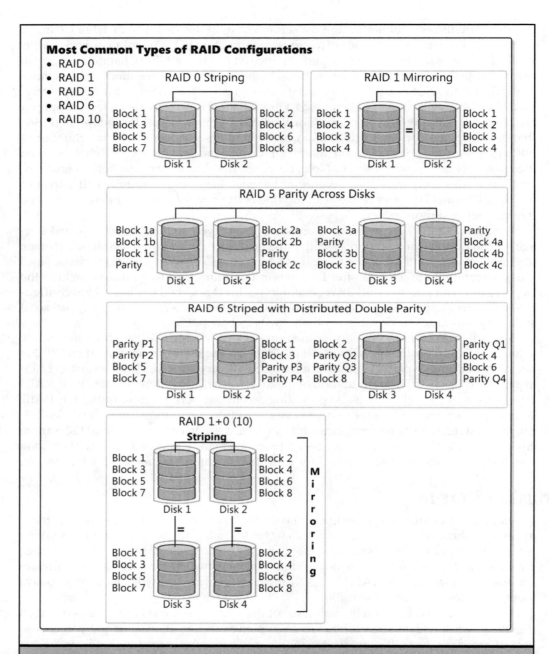

Figure 5-6. Working with different RAID types

When you create a virtual hard disk drive, you'll find that one of the formats is a dynamically expanding disk—a disk that is configured to a maximum size but that only stores the actual contents of a drive and grows with usage. For example, you might create a 100-GB virtual disk drive, but since the actual disk only contains 10GB, the file size is only 10GB. This file will grow to 100GB with usage and may never actually gain the full size of the configured drive.

Thin provisioning does exactly the same thing for physical storage (see Figure 5-7). It creates a storage volume of a given size, but provisions it with only the disks required to contain its actual size. For example, you could configure a volume containing virtual machines to 500GB, but if the total size of the VMs is only 60GB, you only need 60GB of physical disk space. Additional disks are requested by the storage virtualization technology when they are required, saving you enormous costs in actual disks. For this reason alone, storage virtualization is a boon to all shops wanting to move to a virtual infrastructure.

In addition, storage virtualization software will let you configure RAID type at the creation of a volume, but will also let you change it with time. This software will help you maximize actual storage while giving you the best management capabilities.

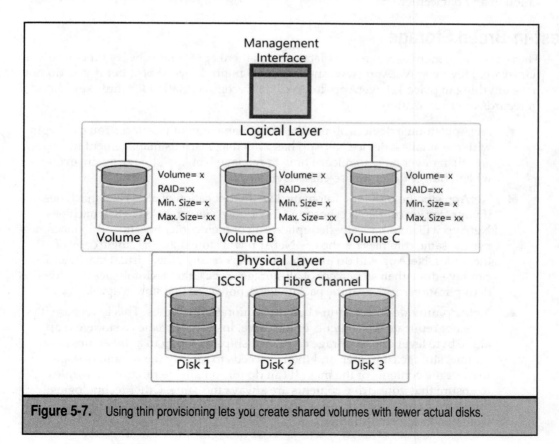

Figure 5-7.   Using thin provisioning lets you create shared volumes with fewer actual disks.

Create a Backup Plan

The final element in your storage configuration should be focused on backup and drive replication. Backup is covered in depth in Chapter 14, but it should be considered when preparing storage. After all, the most important motto in virtualization is to avoid single points of failure. If you have several host servers tied to shared storage in a highly available configuration but you have no protection for the storage LUNs, you will have a single point of failure.

Most SANs will include the ability to take full LUN snapshots during operation to protect the contents of the drives they contain. In most cases as well, SANs will be able to create up to 512 snapshots of their contents, then rely on these snapshots to create backups of the disk in order to avoid any performance impact on the production disks. You will need to determine if this is enough, or if you also require some form of SAN replication to another site.

Basically, the needs of your organization, the importance of the data being protected, and the budget of your project will help you determine exactly which strategy to use. Keep in mind that data protection is one of the most important aspects of storage preparation in any datacenter.

Best-in-Breed Storage

There are many, many storage manufacturers, as there are for most every type of server hardware. However, NetApp (www.netapp.com) might be your best bet if you do not have anything in place yet. NetApp deserves this recommendation for three key reasons in regards to virtualization.

▼ NetApp storage devices all use the same management interface. You can begin with the smallest device NetApp has available, learn its management interface, and then never have to relearn how to manage NetApp storage again, even when you get to enterprise-class devices.

■ NetApp storage provides automatic live deduplication of all virtual machines. If your storage container is hosting 15 Windows Server 2008 virtual machines, NetApp will automatically deduplicate all of their contents. Since all 15 machines use the same core files for the OS, NetApp will store only one single copy of these files. NetApp will do the same for Linux or any other virtual machine. This can save more than 40 percent of all storage costs. Other technologies provide deduplication services at the backup level, not at the live storage level.

▲ NetApp provides the best-in-class replication technologies. This is because it does not replicate the contents of the drive. Instead, it creates a storage map at the byte level of one storage container, ships this map to another, possibly remote, storage container, and then proceeds to modify the remote storage to meet the contents of the map. It can do this on a wide range of schedules to ensure that your drive contents are always the same. Other technologies replicate contents on a byte-per-byte basis, constantly shipping byte contents from one location to another.

NetApp offers these features by default and still provides a competitive price/performance ratio. For these reasons, you should take the time to look at NetApp products if you do not have a shared storage container in place yet. Rely on NetApp representatives to make sure you obtain products that include all of the features you need for virtualization support.

PREPARE HOST SERVERS

When you prepare host servers, most of you will have one major thought in mind: How do I recover existing hardware equipment and reuse it to reduce the cost of my project? This topic has been discussed at length to date, but here are some additional caveats:

▼   First, you'll need to determine if your servers can host virtual machines, which they most likely can, but can they do it with the proper configuration?

▲   The key to host servers is resources—processor, memory, network, and disk. Do your existing servers offer these capabilities? Consider the following:

■   The best host server is one with the most processors or processor cores. If your existing servers are dual-core servers running on AMD processors, you're in luck, because you can simply replace the dual-core processors with AMD's quad-core processors without the need for adapter kits. Simply pop out the old processor and pop in the new one. This should give extra life to your servers. Intel processors do not swap as easily, so if your processors are Intel, you'll need to make a decision.

■   The best host servers use the same processors with similar stepping to support live migrations. If you have several servers with these characteristics, retain them.

■   The best host server is one with tons of RAM. If your servers include a lot of free memory banks, fill them up and reuse the system.

■   The best host server includes lots of NICs. If you have available slots and you can add NICs to the server, then do so.

■   The best host server will rely on shared storage to store VMs. If you can either add NICs in support of iSCSI or host bus adapters to your servers, then retain them.

Basically, if you can add to your server configurations and, at the same time, tie them into high-availability configurations such as cluster configurations, you can retain your servers and reuse them as hosts.

You also need to determine if you will scale up or scale out your host systems. Scaling up implies the use of fewer, larger-capacity servers, either rack-mounted or tower, but mostly rack-mounted. Scaling out implies using more, smaller servers that are either rack-mounted or blade systems. While this question was often moot for application servers because many applications could not take advantage of the multiple processors

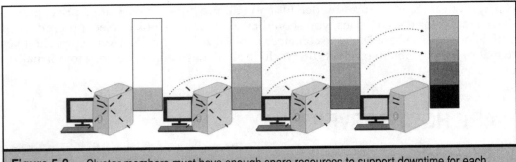

Figure 5-8.   Cluster members must have enough spare resources to support downtime for each of their partners.

or processor cores scale-up systems offered, with virtualization, the nature of the game changes because host servers are designed to use all of the resources of a system. There-fore, it is highly possible to scale up with virtualization.

However, you must take into account host server maintenance. Larger servers will host more VMs, and if you need to shut down the larger system, you could have poten-tial outages. Keep in mind that each time you create a monster server to host dozens or more VMs, you also have to create its twin since you need to create highly available configurations. Because of this, you always need to create host server configurations that have available resources to host their partner server's workload. If four servers are in a cluster, each server must have enough resources to host all of the VMs of their partners (see Figure 5-8). When you decide to scale up, these server configurations can become expensive.

However, you can use a rule of thumb to reduce the server configuration when you scale up. For example, if you assume that in a six-node cluster, only two nodes will fail at the same time, you can host more VMs on each host and ensure that you always have enough resources to cover these failures in the other nodes of the cluster. This rule of thumb will not cover a complete cluster failure, but it will let you create less expensive scale-up clusters and waste fewer resources.

But because scaled-up clusters can be more complex to create, it might be best to scale out, using smaller blade servers that can easily be configured to support their pair nodes in cluster configurations. Blade servers are so much easier to obtain and put in place once their enclosures are set up, that scaling out becomes a simple strategy to support. In fact, the very best host server seems to be one that includes a minimum of two quad-core CPUs, at least 32GB of RAM, at least four NICs (possibly teamed), and no internal disks (see Figure 5-9). The system either runs from an internal integrated hypervisor or it boots from the SAN, avoiding the requirement for DAS disks.

While performing their own virtualization project, processor manufacturer Intel dis-covered that most applications can operate with a single GB of RAM when virtualized.

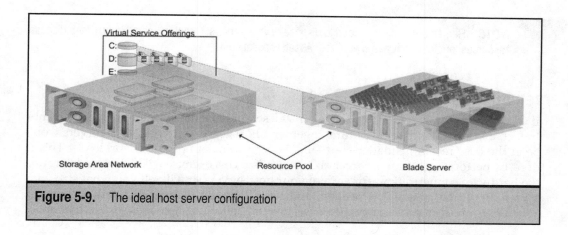

Figure 5-9.   The ideal host server configuration

Out of 3,000 servers in their analysis, more than 1,500 only used 1GB or less. This included mostly file servers, web servers, and backup systems. In some cases, they found that certain e-mail and database servers also had low RAM utilization. They also found that 2-GB Dual Inline Memory Modules (DIMMs) provided the best dollar/RAM value. However, since this study was performed during their own project, which occurred in late 2007, it might be better to opt for 4-GB DIMMs today.

In the end, you'll determine which is best for you. If you have thousands of machines to virtualize, scaling up is the best option to maximize host server workloads; however, if you only have a few VMs to create, scaling out is the best option since smaller servers offer a better price/performance ratio and are much easier to introduce and replace.

When you look to your own existing servers, you'll probably find the following:

▼   Tower servers will most likely be retained only for test and development environments since they do not need to support highly available configurations.

■   Tower servers will also be retained by smaller shops that only have a few workloads to virtualize.

■   Rack-mounted servers may be adapted to support virtualization, but will mostly require upgraded components.

■   Blade servers can also be adapted to support virtualization.

▲   Existing clusters running e-mail or databases can be transformed into host server clusters and can actually form the source of your host cluster pool. However, you must be careful when you convert their current workloads to virtualization.

Whatever you do with existing systems, make sure you configure your host servers in such a way that you will not have to replace or upgrade them in the short term.

Server Sizing for Resource Pools

If you opt to use new servers, you won't install servers that meet minimum requirements. In fact, if you're planning on putting together a host server network, your servers won't be at the base recommendation, but will be sized to meet optimum workloads. This is done by performing a formal server-sizing exercise. This exercise will help you determine the hardware configurations for each of your host servers. It will tell you what size your server should be, where it is needed, and what it should deliver in terms of services. When performing a server-sizing exercise, take the following items into consideration:

▼ **Identify server bases** Rely on the features of the hypervisor you select (see Chapter 7) to identify where your VM groupings will be, how many VMs you will run on each host, how you will team hosts for high availability, and how many host servers will be in a team. You will need to position your servers where you have a concentration of VMs. This can mostly be in central offices since virtualization also supports service centralization.

■ **Number of guest operating systems per server** Identify a maximum number of guest operating systems per host server. To provide a given level of service, you need to ensure that there are never more than a specific number of guests, depending on this server's resources. On average, organizations run between 10 and 30 virtual machines per host.

TIP Remember that all physical hosts must be 64-bit servers if you want to run Hyper-V on them. If you want to reuse 32-bit servers as hosts, you can do so, but you will need to run either Microsoft Virtual Server or VMware Server on top of a 32-bit version of an OS to provide virtualization services. You can also use 32-bit devices to run VMware ESX Server since it is based on 32-bit code.

■ **Maximum acceptable server load** Determine the speed of response you want from a server when providing services. For host servers, this load must take into consideration the maximum central processing unit (CPU) usage. Usually, CPU and RAM are the major bottlenecks. Learn to avoid them. One good way to do this is to continually monitor CPU and input and output (I/O) performance on the server.

■ **Server variance** The location of the server is also important to consider because it often serves to determine the nature of the server. Most host servers are located in central datacenters, but in some cases, you will want to deliver local services to remote offices. The virtual datacenter will run two host machines with shared storage (if possible) in regions and run the appropriate number of guest operating systems to meet demand.

- **Minimum server capacity**   Determine the minimum hardware capacity you want for your host servers. Remember that you don't want to change them for some time. The purpose of your network is to deliver high-quality services to your user base. Take this into consideration when you determine the minimum server capacity. Capacity planning should identify items such as number and size of the processors, amount of RAM, and disk size.

- **Multiprocessing and multicore**   You should use multiprocessing servers (servers that have more than a single processor) as well as multicore processors (processors that have more than one CPU core) for host servers. In fact, right now, you should include at least two quad-core processors in each host. If they can include more, then do so. In a short time, we'll have access to octo-core processors and more.

- **RAM sizing**   The rule is simple: The more RAM you have, the better your server will perform. Thus, RAM is not a place you should skimp on, especially for host servers. Host servers should start with a minimum of 16GB of RAM, but many organizations go straight to 64-GB configurations. Keep in mind that the RAM size will affect the paging file. The best rule of thumb here is to start the paging file at double the size of your RAM and set its maximum size to four times the size of RAM. This rule means that you'll need to reserve a minimum and maximum amount of disk space for the paging file.

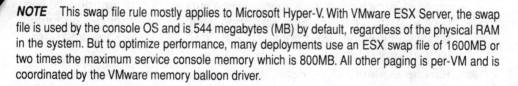

NOTE   This swap file rule mostly applies to Microsoft Hyper-V. With VMware ESX Server, the swap file is used by the console OS and is 544 megabytes (MB) by default, regardless of the physical RAM in the system. But to optimize performance, many deployments use an ESX swap file of 1600MB or two times the maximum service console memory which is 800MB. All other paging is per-VM and is coordinated by the VMware memory balloon driver.

- **Disk sizing**   The size and number of disks you attach to each server will depend on a number of factors. How many partitions do you want to make? How much space do you want to reserve for the operating system, programs, and special elements such as the paging file? How much space for data storage? Do you want to use direct attached storage or remote storage? Whatever you choose, most servers will end up with three, perhaps more, partitions: one for the manufacturer's server utilities, one for the operating system and programs, and one for data.

For host servers, data partitions should always be on shared disks and be separate from system partitions. In addition, data partitions are often significantly larger. Shared disks will allow you to run the hypervisor, if it isn't embedded in your server's hardware, as well as data drives. In addition, shared disks will let you implement high-availability strategies to make sure that your Virtual Service Offerings are always available.

- **Hardware protection**   All of this data needs some level of protection. Local disk drives should be protected by RAID. As mentioned earlier, many people opt for a disk mirroring system (RAID 1) for the system drives, and stripe sets with parity (RAID 5) or mirrored stripe sets (RAID 10) for data partitions.

- **Storage strategy**   The hardware protection system you choose will also depend on your storage strategy. Host servers should share drives. Many manufacturers are delivering innovative all-in-one boxes that include two host servers with shared storage, all in a convenient cooling casing for regional networks. For central servers, you should implement shared storage based on your organizational needs. Small to medium organizations will often opt for DAS with replication or NAS devices, whereas larger organizations will need SANs. Hypervisors will work with several different types of shared storage; just make sure you select something that is on the hardware compatibility list (HCL) your hypervisor provider publishes.

- **Physical location**   The physical location, the actual physical space the server will occupy, will help you determine whether you will choose a rack-mounted or tower server configuration. In most cases, regional servers are tower servers and centralized servers are rack-mounted because they are concentrated in a single physical space. If you opt for rack-mounted servers, consider the blade servers instead. As mentioned earlier, they are perfect for scaling out hosts. In addition, blade servers offer much more compact footprints, often saving as much as 70 percent of rack space, 50 percent power consumption, 80 percent cabling, and 20 percent heat generation compared to other rack-mounted servers. Remember, your physical location should be lockable and offer temperature controls.

- **Backup method**   Once again, the physical location of the server will help determine the backup method selected. Regional servers often used tape drives for backup. Depending on the speed and available bandwidth of your wide area network (WAN) connection, you might just back up all data to a central location. More on this topic will be covered when discussing VM protection strategies.

- ▲ **Growth potential**   You don't want to be replacing this system six months after you put it in place, so make sure it has a capacity for growth. All systems should have the ability to add more processors or at least replace them, more memory, and more disk space. As such, you'll need to consider the server life expectancy—when the server was introduced by the manufacturer, when it will be retired, what its projected growth potential by the manufacturer is, and so on. If you plan carefully, you'll be able to implement servers with a rich life cycle that meet your expectations. In some conditions, this life cycle can last up to five years or more.

This exercise helps you identify the generic size of each server. Several manufacturers such as Dell, HP, and IBM offer sizing tools for host servers on their respective Web sites. Rely on these tools to create your best host server configuration.

Sizing Recommendations for Resource Pools

You already know that host servers should be 64-bit systems using shared storage. They should also be blade servers, if possible, because blades can be implemented faster than other server types once the casing has been configured. They should include multiple NICs so that they will provide sufficient throughput for the multiple VMs they will run. The OS should be stored on the shared storage or within the host hardware, as this will facilitate provisioning. Data—the storage space for the VMs—should be on shared storage and should form the bulk of the disk space allocated to this server. Another smaller partition should be used to store the snapshots that will be required to back up the virtual machines.

Table 5-1 outlines hardware recommendations for host servers.

Components	Recommendation
CPU	3GHz or more
CPU architecture	X64
Minimum number of quad-core CPUs	2
Minimum RAM	32GB, 64GB recommended
Hypervisor	Built-in or on shared storage (remote boot)
Hypervisor configuration	Clustered for HA
Data disk configuration	Two drives in shared storage: bulk for data and small partition for snapshot backups
Shared storage connection	iSCSI
NICs	Minimum of four, with at least 1-GB speed
Server type	Blade or small form factor rack-mounted server

Table 5-1. Sizing Recommendations for Host Servers

Upgrading Host Servers

As you move to the dynamic datacenter, you'll realize that you won't be running upgrades on the host servers. Each host server will most likely be a new installation. Then, the service offerings that will now be virtualized can undergo either upgrades or new installations. We would argue for new installations at all times, but that is obviously your choice. Remember that before you can perform an upgrade on an existing system, you will need to convert it from a physical to a virtual (P2V) installation. Both Microsoft and VMware offer P2V tools, as do others. Microsoft's best P2V tool is found in System Center Virtual Machine Manager (VMM). Information on VMM can be found at www.microsoft.com/systemcenter/scvmm/default .mspx. VMware offers VMware Converter, a graphical tool that converts physical machines to virtual versions and also converts machines between virtual formats. Converter is free and can be found at www.vmware.com/products/converter. Of course, if you own VMware's Virtual Infrastructure, you will already have the Enterprise version of Converter, which allows you to capture running machines and virtualize them. VMware Converter will also convert virtual machine disk formats, for example, from Microsoft's VHD to VMware's VMDK. More information can be found at http://vmtoolkit.com/files/folders/converters/entry8.aspx. There are also third-party P2V tools, such as those offered by PlateSpin (www .platespin.com), that offer much more functionality. More on P2V will be covered in Chapter 9.

Rely on Hardware-Integrated Hypervisors

VMware was the first to make its hypervisor available directly within server hardware. VMware ESXi is a small 32-MB hypervisor that is loaded onto an internal USB thumb drive located within the server hardware. Because of this, it is easy to add a new host server to your resource pool. Use the following process:

1. Mount the server within a rack or blade enclosure.
2. Power it on. The server automatically boots into the hypervisor.
3. Configure the administrative password to secure the system (see Figure 5-10).
4. Configure a static IP address for the host server (see Figure 5-11).
5. Connect the client to the virtual infrastructure through the management console (see Figure 5-12).

As you can see, this process is easy to implement. Adding host servers is a snap, especially now that ESXi is available for free.

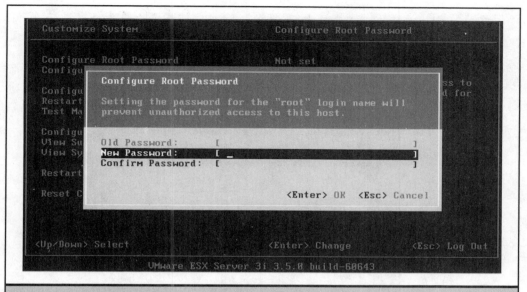

Figure 5-10. Configuring an administrative password in VMware ESXi

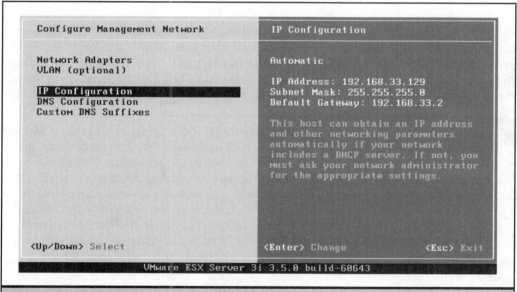

Figure 5-11. Configuring a static IP address in VMware ESXi

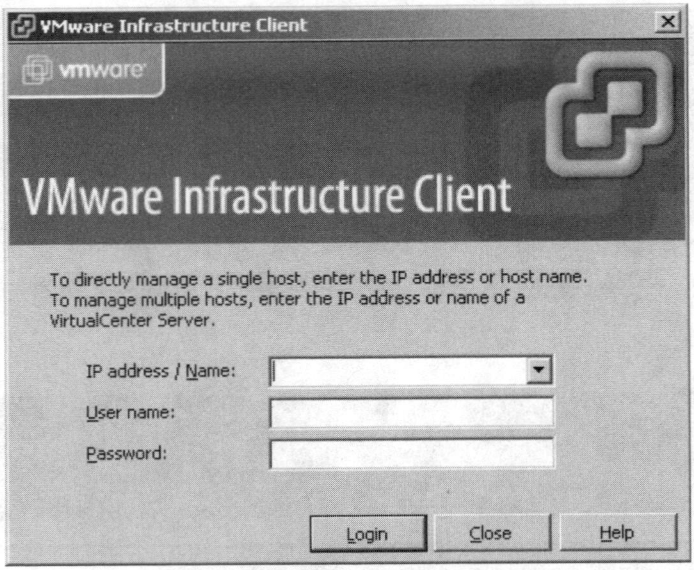

Figure 5-12. Adding a VMware ESXi to a managed infrastructure

VMware is not the only vendor that creates built-in hardware/hypervisor configurations. Citrix also offers an original equipment manufacturer (OEM) version of XenServer, and Microsoft offers a custom built-in version of Hyper-V with certain hardware configurations. Each is as easy and simple to implement as ESXi. For this reason, you should consider obtaining systems with preconfigured hypervisors.

CAUTION If you download and install VMware ESXi, Citrix XenServer Express, or Microsoft Windows Hyper-V Server (not Windows Server 2008 with Hyper-V) on your own hardware, you will not gain access to the complete hypervisor virtualization feature set. VMware ESXi will require the purchase and addition of one of the editions of VMware's Virtual Infrastructure in order to gain a more complete feature set. XenServer Express will need to be replaced by another edition of XenServer in order to gain support for the management of multiple host servers through a single interface. And Microsoft Windows Hyper-V Server will need to be replaced by either the Enterprise or Datacenter Editions of Windows Server 2008 with Hyper-V in order to gain access to features such as high availability.

Build Your Own Hypervisor Hardware

However, you may not always be able to install brand-new servers that already include the hypervisor. For this reason, you need to create standard host server installations.

Creating a VM is easy. Just copy the files of one VM, rename them, repersonalize the server, and you're off. But creating a host server is more complex because it is based on hardware. One of the best ways to do this is to use boot-from-SAN operating system partitions. By booting from the SAN, you do not need any direct attached disks on the server you implement and it is easier to treat the OS partition in much the same way as you would treat a virtual disk. This is because SANs have the ability to create snapshots of disk configurations and duplicate them, much in the same way as you would simply copy a virtual hard disk drive. If you have the means to boot from SAN, use the following process to build host servers:

1. Create the host OS on shared storage.

2. Copy at least one LUN that contains a host OS.

3. Attach this LUN to a host server and depersonalize it. For Windows host servers, this means running the SysPrep command on it. SysPrep will remove the server name, remove the system's globally unique identifier (GUID), and remove the system's security ID (SID). For Linux hosts, you'll have to run a custom script to do the same.

4. Detach this LUN from the host.

5. Each time you need to create a new host, create a copy of this LUN and attach it to the new host. Boot the system and repersonalize it.

As you can see, this process is much faster than using any other means to create a host partition on a physical server.

If you don't have access to a SAN, you'll need to create a standard setup for your servers and possibly rely on disk images to reproduce it on any other host server you need to create.

NOTE   For information on how to create VMware installations, go to www.vmware.com/support/pubs/vi_pages/vi_pubs_35u2.html. For information on creating XenServer hosts, go to http://docs.xensource.com/XenServer/4.0.1/installation/installation.html. For Hyper-V installations go to www.microsoft.com/windowsserver2008/en/us/hyperv-install.aspx.

THE NEXT STEP

Most organizations begin using virtualization in support of testing and development before they move it into production. This is good practice since it lets you become familiar with the virtualization infrastructure in environments that do not require the same type of service level agreements as production does. For this reason, the next chapter focuses on how to prepare your virtualization environment in a laboratory. Once this is complete, you will be more prepared to move virtualization into production.

CHAPTER 6

Begin with the Testing Environment

As you prepare to move forward with the preparation of your host servers, you need to begin working with virtualization technologies in order to master their control before you begin the physical to virtual (P2V) process that will transform your production workloads into virtual machines. The best place to start is with the laboratory. Laboratories consist of workloads that are in constant flux. Machines need to be reprovisioned, systems need to be reconfigured, and entire environments need to be torn down and rebuilt on a regular basis. While this is an arduous task in the physical world, it becomes a snap in the virtual world. Vendors even provide different technologies that facilitate lab management even more than the virtualization engine does, letting you build, use, and tear down entire virtual environments in one fell swoop.

You begin with the testing laboratory because it is perhaps the most important part of any technical implementation project. Testing and retesting solutions before they are deployed is the only way to ensure high quality and avoid problems. After all, you do not want to find yourself in a situation where you are deploying garbage into your network. Garbage aside, you'll quickly find that the lab environment is one of the most exciting aspects of the project. Things move fast, you're playing with new technologies, you're the hub of all technological requests; it's just fun to work in the lab. This is another reason why you want to have everything in place the right way.

Whether it is for training, testing, or development, it's really handy to have a readily available working environment you can just jump into within minutes. That's why you need a virtual laboratory. This laboratory will then become the source of all of your virtualization efforts and will let you maintain a comprehensive testing environment when your project is done.

But for virtual laboratories to provide this kind of support to any IT project, they need to be treated as official systems that have their own place in the production network. This is why you need a structured and standard approach for their creation. That's what this section is all about: how to build a virtual laboratory, set it up, use and reuse it, and manage it for long-term operation. The strategies outlined in this part stem from real-world projects that cover all sorts of usage scenarios. These strategies will help you obtain value from your laboratory and ensure you get a solid return on investment (ROI) from your efforts. For example, one customer was able to build an entire collaboration testing environment in less than 32 hours. Think of it: less than four days to build three physical hosts and more than ten virtual machines playing different roles. In addition, the customer was able to reuse this environment for other testing purposes. And this was the first time they used a virtual laboratory! There is no doubt: this level of ROI is simply not available with physical laboratory environments.

When you're building a laboratory, any laboratory, you need to focus on four different areas.

▼ **Laboratory Description** The first deals with the need to outline the strategy you will use to create and implement the environment.

■ **Laboratory Deliverables** The second helps identify how the deliverables from the laboratory can be used in support of other testing or development scenarios.

With virtual laboratories in particular, it's really easy to include preconstructed machines as deliverables to other projects. That's because virtual machines (VMs) are really only constructed of a few files on a disk—large files admittedly, but files that can be transported, copied, or downloaded from remote locations.

■ **Laboratory Management Practices**   The third needs to focus on the practices you're going to use for the management and operation of the laboratory. Once again, file management will be a big part of this activity.

▲ **Future Plans and Projected Growth**   The fourth looks beyond the immediate and covers both best practices and recommendations for future lab usage, as well as the creation and management of a distributed virtual laboratory structure, as more and more members of the organization require access to running technologies.

These four pillars will help you build and prepare a virtual laboratory that can be used to support any number of scenarios, such as:

▼ **Enterprise Development Environment**   Developers need to have a certain amount of freedom on the machines they work with, but since these machines are enterprise systems, they must be controlled. Within a virtual environment, they can be granted the level of privilege they need without compromising production security.

■ **Test Environment**   New technologies, new products, new patches, new hotfixes…all need to be tested before they are introduced in the production environment. A virtual laboratory can be used to create a low-cost reproduction of the production environment in support of these tests. In this case, this lab will be useful to help you become familiar with virtualization technologies and how they work. Later on, you can rely on it to test the addition of new technologies to your Virtual Service Offerings.

■ **Support Environment**   Help desk operators supporting levels 1, 2, or 3 can use the virtual environment to reproduce any problem. This avoids having to give them multiple systems and lets them test out multiple scenarios without impacting the production environment.

▲ **Training Environment**   A virtual laboratory is the ideal environment for training preparation. You can install any technology and simulate most any situation, which lets you gain practical experience on the technologies you want to be certified in. In fact, the virtual lab will let you test out scenarios that you simply couldn't reproduce in your production network.

You might already be using technologies such as VMware or Microsoft virtualization, but the practices outlined here will help you move from an ad hoc usage of virtual machines to an officially supported implementation, from which multiple members of your organization can profit.

WORK WITH DIFFERENT TESTING LEVELS

Testing is performed in a graduated process, which gradually evolves into more and more complicated testing levels. For virtualization and other IT integration projects, there are five testing levels.

- ▼ Unit
- ■ Functional
- ■ Integration
- ■ Staging
- ▲ Pilot Project

The Unit testing level is designed for information discovery. Its purpose is to let individual technical team members discover how the feature they are tasked with designing works. For example, the team should use this testing level to discover how the creation of virtual machines actually works, play with the virtual files, discover how the options of the virtual machines can be modified, and generally familiarize themselves with the entire virtualization process.

The Functional testing level is designed for initial solution testing. Here, the technical team has determined just how a feature works and now they want to test the automation mechanisms they are preparing.

The Integration testing level starts bringing each individual component of the technical solution together.

The Staging testing level is focused on getting everything right. Basically, this level will provide an environment that is similar to your production environment. While in Integration, you blended every aspect of the solution together; in Staging, you want to make sure you can reproduce every technological aspect from A to Z without a hitch. You'll have to repeat the process until it is absolutely right. This way, you'll know exactly what to do when you move to production and you won't make any mistakes. Technical implementations are 80 percent preparation and 20 percent implementation, but you can only get there if you've fully tested each aspect.

The final testing level is the Pilot Project. While all of the other testing levels focused on technical testing, the Pilot Project focuses on the complete solution, including any administrative aspect of the process. This test will validate the logistics of your solution as well as the technical aspects. Make sure you've completely evaluated each aspect before you move on.

These testing levels require graduation from one to the other (see Figure 6-1). Each level will have both exit and entry criteria. For example, to leave the Unit level, technicians must prove that they have covered all of the activities for this level. To enter the Functional level, technicians must meet key requirements, and so on. You'll build your exit and entry criteria as you learn to work more fully with the lab; but basically, they should aim to make sure that technical teams are fully prepared to move from one level to another. With the high demand you'll have for lab resources, you don't want one team

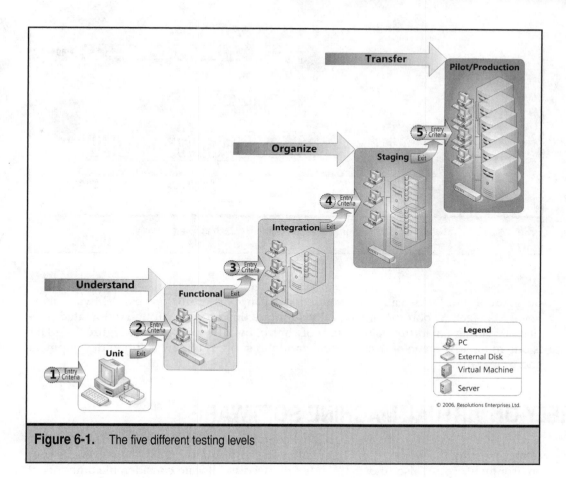

Figure 6-1.   The five different testing levels

to hog resources before they're ready to access them. Also, you want to make sure that no damage is done to any of the high-level environments—for example, Integration and Staging—causing you to have to restore them from backup, or worse, re-create them from scratch. The lab is for the use of all technical team members and should never be monopolized for one single aspect of the technical solution.

NOTE   For a view into the integration architecture—the architecture that is used to build and manage testing levels—as well as a sample Exit Criteria sheet, have a look at "Build the integration architecture" at www.reso-net.com/articles.asp?m=8#g. This article is part six of a seven-part series on enterprise architectures.

This testing structure is accepted industry-wide and helps manage the progression of a solution from start to finish. When you perform these tasks with virtualization software, you move virtual machines from one stage to another, progressively improving

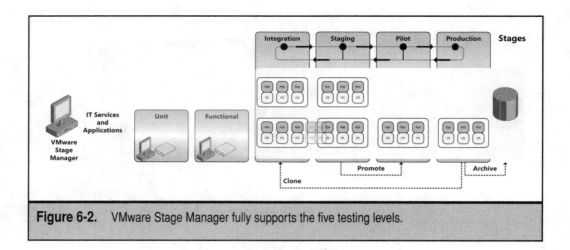

Figure 6-2. VMware Stage Manager fully supports the five testing levels.

the solution until it is ready for production. In support of this process, VMware offers Stage Manager, a coordinator that fully supports this process through automated policies, providing an additional measure of control over the process (see Figure 6-2). This is one more advantage of using virtualization in support of new solution development and preparation.

RELY ON VIRTUAL MACHINE SOFTWARE

Virtual machine (VM) software is an ideal complement to the laboratory. There are lots of reasons why this is the case. First of all, you can virtualize most any servers in your environment. You'll also find that while you need to allocate considerable amounts of RAM to production workloads, laboratory workloads can often get by with much less. For example, Windows Server 2003 workloads can easily run with as little as 256 megabytes (MB) of RAM allocated to the VM, whereas Windows Server 2008 requires at least 512MB. Of course, you may need to increase the amount of RAM when you add more than one role to the server, but if you have the appropriate host, you should easily be able to run any server role you need.

Working with both client PCs and servers through VMs will seriously cut down the cost of building the laboratory. You can rely on virtual technology from Microsoft, Citrix, or VMware, as all offer free copies of their tools, once again reducing lab costs. All three offer full support for running Windows servers or PCs as well as any number of operating systems (see Chapter 7). You will also need to obtain tools for the conversion of physical machines to virtual instances (see Chapter 7 again). This saves a lot of time, as you simply point to the physical machine you want to capture and easily transform it into a virtual instance.

In addition, working with virtual machines, you can "virtualize" the laboratory. Many of our clients buy some large host machines to run their laboratories. As you learned in Chapter 3, the ideal machine will be an x64 server running several multicore processors, lots of RAM, and lots of disk space. In the lab, you might not need shared storage. It all depends on your service level agreements for lab operations. Use an x64 operating system (OS) for this server, install the virtualization technology you've chosen, and you're off and running. When you consider the cost of these machines compared to the cost of having a complete physical lab, they really cut down on your overall costs.

There are a whole series of operations you can perform with virtual machines that you just can't perform with physical machines. For example, you can easily create a source machine. Install a first instance of the OS into a VM, customize its configuration, update its default user profile, update it in terms of patches, and once it is ready, copy it and depersonalize the copy. Voila! You now have a source machine that can be copied and reused to seed any machine role you need. That's a lot easier than working with a physical machine.

Another major benefit is the use of Volume Shadow Copy Service (VSS) on Windows Server 2003 (WS03) or Windows Server 2008 (WS08) if Windows Server is your host OS. Since virtual machines are nothing more than a series of files on a hard disk, you can enable automatic backup protection for them by enabling VSS and then relying on the Previous Versions client to restore any damaged machine almost instantly. VSS automatically takes two snapshots per day and can store up to 64 different snapshots (on WS03) or 512 snapshots (on WS08), which provides an adequate level of protection for your VMs. This doesn't replace proper backups, but it is at least a first line of defense that costs little, if anything.

NOTE VMware started shipping a VSS Writer in ESX 3.5 Update 2, giving ESX similar snapshot capabilities to Hyper-V's.

PHYSICAL VERSUS LOGICAL WORKSPACES

Another advantage of virtual machine technology in the testing lab is that you don't need the physical space a conventional lab usually requires. If you create the lab space in a datacenter by hosting a series of virtual machines on a given set of servers, the host servers can easily be located in the normal datacenter and profit from the standard operations applied to any production server—backup, patch updates, antivirus updates, and so on. Then, your technical team can connect to the VMs these servers host through the normal network. There may be reason for you to provide your teams with a separate network segment to isolate their network traffic, but if everything happens in the datacenter on the same server hosts, network traffic is not really an issue.

DEFINE LAB REQUIREMENTS

Now that you understand the various needs for the lab, you can begin to prepare the lab. This may require some initial acquisitions in order to properly populate the lab. Too many organizations populate labs as afterthoughts, bringing in the oldest machines in the network and leaving lab technicians with having to cannibalize various machines to try to put something decent together. Don't make this mistake! This lab is the epicenter of the project, so make sure you populate it appropriately. Here's an example of what you might need. The scale of the requirements will depend on the scale of your project. Keep in mind that you can run up to eight virtual machines per processor if all of the other requirements—RAM, hard disk space—are met.

Host Server Configurations

The minimal configurations required to support the lab should resemble the following list:

▼ Host Server(s)
   ■ Dual x64 quad-core SMP Server
   ■ 512MB RAM for the host OS
   ■ 256 to 512MB RAM for each VM running on the host
   ■ At least two disks for Random Array of Independent Disks (RAID) 1 (mirroring)
   ■ Preferably three or more disks for RAID 5 (stripe with parity)
   ■ Use the largest disk size you can—currently about 500 gigabytes (GB)
   ■ Retain about 50GB for the system drive
   ■ Assign the bulk of the space to a data drive, which will store the VMs
   ■ Retain about 50GB for a third drive, which will host the shadow copies produced by VSS
   ■ Dual network interface cards (NICs) at a minimum speed of 100 Mbps to support multiple connections to the virtual machines hosted by the server; verify with the virtualization manufacturer to see if you can team the NICs
■ Technician Workstation(s)
   ■ 1-GHz processor (64-bit, if possible)
   ■ 2GB of RAM, minimum
   ■ DirectX 9 support with at least 128MB of dedicated graphics memory
   ■ DVD-ROM drive
   ■ Audio output

▲ External Hard Drive(s)

   ■ External drive of 250GB at 7200 RPM with USB 2.0 or FireWire (IEEE 1394)

These systems should support long-term lab requirements. However, since you are using this lab as the start of your virtualization project, you'll need clustered hosts with shared storage, as outlined earlier. These systems will then move out of the lab once you're ready to move virtualization into production.

Virtual Machine Configurations

Virtual machines should be configured as follows:

1. Standard Server VM

RAM	512MB of RAM, minimum
OS	Your organizational standard
Service Packs	All applicable service packs and hotfixes should be installed
Number of Disks	Depends on the role; can be from one to three
Disk Size	Drive C: 50-GB expandable disk (leaves room for upgrades) Drive D: 70-GB expandable disk (optional based on server role) Drive E: 20-GB expandable disk
Network Cards	At least one NIC per VM
CD/DVD Drive	When providing VMs for use either locally or remotely, you should include ISO files for the installation media; this lets technicians add roles to the machine and generally control its feature set

2. Enterprise Server VM

RAM	512MB of RAM, minimum
OS	Your organizational standard for clustered servers
Service Packs	All applicable service packs and hotfixes should be installed
Disk Size	Drive C: 50-GB expandable disk (leaves room for upgrades) Drive D: 70-GB expandable disk (optional based on server role) Drive E: 20-GB expandable disk Install virtual disks that can be shared between hosts
Network Cards	At least one NIC per VM
CD/DVD Drive	When providing VMs for use either locally or remotely, you should include ISO files for the installation media; this lets technicians add roles to the machine and generally control its feature set

3. Bare-Metal VMs

RAM	512MB of RAM, minimum
OS	No OS
Service Packs	No fixes or service packs
Disk Size	Drive C: 50-GB expandable disk (leaves room for Windows Vista installation)
Network Cards	At least one NIC per VM
CD/DVD Drive	When providing VMs for use either locally or remotely, you should include ISO files for the installation media; this lets technicians add roles to the machine and generally control its feature set

4. Vista PC VMs

RAM	512MB of RAM, minimum
OS	Windows Vista based on the editions you decided to deploy
Service Packs	All applicable service packs and hotfixes should be installed
Disk Size	Drive C: 20-GB expandable disk
Network Cards	At least one NIC per VM
CD/DVD Drive	When providing VMs for use either locally or remotely, you should include ISO files for the installation media; this lets technicians add roles to the machine and generally control its feature set

5. Windows XP PC VMs

RAM	512MB of RAM, minimum
OS	Windows XP based on the editions you are currently running
Service Packs	All applicable service packs and hotfixes should be installed
Disk Size	Drive C: 20-GB expandable disk (leaves room for the upgrade)
Network Cards	At least one NIC per VM
CD/DVD Drive	When providing VMs for use either locally or remotely, you should include ISO files for the installation media; this lets technicians add roles to the machine and generally control its feature set

These systems should be used as source VMs for the reproduction of any system configuration in your network.

VM User Accounts

User accounts are also critical when setting up VMs for distribution to the technical team. With the Unit and Functional testing levels, it is safe to give administrative access to the technicians on your project team in both server and workstation VMs because they are stand-alone environments. But as you proceed through the testing levels, you need to tighten down change control and grant access to high-privileged accounts only to the lab administrator. After all, capturing the changes required to the infrastructure is the purpose of these environments.

When you deliver stand-alone machines for either the Unit or Functional environment, you should endeavor to make servers domain controllers. Their behavior will be different from member servers, but it will be easier to assign different roles to the accounts the technicians will require. In many cases, these testing levels will require either a single PC VM or a PC VM coupled with a server VM, where the server is playing a series of different roles.

When you grant users access to the VMs that make up either the Integration or Staging testing level, you give them accounts with appropriate access rights, as outlined by the information the technical team will provide to you.

Required Server and Workstation Roles

Within each testing level, you'll need to assign or create several different machine roles. As mentioned previously, in the Unit and Functional testing levels, server roles can be integrated into one single VM, but as you move up the testing ladder, you'll want to separate different roles to represent the production environment you're running. For example, your Integration level may still join several roles together into a few machines, but when you get to Staging, it should be as similar as possible to the production environment. Staging is that last technical test before you start making changes in production itself, so you need to get it right (see Figure 6-3).

TIP You can even use VMs to simulate remote sites. Server operating systems include routing capabilities that are similar to those of Cisco's devices. For example, in Windows, you can enable Routing and Remote Access (RRAS) on two different VMs and use them to simulate the routing of data from a local to a remote site. Then you can add branch office server roles to the site located behind the remote routing server.

There are also some good router VMs that you can pull down from the virtual appliance marketplace. If licensing is an issue, these free appliances are a good alternative. Find them at www .vmware.com/appliances.

In the end, your lab will need to provision several different types of levels and several different environments. Remember that when you build the more permanent testing levels or environments, you'll want to build redundancy into the lab infrastructure. For example, the Staging testing level should have at least two domain controllers

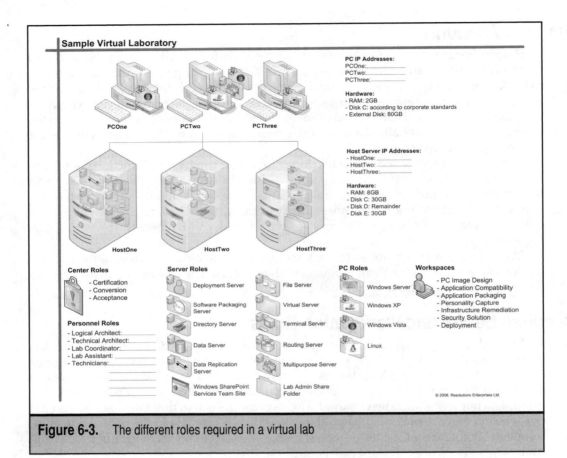

Figure 6-3.   The different roles required in a virtual lab

for redundancy. And if you simulate remote sites, you'll also need to include replication engines in your solution to replicate objects from one location to the next.

Virtual machine software also helps in this process. Once the machines are built and ready, you can use certain tools to automatically provision these machines for users on either a controlled or self-service basis. Microsoft System Center Virtual Machine Manager (SCVMM) is a virtual environment management tool that lets you manage multiple hosts and virtual machines through a familiar interface. It also offers a self-service portal for the creation and generation of virtual machines (see Figure 6-4). This tool, however, only supports the generation of a single machine at a time. If more than one machine is required—for example, for the creation of an entire e-mail environment, including directory servers, mail servers, and end-user devices—you have to build it for the testers. However, this is one of the major advantages of virtual labs: Every machine, every environment is completely reusable.

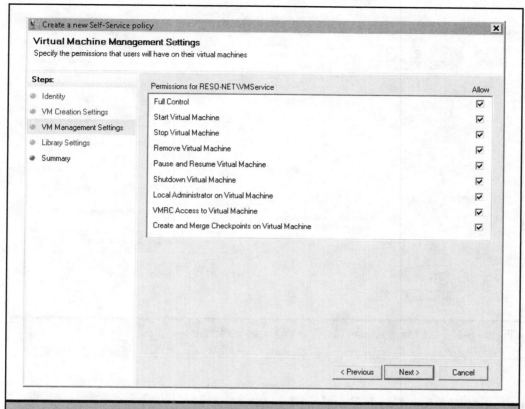

Figure 6-4. SCVMM can allow end-user testers to provision and control their own virtual machines.

Be careful, however, of the policies you put in place for the VMs end-user testers can create. After all, the major reason for this project is to reduce the number of machines in your datacenter, not proliferate them. In order to control the VMs users create, you can set time-limit policies to automatically destroy them once the user's work is complete.

VMware also offers a tool for laboratory management. The VMware Lab Manager is a tool that is designed to manage and maintain complete environments, not just single VMs (see Figure 6-5). Because of this, it is currently much more powerful than the Microsoft counterpart.

TIP If you are not using VMware, you might look up other lab management tools. For example, VMLogix (www.vmlogix.com) and Surgient (www.surgient.com) also offer this type of tool.

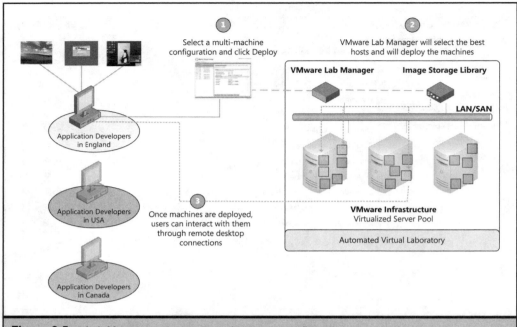

Figure 6-5. Lab Manager can manage entire system configurations.

Requirements for Each Testing Level

Table 6-1 provides guidelines for the requirements for each testing level. Adjust them according to your own needs.

Each of the five environments has its own requirements, but fortunately, you can reuse many of the requirements of a previous level for those of the next. Here's the breakdown of machine reuse.

▼ **Unit level**   Individual technicians work with their own machines stored on an external disk and linked to their own PC.

■ **Functional level**   As team members graduate from Unit to Functional, they reuse the original individual machines they had in Unit since they are no longer needed at that level.

■ **Integration level**   All team members begin to share the same set of virtual and physical machines as they begin to integrate their part of the solution into a single environment. Change control is activated to capture all practices.

Test Level	Objective	Virtual Machines	Physical Machines
Unit	Discovery of new features and feature operation	Host software with several virtual machines	None; use their own PC
Functional	Automate features and obtain peer review	Same as Unit	None; use their own PC
Integration	Link all aspects of the solution together	Several virtualized servers with attached client systems	Use their own PC to access centralized environment
Staging	Finalize all technical procedures and prepare for final-acceptance testing	Servers represent small-scale production environment plus a possible remote site	Same as Integration
Pilot	Finalize all technical and administrative procedures	Production-level machines both virtual and physical environments	Production host servers and production PCs

Table 6-1.   Requirements for the five testing levels

- ■ **Staging level**   All technical team members share an environment that is a scaled-down version of the production environment. Change control is absolute, and no change can be performed without being tracked. Procedures are completely finalized and are tested from end to end.

- ▲ **Pilot level**   All team members, including administrative staff, use production systems to target a deployment to about 10 percent of the population.

CREATE THE LAB ENVIRONMENT

The actual creation of the laboratory environment is simpler once you understand how it should work. If you want to get your technical team members going early, all you need to do is prepare the virtual machines that are required for Unit and Functional testing. These are fairly quick to prepare, but you should still proceed with care. Ideally, you will already have initiated the acquisitions required for these VMs—external drives and perhaps high-performance PCs—and have determined which virtualization technology you want to use as well as obtained the virtualization software. This will be the first of many source installation files that the lab will be responsible for maintaining. You will also need to obtain source installation media for all of the operating systems you will be working with. To make them easier to work with, transform the installation media into ISO files because these act as CD drives in virtual machines.

Once you're ready, prepare these two environments in the following order. Rely on an existing workstation with sufficient capabilities to perform these steps.

1. Install the virtualization technology on a workstation with sufficient capabilities to create virtual machines.

2. Create your first virtual machine, assigning RAM, disk space, and network interface cards. It is best to create a new folder with the machine name and store all VM component files in this folder.

3. Connect the VM's CD/DVD drive to the ISO file for the OS you want to install.

4. Perform the installation, running through your standard procedures for OS installation in your organization.

TIP Since you will be using a physical-to-virtual conversion tool for the actual transformation of your datacenter, you can also create this machine by converting an existing physical machine into a VM.

5. Customize the machine as you normally would, update the default user, and apply any required patches or updates.

6. For any copy of Windows prior to Windows Vista, copy the following files from the Deploy.cab file located on the appropriate Windows installation CD to a new folder called SysPrep on the %systemroot% drive—usually the C: drive:

   ■ Setupmgr.exe

   ■ SysPrep.exe

   ■ Factory.exe

   ■ Setupcl.exe

   For Vista and Windows Server 2008, use the SysPrep tool located in the Windows\System32\SysPrep folder.

   For Linux operating systems, use a custom script to prepare the machine.

7. For versions prior to Windows Vista, run Setupmgr.exe to generate a SysPrep .inf file. Use your organizational standards to provide the answers required for this file. Close Setupmgr.exe.

   For Vista and WS08, run the Computer Image Manager from the Windows Installation Automation Kit (find the WAIK at www.microsoft.com/ downloads/details.aspx?FamilyID=C7D4BC6D-15F3-4284-9123-679830D629F2 &displaylang=en). Once again, for Linux, use custom scripts.

8. Copy the VM's entire folder, rename the folder and the VM files to "machinename SysPrepped," and open the new machine in your virtual machine tool.

9. Run SysPrep.exe on the machine to select the Reseal option, depersonalize it, and shut it down. You now have a source machine from which you can generate a number of copies.

10. Repeat this process until each OS in the datacenter has been reproduced.

11. Document each machine, listing user accounts and capabilities; copy them onto the external disks; and provide the disks to your technical team members.

That's it. Now that your team members are ready to proceed with their own work, you can move on to create and prepare the working environment for the lab, as well as preparing the integration and staging environments.

Virtual Machines and Software Licensing

Even though you're working with virtual machines, you still have to be conscious of licensing issues, especially if you're building a laboratory to last. For this reason, we don't recommend using evaluation copies of software or operating systems. Here are some general guidelines on how you should license virtual machines. You should verify with your vendor to make sure these guidelines meet their licensing requirements.

▼ **SysPrep machine**   A SysPrep machine does not require a license because it is a machine that is used only to seed other machines and doesn't actually get used as-is. Once you've copied the SysPrep machine and start personalizing it, you need a license for the machine.

■ **Running virtual machines**   Each machine that is named and is running on a constant basis needs to have its own license.

■ **Copied virtual machines**   Copies of virtual machines do not need their own license so long as they are not running at the same time.

▲ **Copied and renamed virtual machines**   Each time you copy a virtual machine and rename it, you need to assign a license to it. A renamed machine is treated as a completely different machine and, therefore, needs a license.

For Microsoft products, using either the Microsoft Developer Network (MSDN) or TechNet Plus subscriptions will give you access to ten licenses for each product, though each license needs activation. Both subscriptions support the legal reuse of virtual machines.

If the host operating system is WS03 or WS08 Enterprise Edition, you can run four Microsoft server VMs at no additional cost. This makes a good argument for making the host systems run this OS. More information on virtual machine licensing for Microsoft Windows Server can be found here: www.microsoft.com/licensing/highlights/virtualization/faq.mspx.

When you're ready to build the lab itself, as well as Integration and Staging, you'll need to perform the following activities:

▼ Begin with the base server installation(s) for the host servers.

■ Create file shares for the lab repositories.

■ Install VM software on host servers.

▲ Create or P2V the VMs that simulate production servers and other aspects of the production environment.

You'll find that you need a great deal of storage space. You must plan for storage space, keeping in mind the following requirements:

▼ Space for storing all lab data

■ Space for the installation media for all operating systems and for all required software products

■ Space for the images built during testing—images of both VMs and, if you're not using integrated hypervisors, for host systems

▲ Space for backing up virtual hard disks and duplicating entire virtual environments

On average, a minimum of 500GB of space is required, but this number is affected by the number of disk images, VMs, and applications your project covers and it does not include the storage space required on the host servers themselves.

When you build the Integration and Staging test levels, remember that they need to be as similar to production as possible. Also remember that they don't need to be identical. For example, there is no reason to use the same Active Directory (AD) or identity management forest or domain names since they do not affect the PC deployment process. Ideally, you'll use proper names for AD components, names that make sense and that you can keep on a permanent basis. In our opinion, it is always best to actually acquire proper domain names for this purpose because they are permanent and this low cost is not a burden on the project's budget.

When you work on the client computer portion of the lab, design it to test the same functions and features currently in use or planned for use in the production environment. Include the same types of hardware, applications, and network configurations.

NOTE With the use of the right hardware, the lab can also be transformed into a portable environment. Several manufacturers are now releasing powerful portable hardware. For example, NextComputing, LLC offers a portable lab server through its NextDimension system. This system can include multiple dual-core CPUs, loads of RAM, multiple serial ATA (SATA) drives with lots of space, and even multiple monitors, all in a transportable format. For more information on NextDimension, go to www.nextcomputing.com/.

Build Complete Environments

Now that you have individual machines created, you can use them to build entire environments. The goal is to build an environment that is reusable and easy to repurpose, and that fully supports the simulation of any network infrastructure in your datacenter. This means your lab needs to provide several base services.

▼ Identity management, for example, through Microsoft Active Directory, with a single domain forest running on two domain controllers

■ E-mail capability, for example, through Microsoft Exchange Server

■ Database storage, for example, through Microsoft SQL Server

■ Clustering technologies tied to shared data storage using virtual hard drives

■ Terminal Services for client access to the virtual environment

▲ Other technologies as required for testing/proof-of-concept purposes

All virtual machines should be running on top of a free virtualization engine (see Chapter 7). One of the best ways to give users and participants access to the testing environment is to create a machine to run Terminal Services. The advantage of using Terminal Services is that users have access to the environment as members of the domain, giving them a single-sign-on experience. In addition, no changes are required to their production machines, which is a bonus.

When this is done, you should create a graphical map of where each machine is located and what role it plays in the infrastructure (see Figure 6-6). This type of map will be useful, especially for the technical staff that will be using the lab. It lays out the location of each machine, its name, function, and Internet Protocol (IP) address, as well as providing a global view of how machines interact.

The possibilities for virtual laboratories are almost limitless. For example, a lab made of VMs can also contain and support the following technologies:

▼ **Network Load Balancing (NLB) services for the front-end servers** This lets you test and determine how failover works, as well as which procedures are required to build a duplicate server for the addition of nodes to an NLB cluster.

■ **Windows Server Failover Clusters for back-end servers** This lets you test how server clustering works and how it needs to be set up, as well as test failover policies.

▲ **Independent identity management or Active Directory for the lab** To ensure minimal impact on existing network services, the laboratory should be set up with an independent identity management infrastructure.

This is a great place to let your imagination run. If you have access to all of your organization's technology, you can try any scenario you can think of. When the technical builds of the test levels are complete, they should be fully tested to ensure that they do indeed reproduce the production environment and that they will support testing of your

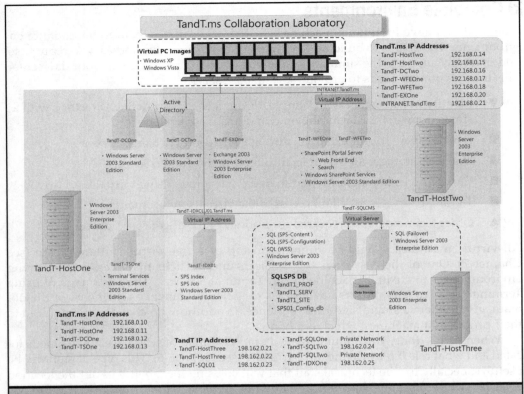

Figure 6-6.   Visual maps of the environment make it easier to use and understand.

entire virtualization solution, including the creation of new VMs as well as the transformation of existing physical workloads. Then, once this is complete, your lab will be ready for prime time and will be able to support all aspects of the solution preparation.

Virtual Laboratory Deliverables

Another area that provides great ROI with virtual machines is the deliverables you can extract from them. Since prepared machines are no more than a series of files in a folder on a disk, they can easily be transported and reused for other purposes than the one intended during their creation. The very nature of virtual machines also allows the use of special administrative and operational procedures that are simply not available or, if they are available, are a lot more complex to perform on physical machines. Here is an example of some of the deliverables you can expect from a virtual lab:

▼   **Core Machines**   These machines are used to generate all of the machines in the lab. You'll want to make sure these machines include the following:

■   The machines are updated with all security patches available, as well as any component update that is required.

■   Update the default user environment in order to facilitate the creation of new user profiles. This default user profile should include the creation of special administrative shortcuts in the Quick Launch area of the Windows toolbar.

■   Add two virtual network interface cards to these machines in order to support special functions such as clustering support.

■   Create a single disk, disk C:, for each machine. Additional disks can be added when the machines are purposed.

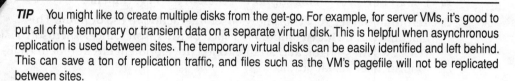

TIP   You might like to create multiple disks from the get-go. For example, for server VMs, it's good to put all of the temporary or transient data on a separate virtual disk. This is helpful when asynchronous replication is used between sites. The temporary virtual disks can be easily identified and left behind. This can save a ton of replication traffic, and files such as the VM's pagefile will not be replicated between sites.

■   Rename the administrator account.

■   Finally, keep these machines in this state to facilitate their update when Microsoft releases new security patches or operating system upgrades.

■   **Two SysPrep Machines**   Next, you keep a depersonalized copy of these machines. You'll use these machines to populate your virtual laboratory. In order to support this, you'll also need to perform the following:

■   Make a copy of both machine images (all files) to a special Virtual Machine\ Source folder on each physical host.

■   Each time a new machine is needed, a copy of the appropriate edition of the local depersonalized machine is made. The new machine is placed in a folder identifying its purpose, and the files that make it up are renamed. The renaming procedure includes the name of the parent folder, the name of the configuration file, and the name of the virtual hard disk drive.

■   Depending on the purpose of the machine, a second or third disk can be added. This could be the case, for example, with an Exchange or SQL Server machine since it will be used to run databases and transaction logs.

■   Once the machine is ready, it is opened in your virtual tool. Because it is a depersonalized machine, it needs to be personalized. This includes a new name for the machine and the inscription of the administrator password. The OS then proceeds with the personalization of the machine and reboots it.

- Once the machine is rebooted, administrators need to reset its IP addresses, determine if a second network interface card is required, join it to a domain (if appropriate), and format the additional disks (if required).

- Once this is done, the machine can be purposed—that is, it can have special software loaded on it to fulfill its purpose in the environment.

- **The Base Environment**   Next, you can construct a base environment using appropriate versions of the SysPrep machines. A standard network should include the following machine builds:

  - **LDAP Server A**   This serves as the first domain controller (DC) in the new AD forest.

  - **LDAP Server B**   This serves as the second DC in the new AD forest. You'll also need to build out the basic structure of the Active Directory.

  - **E-mail Server A**   This supports e-mail in the new domain.

  - **Terminal Server A**   This allows user interaction in the domain. This machine can include components such as Microsoft Office, Microsoft Visio, Windows Messenger, and an integrated development environment (IDE) tool, such as Visual Studio.

  - **Database Server A**   This is the first node that is part of a SQL Server cluster.

  - **Database Server B**   This is the second node that is part of a SQL Server cluster.

  These machines have the following characteristics:

  - All machines are verified for additional patches and service packs required by the software that supports their new purpose.

  - Group Policy objects are created in the domain to facilitate the operation of the machines as well as user access to the environment.

  - Once the machines are ready, a backup copy of all machines is taken to support the reproduction of the environment for other purposes.

- ▲ **The Core Testing Environment**   Using the appropriate depersonalized machine, the core testing environment is constructed. This includes the creation of the following machines:

  - **Web Front-End Server A**   The first node of an NLB cluster hosting collaboration services.

  - **Web Front-End Server B**   The second node of the NLB cluster.

  - **Search Server A**   A server running both indexing and other jobs.

  Once again, these machines can be captured as snapshots and delivered to other projects for testing in their own environments.

These four deliverables can be reused at any time by any other member of your organization (see Figure 6-7). Since each machine can include several gigabytes of information, they're not easy to transport. In some cases, you can copy them to DVDs, but the best way to deliver these machines is to use portable USB disks. Hook the disk up to your server, copy all of the machines for delivery to it, and voilà!, a ready-made networking environment for delivery. You can also store them all centrally and give users access through Terminal Services.

There's a lot you can do with these machines, and there's a lot to be done with them. The first two are easy to reuse since by their very nature, they will produce new and un-named machines, but the third and fourth require more thought. For example, the Lightweight Directory Access Protocol (LDAP) environment needs to be renamed to ensure the protection of your own testing environment as well as renaming machines, modifying their IP addresses to avoid conflicts, and resetting all passwords to make sure no one reuses your own.

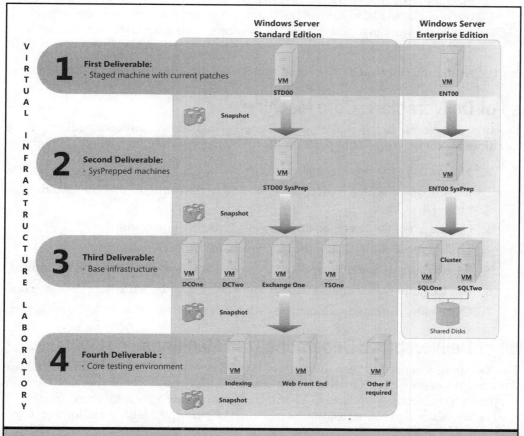

Figure 6-7.   An example of the four core deliverables from the lab and how they can be used

REUSE OF THE LAB DELIVERABLES

Three key items are required for anyone to be able to reuse your deliverables.

▼ They need to have at least two physical hosts with sufficient memory and hard disk space to host the virtual machines. You can also provide them with central VM storage if your lab has enough resources. But you might consider a charge-back program to get testers to pay for the environments they need.

■ The appropriate number of licenses for the virtual engine you run. If you use free virtualization tools, you do not need to worry about this element.

▲ Access to the core images of the virtual machines to reproduce them and copy them to their new environment. Note that these machines are at least 4GB in size—and sometimes considerably more. Because of this, copying these machines can affect network bandwidth. In most cases, the best approach is to use removable disks, such as USB hard drives, for the copy, or to store them on shared storage to use the shared storage's duplication capabilities, which avoids network bandwidth and provides high-speed duplication.

The reuse procedure varies, depending on the deliverable other testers decide to use.

Reuse of Deliverable 1: Core Machines

The first deliverable is the core machines you created. When someone requests these machines for reuse, you should perform the following steps on them before delivery:

1. Make a copy of your original machines.
2. Rename the machine files; rename the folder, the configuration file, and the virtual disk file.
3. Open each of the new machines in your virtualization engine.
4. Modify the IP address and the machine name for each machine.
5. Each machine should be updated. All patches and upgrades should be applied.
6. Next, change the administrative account password to secure the new machines.
7. Optionally, you can depersonalize each machine before delivery to the requestor.

Reuse of Deliverable 2: Depersonalized Machines

The first thing you need to keep in mind is the validity of these machines. You should use these machines only if they are relatively current. That's because you do not want to have to apply several security updates to all of the machines you create from these images.

The use of the depersonalized machines should be performed with the following steps:

1. The machines should be copied to all physical hosts in the new laboratory (if you are moving them to new locations).

2. Appropriate machines should be copied to new folders, and the base files making up the machine should be renamed.

3. The new machines should be opened in the virtual engine and personalized.

4. The core function of the machine should be applied.

5. Each machine should be updated as needed.

Another useful item you might provide to requestors of the depersonalized or core machines is the installation and configuration documentation you used to create your virtual laboratory. One thing to keep in mind on this documentation is to keep it short and to the point, providing a summary of the information required for the installation, then providing crucial details (see Figure 6-8). This will make both the first and the second deliverable much more useful to other groups in your organization.

Prepare the Active Directory

The Active Directory preparation will use the following settings. The Windows Server CD will be required for DNS installation.

Note: Be very careful with the NetBIOS name. It must be different from the one in the production network.

Credentials:	Local Administrator
Source:	DCPromo or Manage Your Server | Add or Remove a Role
Domain Controller:	Domain Controller for a New Domain
Forest:	TandT.NET
NetBIOS Name:	TANDT
Folder Locations:	Defaults on C: drive\
DNS:	Install and Configure DNS on this computer
Default Permissions:	Compatible with only Windows 2000 or Windows Server 2003
Directory Restore Password:	Same as Local Administrator
Domain Functional Mode:	Windows Server 2003
Forest Functional Mode:	Windows Server 2003
Global Catalog Servers:	DCOne and DCTwo
Forest Operations Masters:	on DCOne
Domain Operations Masters:	on DCTwo

The process to create the Active Directory is as follows.

1. Begin by preparing two machines running Windows Server 2008, Standard Edition. The machines should have the following characteristics:
   a. Machine names: DCOne and DCTwo
   b. Machine location: D:\VM Images*MachineName*
   c. Machine files: machinename.VMC and machinename.VHD

Figure 6-8.   An example of the build documentation to be used

Reuse of Deliverable 3: The Base Environment

As you can surmise, use of this environment requires some special procedures to protect other existing environments, including your own laboratory, from potential damage. When you choose to deliver the base environment to other groups, saving them considerable time in preparation, you'll need to prepare it according to the following steps:

1. A formal request to the virtual lab manager must be sent. This request must include:
   - The name for the new environment
   - The DNS name of the new domain
   - The down-level name for the new domain
   - A three-character prefix for machine names
   - A list of IP addresses to use for each machine

2. A generic administrative password that can be used in the preparation of the machines. This password can be changed once the machines are delivered.

3. Once this request has been received, the virtual lab team can proceed to the preparation of the delivery. All machines need to be renamed. The addition of the three-letter acronym representing the purpose of the new lab to the existing machine name should be sufficient.

4. The domain/forest/security context also needs to be renamed to avoid duplication on the internal network. For Active Directory, tools and procedures for performing this operation can be found at www.microsoft .com/windowsserver2003/downloads/domainrename.mspx.

5. All administrative passwords need to be changed.

6. All IP addresses need to be changed.

Once this is done, the new environment can be delivered for use. The ideal mechanism for this delivery is a removable USB hard disk since the environment is made up of several virtual machines, or central storage if you have it.

Reuse of Deliverable 4: The Core Environment

Like Deliverable 3, this deliverable requires special procedures for reuse. There are two ways to reuse this set of machines. The first consists of renaming the security context and all of the machines, just like for the reuse of Deliverable 3 and using the same steps. The second is to simply provide this entire environment as-is. The issue with this second approach is to find a way to reuse the entire set of machines without impacting any other existing environment. This can be done if you set up an isolated network to run this new instance of your lab. But since it is easy to make mistakes and you don't want to cause any downtime to your own lab, the best way to provide this deliverable for reuse is to use the same procedure as for Deliverable 3.

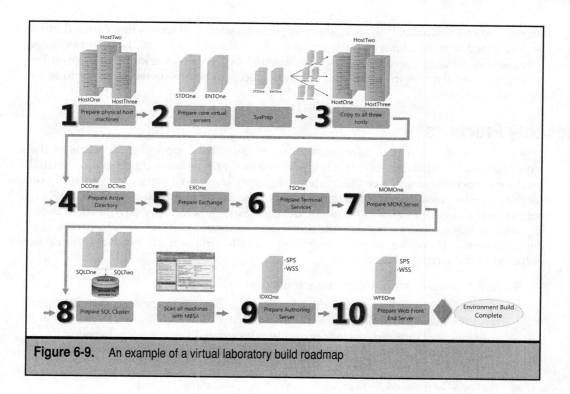

Figure 6-9. An example of a virtual laboratory build roadmap

Another useful tool you can provide with both of these deliverables is the laboratory build roadmap (see Figure 6-9). This roadmap graphically portrays what was done to create both these deliverables and, therefore, lets other users better understand the complexity of your deliverable.

One of the key advantages your organization will gain with this approach and the reuse of your laboratory deliverables is a significant return on investment (ROI) and a vastly reduced total cost of ownership (TCO) for these laboratories. Imagine, now with two physical machines you can run complex testing and training environments that used to require one single physical machine for each role. Before, you had to scrounge around to find leftover hardware just so you could create a laboratory. Now, you don't need to use this approach because you can justify the low cost of two properly sized machines, especially given the results you can deliver with them.

VIRTUAL INFRASTRUCTURE LABORATORY MANAGEMENT PRACTICES

Another area that can provide lowered TCO is in your laboratory management practices. Because this is a production laboratory that provides constant service levels, you'll need to design proper processes for the management and administration of the lab. Since the lab runs on free virtualization tools, there are several special practices that can and must be performed to ensure both stability and security of the environment. These procedures cover several different areas: security, special build procedures, backup and disaster recovery, and finally, maintenance. Each of these needs to be addressed in order to meet the goals of the lab.

Security Practices

One key area of the virtual infrastructure is security. This applies at all levels of the environment. For example, because it is a laboratory, and because it is based on virtual machines, operators may have the tendency to apply lax security rules or even apply no security at all—passwords are freely exchanged, the same password is applied to all accounts, and so on. But this should not be the case. Since a laboratory environment is designed to represent reality, it should be as secure as possible, just the way the production environment is. Therefore, as a starting point, the following security practices should be enforced in the virtual laboratory:

▼ All administrator accounts are renamed from the defaults.

■ Critical passwords, such as those for the local administrator on each machine and the domain administrator in the security context, are known by only key people: the laboratory manager and the designated system administrator. Only the laboratory manager is allowed to divulge this password to others, and this only in an extreme emergency.

■ Whenever a password is compromised, it is reset immediately.

■ All service accounts are assigned a special complex password, which is distributed to only the core administrators. This password is completely different from that of the administrative accounts.

■ User accounts use a generic password, which is distributed to the user through internal e-mail but requires an immediate reset once they log into the system.

■ A proper delegation-of-authority strategy is in use in the environment, granting operators only those rights that they absolutely need to perform their job.

■ A proper organizational unit structure is created in the LDAP environment to support this delegation model.

■ The delivery of security patches should be managed through proper infrastructures. For example, in Windows environments, you can use Windows Server Update Services in order to keep the machines up-to-date at all times.

■ A corporate antivirus tool should be installed and used to automatically update all of the definitions on each machine in the environment.

▲ The physical hosts are part of a workgroup and are not part of the security context managed by the virtual laboratory. Specific operator accounts need to be created on these machines to enable operator logon without the use of the local administrator account.

This last item is very important since the security-context servers for the virtual lab are virtual machines. Since the virtual machines cannot start until the host machines are started, joining them to this security context causes logon issues on the physical hosts. These host machines can be part of your production domain instead of a workgroup, but practice has found that it is often simpler and easier to set the physical hosts to be members of a workgroup that has the same name as the down-level name of the lab's security context. This way they all show up together in the Network Neighborhood.

The practices outlined here are by no means a complete list of the activities required for securing an environment; they need to be supplemented with the normal professional practices you use to enforce a secure environment. They are brought to your attention to highlight some of the specific items required for virtual laboratories.

Special Build Procedures

The very nature of virtual machines makes it easier to support complex system build procedures. This means that at each time you perform a critical operation during a complex build process, you can take a backup copy of the files making up this machine or, even better, take a snapshot of the machine. Snapshots let you return to a specific point in time on a VM. So, for example, when you're building a complex system, you can take several backup images or snapshots.

The advantage of these temporary backup copies and snapshots is that whenever an operation fails, the backup copy makes it easy to simply go back one step and start over again. This is something that is impossible on a physical server—unless you use a disk imaging tool, which takes much more time than a simple disk copy of a virtual machine. Once the complex installation operation is complete, these temporary backups can be discarded. Consider this strategy during your machine builds.

Backup and Disaster Recovery

Backup is also a place where you can take advantage of virtual technology. One of the great advantages of working with virtual machines is that they are made up of files located within folders. This enables the ability to include several types of protection levels.

▼　The first level of protection is provided by **manual machine backups**. Each time a critical event is set to occur on any given machine, it is paused, its state is saved, and a copy is made of the folder that contains its files. Then, the machine is restarted, the operation is performed, and if all goes well, the manual backup machine is deleted. If not, operators can quickly return to the previous version of the machine.

■　The second level of protection is offered by a powerful feature of Windows Server (if your host is running Windows): **Volume Shadow Copy Service (VSS)**. VSS is a default service that automatically protects data stored within a shared folder. Snapshots are created twice a day by default, and multiple snapshots can be stored for any drive or volume where the service is activated

(64 for WS03 or 512 for WS08). To recover a damaged machine, you go to the Properties of its folder and restore a previous version. To ensure this service applies to all virtual machines, their folders are all stored within a shared folder, and since disks are shared by default, each volume is automatically considered a shared folder by VSS.

- The third level of backup is the **default backup technologies**, which take backups of the internal contents of the VMs. These are used whenever a critical event has occurred on a system.

- A fourth level of backup can be provided by utilities such as Robocopy from the Windows Server 2003 Resource Kit. If you have two hosts, you create a scheduled Robocopy job that takes all of the virtual machines from one host and copies them to the other and vice versa. Since Robocopy is intelligent enough to copy only changed files, this does not take up too much overhead.

- ▲ A fifth level of backup can be provided by your enterprise backup tool. Since virtual machines are only files, the use of a file system agent should be sufficient to protect these machines on tape.

In production labs, backups are a crucial part of the operation of the lab as a whole.

Lab Maintenance Procedures

Special maintenance practices are also required for the virtual laboratory because of its nature. These include many variations on traditional machine management practices, such as the following:

- ▼ **Weekly Security Scan** For Windows systems, the system administrator must perform a Microsoft Baseline Security Analyzer scan on the entire domain once a week to ensure all machines are secure. This can be mitigated by the use of Windows Server Update Services, since this update service protects more than just the operating system. Use appropriate tools for non-Windows environments.

- **Weekly Antivirus Verification** Once a week, the system administrator should ensure that proper virus definitions are applied to all machines and that no machine remains unprotected. Also, the schedule in which antivirus (AV) scans run should be staggered. This prevents performance issues on a physical host when all VMs try to run AV scans at the same time.

- **Weekly Maintenance Window** Once a week, if required, a special maintenance window is reserved to perform major maintenance activities on the environment.

- **Weekly Free Space Verification** Once a week, the system administrator verifies that there are appropriate amounts of free space on the disks of both the physical hosts and the virtual machines.

- **Weekly Event Log Verification** Once a week, the system administrator verifies that there are no untoward events in the event logs of the various machines in the laboratory.

■   **Weekly Backup Verification**   Once a week, the backup administrator ensures that backups are properly performed on all machines and reports to the system administrator. In addition, the system administrator verifies that shadow copies are working properly on both physical and virtual machines.

■   **Change Log**   Each time a modification is performed on the environment, an entry is written to the laboratory change log. This helps ensure that events are properly recorded.

▲   **Special Machine Deletion Procedure**   Manual machine backups are performed every time a significant event occurs on a machine. If the event or modification is successful, this special backup should be deleted, but sometimes this backup is not removed. Therefore, regular deletion events must take place. Because of the confusing nature of working in the file system without any real link to the virtual engine, it may be possible to delete the wrong machine. To ensure this does not occur, machines that need to be deleted should be moved to a special **To be deleted** folder prior to deletion. Then an overall system check should be performed. If all machines are operating properly in your virtual engine, deletion can proceed. If the wrong machine is copied to this folder, one or more machines will no longer be available in the virtual engine. The same applies to snapshots. Most virtual engines can store up to 512 snapshots of a virtual machine. You must manage these snapshots in order to retain only valid copies.

These procedures are added to normal maintenance procedures that apply to all IT environments.

VIRTUAL LAB BEST PRACTICES SUMMARY

One of the most important findings you should come away with from working with virtual technologies is that it is possible *to build and test almost any functionality in a network environment within a matter of a few weeks, sometimes even a few days*. Now that you have core virtual machines to work with as well as a comprehensive installation instruction set, the time required to prepare a working environment should be greatly reduced. In addition, here are some recommended best practices.

▼   To increase the speed of the implementation of a testing environment, reuse the deliverables from the virtual laboratory.

■   The process of acquiring hardware in support of a testing environment should be streamlined. Perhaps you could consider having a bank of machines on hand at all times. This bank of machines can then be used as a pool for allocation to different testing environments. To facilitate the creation of this pool, you may consider moving all of your current testing environments to a virtual infrastructure. This should free up several machines. You can also add more machines to this pool as you virtualize your production servers.

- P2V tools, which are discussed in Chapter 9, must be part of the overall lab toolkit. They also will be required for the actual migration you will perform.

- Machines used in support of testing should be multiprocessor systems that include lots of RAM and large amounts of disk space so that they can support multiple virtual machines.

- Training or familiarity with virtual machines is essential to the success of any virtual lab. Technical staff with little or no experience with virtual machine technology will find it confusing at first.

- A glossary of terms and terminology is a good idea to ensure that everyone is on the same page.

- Keep the host machines out of the security context you create in your testing environment. Otherwise, this may become a problem since the machines managing the security context are virtual machines and don't run until the physical host is up; yet, to log into the physical host, you need access to these machines.

- It is a good idea to have a communication plan in place. For example, an introductory document could be crafted from these two articles. Such a document is useful to bring new technical staff quickly up to speed on virtual technologies.

- It is a great idea to have a graphical representation of the virtual lab to provide to technical staff. This graphical map is often the single most important piece of documentation operators use.

- Also, keep a change log for all activity within your testing environment. This log can be invaluable when trying to troubleshoot your systems.

- ▲ Finally, you might consider giving your staff some hands-on experience with virtual machines. For Windows environments, you can access VMs that Microsoft is currently hosting through either MSDN or TechNet. Both provide the ability to run through specific exercise sets directly on a virtual machine, letting you gain valuable experience at no other cost than the time it takes. This might be the best way for your technical staff to get up to speed on this technology, and it's completely free. Find out more about TechNet VMs at http://technet.microsoft.com/en-us/bb738372.aspx.

Now that you're up and running in your virtual lab, you can start to reap its benefits. This section outlines quite a few, but the one you'll certainly appreciate the most, or rather, the one that will make your superiors appreciate you the most is the cost savings you'll gain from moving all testing environments from physical to virtual environments. That, coupled with the flexibility of virtual machines compared to physical ones, will greatly enhance the way you work with and learn new technologies from now on.

MOVE ON TO THE VIRTUAL DATACENTER

Building a virtual lab is the best way to get used to virtualization technologies. You become familiar with VM contents, VM builds, VM management practices, and more. Practice well. The next step is to move forward with the build of your host systems to create the start of your resource pool. In this case, you'll most certainly use hypervisors and shared storage. Then, you'll be ready to test the P2V migrations that will transform your datacenter into a virtual infrastructure.

The next chapters will take you through these processes. Chapters 7 and 8 outline how server virtualization works and help you choose your virtualization solution. Chapter 9 lets you learn how to work with P2V. Chapter 10 outlines how desktop virtualization works and how you can choose your own solution. Chapters 11 and 12 outline how application virtualization works and how it integrates with the former two to create a completely dynamic datacenter.

CHAPTER 7

Work with Server Virtualization

S erver virtualization technologies are the driving force behind the move to dynamic datacenters. While the concept of building a datacenter that could respond dynamically to business requirements has been around for decades, it was not until VMware introduced production-level server virtualization technologies that the true dynamic datacenter became possible.

For years, the analyst firm Gartner has been touting the four stages of IT maturity as being:

▼ **Basic**   Organizations use ad hoc IT procedures. Most administrators do things on their own and there are few, if any, standard procedures.

■ **Standardized**   Organizations begin the use of standard operating procedures (SOP), and all administrators rely on them to run the datacenter. Issues are easier to deal with because everyone knows the starting point of a problem.

■ **Rationalized**   Organizations begin to remove extraneous equipment and services from the network. While organizations in previous stages simply have a tendency to add to the infrastructure when the need arises, the rationalized organization puts rules and guidelines in place to avoid adding to the infrastructure unless it is absolutely necessary. For example, instead of adding more storage space to central file shares, the organization will review the files it has in storage, determine their validity, archive outdated and unused files, and therefore make additional space available from existing resources.

▲ **Dynamic**   Organizations can respond dynamically to business needs. Volatile workloads can be generated as needed and removed from the datacenter once their requirement has been fulfilled. Workloads automatically run when required based on established policies. All operations are streamlined, and issues are rarer, but often more complex and, therefore, more interesting for IT personnel to deal with.

Each of the four stages serves as the foundation for the next. Operations are based on three key elements—People, PCs, and Processes—or the three Ps of IT (see Figure 7-1).

▼ People make up the core of any datacenter. They are the driving force of the standards that are implemented to streamline operations.

■ PCs represent the technology aspect of the datacenter. By choosing the right technologies, organizations reduce overhead and simplify IT management.

▲ Processes form the core of the operations practice. Standard processes are based on SOPs to make sure all personnel respond in the same manner whenever a task needs to be performed.

When you move to server virtualization, you immediately gain the advantages of a dynamic IT, but if you do not have the other elements of the foundation in place, you will simply add to the complexity of your operations and may well find yourself in a situation where you proliferate technologies even more than ever before.

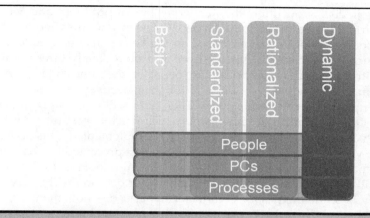

Figure 7-1. The four stages of IT maturity and their foundation

NOTE For more information on how to build a dynamic datacenter based on standard operating procedures, see *Windows Server 2008: The Complete Reference* by Ruest and Ruest (McGraw-Hill, 2008).

As you decide how to implement the dynamic datacenter, you will find that you need to address four key aspects of server virtualization before you can run the technology in your datacenter. These include:

▼ How to choose a server virtualization technology

■ How to work with virtual workloads

■ How to provision new virtual machines

▲ How to provision virtual machines from existing physical workloads

As you address each of these aspects, you become more and more familiar with how you will need to manage your datacenter once your server virtualization technology is in place.

CHOOSE A SERVER VIRTUALIZATION TECHNOLOGY

The server virtualization technology you choose must meet all of your requirements. For you to make the right choice, you must be aware of and understand what the major choices are and which technologies offer the most features based on your own requirements. Chapter 2 introduced the concept of server virtualization and outlined the major players in this field. While there are several different manufacturers offering virtualization engines, there are really only three that offer extensive feature sets: VMware, which was the founder of server virtualization on x86 technologies; Citrix, which, with its purchase of XenSource in 2007, now offers the XenServer line of products; and Microsoft, who now offers virtualization through the Hyper-V code in Windows Server 2008. Most other vendors offer technologies that are based on the Xen open-source code. This means that vendors such as Oracle, Sun, Virtual Iron, and more, really offer nothing much different than Citrix, since all of their offers are based on the same code.

But in order for you to choose the right product for your needs, you must first be aware of what makes up what each vendor offers. Then, you will look to pricing and implementation costs. Once you begin to understand which product best fits your bill, you must look to what you need to do and how best it can be implemented. This decision process is based on the virtualization implementation flowchart presented in Chapter 3, but this time, with a focus on server virtualization. Once again, looking to the offerings of each vendor will assist you in the process. Finally, your decision will be crystallized through the analysis of the metrics for each major hypervisor—how many virtual machines can run on one host, how hosts are managed, which operating systems are supported in the virtual layer, and so on—which will help position each vendor in the marketplace and view its long-term value.

TECHNOLOGIES AND SCENARIOS

The three major virtualization vendors offer several different solutions for virtualization. Table 7-1 provides a review of the different offerings each vendor has and categorizes them as either software virtualization (SoftV) or hardware virtualization (HardV).

Two of these major vendors—VMware and Microsoft—also offer other desktop-based products that emulate SoftV and can run on a variety of operating systems. For example, VMware first made its name through VMware Workstation, its flagship product and the one they use to introduce most new feature sets for their virtualization engine. Each of these engines, SoftV and HardV, makes up part of the virtualization solution you implement. For example, in Chapter 6, you relied mostly on free virtualization technologies to transform your laboratory into a virtual development and testing ground. This is the process most organizations use to begin working with virtualization engines. In fact, most organizations use a standard process for the implementation of server virtualization technologies (see Figure 7-2).

They begin with testing and development environments. Then, when they have become more familiar with these technologies, they move on to the virtualization of their production workloads. Almost all workloads can be virtualized, and doing this greatly reduces the physical footprint of your datacenter so long as you get the preparation of the hosts right (as per Chapter 5). Once your server workloads are virtualized, you can then look to business continuity solutions. Since all your workloads are nothing but files in a folder, these strategies are much simpler to implement. Finally, once your infrastructure is secured and protected, you can begin to work with more advanced virtualization strategies, transforming your workloads into dynamic services that run based on policies. These policies dictate where the workload must be placed, how many resources must be allocated to it, and when it should run. At this stage, you enter the realm of the dynamic datacenter and begin to truly provide IT as a service to your end-user customers.

Manufacturer	Product	Software Virtualization	Hardware Virtualization
VMware	VMware Server	Free software-based virtualization tool; version 2 includes its own web server (Apache) for management; runs x86 or x64 virtual machines (VMs)	
VMware	ESX Server		32-bit hypervisor, but 64-bit memory manager; most used and most proven on the market; runs x86 or x64 VMs
VMware	ESXi		Free integrated hypervisor; available with hardware or as a separate download; runs x86 or x64 VMs
Citrix	XenServer all versions		64-bit hypervisor; based on open source; relies on Microsoft Virtual Hard Drive (VHD) format; also includes a free version (XenServer Express); runs x86 or x64 VMs
Microsoft	Virtual Server	Free software-based virtualization tool; relies on Web interface; if used with System Center Virtual Machine Manager (SCVMM), Internet Information Services (IIS) is not required; runs only x86 VMs	
Microsoft	Hyper-V		64-bit hypervisor; integrated with Windows Server 2008; runs on either Server Core or the Full Installation; interoperates with Citrix; runs x86 or x64 VMs

Table 7-1.   SoftV and HardV Offerings from the Three Major Vendors

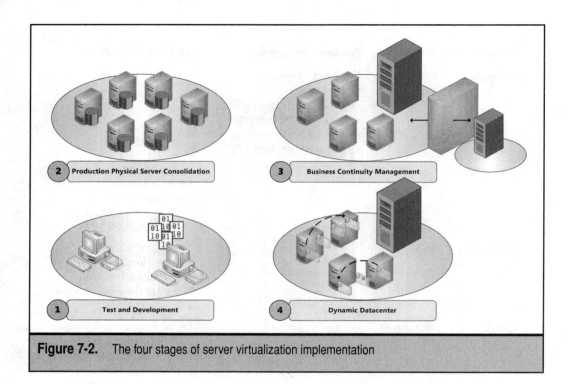

Figure 7-2. The four stages of server virtualization implementation

There are, however, several stages of implementation before you get to the point where your workloads are dynamically generated and managed, but each step is rewarding in itself, as you will discover.

Server Virtualization Scenarios

As you can see, several scenarios can be supported through the implementation of server virtualization machines. They range in cost and capabilities, but each offers features that simply cannot be supported when using physical machines.

▼ **System Testing**   Every IT organization has put in place some form of testing laboratory for the purpose of examining and understanding new technologies and how they could fit into their network. Usually, these testing environments are scrounged together from bits and pieces that are left over from the production network. The result is a low-cost, but not very functional testing environment. As seen in Chapter 6, virtualization can help by allowing IT to build comprehensive laboratory environments using only a few physical devices to host a plethora of virtual machines. Using undoable disks and virtual machine duplication, IT can reproduce any scenario and create complex virtual testing environments. It is even possible to use physical-to-virtual capture engines to make a virtual duplicate of physical machines running in production.

- **Software Development**   Every software developer has been faced with the need for high privileges on their system. This is completely understandable because developers need to install and test software as they develop it. In locked-down environments, this can become a significant issue, but not if you are using virtual machines in support of the development effort. With a virtual machine running on a developer's workstation, the developer can be free to have complete access rights in the virtual machine while the physical workstation can remain completely locked down. Best of all, all you need to do is support the original virtual machine. If the developers break it, you just give them another copy of the original machine.

- **Training**   Every technician that is responsible for the support of computer training centers will most definitely profit from virtualization. That's because normally, each time a course is run, you have to devise a means to return each PC to the course starting point. In addition, you need the means to repurpose the PC in support of other courses. Virtual machines are ideal for this for several reasons. First, they are easy to repurpose—all you need to do is create a copy of an original machine for the course and then simply throw it away once the course is complete. Second, virtual machines can contain any x86 operating system. This means that even a classroom that was originally created to support productivity training on tools such as office automation software can become a complete and comprehensive technical training center that can even teach advanced operating system installation courses. All you need is the proper amount of RAM on the PCs, larger disk drives to contain virtual machine images, and a fast network to copy machines from a central location. Once this is done, your training rooms can support operating system, complex IT infrastructure, and even development training. Of note: Several firms offering technical training courses now rely exclusively on virtual machines.

- **Help Desk**   In environments that offer help desk and support services, virtualization can bring huge benefits, especially if the technician needs to support multiple operating systems. Formerly, technicians needed to have access to multiple PCs with keyboard, screen, and mouse switches to change from one to another. Today, each support technician only needs one single PC with multiple virtual machines on it to support any number of clients. This is especially useful in outsourced support centers that have multiple clients, each with their own particular desktop environment.

- **Environment Standardization**   One additional use of virtualization is in the control and deployment of custom applications. Using virtual machines, IT groups can prepare a working version of an application and instead of deploying the application on a physical machine, deploy a complete virtual machine to end users. This ensures standards compliance and can help keep support costs down. More on this will be covered in Chapter 10 as we discuss virtual desktop infrastructures.

▲ **Physical Server Consolidation**   Over the past decade, organizations have seen a proliferation of server machines for several different reasons. In many cases, these machines run with minimal utilization of their resources. Virtualization offers the opportunity to consolidate server hardware, reducing the number of physical hosts running in a data center, but maintaining independent virtual machines for each function currently deployed in the organization. In addition, the availability of physical-to-virtual machine migration tools makes this scenario attractive and simple to deploy in any data center. This is the most cost-effective reason for deploying server virtualization.

The most important point to remember about virtualization is that each virtual machine can be treated as a physical machine within the network—a machine that can communicate with others, either virtual or physical. IT can manage virtual machines the same way it manages all other machines. In fact, IT can even send a command to the physical host machine to wake up a virtual machine before initiating an operation, such as a software deployment. And as you'll see, many virtualization vendors have taken extra steps to include comprehensive virtualization management tools to cover any situation you'll run into when working with both physical and virtual engines.

Other Vendor Offerings

Chapter 1 outlined that it may well be that you end up having to run more than one hypervisor in your datacenter. The impact is not so overwhelming when you run hypervisors from the three major vendors, since each has invested heavily in making sure their management tools support the others' products. But issues will arise if you have to run hypervisors that are not supported by the management interfaces you have selected, because then you'll have to maintain and run more than one management interface. This will have a negative impact on the dynamic datacenter since you will not be able to centrally manage virtual workloads through policies.

Oracle, for example, has officially stated that they will not support their products on any other hypervisor than Oracle VM (see Oracle VM Frequently Asked Questions at www.oracle.com/technologies/virtualization/docs/ovm-faq.pdf under "Support Details"). In fact, they are now offering prepackaged versions of their applications in "templates," which are ready to run (only on Oracle VM) and do not require installation. This is odd, since they offer their products on a variety of server platforms—IBM, HPUX, Microsoft Windows, varieties of Linux, and more—however, because of this policy, organizations choosing to use Oracle applications will have to seriously consider if the need for these applications justifies the introduction of another, non-mainstream hypervisor and its accompanying management tools in their datacenter. Oracle VM is yet another version of the free Xen-based open-source hypervisor, but because of the changes Oracle has made to this code, you must rely on the custom browser-based management utility Oracle offers with Oracle VM to control its operation. For enterprise Oracle customers, Oracle offers Enterprise Manager, which has been updated to include Oracle VM management.

Novell and Red Hat also offer a Xen-based virtualization engine in their Linux distributions. Once again, these are not versions that are managed by mainstream virtualization management engines and, because of this, will require the addition of other management tools.

Parallels (www.parallels.com) offers Virtuozzo, which is a partitioning platform that supports the division of hardware resources into separate containers, letting several different virtual machines run on the same hardware. Originally, this product was designed to run multiple instances of their custom operating system. Parallels (formerly SWSoft) has been working at developing a more general-purpose virtualization engine to compete with the VMwares of the world. With this new virtualization engine, Parallels has partnered with other organizations—for example, Quest Software—to support virtual desktop infrastructures. Their real virtualization engine is new to the market though and seems untried as of yet.

Of all the other vendors on the market, Virtual Iron (www.virtualiron.com) offers the most advanced selection of features for its virtualization platform. For many years, Virtual Iron has been marketing its products as low-cost datacenter virtualization solutions, but with the competition heating up between the three major vendors, Virtual Iron's offerings have lost this edge in many respects.

One thing is sure: Large datacenters will end up managing more than one hypervisor for a variety of reasons. Because of this, it will be important for these organizations to make a careful selection when they choose which virtualization management system to use. More on this topic is covered in Chapter 16.

VMware Technology Components

VMware offers its virtualization technologies through the VMware Virtual Infrastructure (VI), which builds on its free hypervisor product (ESXi) or its paid hypervisor product (ESX Server) to create a complete complement of management tools for the dynamic datacenter. In fact, VMware is the vendor that currently offers the most complete selection of virtualization management tools, covering the most important management activities any datacenter running virtual workloads requires. These functions include the following:

▼ Central management console

■ Update management for both the hypervisor and the virtual workloads

■ Backup technologies for both the host and the virtual workloads

■ Disk-sharing technology for host servers in support of high availability

■ High-availability components to manage host and site failovers

■ Live migration components to move a working virtual machine from one host to another

■ Live storage migration components to move a working virtual machine from one storage container to another

■ Host resource management components to move resource-intensive virtual machines to hosts with available capabilities

- ■ Power management components to power on or off host servers as needed
- ■ Lab management components to support the generation and management of entire working environments as well as individual virtual machines
- ■ Stage management components to move IT solutions through various testing and development stages
- ▲ Scripting components to manage and automate VM and host management

This selection of tools is currently the most comprehensive on the market. VMware has been in the virtualization market for over a decade and because of this, their offering is still the most mature that is available.

In addition, VMware offerings scale with user requirements (see Figure 7-3). Organizations can begin with free virtualization technologies, relying on ESXi as a free integrated hypervisor. The ESXi download discussed in Chapter 5 gives organizations access to the VMware Infrastructure Client (see Figure 7-4), which allows them to manage host servers on an individual basis. However, ESXi is a true hypervisor that is designed to maintain a small footprint and yet act as an orchestrator to expose hardware resources to virtual machines (see Figure 7-5). Organizations working with ESXi will automatically gain access to the Virtual Machine File System (VMFS) discussed in Chapter 2 to create shared storage containers, as well as the Virtual Symmetric Multiprocessing (SMP) engine to allow VMs to access more than one processor core. Together, these tools make up a good starting point for any organization, especially considering that they are free.

Note that support incidents are charged separately when using the ESXi components. Organizations can purchase them on an incident-by-incident basis, purchase incident packs in three or five bundles, or acquire Gold or Platinum Support for each host server.

		Free ESXi	VI Foundation	VI Standard	VI Enterprise
Resource Management Power Management					DRS DPM
Live VM Migration Live VM Disk File Migration					VMotion Storage VMotion
Availability				High Availability	High Availability
Backup			Consolidated Backup	Consolidated Backup	Consolidated Backup
Patch Management			Update Manager	Update Manager	Update Manager
Central Management			VC Agent	VC Agent	VC Agent
Storage Enterprise VMs	VMFS Virtual SMP		VMFS Virtual SMP	VMFS Virtual SMP	VMFS Virtual SMP
Next-generation Hypervisor	VMware ESXi		VMware ESXi or VMware ESX	VMware ESXi or VMware ESX	VMware ESXi or VMware ESX

Figure 7-3. The base offerings from VMware

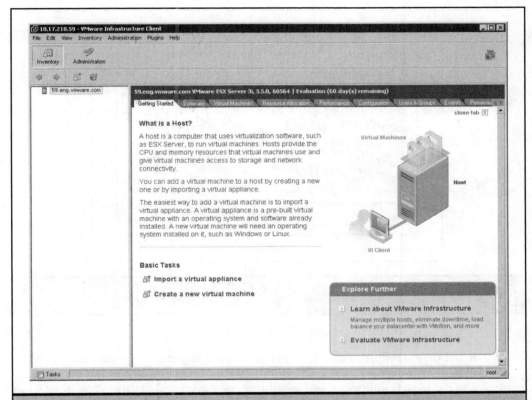

Figure 7-4. Managing hosts and VMs through the VMware Infrastructure Client

The difference between VMware ESXi and ESX is that the ESXi image only includes the hypervisor, while the ESX image contains both the hypervisor and the management partition for the server. When you run ESXi, you must use a remote machine—physical or virtual—to manage the host. When you use ESX, you can rely on the management partition to manage and maintain the host locally.

One of the most powerful features of both VMware ESX and ESXi is the support for key memory management features. These include:

▼ **Min/Max Memory Settings on VMs**   This feature lets you assign a minimum and a maximum memory setting to a VM. When the VM is running, ESX will begin by assigning the minimum amount of RAM to the VM. If the VM requires it, ESX will increase the amount of RAM for the VM until it reaches the maximum setting.

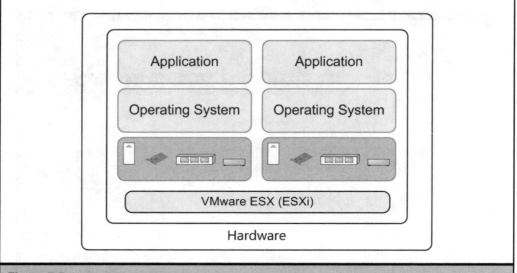

Figure 7-5. The VMware ESX and ESXi architecture

- **RAM Overcommitment** This feature lets you allocate more memory to VMs than exists on a host. When you build a VM or transfer a VM to an ESX host, you can assign minimum and maximum memory values to the VM through the Min/Max Memory Settings. The maximum memory value lets you even assign more memory than is available on the host. Then, ESX will rely on policy-based VM management to move the VM to another host with appropriate resources should the VM require all of the memory you allocated to it.

- **Transparent Page Sharing** This feature stores only one copy of a duplicate file in host RAM. This feature is powerful and is the reason why VMware hosts can run massive numbers of VMs on hosts with significantly less memory than other hypervisors. For example, if your system is hosting ten Windows Server 2008 VMs, each VM will store only one copy of the files that make up its core processes during operation in RAM. This can save as much as 40 percent of the RAM required to run VMs in some scenarios.

- ▲ **Memory Ballooning** This feature lets you recover memory from VMs that are not using it and allocate it to others. This lets ESX manage more workloads by dynamically modifying memory allocations to the VMs it manages.

These features make ESX and ESXi the powerful hypervisors that they are today.

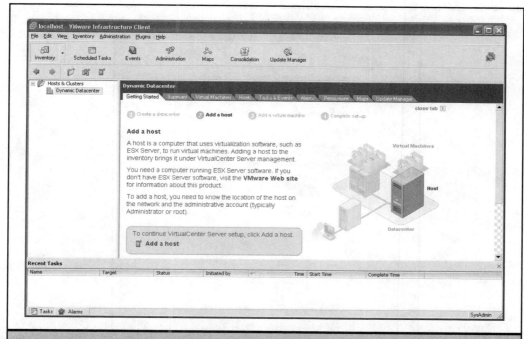

Figure 7-6.   The VMware VirtualCenter management interface

Once organizations are more familiar with ESXi, they can move up to the Virtual Infrastructure Foundation, which includes three additional tools. The first is VirtualCenter (now vCenter), the hub of all VMware VI management (see Figure 7-6). VirtualCenter is designed in such a manner that it grows with an organization's needs, adding features and functionality as new tools are added to the infrastructure. Because of this, administrators never need to learn another tool, only become familiar with the additional functions it can host.

In addition, Foundation includes both Update Manager and Consolidated Backup, options that also are made available as additional features within VirtualCenter (see Figure 7-7). Update Manager can manage updates for both host components and virtual machines (see Figure 7-8). For example, when changing or updating ESXi, it replaces the entire firmware image, but also provides a rollback path should something go wrong with the update. When working with virtual workloads, it relies on the internal update engine within the client, such as Windows Update within Windows VMs.

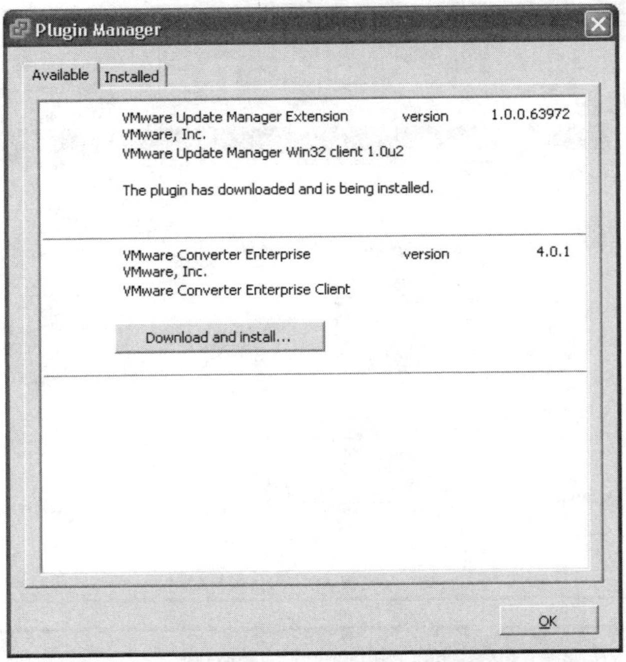

Figure 7-7. VMware VirtualCenter supports additional feature plug-ins.

For backup of VMs, you can rely on VMware Consolidated Backup (see Figure 7-9). Consolidated backup works with shared storage technologies to support the creation of snapshots, then the generation of backups from the snapshots, having little or no impact on the operation of the VMs and the hosts that manage them.

VI Standard Edition moves up the scale to offer additional services. The most significant addition available through the Standard Edition is High Availability, which, as discussed in Chapter 5, combines with the VMFS to provide cluster-like services for host machines. If one host fails, all of the VMs it was managing are automatically failed over and restarted on another host in the cluster. VMs are restarted because when the original host fails, they also fail until they are moved to another host. Note that this does not work like the live migration feature of VMware, which moves the VM while it is in operation.

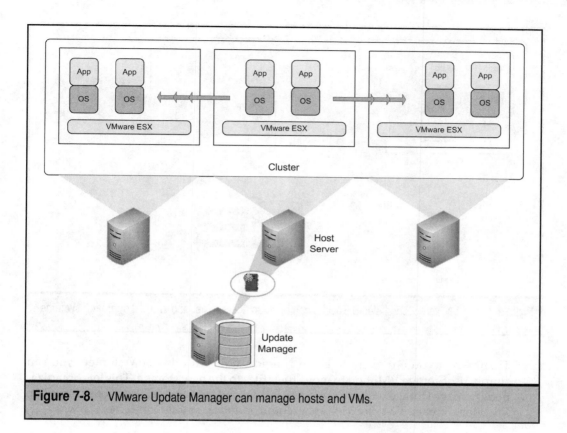

Figure 7-8. VMware Update Manager can manage hosts and VMs.

VI Enterprise provides organizations with the most advanced tools in support of the dynamic datacenter. First, this edition adds VMotion, the live migration feature that VMware first made famous (see Figure 7-10). VMotion moves VM contents from one host to another while the machine is in operation. For this to work, your host systems must use the same processors with the same stepping or rely on the Enhanced VMotion Compatibility feature of ESX Server, as discussed in Chapter 5.

In addition, the Enterprise Edition adds Storage VMotion, which is similar to VMotion and will work in conjunction with it to move a working VM from one storage container to another (see Figure 7-11). The capability to move virtual machine files from one location to the other in a nondisruptive fashion liberates administrators from traditional shared storage constraints. This means that if you need to add additional shared storage to your host servers, you can add the new containers without impairing VM operation.

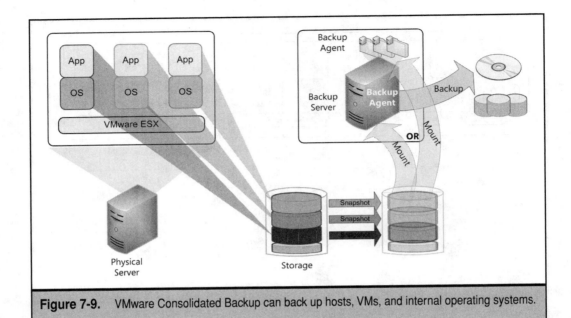

Figure 7-9.   VMware Consolidated Backup can back up hosts, VMs, and internal operating systems.

Then, when you are ready to begin running VMs with this new storage, you can simply use Storage VMotion to move their files to the new storage. This lets organizations manage storage without impacting actual end-user operations. Note that unlike VMotion, Storage VMotion does not require identical storage containers to work.

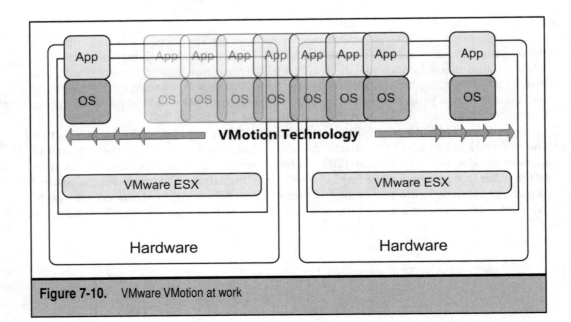

Figure 7-10.   VMware VMotion at work

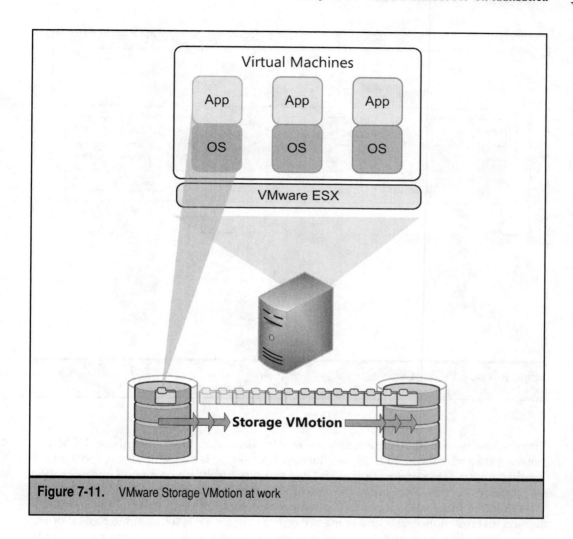

Figure 7-11. VMware Storage VMotion at work

With these VMotion technologies, the Enterprise Edition of VI adds two powerful tools. Distributed Resource Scheduler (DRS) lets you assign resource management policies to your virtual workloads. Because VMware supports the ability to assign resources to a VM through minimum and maximum values, it can constantly monitor the requirements of a VM and, should the VM require more resources than are available on the host, move it through VMotion to another host server. DRS regularly scans VMs and host servers to maintain the optimum performance for each (see Figure 7-12). Distributed Power Management (DPM) works along with DRS to monitor host server requirements. Should a host server not be required, it will automatically be moved to a power-saving state.

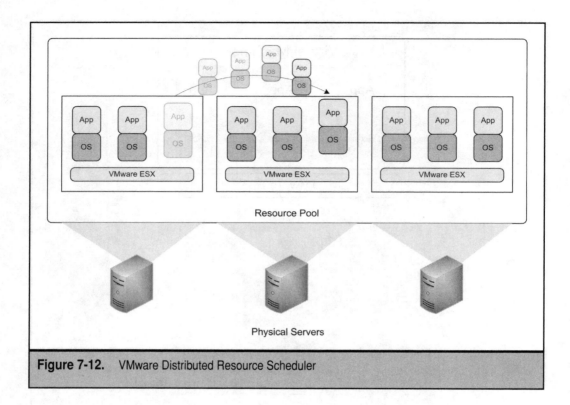

Figure 7-12. VMware Distributed Resource Scheduler

Then, when workloads increase and the system is needed to support them, DPM will power it up and indicate to DRS that the new host server is available. These tools intelligently monitor datacenter resources and dynamically turn them on and off in conjunction with business cycles. They are at the core of the concept of a dynamic datacenter.

While the three paid VI editions offer a complement of tools, each tool is also available on a stand-alone basis and some are only available on a stand-alone basis. For example, Stage Manager and Lab Manager, two tools discussed in Chapter 6, are only available as stand-alones. You must, however, have some version of VI in place to make the most of these additional tools.

VMware also offers bundles for small to medium organizations (see Table 7-2). These bundles combine a series of different components and provide support for a minimum number of host servers. In addition, you can use VMware's Total Cost of Operations (TCO) Calculator, mentioned in Chapter 5, to quantify the potential cost savings that can be obtained through the purchase of VMware solutions.

NOTE For more information on VMware's scalable solutions, go to www.vmware.com/solutions/ smb/whats_new.html. For access to the VMware TCO Calculator, go to www.vmware.com/products/ vi/calculator.html.

	VMware Infrastructure Foundation	VMware Infrastructure Standard HA	VMware Infrastructure Midsize	VMware Infrastructure Enterprise
Description	VirtualCenter Foundation + 3 VMware Infrastructure Foundation	VirtualCenter Foundation + 2 VMware Infrastructure Standard	VirtualCenter Foundation + 3 VMware Infrastructure Enterprise	VirtualCenter Management Server + 4 VMware Infrastructure Enterprise
Management Solution	VirtualCenter Foundation	VirtualCenter Foundation	VirtualCenter Foundation	VirtualCenter Management Server
VirtualCenter Foundation	☑	☑	☑	☑
ESX or ESXi	☑	☑	☑	☑
Virtual SMP	☑	☑	☑	☑
VMFS	☑	☑	☑	☑
VirtualCenter Agent	☑	☑	☑	☑
Update Manager	☑	☑	☑	☑
Consolidated Backup	☑	☑	☑	☑
High Availability		☑	☑	☑
Storage VMotion			☑	☑
VMotion			☑	☑
Distributed Power Management			☑	☑
Distributed Resource Scheduler			☑	☑

Table 7-2.   VMware Infrastructure Acceleration Kits for Small and Medium Businesses

Once again, each bundle offers a variety of choices and tools to organizations of all sizes. Table 7-3 provides a summary of the capabilities of VMware's Virtual Infrastructure components.

NOTE For more information on VMware Infrastructure, see www.vmware.com/solutions/consolidation.

Tools	Description
VMware Consolidated Backup	Performs virtual and host machine backups.
VMware DPM	Dynamically manages host servers by powering them on or off as needed.
VMware DRS	Monitors utilization across resource pools and allocates available resources among the virtual machines on pre-defined rules that reflect business needs and changing priorities.
VMware ESX	Hypervisor that abstracts server processor, memory, storage, and networking resources into multiple machines.
VMware ESXi	Free hypervisor that offers the same functionality as VMware ESX, but with a thin 32-megabyte (MB) footprint designed for server integration.
VMware HA	Provides high availability for any application running in a virtual machine, regardless of its operating system (OS) or underlying hardware configuration.
VMware Lab Manager	Manages either single VMs or entire environments for the purpose of testing or development.
VMware Lifecycle Manager	Manages virtual machine provisioning from start to end. Supports single VMs or complete VM environments.
VMware Distributed Power Management	Manages power states for host machines based on VM workload lows and peaks.
VMware Site Recovery Manager	Manages disaster recovery scenarios from site to site in the event of a full site disaster.

Table 7-3. VMware Virtual Infrastructure Tools

Tools	Description
VMware Stage Manager	Manages solutions as they are developed or prepared from one staging level to another throughout the solution graduation process until solutions are thoroughly tested before entering production.
VMware Storage VMotion	Enables live migration of virtual machine disk files across storage arrays. Allows you to relocate VM disk files between and across shared storage locations while maintaining continuous service availability and complete transaction integrity.
VMware Update Manager	Manages patches and updates of VMware ESX hosts, as well as select Windows and Linux virtual machines.
VMware Virtual SMP	Allows a single VM to use up to four physical processors or processor cores simultaneously.
VMware VMotion	Moves running virtual machines from one physical server to another with no impact to end users.
VMware VMFS	Simplifies VM provisioning and administration with a high-performance cluster file system optimized for VMs. This is the default storage system for virtual machine files on physical disks and partitions.
VI Toolkit for Windows	Provides support for task automation through the use of the Windows PowerShell command language. Requires the .NET Framework to operate.

Table 7-3.   VMware Virtual Infrastructure Tools (*continued*)

As you can see, VMware offers quite a few tools in support of dynamic datacenters. It is no wonder that most of the datacenters that have already implemented server virtualization have come to rely on this technology.

Citrix Virtualization Technologies

Citrix also offers several different tools for its virtualization engine. Citrix acquired Xen-Source, the makers of XenServer, in late 2007 and relied on this acquisition to create the basis of its virtualization offerings. XenSource was created as a company by bringing together several of the developers that worked on developing the Xen extensions for

Linux through an open-source project. These developers wanted to take Xen to the next level by bringing additional technologies to the fore and enhancing the capabilities of the Xen hypervisor.

Terminal Services vendor Citrix bought into the hypervisor game by purchasing XenSource and rebranding it as its own. This enabled Citrix to enter the virtualization fray with four key virtualization offerings.

▼   XenServer is its line of hypervisor offerings.

■   XenDesktop is its solution for centralized virtual desktop management.

■   XenApp (formerly Presentation Server) is its solution for virtualizing applications.

▲   XenApp also supports Terminal Services and application sharing, supporting its Presentation Virtualization offerings.

While it offers a free version of XenServer, the Express Edition, Citrix does not offer any SoftV products, as all of its server virtualization offerings rely on HardV to operate. Therefore, it differs from both Microsoft and VMware in this regard. Table 7-4 outlines the Citrix XenServer offerings.

Feature	Express	Standard	Enterprise	Platinum
Native 64-bit Xen hypervisor	X	X	X	X
Windows and Linux guests	X	X	X	X
XenAPI management and control scripting interface	X	X	X	X
XenCenter unified virtualization management console	X	X	X	X
Multiserver management		X	X	X
Subscription Advantage— first year included		X	X	X
Virtual LAN (VLAN) configuration		X	X	X
Resource pools			X	X
XenMotion live migration			X	X

Table 7-4.   Citrix XenServer Editions

Feature	Express	Standard	Enterprise	Platinum
Shared Internet Protocol (IP)-based storage			X	X
Resource Quality of Service (QoS) controls			X	X
Dynamic provisioning of virtual and physical servers				X
Administrative model	Single server	Multiple servers	Multiple servers and resource pools	Multiple physical and virtual servers and resource pools
Maximum physical memory	128GB	128GB	128GB	128GB
CPU sockets	2	Unlimited	Unlimited	Unlimited
Guests active simultaneously	Unlimited	Unlimited	Unlimited	Unlimited
Maximum RAM per virtual machine	32GB	32GB	32GB	32GB

Table 7-4.   Citrix XenServer Editions (*continued*)

Unlike VMware, Citrix does not offer additional management or operational tools along with its hypervisor (at least not at the time of this writing). However, Citrix has announced that it would be working on additional tools, especially tools that would support the interoperation and management of virtual machines across multiple hypervisor platforms through known standards. It also announced that it intends to make these tools available for free. This is definitely something that you should look into as you review the capabilities of different virtualization engines.

One significant advantage Citrix XenServer had over both Microsoft and VMware offerings was the ability to generate virtual machines as differentials from a core VM image. This means that instead of generating VMs, which are multiple gigabytes in size, you can rely on XenServer to generate machines from one single VM and only capture the differences in each VM file. This software-based feature can save up to 50 percent of the storage space you require for VMs and can have a positive impact on your storage bottom line. VMware added this feature to its latest version of ESX Server. Microsoft, however, still does not support this feature.

NOTE Citrix XenServer information is available at www.citrix.com/xenserver.

Microsoft Virtualization Technologies

Microsoft has been in the server virtualization business ever since it acquired Connectix in 2003. At the time, Microsoft was looking to buy VMware, but the deal was nixed by its legal team on the grounds that if Microsoft bought VMware, it would become the largest single owner of Windows licenses in the world because, at the time, VMware sold virtual machines containing Windows operating systems as part of its product line. VMware has since stopped releasing virtual appliances prebundled with Windows operating systems, but that still left Microsoft with the need to obtain a virtualization technology to bring it into its software portfolio. This left Connectix, the original makers of Virtual PC.

Connectix made the papers through the original release of virtualization software that would let Macintosh users run Windows applications on their systems. Later, Connectix ported their virtualization software to the PC. When Microsoft acquired Connectix, it focused on the PC version of Virtual PC and quickly turned it into two products: Virtual PC and Virtual Server. Both were of the SoftV variety. In addition, Virtual Server required the installation of Internet Information Services (IIS) to operate since its management interface was Web-based (see Figure 7-13).

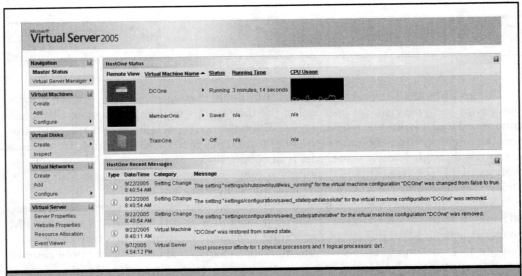

Figure 7-13. Microsoft Virtual Server can run multiple 32-bit VMs.

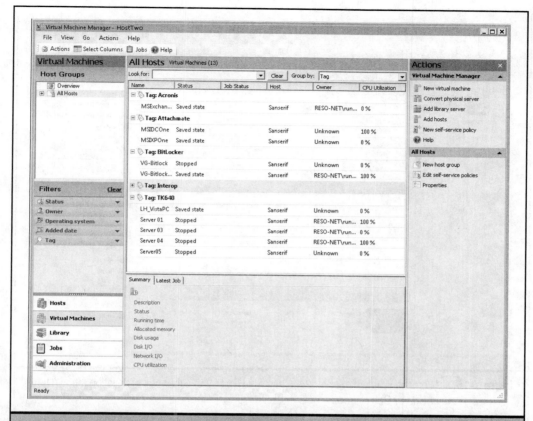

Figure 7-14. Microsoft Virtual Machine Manager is part of System Center.

Microsoft later released an integrated version of Virtual Server along with its System Center Virtual Machine Manager (SCVMM), which could be used to deploy Virtual Server without the IIS requirement (see Figure 7-14). In 2008, about four-and-a-half months after releasing Windows Server 2008 (WS08), Microsoft released Hyper-V, a HardV hypervisor that was integrated to the WS08 OS. This is Microsoft's flagship virtualization technology (see Figure 7-15). Hyper-V can run on either the Server Core (recommended) or the Full Installation version of WS08. In addition, the Hyper-V management tools can be deployed as standalone tools to manage multiple Hyper-V hosts.

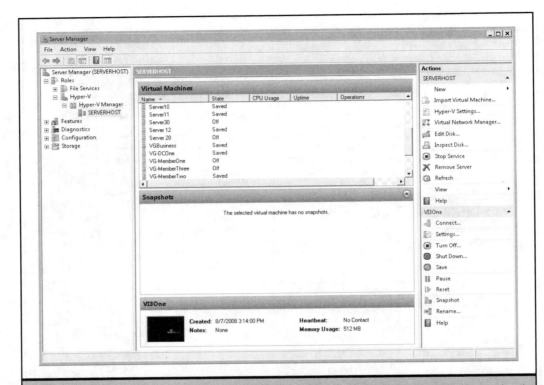

Figure 7-15. Microsoft Windows Server 2008 can run Hyper-V in either Full Installation (shown here) or Server Core mode.

Microsoft then adapted several of its existing management tools to interact and operate with Hyper-V and its other virtualization technologies. Table 7-5 outlines the Microsoft virtualization toolset.

Tool	Purpose
Microsoft Application Virtualization (MS App-V)	Virtualizes applications and delivers them as on-demand, streaming services to desktop users and Terminal Services servers. Applications are available both online and offline. Formerly SoftGrid.
Microsoft Desktop Optimization Pack (MDOP) for Software Assurance	Licensing scheme that provides additional resources to IT administrators for the management and deployment of desktops so long as they obtain Software Assurance for their Microsoft products. Includes MS App-V among other tools.

Table 7-5. Microsoft Virtualization Toolset

Tool	Purpose
Offline Virtual Machine Servicing Tool	Supports the configuration of updates on virtual machines that are kept in an offline state.
System Center Configuration Manager	Supports system deployment, task automation, compliance management, and policy-based security management.
System Center Data Protection Manager	Lets IT administrators and end users recover data by delivering continuous data protection for Microsoft application and file servers.
System Center Essentials	Lets IT administrators monitor and manage smaller environments. Manages both virtual and physical machines. Manages up to 500 clients and 30 servers.
System Center Operations Manager	Monitors environments, applications, and clients to provide a complete view of the health of your IT environment and to enable rapid response to events.
System Center Virtual Machine Manager	Enables the increase of physical server utilization; provisions and centralizes management of virtual machines. Supports the management of Hyper-V, Virtual Server, and VMware ESX. Citrix XenServer support is in the works. Can also convert physical servers to virtual machines.
Terminal Services	Virtualizes the presentation of entire desktops or specific applications (only in WS08). Local and remote users must be online to access Terminal Services.
Virtual PC	Designed to host legacy line-of-business (LOB) applications and applications that are not compatible with a given desktop OS.
Virtual Server	SoftV engine that can be used to virtualize 32-bit workloads. Runs on both 32-bit and 64-bit hardware.
Windows Server 2008 Hyper-V	HardV engine that is integrated to the WS08 OS. Runs both 32-bit and 64-bit workloads, but runs only on x64 hardware.
Windows Unified Data Storage Server	Network attached storage engine that can either be used to provide storage services or as a front-end virtual storage manager for storage area networks. Also supports virtual hard drives as iSCSI targets, letting you cluster virtual machines.
Windows Vista Enterprise Centralized Desktop	Licensing scheme that supports the centralization of Windows desktops. License is for Vista, but supports any Windows desktop OS. Users are allowed to run up to four virtual machines each with the same Vista license.

Table 7-5.   Microsoft Virtualization Toolset (*continued*)

NOTE Microsoft virtualization information can be found at www.microsoft.com/virtualization/products.mspx.

Microsoft has been working at integrating its management strategies for some time and because of this, has been able to ramp up rapidly to provide extensive virtualization management tools. As such, it provides a comprehensive approach to virtualization for both its own and other hypervisors (see Figure 7-16).

Virtual Machine Formats

One of the challenges IT administrators face when they are implementing virtualization, especially if they implement more than one hypervisor, is the virtual machine format. As outlined in Chapter 2, several different files make up virtual machines—configuration, disks, in-memory contents, log files, and more. However, each virtualization engine has a tendency to include its own format for these files. For example, Microsoft uses the VHD format for hard disk drives, while VMware uses the Virtual Machine Disk (VMDK) format.

In order to foster a single standard for virtual machines, VMware worked with the IT industry to introduce the Open Virtualization Format (OVF). OVF has been accepted by the Desktop Management Task Force (DMTF), and several vendors are moving forward with this format. For example, as mentioned previously, Citrix is one of the first vendors to develop an OVF management tool. VMware also has a virtual machine conversion tool, VMware Studio, that lets you bundle a virtual machine into OVF format.

NOTE For more information on OVF and to access VMware's OVF conversion tool, go to www.vmware.com/appliances/learn/ovf.html.

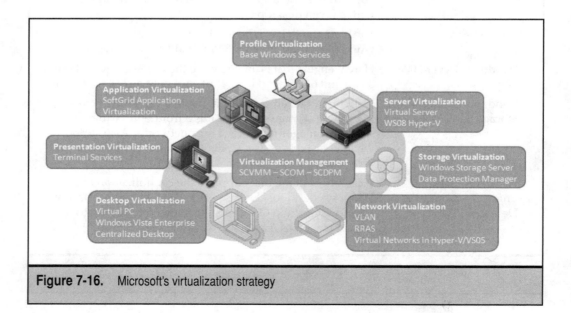

Figure 7-16. Microsoft's virtualization strategy

OVF is a single file format that can be used to bundle all of the files that make up a virtual machine into a single, transportable entity. It can also be used to bundle a series of virtual machines into a single file. This makes it useful for the creation not only of single virtual machines containing virtual appliances, but also for the creation of entire computing environments, all bundled as single files. OVF is based on the Extensible Markup Language (XML) standard. Note that virtual hard disk drives are converted during the creation of an OVF file and converted back when the OVF file is imported into a hypervisor.

The advantages of OVF are:

▼   It simplifies distribution of VMs. It relies on public key infrastructures to provide content verification and integrity. In addition, it provides a basic scheme for the management of software licenses within VMs.

■   During installation, OVF package contents are validated. In addition, the OVF standard can include user-oriented documentation, which can be accessed through the virtualization engine importing the file to provide additional implementation instructions for the packaged content.

■   Can be used to package single or multiple VMs into one single container.

■   OVF is hypervisor-neutral, supporting all current virtual disk formats, making it the ideal format for machine transportation. It is also extensible and can support additional virtual disk formats should they arise in the future.

■   Virtual appliances (VAP)—preconfigured virtual machines containing a specific application—can be configured as OVF files to make them available to any hypervisor. Vendors only need to configure the VAP once.

■   The design of OVF was intentionally made extensible to support future usage of VAPs and new hypervisor technologies.

■   OVF supports localization, letting vendors create language-specific VAPs for worldwide markets.

▲   OVF is an open standard, having been created jointly by virtualization market leaders and, as such, it is now under the responsibility of the DMTF, a standards-based body.

In short, OVF is similar to the Microsoft Installer (MSI) format Microsoft uses for Windows Installer installation files. Of course, the MSI format is not an open standard, but it is a special packaging format that vendors use to provide their applications to users of Windows. With OVF, vendors will use a similar process to package ready-to-run applications into a standard format.

Today, both VMware and Citrix offer support for OVF, while Microsoft intends to add support for this format in future versions of Hyper-V. Machines in OVF format can either be imported into a hypervisor, converting them to the hypervisor format, or run as-is. However, since OVF is a format that is designed to support transportability and the integrity of VM contents, if you run a machine as an OVF, these two purposes are invalidated. Once an OVF file has been modified by running it as-is, it can no longer be considered a golden image of the VAP it includes. As you can see, OVF is once again similar to an MSI, since you must install the MSI in order to use the application it contains.

VM Disk Types

Since OVF is best used to transport VMs, you will need to understand and work with the actual disk formats supported by the hypervisor you implement. Table 7-6 outlines the different types of disks you can use in server virtualization technologies.

On high-performance storage volumes, you should aim to use dynamically expanding disks as much as possible; however certain workloads will operate better with fixed-size disks. And as mentioned in Chapter 5, tying a dynamically expanding disk to virtualized storage using thin provisioning can save you considerable amounts of physical hard drive space.

VM Disk Type	Format	Impact	Manufacturer
Raw, Linked or Pass-through	Physical Disk or SAN LUN	Machine is tied to a physical disk drive and cannot be moved from site to site or cluster to cluster; however, tying the machine to RAW disks lets you easily cluster it.	VMware, Citrix, Microsoft
Dynamically Expanding	VHD or VMDK	Disk expands as machine needs more space. Disk file only contains existing information and nothing more.	VMware, Citrix, Microsoft
Fixed-Size Disk	VHD or VMDK	Disk is created with a set size when you create the machine. File may contain considerable empty space.	VMware, Citrix, Microsoft
Differencing Disk	VHD	Disk is tied to another parent or source disk. Only changes are stored in this disk type (the child). Has significant performance impacts.	Citrix, Microsoft

Table 7-6.   Disk Formats Supported by Various Hypervisors

Virtual machine disks use a flat file format, which provides fast access to contents. VM disks are very much like database files and will add to the container as new data is added in the VM; however, they will not automatically recover unused space when the contents are deleted. In order to recover unused space, you must compress and defragment the disk through special interfaces within the VM management tool you use. For example, in WS08 Hyper-V, disk management is performed by editing the properties of a disk (see Figure 7-17), while in VMware, it is performed by editing the properties of a virtual machine (see Figure 7-18). In both cases, the machine must be stopped to be able to control a disk's properties.

Note the following when working with virtual disk drives:

▼   Virtual hard disks can also be set to undoable disks. In this case, they are either persistent or nonpersistent.

■   Undoable disks ask if the changes are to be saved when the VM is closed. If you want to commit the changes, reply yes; if not, reply no and the machine will revert to its last saved state.

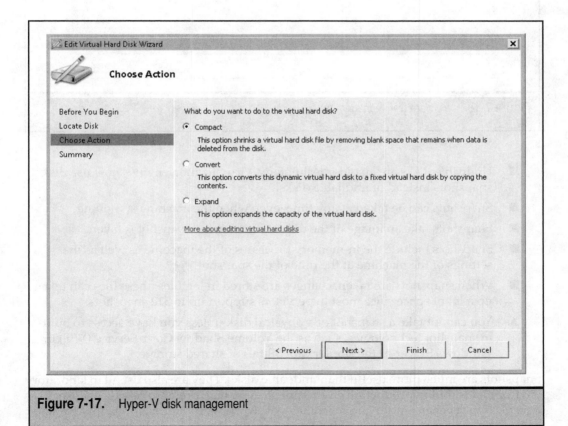

Figure 7-17.   Hyper-V disk management

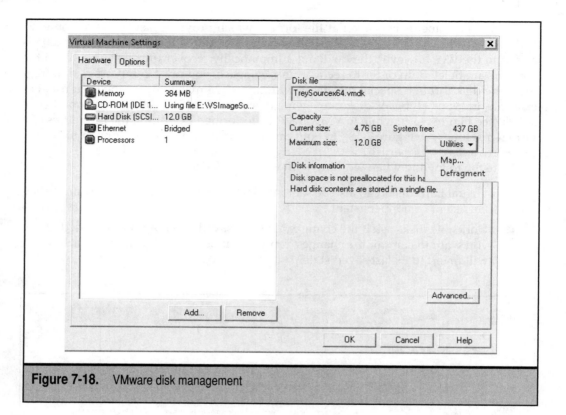

Figure 7-18. VMware disk management

- Undoable disks are an older technology. Virtualization engines now use disk snapshots instead of undoable disks.
- Snapshots can be taken at any time, even when the machine is running.
- Snapshots take an image of the disk at the time the snapshot is taken.
- Snapshots include the in-memory processes of the machine as well as the settings of the machine at the time of the snapshot.
- When snapshots are taken, changes are stored in log files; these files can take up a lot of space since most hypervisors support up to 512 snapshots.
- ▲ You cannot take a snapshot of a physical disk unless you have access to built-in snapshot technologies, such as the Volume Shadow Copy Service (VSS) in Windows Server or the similar capabilities of shared storage.

Snapshots are much more useful than undoable disks. They are also useful in laboratory environments. But in production environments, you may prefer to rely on snapshots as a protection mechanism for the machines you work with. For example, make a habit of taking a snapshot of a machine before you apply updates to it. If the updates do not work, revert to the snapshot image of the machine.

You'll learn that because of these features, virtual hard disk drives are much more practical than physical drives.

VIRTUALIZATION TECHNOLOGY PRICING

Pricing is always subject to change, and because of the type of market virtualization vendors are in, the competition is fierce. But as you make your choices for your datacenter, you must at least gain an idea of the costs of each technology. Table 7-7 lists a sample of the pricing for various products at the time of this writing. While the prices will most likely be considerably different by the time you have this book in hand, this table still can serve as a guideline for what to expect from the three market leaders.

Technology	Citrix	Microsoft	VMware
Hypervisor	Citrix XenServer Enterprise Edition $2,000 Citrix XenServer Perpetual Server with Subscription $3,000 Citrix XenServer Express Edition free download	Windows Server 2008 Enterprise Edition License $2,500 Microsoft Virtual Server free download	ESX Enterprise Edition License $5,750 VMware ESXi free download
Live Migration	XenMotion Live Migration only with Enterprise or Platinum editions	Not applicable; use failover clustering	VMotion included in the Enterprise Edition or $1,400 Virtual Center Management Server on its own $5,000
High Availability/ Clustering	Third party, such as SteelEye Protection Suite or Marathon Technologies	Included	Additional charges for DAS $2,000; included in VI Standard
Dynamic Resource Management	Third party, such as Platform VM Orchestrator (VMO)	See Management	Additional charges for DRS $2,000; included in VI Enterprise

Table 7-7. Citrix, Microsoft, and VMware Pricing Comparison

Technology	Citrix	Microsoft	VMware
Management		System Center Enterprise Edition $860	Additional charges $3,750; included in VI Foundation
		VM Manager	VI Enterprise is $5,750 plus Virtual Center Management Server $5,000
		Configuration Manager	
		Data Protection Manager	
		Operations Manager	
Capacity Planning	XenConvert	Included in SCVMM	Additional charges for VMware Capacity Planner
P2V/V2V	XenConvert	Included in SCVMM	VMware Converter included
Library	Included	Included	Included
Windows Server Guest Licenses	Windows Server Enterprise Edition License $2,500	Included	Windows Server Enterprise Edition License $2,500
Windows Desktop	Vista Enterprise Centralized Desktops (VECD) licensing required	VECD licensing required	VECD licensing required

Table 7-7. Citrix, Microsoft, and VMware Pricing Comparison (*continued*)

As you can see, each of the vendors requires different components to provide a complete virtual and physical infrastructure management environment. Citrix relies heavily on third-party products. Microsoft relies heavily on its existing management tools for Windows environments. VMware has been working at creating a complete VM management suite for some time.

In all cases, you will need Microsoft Windows Server licenses if you decide to run a Windows infrastructure. One advantage Microsoft has is that by buying the Windows Server license, you obtain a license both for the host and for the virtual machines. Note, however, that the VM licenses supported by the Windows Server edition are also available should you decide to use a non-Microsoft hypervisor (see Table 7-8).

Microsoft Edition	Number of VM
Windows Server 2003 R2/2008 Standard Edition	Rights to run one instance
Windows Server 2003 R2/2008 Enterprise Edition	Rights to run four instances under one physical license
Windows Server 2003 R2/2008 Datacenter Edition	Unlimited instances
	Any virtualization technology or host operating system
	Per processor licensing

Table 7-8. Number of VMs Supported by the Windows Server License

If you wanted a low-cost environment, you could rely on any of the free technologies from Citrix, VMware, or Microsoft. Citrix XenServer Express will only support four VMs per host. VMware ESXi will give you all of the capabilities of the VMware hypervisor for free. And Microsoft Virtual Server will also run several virtual machines on each host, but it only supports 32-bit virtual machines. In each case, the free technologies only provide tools to manage one single host at a time. While it is possible to run small shops in this manner, it is cumbersome and will not be efficient in the long term for anyone with a significant number of VMs. In addition, using free technologies does not provide you with support.

But price alone is not enough to determine which technology you should rely on. Make sure you fully understand the capabilities of each environment and each tool before you make the decision. For this reason, the next section, "Market-Leader Hypervisor Metrics," will provide valuable input to your decision since it compares the feature sets of each hypervisor and outlines just what each can do in terms of virtual machine support.

MARKET-LEADER HYPERVISOR METRICS

All hypervisors are not created equal. Some are native x64 hypervisors, while others may be 32-bit but include x64 components for important tasks, such as memory management. Table 7-9 outlines some of the core metrics for each of the three major vendors. Use this table to determine how many VMs to run per host and how to configure your hosts. Rely on these values to make an informed decision on how each hypervisor stacks up and which one you should use in your own network.

Metric	VMware	Microsoft	Citrix
Hypervisor Operation Overhead	Negligible	One CPU core	One CPU core
Maximum Memory (Host)	256GB	32GB to 2 terabytes (TB)	128GB
RAM for Hypervisor	32MB+	512MB+	256 to 512MB+
Maximum CPU Sockets (Host)	32 cores	24 cores	Unlimited
Maximum CPU Sockets (Guest)	4	4	8
Required Management NIC(s)	1	1	1
Maximum number of servers in a pool or cluster	32	16	16
Number of VMs per CPU Core	8 to 11	8	2 to 8
Maximum Memory (Guest)	64GB	64GB	32GB
Simultaneous Active Guests/Host	192	192	Unlimited

Table 7-9. Market-Leader Hypervisor Metrics

Table 7-9 requires some caveats.

▼ Because VMware uses an integrated hypervisor, ESXi, which has a very small footprint, its overhead is negligible. Both Hyper-V and XenServer require 1 CPU core to operate because they also include a parent partition with the hypervisor.

■ Of the three, Hyper-V supports the most host memory because it is based on Windows Server code. However, no physical host with 2 TB of RAM currently exists.

■ Each host requires some RAM for the hypervisor as well as some overhead RAM for each virtual machine. In the case of VMware, VM overhead is 30 MB plus 15% of the RAM allocated to a VM for each VM. Microsoft requires 32 MB of RAM for each VM. Citrix calculates overhead as a percentage of RAM. And, in order to limit the host server RAM overhead in Hyper-V, you would want to make sure you are running it on Server Core only, not the full installation of Windows Server 2008.

- The maximum number of CPU sockets supported in host servers is calculated in number of logical cores—normally a physical core—and addresses the maximum number of cores in certain server configurations. Note that Microsoft updated Hyper-V on October 24, 2008 to support up to 24 cores in support of Intel's new six-core processors. And while XenServer states that it supports 'unlimited' cores, this is only a factor of the Enterprise license for the product. The actual number is limited to physical box configurations.

- The maximum number of virtual CPU cores per guest is often a factor of the guest operating system. In VMware, most guest operating systems that support multi-processing will support up to 4 virtual cores. The same applies to XenServer, but its guest operating systems can run with up to 8 virtual cores. In Hyper-V, the only multi-processing OS that will run with 4 virtual cores is Windows Server 2008. Other supported versions of Windows Server will only access 2 virtual cores.

- Each hypervisor requires at least one management NIC.

- Pool or cluster numbers are limited by the functionality of the hypervisor. VMware supports pools through its High Availability (HA) and Virtual Machine File System (VMFS) features. Citrix has a built-in resource pool feature. Microsoft relies on the Failover Clustering feature of Windows Server 2008 which is limited to 16 nodes in a cluster, however, these nodes can either be within the same site or in separate sites.

- Each hypervisor supports a maximum amount of RAM for guests, however, it is rare that organizations allocate the maximum to a guest OS since it does not leave a lot of memory for the host. Allocating the maximum often creates what is called a 'single-VM' host—a host that runs only one single VM—and this is often cost prohibitive.

- ▲ The number of virtual processor cores per logical (read physical) processor core usually equates to the number of single virtual processor core VMs you can run on a host. This number is often linked to the following value: Simultaneous Active Guests/Hosts. However, other factors such as available RAM limit the possible number of VMs you can run. Citrix XenServer has been configured with 32 cores and 50 VMs in the past. Microsoft and VMware have not announced hard limits for the number of VMs they can run, but VMware has an edge over both Hyper-V and XenServer because of its memory management features which neither of the other two have. Because of these features, it is possible to over-commit resources to VMs on an ESX host server, assigning more resources to the VMs than are actually available on the host. VMware supports Variable Resource VMs, while the other two support only Fixed Resource VMs. In the Fixed Resource VM model, the hard limit for number of VMs is memory, not CPU cores.

In actual fact, each hypervisor has similar features as far as the numbers are concerned. But in real life, organizations will have a tendency to run more VMs in VMware than in the other two on similar hardware configurations. This is because of the resource over-commitment features it supports. After all, the main reason why organizations move to virtualization in the first place is because their physical server resources are underused most of the time. So creating a virtual machine with a minimum and maximum resource setting makes a lot of sense—it runs with minimal resources at low loads and uses maximum resources during peak loads. However, for this to work, you must run a pool of servers with room to spare. This will let you move a VM to another host server when it requires more resources than are available on the current host. You would need an additional host in your resource pool anyway to support high availability for all of your VMs.

In addition, host support for different operating systems within guest machines is not the same. Table 7-10 lists the guest OS support for each hypervisor.

Metric	VMware	Microsoft	Citrix
Guest OS Support	Microsoft Windows 3.1/3.11/95/98/Me/ NT/2000/ 2003/2008/ XP/Vista x86 or x64	Microsoft Windows 2000/2003/ 2008/XP Pro/ Vista x86 and x64	Microsoft Windows 2003 SP2 x64
	MS-DOS 6.x	SUSE Enterprise Linux Server 10 SP1	Microsoft Windows 2000 SP4/2003/SBS 2003/2008/XP SP2/Vista x86
	Red Hat Enterprise Linux 2.1/3/4/5		
	Red Hat Advanced Server 2.1		CentOS 4.1/4.2/4.3/ 4.4/4.5/5.0/5.1 x86 and 5.0/5.1 x64
	Red Hat Linux 7.2/7.3/8.0/9.0		Oracle Enterprise Linux 5.0/5.1 x86 and x64
	SUSE Linux Enterprise Server 8/9/10		
	SUSE Linux 8.2/9.0/9.1/9.2/9.3		Red Hat Enterprise Linux 3.5/3.6/3.7/ 4.1/4.2/4.3/4.4/5 x86 and 5.0/5.1 x64
	FreeBSD 4.9/4.10/4.11/5.0		
	TurboLinux 7.0, Enterprise Server/Workstation 8		SUSE Enterprise Linux Server 9 SP2/9 SP3/10 SP1 32-bit
	Novell Linux Desktop 9		
	Sun Java Desktop System 2		Debian Sarge 3.1/ Etch 4.0 32-bit
	NetWare 6.5/6.0/5.1 Solaris 9/10 for x86		
64-Bit Guest Support	Most x64 operating systems	Windows 64-bit operating systems	Windows 64-bit operating systems

Table 7-10. Market-Leader Hypervisor Guest OS Support

Once again, VMware supports many more guest operating systems than either of the other two 64-bit hypervisors. It also supports more x64 guest operating systems than the other two. While this may not be important to you, you must be aware of these facts before you can make a decision on which hypervisor to implement.

Market-Leader Hypervisor Positioning

Given the feature set of each hypervisor, it is obvious that each vendor has something to offer. Microsoft offers virtualization democratization. By putting their hypervisor directly within their OS, Microsoft gives its customers access to server virtualization. Many shops will opt for this tool simply because it is easy to access. Citrix, on the other hand, focuses on low-cost enterprise virtualization. However, shops using Citrix will often have to rely on third-party tools to create a completely dynamic datacenter. Currently, VMware is still the market leader. Their offerings may appear to be the most expensive, but their hypervisor offers more physical server density. If greening the datacenter is foremost on your mind, VMware may be your only choice since it offers higher numbers in terms of physical server consolidation.

The three are therefore positioned to gain some level of market share and continue to do so in the near future.

CHAPTER 8

Work with Virtual Workloads

Now that you understand the basic feature sets of each hypervisor, you're ready to move on to working with the virtual machines themselves. To do so, you need to first understand how the virtualization decision process should work. Basically, this process matches business requirements with the type of virtualization that meets them best. The overall virtualization decision process was introduced in Chapter 3, but here, you'll focus on the server virtualization contents of this process.

In addition, you need to understand the structure of the Virtual Service Offerings you will be running in the virtualization layer. How will you structure these virtual machines? How will you assign VM priorities, and which types of policies should you attach to each VM? These are decisions you must consider now before you begin to run full workloads within the virtual layer.

Finally, you need to consider how you allocate resources to your VMs. Will a certain VM contend for the same resources as another? How will your host servers determine how to assign resources to each VM, and how will they decide where to place a VM? Finally, how do you configure the hosts and just how many VMs should each host run?

The answers to these questions help you understand how virtual workloads operate and how to best use the physical resources you make available to them.

THE SERVER VIRTUALIZATION DECISION PROCESS

The reason why you engage in virtualization is, of course, to save on power, cooling, space, and, of course, money. But even if you gain such powerful advantages by moving to a virtual infrastructure, your purpose is to continue and perhaps improve the way your datacenter responds to business requirements. As you've seen so far, working with virtual machines is much faster than working with physical machines, yet you must be careful of VM sprawl and, as such, each VM you create must meet a specific purpose, and, if possible, be time-based so that it can be removed from the datacenter once its purpose is complete.

The best way to manage this process is to rely on a given decision process. In this case, it is the server virtualization decision process (see Figure 8-1). You begin by first

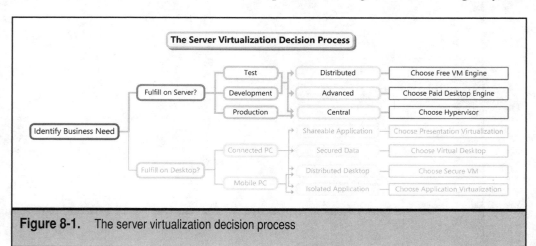

Figure 8-1. The server virtualization decision process

identifying the business requirement; then you determine if you will fulfill this business requirement on the server or on the desktop. Since you are currently considering server virtualization requirements, you know that in this case, you will fulfill the business needs that arise through server virtualization technologies.

Next, you need to determine if the requirement is for a test, development, or production environment. Both test and development requirements will be addressed in one of three ways:

▼ Will you be using a distributed solution, one that could be running either on the requestor's desktop or on server hardware that is managed outside of the datacenter? If so, you should rely on free virtualization technologies and, most often, on software virtualization (SoftV) products. For example, depending on your choice of hypervisor, you could use VMware Server, Microsoft Virtual PC, or Microsoft Virtual Server to respond to this need. Keep in mind that the Microsoft products will, of course, produce machines in the virtual hard disks (VHD) format, but will also only support 32-bit VMs. The VMware solution, however, can easily run either 32- or 64-bit VMs so long as it has been installed on top of an x64 operating system.

Machines of this type are best prepared centrally, possibly through the virtual lab you created in Chapter 6, and distributed to end users with a specific service level: The machine is available as-is and will be provided again as-is should anything happen to it.

And, as discussed in Chapter 6, the ideal configuration for the workstations your testers and developers will work on should be:

■ An advanced workstation with 4GB or more of RAM

■ A separate external USB disk or, even better, a separate external serial advanced technology assessment (SATA) disk. Running the VMs on a disk that is separate from the system volume gives much better performance (see Figure 8-2).

Figure 8-2. Running VMs on a separate disk gives much better performance for testers and developers.

■ If your customer requires more advanced features than the free SoftV products offer, you might consider providing them with a paid virtualization engine. VMware Workstation, for example, is the flagship SoftV product from VMware and includes powerful features that are not found in the free VMware Server. For example, you can use VMware Workstation to record both pictures and movies from within virtual machines directly through the Workstation interface (see Figure 8-3). Screens are captured as BMP files, and movies are captured as AVI. Movie capturing will even omit blank screens during the capture. In addition, using the Team feature in Workstation makes it much easier to create collections of VMs that may be linked together for multitier applications. For these reasons, providing your customer with a paid copy of VMware Workstation would best meet their advanced requirements. You should, of course, use a chargeback system to make sure their project's budget will pay for this service.

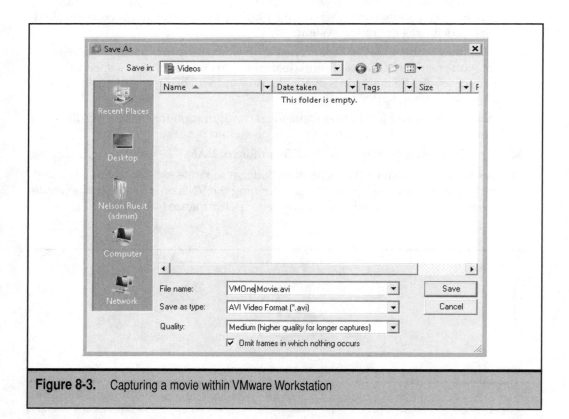

Figure 8-3.　Capturing a movie within VMware Workstation

▲   If the requirement is for a complex testing or development environment, such as the Integration or Staging levels discussed in Chapter 6, the only solution is to provide them with remote access to a hosted VM environment. In this case, you may also call upon either VMware Lab Manager or VMware Stage Manager to further refine the service offering you are making available.

If the requirement is for a production solution, the answer is much simpler: You will provide the customer with a centrally hosted VM or VMs that will be managed as production workloads on your datacenter's hypervisor.

VIRTUAL SERVICE OFFERINGS STRUCTURE

In production, you'll want to obtain the topmost performance from both hosts and virtual machines. After all, even if you want to improve physical resource utilization, you'll still want to make sure all systems perform at their best. For this reason, you need to look at the Virtual Service Offerings you will be running. The best way to do this is to take a structured approach. Begin by categorizing the server workloads in your Virtual Service Offerings. You'll find that there are generally eight main production server categories (see Figure 8-4). You'll also need test systems and development systems, which should be running in your laboratory, but even these fit into the eight main categories.

As you can see, the eight categories are brought together by grouping service types by service affinity. Certain types of services or functions do not belong together, while others naturally tend to fit in the same category. As a result, you will have roles that are

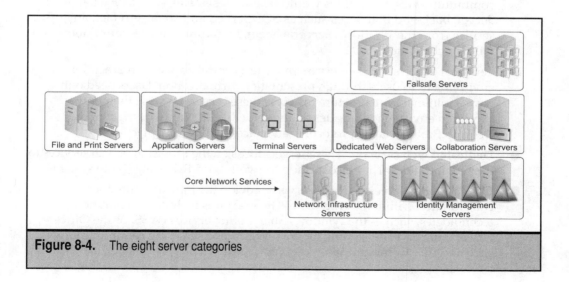

Figure 8-4.   The eight server categories

defined by the type of software servers run and the type of service they deliver. The resulting categories include:

▼ **Network infrastructure and physical servers**   These servers provide core networking functions, such as Internet Protocol (IP) addressing, for example Dynamic Host Configuration Protocol (DHCP), or name resolution, especially for legacy systems such as the Windows Internet Naming System (WINS). However, this is no longer really required since single-label naming is now available through the Domain Name System (DNS) in Windows Server 2008. These servers also provide virtual private network (VPN) and Routing and Remote Access Services (RRAS). And, because they are a base-level service, they run the virtualization role on physical machines through technologies like hypervisors.

■ **Identity management servers**   These servers are the core identity managers for the network. They contain and maintain the entire corporate identity database for all users and user access. For Windows Server 2008 (WS08), these would be servers running Active Directory Domain Services (AD DS). This function should not be shared with any other as much as possible, unless it is a core networking function, such as name resolution—in this case, DNS.

■ **File and print servers**   These servers focus on the provision of storage and structured document services to the network. They include both the Network File System (NFS) and the Common Internet File System (CIFS). They also include standard and Internet print servers.

■ **Application servers**   These servers provide application services to the user community. WS08 examples would be e-mail systems such as Exchange Server, back-end databases such as SQL Server, and so on—in fact, any service from the Windows Server system, including middle-tier systems and failover clusters.

■ **Terminal servers**   These servers provide a central application execution environment to users through presentation virtualization. Users need only have a minimal infrastructure to access these servers because their entire execution environment resides on the server itself. Note that the Remote Desktop Protocol is the protocol used to access all virtual machines.

■ **Dedicated web servers**   These servers focus on the provision of web services to user communities. They also include Network Load Balancing (NLB) systems.

■ **Collaboration servers**   These servers provide the infrastructure for collaboration within the enterprise. Their services include collaboration technologies, such as the Windows SharePoint Services (WSS) or the Office SharePoint Server, streaming media services, and real-time communications, such as Office Communications Server.

▲ **Failsafe servers** This eighth role focuses on redundancy and provides business continuity by having identical images of production servers in standby mode. When a production server fails, the failsafe version automatically comes online. The most important aspect of this server construction is replication technologies, ensuring that failsafe servers are always up-to-date and that no data is lost. This category is now extremely easy to create, since virtual servers are nothing but files that need to be replicated in another location. Physical servers are also easy to reproduce, since they run only a single role and can come with an integrated hypervisor.

In addition, server placement comes into play. Placement refers to the architectural proximity or position of the server in an end-to-end distributed system. Three positions are possible:

▼ Inside the intranet

■ In the security perimeter—often referred to as the demilitarized zone (DMZ), though for large organizations, the perimeter often includes more than just a DMZ

▲ Outside the enterprise

With the coming of virtualization, server placement tends to blur, as virtual machines on a physical host may be in one zone, while others on the same host are in another. Make sure you keep server placement in mind when you position the virtual servers for each zone in your network.

NOTE For those running Windows workloads, Microsoft offers a Windows Server Virtualization Validation Program. This program enables vendors to validate various configurations so that Windows Server customers can receive technical support in virtualized environments. Customers with validated solutions benefit from Microsoft support as a part of the regular Windows Server technical support framework. To learn more, go to www.windowsservercatalog.com/svvp.

If you plan well, you should be able to virtualize 100 percent of your workloads. Today, virtualization infrastructures can run almost any workload. In a survey of VMware customers conducted in July 2007, VMware found that out of 361 polled customers, most of them ran advanced workloads on their virtualization engine (see Figure 8-5).

There should be few reasons why you cannot virtualize a service offering. For example, you may decide to continue running some service offerings on older 32-bit hardware just because you're not ready to move off of those systems. But consider the advantages of running virtual machines. Because they are virtual, they can be loaded on any hardware system. In addition, they are easy to deploy and protect—just copy the disk files to another location.

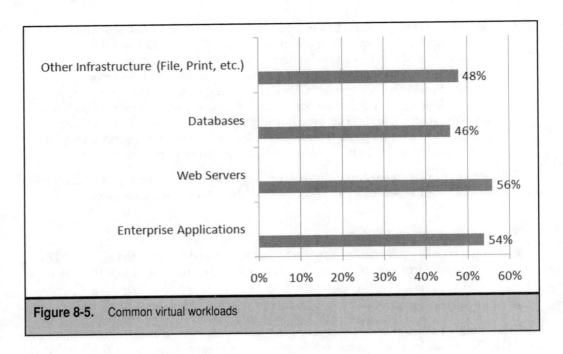

Figure 8-5.   Common virtual workloads

Another reason for maintaining physical service offerings may be to use older 32-bit hardware in regions. Once again, you should run these as virtual instances as much as possible. If you do find that you need to maintain older hardware and run it in your datacenter, why not make them host systems anyway? It's true that Hyper-V does not run on 32-bit platforms, but you can still rely on tools such as Microsoft Virtual Server, System Center Virtual Machine Manager, or VMware Server. All will run on 32-bit systems, giving them more life as physical hosts instead of actually delivering service offerings to users. This way, all of your physical machines—32- and 64-bit—are hosts, and all your service offerings are virtualized.

VIRTUAL RESOURCE ALLOCATION RULES

Now that you have categorized the various server workloads, you need to consider how you will assign them to hosts. If a host server is going to run up to 20 VMs, the VMs cannot or should not contend for the same resources at the same time. In fact, you want to configure heterogeneous virtual workloads as much as possible and avoid configuring homogeneous workloads on host servers. To do this, you must look at the workloads and identify which processes and resources they need and when they require them.

For example, if you're running Windows services in your network, you can expect them to behave as follows (see Figure 8-6):

▼   Domain controllers (DCs) require network and processor resources at peak times (early morning, after lunch).

■   File and print servers require processor and network resources at off-peak times (mid-morning, mid-afternoon).

■   Web servers focus on network resources and, if properly constructed, will require a steady stream of resources.

■   SQL Server and Exchange Server both require a steady amount of resources throughout the day and focus mostly on disk and processor resources.

■   Test and development systems are often used during off-hours.

▲   Corporate applications often have scheduled resource requirements. For example, a payroll application will run on bimonthly or biweekly schedules.

You'll notice that not all workloads are busy at all times. In fact, some workloads are "parked" and rarely run. These are good candidates for rationalization.

Because server workloads require different resources at different times, you should configure your workloads in a heterogeneous manner (see Figure 8-7). This means one host server could run a DC, a network infrastructure server, a file server, one or more

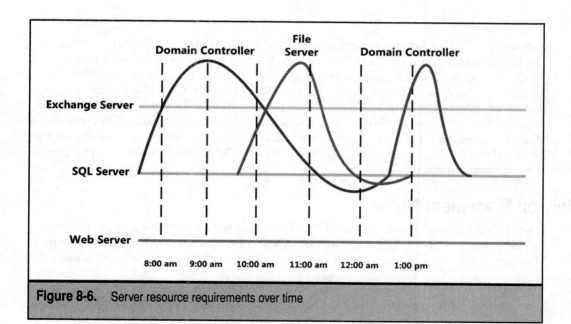

Figure 8-6.   Server resource requirements over time

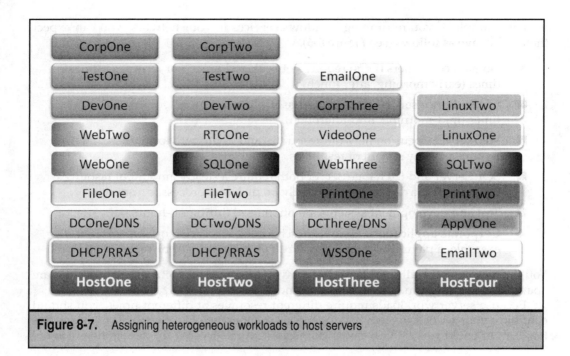

Figure 8-7. Assigning heterogeneous workloads to host servers

web servers, test and development servers, and perhaps even a corporate application. The key is to focus on workloads that require different resources at different times.

Of course, if you run a monitoring tool, such as VMware's Distributed Resource Scheduler (DRS), and assign appropriate policies to your VMs, the system will automatically move the workloads from one host to another in order to guarantee the required resource levels. Similarly, using a combination of System Center Virtual Machine Manager (SCVMM), Operations Manager, and Hyper-V, you can rely on the Performance & Resource Optimization feature of SCVMM to optimize the placement of your virtual machines.

Rely on Placement Rules

When assigning workloads, you need to rely on host server placement rules. For example, each time you create a virtual machine in Microsoft's System Center Virtual Machine Manager, it relies on placement rules to assign the new VM to a host (see Figure 8-8).

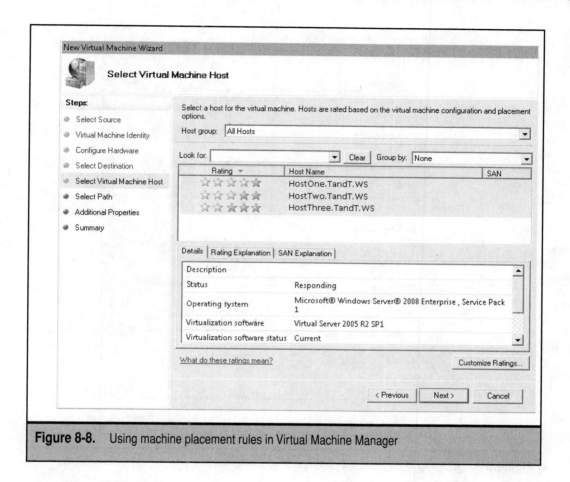

Figure 8-8. Using machine placement rules in Virtual Machine Manager

To do so, it assigns a star rating to each host server. Host servers with available resources are granted up to five stars, while host servers with existing workloads or with fewer available resources are granted fewer stars.

These ratings can be customized. By default, SCVMM relies on load balancing, making sure each host server runs approximately the same amount of workloads or, at least, uses up the same amount of resources. Resources focus on processor, memory, network, and disk input and output (see Figure 8-9). You can also focus on a second placement goal: resource maximization. In this case, SCVMM will continue to assign VMs to a host until all of a host's resources are consumed.

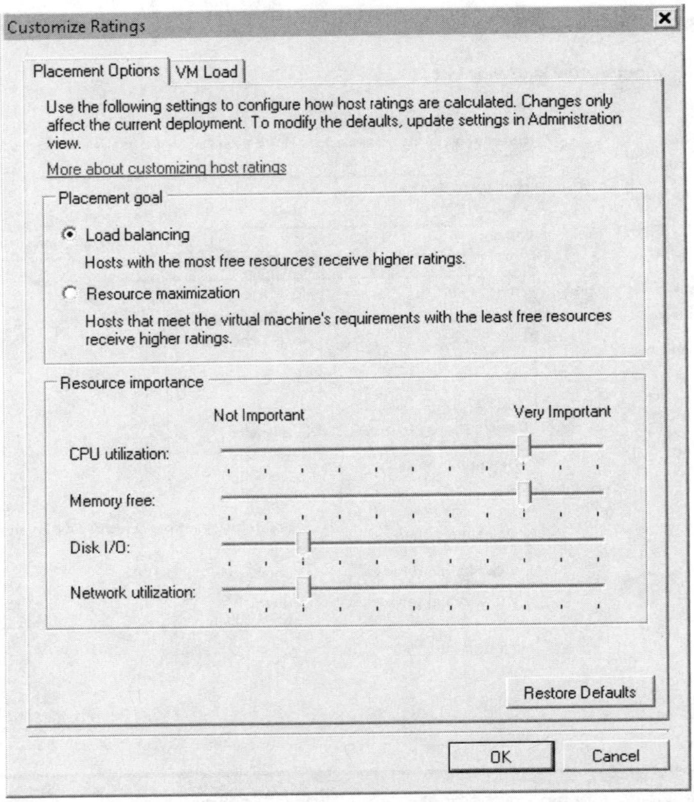

Figure 8-9. Working with placement options in Virtual Machine Manager

SCVMM also lets you customize host ratings by controlling just how much you expect to draw from a host server's CPU, disk I/O, and network usage (see Figure 8-10). Using these resource assignments lets you maximize how host resources are consumed by your systems. This is how you guarantee that your physical servers run workloads that use up to 80 percent of their capabilities.

Each virtualization engine lets you manage resources in this manner. Make sure you work with your hypervisor management tool to properly configure and assign these resources.

Single Versus Multi-VM Hosts

When organizations first began to run virtual workloads, they wanted to maximize hardware usage. In addition, in the first days of server virtualization, hypervisor technologies

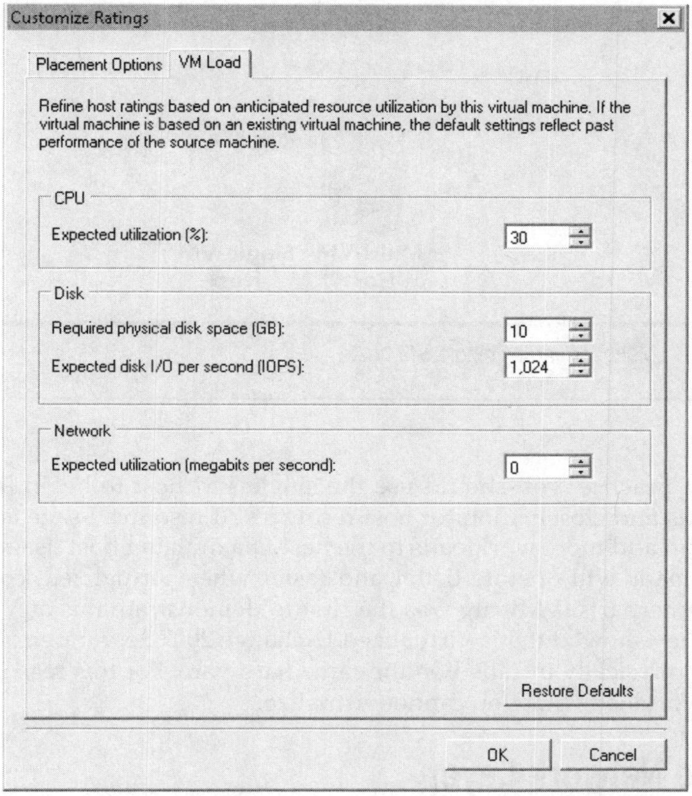

Figure 8-10. Customizing host ratings in Virtual Machine Manager

were very, very expensive. In fact, many vendors, such as Virtual Iron and XenSource (now Citrix), made their entry into the hypervisor market by providing less expensive solutions. Now, with many hypervisors available for free or for a mere pittance, organizations are looking at server virtualization in a different light.

Before 2007, organizations only virtualized workloads that had low-resource requirements so that they could load up as many VMs as possible on a host server to maximize their investment. Today, with the advent of low-cost virtualization, you can virtualize any workload, even workloads that are highly resource-intensive. While pre-2007 virtualization focused on multi-VM host servers, today, you can also consider the single-VM host (see Figure 8-11). By virtualizing workloads, they become liberated from the physical server. They can then be more easily provisioned, protected, and managed.

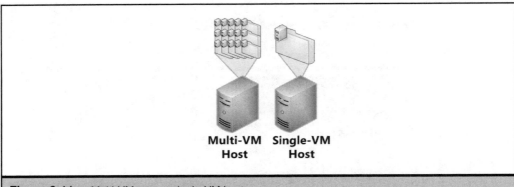

Figure 8-11.   Multi-VM versus single-VM hosts

As a best practice, you should use the single-VM host to begin hosting resource-intensive VMs and closely monitor host resources. If resource usage is less than anticipated, you can add more workloads to the host, maximizing host usage. In many cases, server workloads will operate better and faster when virtualized, compared to their physical counterparts. VMware was the first to demonstrate this at VMWorld Europe 2007 when they showed that a virtualized Exchange 2007 Server performed better than when it was physically installed on the same hardware. For this reason, there are very few, if any, workloads that you cannot virtualize.

Work with the Network Layer

As mentioned in Chapter 5, you can provision multiple virtual networks through the properties of the hypervisor. Three networks can be provisioned: public, private, and host-only. VMs can use these different networks in a variety of ways and, therefore, you should provision each of these networks within the host systems you prepare.

For example, each VM that is designed to provide service offerings to end users must do so through the public network. Therefore, these VMs must have at least one connection to the public virtual network interfaces you create on the host servers. Public networks also allow virtual machines that are located on different hosts to communicate with each other. It is a good practice to create multiple public network paths on each host to provide redundancy in the services.

Host-only virtual network cards are used to provision the VMs through the host. For example, if you need to update the VM, you can do so through the host-only communication channel, avoiding additional traffic on the public interfaces. Host-only communications are performed directly from the host to the VMs and use the host's internal communication channels to operate.

Private virtual network cards can also be used to avoid traffic on the public interface. For example, when you build a failover cluster, you must create a private communication channel between all of the nodes of the cluster. This private link is used to exchange heartbeat information between each node of the cluster to ensure that the nodes do not fail over unnecessarily. By using a private virtual network interface card (NIC) for this channel, you rely on the internal capabilities of the hypervisor to support the communication. Note that when you host cluster nodes on two different hosts, you must use a public channel for this communication.

Another example of private communications between VMs is the communications between Exchange Transport Servers and domain controllers. All of the Exchange configuration is stored within AD and is queried on a regular basis to provide Exchange with topology information. Directing this communication onto private networks will free up the public network for other traffic.

For this reason, you should provision each host with each network type and then link various VM components to the appropriate virtual NIC.

BEST PRACTICES IN SERVER VIRTUALIZATION

As you can see, there is a lot to server virtualization. You'll quickly learn that it is a powerful operational model and that the return on investment is extremely worthwhile. In addition, the administrative workload will decrease and become more interesting. There is so much you can do with a VM that you just can't do with a physical server.

Remember to standardize all of your host servers as much as possible. Choose servers that will meet and grow with the needs of your VMs. You might consider putting your virtualization management system on a physical server to ensure constant availability. If not, make sure the VM that includes this tool is set to autostart with the host server so that you can quickly and easily get into the management environment.

Configure your VMs with appropriate policies. For example, if you are running VMware, assign a high Distributed Resource Scheduling priority to applications that are hit hard at specific times. Also, make sure your ISO files are easy to access. It might be best to create a central library on a file share to make them available to any device and any machine.

Finally, pay close attention to Microsoft licensing. Virtual machines require fewer licenses than physical machines, and this is one of the reasons why it is so rewarding to move to a dynamic datacenter, but virtual machines are also easy to generate. Keep this in mind whenever you create a new VM. You don't want to cause problems with virtualization; you aim to solve them.

CHAPTER 9

Provision Virtual Machines

All machines have a life cycle, whether they are physical or virtual. This life cycle is made up of four phases, which differ slightly between physical and virtual machines. In the dynamic datacenter, physical machines are host servers only, so their life cycle is greatly shortened and simplified. But Virtual Service Offerings continue to require a more extensive life cycle (see Figure 9-1).

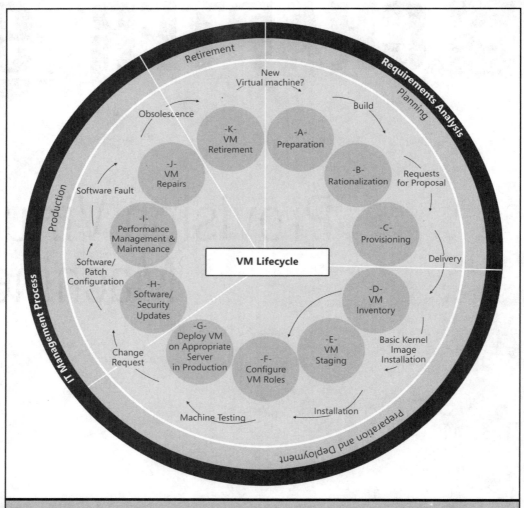

Figure 9-1. The four phases of the service life cycle: planning, preparation and deployment, production, and retirement

This life cycle includes four different stages, as follows:

- ▼ **Planning**   Identifying and preparing solutions for deployment
- ■ **Preparation and Deployment**   Acquiring, packaging, configuring, installing, and testing deployment strategies
- ■ **Production**   Problem, change, optimization, and administration management within the production network
- ▲ **Retirement**   Replacement/upgrade planning and removal of obsolete technologies and processes

The planning phase is focused on identifying the business requirement and which technologies will help fulfill it. For virtual machines, there is no need to purchase a physical server, unless, of course, there are no existing hosts for this new virtual machine (VM). This is where host servers must be transformed into shared infrastructure costs. Because you no longer need to purchase VMs, the purchasing process turns into a requirements analysis process. Since virtual machines include reduced licensing costs, provisioning a virtual instance of an operating system (OS) is simpler and easier than a physical instance. Here, you need to focus on system requirements—number of processor cores, random access memory (RAM), disk space, and network interfaces required by the VM—before you create the instance of the OS. You may, however, have to obtain separate licenses for the actual workload the machine will run.

NOTE   This service-offering life cycle was originally presented in *Windows Server 2003: Best Practices for Enterprises Deployments* by Danielle Ruest and Nelson Ruest (McGraw-Hill, 2003). The model was derived from an original model presented by Microsoft in a white paper entitled "Planning, Deploying, and Managing Highly Available Solutions" released in May 1999. The original Microsoft IT service life cycle model can be found at www.microsoft.com/technet/archive/ittasks/plan/sysplan/availsol.mspx?mfr=true.

The preparation and deployment phase focuses on the technical architecture process, which either follows or can occur at the same time as the planning process. The technical architecture provides the specific technical parameters that will be applied to the service offering during its installation and during the rest of its life cycle within the network. It is based on the orientations outlined in your enterprise architecture and should detail the specifics of the implementation.

The life cycle then moves on to installation and initial configuration and packaging/staging. Packaging is used if the service offering relies on a software product or an addition to the current network. Staging is used if the service relies on a feature of the new operating system. For example, with Windows Server 2008, you will need to rely on both packaging and staging, since you will have a tendency to begin with initial installation or staging of your servers and then follow with the application of the specific function or role the server will play in your network. Packaging is often used to automate the software or service-offering installation process, or even to turn the VM into a virtual appliance that can be used as a source for other, similar requirements.

Testing is the next stage, and it is vital because it ensures the stability of any new service offering introduced into your production network. Finally, the service offering is ready for deployment. This deployment can be done in several stages. Another proof of concept (POC) can be used to perform a final validation of the service offering in operation. The target audience for this POC usually consists of the project team and some of its closest associates. This is followed by a pilot project that tests all aspects of the deployment methodology, including technical and administrative procedures. Massive deployment follows a successful pilot project. In addition, the VM must be properly positioned on a host that has sufficient resources to run the workload. At least one additional server should be earmarked to provide failover for this workload should either maintenance or mishaps occur on the original host.

Once the service offering is deployed, it enters the production phase of its life cycle. Here, you manage and maintain a complete inventory of the service, control changes, deal with problems, and support its users. You must implement and manage service level agreements (SLAs) for each service offering you deploy. SLAs focus on performance and capacity analysis, redundancy planning (backup, clustering, failsafe, and recovery procedures), availability, reliability, and responsiveness of the service.

The final phase of the IT service-offering life cycle is retirement. When the service reaches a certain degree of obsolescence, it must be retired from the network because its operation costs often outweigh its benefits. With VMs, this process is easy to implement and can even be automated in some instances.

Workflow products are often good tools to use to implement this type of provisioning process. For example, you could build such a process through the Windows Workflow Foundation that is part of the Microsoft Office SharePoint System; or you could rely on VMware's Lifecycle Manager, which includes built-in workflows for VM life cycle management (see Figure 9-2). As you can see, it tracks the original VM request

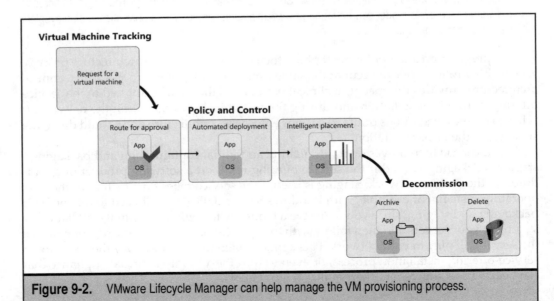

Figure 9-2. VMware Lifecycle Manager can help manage the VM provisioning process.

from beginning to end and then relies on the placement rules you have defined to intelligently place the machine on the most appropriate host.

You rely on VM life cycles to make sure that you do not proliferate server VMs. It is easy to fall into the VM sprawl trap since VMs are so easy to create. With a standard life cycle process, you will control the urge to create VMs as needed, or at least give them time-based policies so that they will automatically be removed from the network once they are no longer required.

CAUTION   In environments where users have administrative rights on their systems, it is easy for them to download and install a free SoftV product and begin to create their own VMs. The problem with this is not so much that these users have access to VMs, but more the fact that they are not trained to properly configure complex operating systems. In this case, it is best for you to create standard VMs that you make available to them on an as-needed and justified basis. This way, you won't find out that you have rogue systems running in unpatched mode in your network.

One of the most important parts of the four-phase VM life cycle is machine provisioning. There are two ways to provision machines.

▼   Provision machines from new source templates

▲   Provision machines through the physical to virtual (P2V) conversion process

Each process has its own particularities.

BEFORE YOU BEGIN

Your goal is to transform the physical machines in your datacenter into virtual service offerings. But to achieve this goal, you need to know where to start. One good way to do this is to rely on SCOPE, a conceptual classification tool (see Figure 9-3). SCOPE lets you quickly identify which workloads to start with. SCOPE is simple to use; it begins with the easiest workloads to convert, then moves upward through the most complex and critical to your business.

SCOPE divides workloads as follows:

▼   Easy workloads include lab machines or machines used for test and development. Training machines also fit into this category, as well as systems running Web services, domain controllers in Windows networks, and network infrastructure systems such as DHCP servers. Web servers are ideal in this category because they often run stateless workloads or workloads that are read-only.

■   Productivity workloads include systems that run printers, file shares, collaboration services such as Office SharePoint Server and other servers that act as front ends to *n*-tier applications. Also included are any systems used to share applications centrally, such as Terminal Servers.

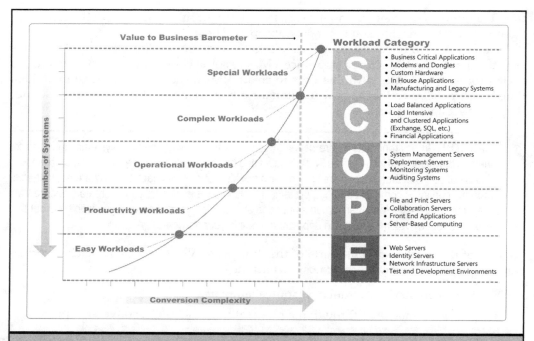

Figure 9-3. The SCOPE Curve helps determine which servers to virtualize first.

- Operational workloads include any system designed to manage your infrastructure. These are often complex implementations, but are still relatively easy to migrate because they often include the capability of transferring a role from one server to another, making the transition from physical to virtual—known as P2V—simpler.

- Complex workloads include systems that run high-availability or load-balancing services, as well as those that have high I/O throughputs, such as databases. If a system is load balanced, migration is simplified since you can add new VMs with the role and integrate them into the load balancing cluster. When enough machines have been virtualized, you can decommission the physical nodes.

  Clustered machines also use this model. For example, with Windows Server 2008, you must migrate clusters from previous versions of Windows Server. Migrating to a cluster made of VMs is just as easy as migrating to a physical cluster. High I/O workloads present a trickier migration, but by the time you get to these workloads, you should be very familiar with the capability of your virtualization infrastructure and with VMs in general.

▲ Special workloads are reserved for last, giving you the opportunity to gain experience in the process. These workloads are usually fewer in number and will include items such as business critical, manufacturing and legacy applications. Here you have to look to special procedures for virtualizing the workload to make sure it still runs properly once converted.

At some point in time, you'll hit the Value to Business Barometer—the point at which conversion takes more effort than normal and you begin to wonder if it's worthwhile. We would argue that conversion of 100 percent of your infrastructure is the goal. Once all systems are converted, you'll have a truly dynamic datacenter; one where all end user-facing workloads are virtualized, and the only role hardware has in your network is to act as host servers running virtual workloads.

Now you're ready to move on to provisioning your virtual workloads.

PROVISION NEW VIRTUAL MACHINES

When you provision virtual machines, you should create custom templates that you can reuse over and over on an as-needed basis. In the physical world, organizations rely on system images to simplify machine provisioning. In the virtual world, you rely on a VM template. Using VM templates makes life so much simpler because all you need to do to create a new VM is copy the files that make it up and boot it up. You must, however, create standard virtual machine configurations. These configurations must identify the following items for each VM:

▼ Number of processors or processor cores per VM

■ Amount of RAM per VM

■ Number of disks and disk space per VM

▲ Number of network interface cards (NICs) per VM

Over time, you will be able to extend these standard configurations to different workloads, knowing exactly just how many resources you need to assign to each server category to provide adequate service—service that will meet the service level agreements you have set with your users.

You must also identify how VMs are provisioned. If you don't use a life cycle, as recommended earlier, you have to implement a standard request process. This process should have two aspects:

▼ **Administrative** Requestors of virtual machines must go through a process similar to the request of a physical machine. The new VM must be costed out to the client. And you must have a stipulation with regard to infrastructure costs. When a new host or a new blade enclosure is required, the cost must be borne by the entire organization, but shared by each client.

▲ **Technical** You must use a standard machine creation process. Ideally, you will rely on precreated virtual machines as a seed for new VMs.

This process will help you control internal VM sprawl.

Create Seed Virtual Machines

Seed machines may not be simple to create, but in the virtual world, you only need to create them once. While you relied on system images in the physical world, you rely on virtual disk drive copying in the virtual world to seed new machines. Therefore, you must create the right source virtual machines in order to avoid propagating garbage into the network. Basically, your seed machine should be created with the same process you would normally use to create a reference server prior to generating a disk image of the server.

For example, in a Windows network, you might need sources for several different operating systems and/or OS editions, such as the following:

▼ Windows Server 2008 (WS08) Standard, WS08 Enterprise, WS08 Web

■ Windows Server 2003 (WS03) Standard, WS03 Enterprise, WS03 Web

■ Windows 2000 Server (W2K) Standard, Advanced

▲ Windows NT Server (hopefully not)

If you created a source machine for each of these server operating systems, you would need nine different seed machines, and this doesn't even include any of the various Linux distributions. For this reason, it is a good idea to standardize the infrastructure OS for VMs, reducing the number of server operating systems that are found in your network. Once again, standardization and rationalization are two core processes found in any dynamic datacenter.

You will need two copies of each source virtual machine you create. In the physical world, you create a reference system, prepare it for duplication, and then capture a system image from the reference system. However, each time you need to update the reference system, you need to reapply the system image, personalize the machine, update it, and repeat the entire preparation process once again. With virtual machines, you simply keep two versions of each machine: one that is the reference system and one that is ready for duplication. The source VM is used to support monthly patching and updates, and the SysPrepped, or depersonalized, machine is used to support multimachine provisioning.

Make sure you inject virtual machine drivers into the machine. In some cases, the operating systems have been "enlightened"—that is, they have been made aware that they are running in a virtual environment. These operating systems are intelligent enough to share core resources and will already include many of the required drivers to run. In others, they are still standard operating systems and must be injected with the appropriate drivers. During the preparation process, you would install components such as VMware Tools, Hyper-V Integration Components, or other hypervisor components based on which hypervisor you run.

Provision Using Seed Machines

When your source servers are ready, you can use a standard process to seed new VMs (see Figure 9-4).

1. Keep the reference VMs on standby until patches are needed.

2. Update the source machine each Patch Tuesday (monthly).

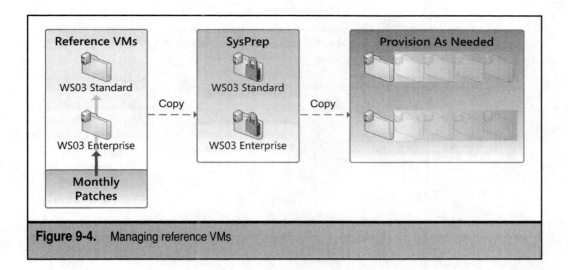

Figure 9-4.   Managing reference VMs

3. Inspect and compress the virtual disk(s) that make up the machine.

4. Reapply SysPrep as needed, such as each time patches are applied to the reference VMs.

5. Copy and repersonalize the SysPrepped VM to provision a new system.

You can standardize this process and use a monthly cycle to update your source VMs 12 times per year.

Several tools will automatically update the source VMs. For example, Microsoft's Offline Virtual Machine Servicing Tool will automatically launch shutdown VMs, patch them, and then turn them off again on a schedule. VMware's Update Manager performs a similar task using a similar process. Look to your hypervisor toolkit to reduce the overhead of having to manage multiple VM images.

Physical Versus Virtual Provisioning

As you can see, provisioning a virtual machine is much faster than working with a physical machine. In the past, you had to begin by obtaining the hardware for the new server, configure it once it came in, install the OS, and then install and configure the application designed to provide the expected workload. Once this was done, you would test the system, assign an Internet Protocol (IP) address to it, and possibly configure the network to support it. This could easily take up to six weeks before a system would be ready. Today, with the proper seed machines, you can provision a server much faster, sometimes in as little as 20 minutes (see Figure 9-5).

This has a serious impact on the amount of work required to create new service offerings. This workload is reduced even further when you rely on virtual appliances.

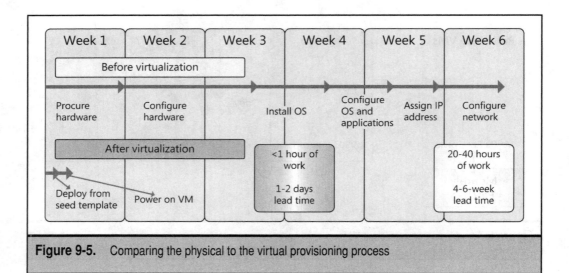

Figure 9-5.   Comparing the physical to the virtual provisioning process

Rely on Virtual Appliances

Virtual appliances (VAPs) are virtual machine templates, sometimes in the Open Virtualization Format (OVF), that contain preconfigured operating systems and applications. Since VMs are self-contained and transportable, they can be delivered in a preconfigured state as virtual appliances. VAPs are most often designed to run on Linux operating systems because of the licensing cost. Few vendors have created VAPs based on Microsoft technologies because they have to become Windows resellers to do so.

However, VAPS further decrease the time to production of a new application because they are preconfigured and ready to run. Given this, you may never need to install another product again; just get it in a VAP and run it.

Virtual appliances offer several benefits. Physical IT appliances have been around for quite some time. Several different types of appliances are available: network intrusion detection systems, search engines, firewalls, storage servers, configuration management servers, Network Load Balancing servers, and much more. What's great about these devices is that they are really easy to deploy and use; mount it in a rack, give it an IP address, and then log into it to configure it—a process that is much like that of a host server with an integrated hypervisor. Configuration is usually performed in a web interface through a browser: Use the IP address you assigned the device to go to the configuration page, change or assign an administrative password, and move on to the configuration of the features included in the device.

Virtual appliances are even easier to set up than physical appliances. Copy the files that make up the VAP into a file folder on a server, or import them if they are in OVF form, and then launch the virtual machine that makes up the appliance to finalize the configuration. But even if they are easy to set up and install, your virtual appliances still need to be prepared carefully. In the physical world, your main concern is if the appliance will fit into your racks. But in the virtual world, you must ensure the virtual appliance you obtain relies on the virtualization technology you have decided to deploy in your network. For example, if you chose to standardize with VMware as your virtualization provider and the virtual appliance you select comes in another format, you'll most likely choose not to obtain it. After all, you don't want to run multiple virtualization engines if you can help it. Of course, you could always convert the appliance, but doing so may well void any warranties provided by the manufacturer because you'll be changing the very nature of the VM, unless, of course, it is packaged with OVF, which is designed to support the creation of VAPs for any hypervisor.

In addition, when you rely on an appliance that is provided to you through a trusted manufacturer, you won't have to worry about licensing issues since these concerns are part of the warranty the manufacturer provides with the product. You know you can safely deploy the appliance and use it risk-free because the manufacturer will have taken any potential licensing issues into consideration in the fabrication of the appliance.

Another issue you face with any product, server or not, is the updating process. When you obtain and install your own tools, you also have to devise a strategy of your own to keep them up-to-date in terms of patches and service packs. With a commercial appliance, you don't need to worry about these updates because they are part and parcel of the appliance itself and the support program that comes with it. Of course, you have to make sure you can support the update process, but you don't have to devise it yourself.

Keep the following considerations in mind when you select a commercial VAP:

1. Is the virtual appliance fully configured and secured?

   ■ Does it include a minimalist version of the operating system, including only those components required to support the application, or does it include additional, unused components?

   ■ Is the operating system hardened and, if so, how is this hardening documented?

   ■ Is the operating system up-to-date and does it include the latest patches and updates?

   ■ What other security measures has the manufacturer applied to the appliance?

2. What are the vendor's update and upgrade policies?

   ■ Does the vendor have a documented update and upgrade policy?

   ■ Do vendor updates address only the application within the appliance, or do they also address the underlying operating system?

   ■ What is the vendor's update schedule and how are update notifications sent?

- Are updates included as part of the support costs for the appliance, or is there an additional cost?

- Are there any impacts, licensing or operational, when the VAP is moved from one host to the other?

- What is the impact, cost or otherwise, of creating virtual machine snapshots of the VAP?

- Is the VAP certified by the virtualization vendor you have selected to use?

- Is it possible to recover existing configuration and management data during the upgrade process?

- What is the upgrade process? Can it be as simple as implementing a new VAP, synchronizing data, and deleting the old VAP?

3. What is the vendor's preferred deployment process?

- Which options does the vendor offer for VAP evaluation?

- What are the requirements for an evaluation and test of the VAP?

- What is the duration of an evaluation period for the product?

- Is it possible to retain data generated during the evaluation period when you move the VAP to production?

- How do you move from evaluation to production? Can it be as simple as entering a valid license key into the VAP?

4. What if you need to scale your deployment?

- Which options does the vendor offer for the implementation of additional VAPs? Can it be as simple as deploying the same VAP with a different license key?

- Does the vendor offer a single centralized console that lets you configure multiple VAPs in one place?

- Is it possible to synchronize multiple configurations with the same settings?

- How does a scaled deployment affect licensing and support costs?

5. How easy is it to manage and maintain the VAP?

- Can all VAP features be accessed via a single web-based interface, or is console access required?

- Does the VAP help automate common maintenance tasks, such as backup and disk defragmentation?

- Does the VAP provide alerts and notifications regarding its status?

Relying on these considerations will ensure that you select the very best VAP, a VAP that will provide operational support for as long as you need it.

Virtual Appliance Benefits

Appliances that meet the considerations that have been outlined earlier will ensure that organizations can quickly realize the many benefits of VAPs.

▼   **Rapid Deployment**   One of the biggest benefits of an appliance is that you do not need to run through the installation process for the software it contains. Just compare any appliance with any product that is available through traditional distribution means. In addition, virtual appliances work just the same way as a physical appliance. The major difference is that they come in a software version instead of as a physical device, making them even easier to deploy. For administrators who want to reduce the physical footprint of their datacenter, the virtual appliance might make more sense.

■   **Ease of Use**   Another major benefit of virtual appliances, or appliances in general, is that they save enormous amounts of time. For mid-market IT professionals, system management appliances—physical or virtual—are a major boon because they let you control change in your network without adding any significant workload. In fact, they often reduce your workload since the appliance can help centralize all management and administrative tasks.

■   **Best Practices and Secure Configurations**   In addition, appliances provide you with a secure implementation by default. That's because appliances are built and configured by the manufacturer of the product. Who could do it better? The manufacturer knows the ins and outs of their product and can ensure that all preconfigurations are performed using best practices. If the manufacturer can install and configure the product and then deliver it in a preconfigured state, why should you bother with the hassle of trying to figure it out yourself? By relying on appliances, you may never have to install a server product again. Preconfiguration by the manufacturer also ensures a secure and bulletproof installation that is ready to run as soon as you connect it.

■   **Supportability**   Since the manufacturer creates and controls the configuration of the product, you can be sure that every aspect of it will be completely supported. Manufacturers can provide this level of support for their products because they know it was set up right in the first place.

■   **Scalability**   Because of their virtual nature, it becomes easy to upgrade the resources for a virtual appliance. Just stop the machine; add more processors, more RAM or additional disks, and network cards; and restart it again. It will automatically take advantage of the new resources. Just add a few configuration changes, such as mapping an IP address to a network interface card, and it's ready to go. In some cases, you don't even need to stop the virtual appliance to add new resources. It all depends on the virtualization engine you use and the type of resource you need to add.

■ **Transportability**   Virtual appliances, like virtual machines, run on physical host servers. Because of this, they are transportable and can be moved from one hardware resource to another. Pause the machine, move it, and then start it up again. This makes it easy to provide the virtual appliance with the resources it requires during peak loads. Some virtualization infrastructures will even move the virtual machine automatically based on a set of policies.

■ **Business Continuity**   Hardware resources can be linked to shared storage, and virtual appliances can be contained within this shared storage. When problems arise with a hardware host, the virtual appliance is automatically moved from one host to another in a process that is transparent to end users. Some virtualization infrastructures will even move the VAP without any service interruptions. You can also use replication technologies to replicate the virtual appliance's disk files to a remote location for longer-term business continuity.

■ **Disaster Recovery**   Because of the nature of virtual machines, VAPs can be backed up on a constant basis through snapshots, or the ability to capture the state of a virtual machine at a given point in time. You can then return to these snapshots if something goes awry with the virtual appliance during critical maintenance, update, and patching processes. This can improve the reliability of the VAP.

▲ **Affordability**   Because they do not require dedicated hardware, VAPs can be much more affordable. In addition, it becomes simple to deploy additional versions of the VAP, providing scalability when workloads increase.

VAPs are the way of the future. In a short time, all applications will be provided as VAPs and you will no longer have to worry about installing and configuring a complex application again.

Create Virtual Appliances of Your Own

As you saw earlier, VAPs are downloadable when it comes to open-source systems. But when it comes to Windows, few VAPs are available. Because of this, you must create your own Microsoft VAPs. The process for creating your own VAPs is very much like that of creating a seed machine for new VMs, except that in addition to installing the OS and configuring it for use, you install the application before you depersonalize the machine. With this process, you can create quite a few different types of Microsoft VAPs.

▼ Web servers running Internet Information Server (IIS)

■ SQL Server back-end database servers

■ Windows SharePoint Services front-end servers

■ Streaming media servers

▲ DHCP servers and more

Once the VAP is prepared, you use the same depersonalization process as with seed VMs; then you copy and personalize the VAP as needed when you reuse it.

NOTE   Look up how to create a SQL Server VAP at http://itmanagement.earthweb.com/article .php/31771_3718566_2.

Keep in mind that you cannot create a VAP for anything that must be in a domain first, for example, domain controllers, some Exchange server roles, and so on. Because of the domain association, these workloads cannot be depersonalized and copied. You should, therefore, document and automate the installation of these roles as much as possible.

PERFORM PHYSICAL-TO-VIRTUAL CONVERSIONS

The second method for the creation of virtual machines is the physical-to-virtual conversion process. The P2V conversion process decouples and migrates a physical server's operating system, applications, and data from its physical container to a virtual machine guest hosted on a virtualization platform. During the conversion process, drivers are converted from physical to virtual and the machine is adapted to the hypervisor.

There are three P2V methods.

- ▼ **Manual P2V**   Manually create a virtual machine and copy all the files from the operating system, applications, and data from the source machine to the VM. This process has the advantage of running on an OS that is optimized for VM operation.

- ■ **Semi-automated P2V**   Use a tool to move the servers from the physical state to a virtual machine, such as Microsoft's System Center Virtual Machine Manager or VMware's free Converter.

- ▲ **Fully automated P2V**   Use a tool that migrates the server over the network without user interaction. There are several such tools on the market, such as PlateSpin or Vizioncore, which all support VMware, Citrix, and Microsoft platforms in addition to the tools from the vendor.

In each case, you must carefully prepare the physical machine before the transformation.

P2V Preparation Tasks

As mentioned in Chapters 1 through 5, you need to fully understand your environment before you begin to transform it into a virtual datacenter. Then, you need to perform a cleanup of the environment as much as possible. For example, you don't want to find yourself in the midst of a massive file server conversion only to discover that 90 percent of the files on the server haven't been accessed in months and are ready for archiving. Use the the SCOPE curve to best determine which machines should be migrated first. Also rely on metrics such as hardware requirements, software dependencies, licensing requirements, and current resource utilization ratios to do so.

Migration relies heavily on the network to move the data from one machine to the other. Basically, the migration process copies the contents of the physical disk drives to virtual disk drives, but to do so, all of this content needs to move through the network.

This may cause some downtime. While several technologies support live conversion from P2V, in most cases, you will perform these conversions offline during maintenance periods. You may even need to put in a request for a special migration period, which will allow you to move all of the target machines to VMs.

When machines have redundant services, the risk of downtime will be considerably less. For example, if you migrate a domain controller with its accompanying Domain Name System (DNS) service, you should not experience any downtime since you will most likely have another DC in production that can take the load in the meantime. Keep in mind that this strategy does not work for organizations that use all-in-one servers, such as Microsoft Small Business Server (SBS). Since all server roles run on the same machine, virtualizing SBS will most certainly cause some downtime.

Also make sure you are prepared for the migration. Do you have enough storage to virtualize all of the machines you are targeting? You should be using storage virtualization with thin provisioning and target the creation of dynamically expanding virtual disks in order to minimize the required amount of storage. Will your network be able to take the load during the conversion? If you are at peak performance today, adding a conversion workload may overly stress your network.

Finally, it is a good idea to check with vendors to see if they support virtualizing their applications. Vendors that do not support virtualization are becoming rare indeed, unlike ten years ago, but it is always good to check. For example, vendors such as Oracle support the virtualization of their applications, but only on their own virtualization platform. In other cases, some vendors will offer a best-effort support policy. Microsoft, for example, offers a best-effort policy for the support of their applications within non-Microsoft virtualization environments. Other vendors may actually request that you convert the workload back to a physical platform in order to provide you with support for special problems. Keep this in mind when you choose the P2V tool you will use. Because of this, you should also consider the benefits of integrating the backup tool you select with the ability to convert machines from one state to another.

NOTE   Microsoft's support policy is documented in Knowledge Base article number 897615 at http://support.microsoft.com/kb/897615.

Physical-to-virtual conversions are usually straightforward: Point to a physical server and transform it into a virtual machine. Of course, the tool you use to carry out a P2V conversion must support the transformation of the drivers that were included in the physical installation of the operating system to those required for the virtual machine engine or hypervisor you are relying on. This is usually the most difficult aspect of a conversion. You should also aim to be able to perform reverse conversions; instead of going from physical to virtual, you go from virtual to physical. While the need for these reverse conversions will disappear with time, it may still be a necessity in the early stages of your dynamic datacenter implementation.

Because of this, you may need a tool that can not only perform P2V conversions, but also V2P conversions. Then, perhaps the best strategy you can use is to combine the requirements for backup and restore with the requirements for machine conversions.

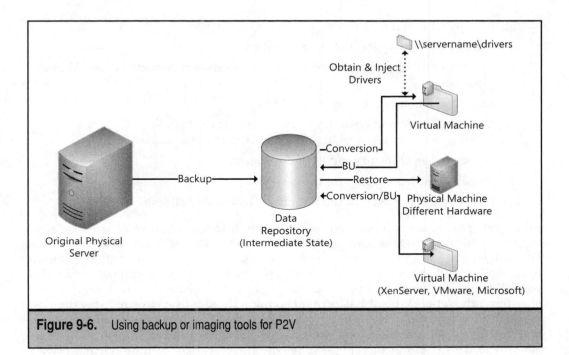

Figure 9-6. Using backup or imaging tools for P2V

When you think of it, a P2V conversion is really nothing more than a backup of the physical drives. Ideally, you can use a tool that backs up any machine—physical or virtual—then stores this backup in a central location. In this case, disk image backups are often the best. When the time comes to restore the machine, you can move the image from this central backup location to any potential target, once again physical or virtual. The key feature you need to identify is the ability to update OS drivers when the restoration process is run. Many such tools will be able to point to a central driver store to first obtain them and then inject them into the image as it is being restored (see Figure 9-6). From then on, this tool will continue to support backups, restores, and conversions from any machine, whether it be in the resource pool or in the Virtual Service Offerings.

Several tools on the market offer support for this. Look to disk-imaging vendors such as Acronis, which offers the True Image line of products, or Symantec, which offers the Ghost line of products, to evaluate the best tool for your needs.

Perform the P2V

When you're ready to perform the actual P2V operation, use the following approach:

1. Determine the validity of the candidate for migration.
2. Clarify vendor support for the virtual workload.
3. Consider licensing costs and make adjustments if necessary.
4. Identify the appropriate host for the VM.

5. Identify CPU and memory requirements for the VM.

6. Identify the storage location for the VM's files.

7. Identify network requirements and make sure the appropriate virtual NICs are available on the host.

8. Identify the failover strategy for this VM.

9. Use a standard naming strategy to differentiate the new Virtual Service Offering from the physical host that used to run the workload.

10. Schedule downtime in support of the migration.

11. Prepare your testing plan for the new VM.

12. Prepare a go-live plan for the VM once it has passed all tests.

Select the appropriate candidates in order of importance. Begin with low-risk, non-business-critical workloads, such as the test and development environments you run. This will let you learn the ins and outs of the P2V process without any negative impact to the business. Web servers are also often good candidates for initial conversions. If your Web site is properly set up, you may already have redundant web servers running through Network Load Balancing. Having redundant services reduces the risk, especially for your first P2V experiments. Then, move on to low-utilization systems that host less critical applications. Next, work on higher-utilization systems that are not critical. This could include application-specific servers or routing/virtual private network (VPN) servers.

Migrate servers running critical workloads last. By then, you should be quite familiar with the process and be ready for any eventuality. This would include applications such as Exchange, SQL Server, and business-critical applications.

You'll find that there are several products, both free and paid, that support the physical-to-virtual move process. Select the one that best fits your needs. Some of the most popular ways to perform a P2V conversion include:

▼ VMware Converter

■ PlateSpin PowerConvert

■ Ultimate-P2V plug-in for BartPE

▲ Microsoft conversion tools

Each provides its own features and performance level.

Work with VMware Converter

VMware Converter comes in two flavors: Converter Starter and Converter Enterprise. Starter is a free version that lets you perform single conversions on a one-by-one basis. Converter Enterprise supports both online real-time and offline conversions. The differences between the two tools are outlined in Table 9-1.

This tool can be run on a variety of hardware and supports most commonly used versions of Microsoft Windows operating systems. VMware Converter can convert local

Feature	VMware Converter Starter	VMware Converter Enterprise
Description	Free product to convert physical machines into virtual machines	Enterprise-class product to manage and automate large-scale conversions
Support	To be purchased on a per-incident basis	Included in support for VirtualCenter Management Server
Target	Small-scale, single-server conversions	Large-scale server consolidation projects
	Quick backup/clones of a small number of servers	Centralized management of multiple simultaneous conversions
Hot cloning (convert physical machines while they are still running)	Included	Included
Cold cloning (using a boot CD)	Not applicable	Included
Multiple simultaneous conversions	Not applicable	Included
Local conversions	Included	Included
Remote conversions	Included for destinations under: ■ VMware Workstation ■ VMware Server ■ VMware Player ■ VMware GSX Server	Included for all destinations, including VMware ESX and ESXi
Licensing	No license required	License file is required for Enterprise features

Table 9-1.   A Comparison of VMware Converter Editions

and remote physical machines into virtual machines without any disruption or down-time (see Figure 9-7). This tool can also complete multiple conversions simultaneously through a centralized management console and a conversion wizard. Note that performing several conversions at once puts a heavy strain on the network.

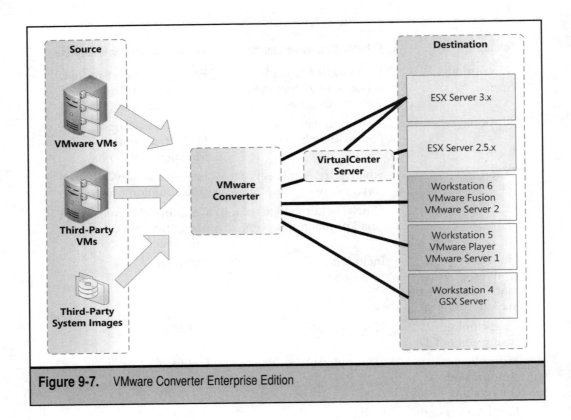

Figure 9-7. VMware Converter Enterprise Edition

Converter can also be used to convert other virtual machine formats, such as Microsoft Virtual PC and Microsoft Virtual Server, or backup images of physical machines, such as Symantec Backup Exec System Recovery or Norton Ghost 12, to VMware virtual machines. This process is called a virtual to virtual (V2V) conversion. Moreover, it can restore VMware Consolidated Backup (VCB) images of virtual machines to running virtual machines, or clone and backup physical machines to virtual machines as part of a disaster recovery plan.

NOTE For more information on VMware Converter, see www.vmware.com/products/converter/overview.html.

Work with PlateSpin PowerConvert

For more comprehensive environments that may even be using multiple hypervisors, look to tools such as PlateSpin PowerConvert. This tool can migrate and protect workloads over the network between physical servers, regardless of platform or virtual hosts and image archives. It can remotely decouple workloads from the underlying server hardware and stream them to and from any physical and virtual host with a simple drag-and-drop operation.

The move can be done in any direction between physical and virtual hosts: physical-to-virtual (P2V), virtual-to-physical (V2P), virtual to virtual (V2V), physical-to-physical (P2P), in and out of imaging format, and so on. This tool supports any virtual engines: Citrix, Microsoft, or VMware. It can convert Microsoft Windows server and client operating systems as well as Linux. It can even target image archives from Acronis or Symantec, or backup solutions such as Double-Take.

NOTE For more information on PowerConvert, see www.platespin.com/products/powerconvert/overview.aspx.

Rely on the Ultimate-P2V Plug-in for BartPE

BartPE is a free pre-execution environment that is commonly used by IT administrators and technicians to replace DOS when working with machines that have no operating system installed. Ultimate-P2V is a free plug-in created by Qui Hong, Chris Huss, and Mike Laverick. This plug-in allows you to clone a physical machine into a virtual machine and perform the system reconfiguration tasks required to make it bootable. It comes with two user guides. The first one explains the manual creation of the plug-ins and drivers, and the second gives you all the plug-ins and drivers you can download. Unzip these drivers and plug-ins to the BartPE installation and build a CD ready to work with Ultimate-P2V. This tool supports both VMware and Microsoft virtual disk formats as targets, letting you convert machines for use with VMware, Citrix, or Microsoft hypervisors.

NOTE For more information on Ultimate-P2V, see www.rtfm-ed.co.uk/?page_id=174.

Microsoft Conversion Tools

Microsoft also offers conversion tools. The Microsoft Virtual Server 2005 Migration Toolkit (VSMT) is a free download that allows you to convert physical machines to Microsoft's virtual machine format, VHD (virtual hard disks). But you can import this format into VMware Server or VMware Workstation since both tools can convert VHD files to the VMware virtual machine disks (VMDK) format.

In order to be able to use the VSMT, you need access to the Windows Server 2003 Automated Deployment Services (ADS), which is also free but can be run only on Windows Server 2003 Enterprise Edition. Of course, this tool is designed to convert Microsoft workloads into virtual machines.

NOTE For more information on the VSMT tool, see www.microsoft.com/technet/virtualserver/downloads/default.mspx.

Microsoft also supports P2V conversions with System Center Virtual Machine Manager (SCVMM) through a wizard interface (see Figure 9-8). However, for you to be able to perform conversions with SCVMM, you must also have access to the Windows Automated Installation Kit (WAIK) because SCVMM relies on Windows PE—included in the WAIK—to boot to an alternate OS before copying the server contents to a virtual hard drive. SCVMM conversion does not work with all versions of Windows. In addition, the machine must be reachable through DNS or you must use its IP address for SCVMM to locate it. Basically, the wizard locates the machine, gathers information about it, lets you rename the VM if need be, lets you configure virtual disk volumes, lets you select the target host and path for the new VM, and finally lets you assign additional properties to the VM. Note that SCVMM is not free and must be acquired as part of your virtual infrastructure.

NOTE For more information on P2V with SCVMM, go to http://technet.microsoft.com/en-us/library/bb963740.aspx.

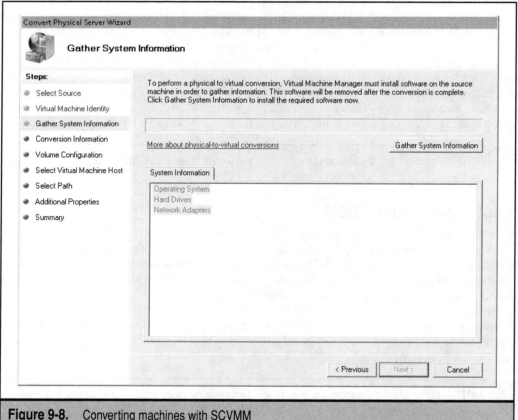

Figure 9-8. Converting machines with SCVMM

PROVISIONING BEST PRACTICES

As you can see, there are a lot of different methods and tools you can use for P2V conversions. One of the best is to create a new VM and either restore the contents of a physical server into the VM or, even better, migrate the VM's workload into the new machine. Migrating contents from a physical server to a virtual machine may be best because it lets you build pristine machines that are based on standard configurations and then load them with the appropriate workload. Several tools exist to migrate anything from file servers to Exchange workloads.

NOTE For a step-by-step guide outlining how to convert enterprise network workloads from the physical to the virtual through workload migrations, see *Windows Server 2008: The Complete Reference* by Ruest and Ruest (McGraw-Hill, 2008).

Consider your P2V strategy carefully because you do not want to convert machines that are not running at their very best. When the VMs are in production, they will be sharing resources. There is nothing worse than a VM that is improperly configured and begins to hog all of the host server's resources. You don't want to transfer problems from the physical to the virtual world. In addition, consider the following best practices before you perform a P2V conversion:

▼ Make sure you can convert to the target machine. For example, if you are running Microsoft Virtual Server, you cannot convert 64-bit machines.

■ Determine if you can perform an online migration before you begin. Some workloads do not lend themselves to online migrations. In some instances, you must perform the migration while the source (physical) server is offline.

■ Make sure the host systems include enough space and resource capacity for the conversion. When you convert a system, you must have space to host a running instance plus space to host the VM elsewhere in support of high availability.

■ Prepare the source server before you perform the conversion. Perform a checkdisk to identify bad sectors. Perform a defragmentation to speed up the conversion process. And use dynamic virtual disks to minimize space.

▲ Verify the target server after the migration. Perform a post P2V cleanup. This cleanup includes items such as removing all vendor agents, removing drivers that are not used in a virtualized environment, and removing any unnecessary devices.

Using these practices will help you build the best dynamic datacenter and perform error-free P2V conversions.

CHAPTER 10

Work with Desktop Virtualization

Desktops have been the bane of the administrator's existence ever since they first appeared on the market. Desktops are distributed points of access to system resources and as such must be standardized as much as possible to reduce potential issues. However, too many organizations do not lock down their desktops even if they do standardize them. Open desktops, or desktops where the end user is a local administrator, are impossible to manage since they change from the very moment they are deployed. In fact, they can be the cause for virtual machine (VM) sprawl, as users that are local administrators can easily install virtual machine software and begin creating their own VMs, causing even more problems for desktop administrators and technicians.

If desktops are not locked down, there can be no control and there always are a lot of issues. Yet it is possible to lock down systems and still allow them to work. One of our customers locked down their desktops with Windows NT in 1996. The result: They reduced desktop-related help desk calls by 800 percent! If it was possible for them to lock down the desktop with an archaic operating system like Windows NT, it is possible for everyone else to do it with either Windows XP or Windows Vista, both of which have massive built-in improvements for just this issue. Yet administrators today still don't bother even trying because it is just too much work. Users have become used to controlling everything on their desktop, and they just won't give up this freedom since they now consider it an acquired right.

The problem has always stemmed from the very name we use for desktops: personal computers (PC). Instead of personal computer, organizations should make a point of calling their systems *professional* computers. Using the term PC in its original sense gives every user the impression that the computer is theirs in the first place. Well, that is not the case. The computer, like the desk it sits on, belongs to the organization, not the individual, and because of this, it should be locked down and controlled centrally. The key to such a project is the proper negotiation of who owns what on the PC. Where do the user's rights begin and where do they end? What belongs to the corporation and what belongs to IT? Defining each of these property zones on the PC and making them very clear through massive communications with the user makes a locked-down project work.

WORK WITH A SYSTEM STACK

Another major problem of distributed PCs is the amount of applications to manage and deploy to them. While organizations range in size and number of users, they are usually rather constant in the number of applications they run on a per-user basis. In the worst case, they manage more than one application per user; in the best, they have less than one per user, but when you think that an organization with 1,000 users can have to manage 1,000 or more applications, you know and probably share their pain. One thousand applications to package, deploy, update, license, monitor, and support. That's a lot of work. What is worse is trying to get the applications to coexist properly on the same system. Now that is a challenge.

This is why you need to create a standard system stack. Using a system stack simplifies the way you construct PCs as well as the way you manage applications because it structures how computer systems are built from the ground up. Few organizations will ever need to install 200 or 500 products on the same computer. Using a model for system design will ensure that applications are categorized properly and regrouped into families that work together to provide the functionality required to fulfill specific job roles within your organization. For this reason, we have been promoting the Point of Access for Secure Services (PASS) model for more than 15 years (see Figure 10-1). Organizations relying on this system stack have a proven track record of proper system and application management.

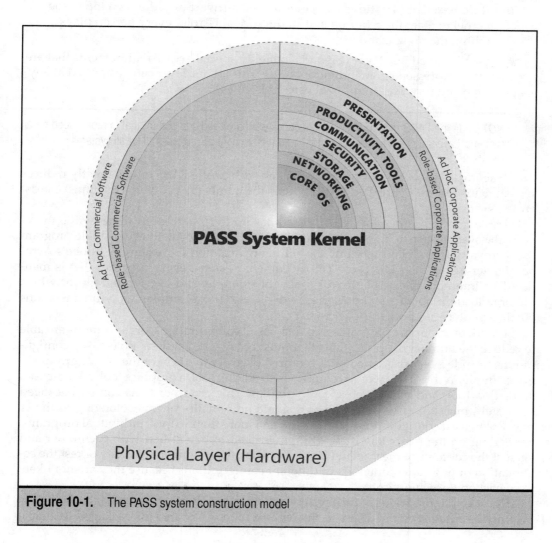

Figure 10-1. The PASS system construction model

This system stack is based on the construction of a computer system that responds to corporate needs in three ways:

▼ The **PASS system "kernel"** is designed to meet the needs of the average or generic user. It contains all of the software components required to perform basic office automation and collaboration tasks. In addition, it is divided into a series of layers similar to the Open Systems Interconnection (OSI) networking model. Like the OSI model, it uses seven layers to provide core corporate services. Because its functionalities are required by all personnel, this kernel is installed on all computer systems.

■ **Role-based applications and commercial software** are added on top of the kernel to meet the requirements of the special IT roles every person plays within the organization.

▲ Finally, an **ad hoc layer** responds to highly specialized IT requirements that are often expressed on an individual basis. This ad hoc layer can be applied at any time and traverses traditional vertical IT roles.

NOTE   In the PASS model, the kernel is considered a closed component that is reproduced on all systems. Layers that are located beyond the kernel are considered optional for all systems.

Constructing systems based on a system stack such as the PASS model greatly reduces system management efforts because it reduces the number of programs that must coexist on any system.

First, a good portion of systems, sometimes up to 50 percent or more, will only require the system kernel. Remember that the kernel should contain every single program that is royalty-free and required by the entire organization (for example, Adobe's Acrobat Reader or the new Microsoft XPS Document Reader); every program that is mandated by internal policies—antivirus tools, for example; and every program for which the organization obtains an enterprise-wide license (for example, many organizations obtain an enterprise license for Microsoft Office).

Second, by grouping programs into role-based configurations, organizations are able to reduce the number of applications that must coexist on a system. Role-based configurations include every program that is required by every member of the IT role grouping. For example, Web editors would require a Web editing tool, a graphics tool, a Web-based animation tool, and other Web-specific utilities. This group of tools can be packaged separately, but should be delivered as a single unit on all systems belonging to the IT role. Role-based configurations often include no more than 10 to 30 individual programs, depending on the role. Only these groupings need to be verified with each other and against the contents of the system kernel. There is no requirement to verify or test the cohabitation of programs contained in different configurations because they are not likely to coexist on the same system.

Third, ad hoc programs reduce system management efforts even further because they are only required by a few users in the organization. They are still packaged to enable centralized distribution and automated installation, but once again, they only require testing against both the kernel and the configurations they will coexist with; however, because of their ad hoc nature, they may coexist with all possible configurations.

Each application has a life cycle of its own that is independent of its location within the system construction model. The difference lies in the rate with which you apply life cycle activities to the application. Components of the kernel will have an accelerated life cycle rate—since they are located on all systems, they tend to evolve at a faster pace than other components because they are supported by corporate-wide funding—while products within the outer layers of the model will have slower life cycle rates, which will be funded by the groups that require them. Ideally, the rate of evolution of these products will be monitored by the subject matter experts or application sponsors your organization identifies for each non-kernel application.

NOTE   Application sponsors are responsible for several activities, four of which are subject matter expertise for the application; acceptance testing for application packaging; application monitoring, or watching for new versions or patches; and rationalization justifications, or justifying why the application should be in the overall software portfolio in the first place.

Using these strategies will reduce the overall issues you face when you build and manage distributed systems, but they will not reduce them all.

DESKTOP MANAGEMENT ISSUES

Systems weren't locked down and they were rarely standardized until organizations moved to Windows XP. But given that most organizations recently finished standardizing on Windows XP, are they ready to begin again just to lock down their systems? The answer is no. And this is the same answer for a move to Vista. Performing a massive distributed desktop deployment is a daunting task, mostly because each and every application that is managed in the organization needs to be revisited to verify compatibility, possibly upgrade it, repackage it, and then deploy it on the new operating system (OS). That's just a lot of work for very little profit. Just what is the status of Vista deployments today? Just what is a desktop anyway? The answers to these questions help understand the move to desktop virtualization or the creation of standard desktop images that are run inside virtualization software, not on physical hardware.

Vista State of the Union

Few organizations have deployed Vista to date, and despite Microsoft's best efforts, that is unlikely to change until Windows 7 is released. Yet, according to Microsoft, Vista is the fastest-selling operating system in the company's history.

▼   More than 100 million copies were sold by mid-2008.

■   In 2008, 2,500 applications were certified for Vista, compared to 254 in 2006.

- Ninety-eight of 100 of the best-selling applications are on Vista today.
- One hundred fifty enterprise-class applications are available to run on Vista.
- ▲ In 2008, 78,000 devices were certified for deployment with Vista.

Given these statistics, you would think that Vista is the most popular OS Microsoft has released in quite a while, but that does not seem to be the case—or at least that is what seems to come out of a survey performed by Kace Systems in mid-2008.

- ▼ Ninety percent of administrators are concerned about Vista, but only 13 percent had definite plans in regard to Vista deployment.
- ▲ Forty-four percent were considering another OS, but more than 50 percent of these were saying that system management issues with other operating systems were stopping them from doing so.

However, whether it is with Vista or any other desktop operating system, distributed desktops are hard to manage, period. They are distributed throughout the organization's office. They can be desktops or mobile systems. They can be inside the office or outside the office. And, of course, when users have administrative rights, you never know what the status of your OS is as soon as it leaves your desk.

NOTE If you are one of the very few who are actually deploying Vista, turn to two books for help: the free *Definitive Guide for Vista Migration* by Ruest and Ruest, which can be obtained at www.altiris .com/campaigns/vista/vista_ebook.aspx, and the *Deploying and Administering Windows Vista Bible* by Kelly, Ruest, and Ruest (Wiley, 2008).

The Anatomy of a Desktop

When it comes right down to it, a desktop has three core components (see Figure 10-2):

- ▼ The core OS layer, which includes the OS itself and any patches it requires. This covers the PASS model kernel without the productivity layer.
- The application layer, which is designed to provide added functionality to the end user. This includes the productivity application layer, the role-based layer, and the ad hoc layer of applications contained within the PASS model.
- ▲ The user data layer, which contains all of the user's data, including user-produced documents, presentations, and more, as well as application configuration settings and desktop personalizations.

These are the three key components of a desktop, and if you can abstract these layers from one another, you can significantly reduce desktop management overhead. This is where desktop virtualization products can help. Because the desktop is contained within a virtual machine, you gain all of the advantages and few of the issues that come with machine management when a machine is transformed from the physical to the virtual.

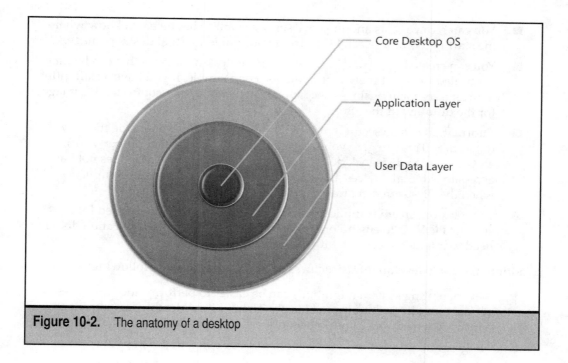

Core Desktop OS

Application Layer

User Data Layer

Figure 10-2. The anatomy of a desktop

MOVE TO DESKTOP VIRTUALIZATION

More and more organizations are turning to a virtual desktop to simplify the desktop management model. There are several reasons why desktop virtualization often makes more sense than managing physical desktops.

▼ First, you can provide centrally managed desktops to users on any endpoint device—desktops, thin clients, Web clients, and more.

■ Second, you can lock down virtual desktops because they are controlled centrally and, therefore, are easier to provision—just create one single desktop image and copy it as often as needed.

■ You spend less time on endpoints—the actual physical PCs—because they no longer need to be managed as tightly. After all, you only need these endpoints to provide a remote desktop connection to the virtual desktop.

■ You can provide service level agreements (SLAs) only for the central desktop and not for the endpoint itself. Users can be administrators on the endpoints, but locked down on the virtual desktop. This lets them do what they want to the endpoints, but remain controlled within the corporate PC.

- You can reduce costs and improve service stability because you know where the starting point for each PC is: from your golden virtual desktop image.

- You can create locked and encrypted virtual desktop images that can be time-controlled to meet timely requirements. For example, if you have a staff influx to meet a seasonal business need, you can generate time-controlled PC images for the duration of the effort.

- Information can be secured by keeping the virtual desktop inside the datacenter. This can give you more control over intellectual property (IP); all you have to do is lock down the image you create so that it does not have access to external devices. It is considerably easier to maintain compliance when the IP is stored centrally and does not leave the datacenter.

- ▲ Complex or sensitive applications can be encapsulated and isolated into specific PC VMs to ensure proper operation. This way, the application does not need to interact or coexist with any others.

In addition, virtual desktop infrastructures (VDIs) can support the following:

- ▼ New operating system migrations can be easier to perform since resources are only required centrally, not locally. There is considerably less impact on hardware refresh since endpoints only need remote desktop capabilities.

- Mergers and acquisitions are easier to manage since all desktops are centralized.

- Alternative workspaces can be provided on an as-needed basis to employees.

- You can use custom virtual desktops to provide contractors with secured, encrypted machines to work in your environment. This way, their own machines never need to connect to your network.

- ▲ Virtualized PCs can also support testing and development environments, as seen earlier in the construction of the virtual laboratory (see Chapter 6).

But what is a virtual desktop, and how do you make it operate?

NOTE   For more on the pros and cons of VDI, lookup VDI Makes Sense by Ruben Spruijt at www .virtuall.nl/articles/PublishedArticles/LanVisionVDIenglish.pdf.

Available Desktop Virtualization Products

There are several different types of desktop virtualization engines. They usually fit within two different virtualization models: local versus centralized. The local desktop virtualization model, often called Client-side Desktop Virtualization, focuses on using the endpoint's own resources for running the virtual desktop. Virtualization software is installed on the physical desktop, and a corporate virtual desktop image is provided to the end user. The end user then runs the virtual desktop on top of their physical desktop.

The second model is centralized and is often called Server-hosted Desktop Virtualization. Here, the virtual desktop will run on top of a production hypervisor and will be accessed remotely by the end user. All the end user requires is any device that supports a remote desktop connection. The virtual desktops run on top of host servers using shared storage to ensure desktop availability.

In addition, the local model supports both managed and unmanaged product usage. Managed product usage means that PC images are provided from a central authority and are centrally controlled. Unmanaged means that the user can create and run their own versions of virtual desktop images because the software they use supports this ability. Table 10-1 outlines a selection of the different products provided by various manufacturers for both local and centralized virtual desktops. Desktop virtualization is a market that is very vibrant and may well include several additional offerings by the time you read this. However, the vendors listed in Table 10-1 have been on the market for some time and offer a good variety of products.

As you can see, there are several different types of products and platforms for the control of virtual desktops, both locally and centrally.

Virtual Desktop Licensing

When working with virtual desktops, as when working with virtual servers, you must always consider licensing and make sure each user's desktop has an appropriate license, whether it is physical or virtual. If you're working with Windows, you will get a break from Microsoft because Microsoft has released the Windows Vista Enterprise Centralized Desktop (VECD) license. VECD provides unique licenses to run virtualized desktops, both locally and centrally. It also includes the following features:

▼   Unlimited installs of Windows Vista Enterprise or of a downgraded desktop OS on a server.

■   Virtual desktops are licensed by access device, whatever the device.

■   Each user can have up to four virtual instances running on the access device at one time.

■   Organizations can run either static or dynamically hosted desktop architectures.

▲   Virtual desktops can run on Microsoft or non-Microsoft infrastructures.

As the name implies, the license relies on the Enterprise Edition of Windows Vista, which by default requires an Enterprise Licensing Agreement with Microsoft.

Note that obtaining an Enterprise Agreement with Microsoft also gives you access to Microsoft's Software Assurance program, which includes several benefits for organizations, notably the Microsoft Desktop Optimization Pack (MDOP) for Software Assurance. MDOP includes several tools that are specifically designed to support organizations running Windows desktops. Tools such as Microsoft Application Virtualization, Microsoft Enterprise Desktop Virtualization, Advanced Group Policy Management, Asset Inventory Service, the Diagnostics and Recovery Toolset, and Desktop Error Monitoring are at the core of the MDOP package.

Manufacturer	Product	Managed	Unmanaged
VMware	VMware Player		Provides a free engine for running VMs on desktops
VMware	VMware Workstation		Provides the most advanced VM feature set from VMware
VMware	VMware Fusion		Runs VMs on Macs
VMware	VMware Ace	Provides secure, locked, and encrypted VMs to run on the user's desktop	
VMware	Virtual Desktop Infrastructure (VDI)	Centrally controlled desktop management and provisioning	
Microsoft	Virtual PC		Provides a free engine for running VMs on desktops
Microsoft	Kidaro	Provides secure, locked, and encrypted VMs to run on the user's desktop	
Citrix	XenDesktop	Centrally controlled desktop management and provisioning	
InstallFree	InstallFree Desktop	Centrally controlled desktop management and provisioning with offline capabilities	
Desktone	Virtual-D Platform	Centrally controlled desktop management and provisioning	
Quest Software/ Parallels	Bundled Virtual Desktop Infrastructure	Centrally controlled desktop management and provisioning	

Table 10-1.   Desktop Virtualization Technologies and Vendors

If you are running non-Windows desktops, you must work with your manufacturer to ensure you have appropriate licensing for each user and each instance of the desktop.

NOTE More information on VECD can be found at www.microsoft.com/virtualization/solution-product-vecd.mspx. More information on MDOP can be found at www.microsoft.com/windows/products/windowsvista/enterprise/benefits/tools.mspx.

Potential Desktop Virtualization Scenarios

There are different scenarios for desktop virtualization, as outlined in the sample list of products included in Table 10-1. Some are focused on running the virtual desktop through the user's desktop's capabilities; others are focused on running virtual desktops on server virtualization platforms in a central datacenter. In fact, you can rely on virtual desktops in four different models.

The first model focuses on locked and encrypted desktop virtual machines. Machines are centrally prepared and then encrypted to protect their content. They are distributed to end users on portable devices, such as USB memory sticks, DVDs, external USB disk drives, or other removable storage devices. Because they are encrypted, they are completely protected from tampering. The user must provide the appropriate unlocking key to launch the VM. Because it runs on the user's own desktop, this model provides you with the ability to create a standard locked-down VM that meets all corporate requirements (see Figure 10-3). Products that support this model include VMware ACE and Microsoft's Kidaro—renamed to Microsoft Enterprise Desktop Virtualization—virtual desktops. ACE runs on top of VMware Player since the user only needs the ability to execute the virtual machine, not create it. Kidaro relies on a locked-down version of Microsoft Virtual PC to execute machines. Both the Player and Virtual PC must be pre-deployed to the user's desktop or the user must have the administrative rights required to run the installation when they receive the virtual machine.

Figure 10-3. Locked and encrypted desktop virtual machines rely on desktop capabilities to run.

Unmanaged desktop virtualization stems from the use of tools such as VMware Workstation or Microsoft Virtual PC. Both tools are installed locally on the user's desktop and rely on the desktop's processing capabilities to run VMs. Users can also rely on other tools, such as VMware Server or Microsoft Virtual Server, but these tools also require the installation of a web server, which consumes even more resources from the PC. Therefore, it is best to use the desktop tools to maximize the PC's resources and run as many VMs as possible.

This form of virtualization is called unmanaged, though it could be managed. In unmanaged mode, the user installs their own version of the virtualization software and creates and runs his or her own virtual machines (see Figure 10-4). The most significant problem with this model is that the users who perform these installations are often not trained to do so. This can lead to rogue virtual machines that may run either unpatched and unprotected or, worse, unsupported operating systems that could provide an entry point for malicious users.

For example, one of our customers had a user who installed his own virtualization software and then installed an unpatched version of Linux within a virtual machine. What was worse was that the machine also had a series of open Transmission Control Protocol/Internet Protocol (TCP/IP) ports running e-mail services, which were broadcast on the Internet. Of course, the organization's firewall had open ports for their official e-mail service, which was protected, but the Linux machine's e-mail service was wide open. Because of this, it was taken over by spammers who used it as an e-mail relay. So much e-mail was sent through this server that an Internet service provider's (ISP) entire e-mail service was brought down. The organization only learned of the rogue Linux machine when the ISP contacted them to find out just what was going on. Needless to say, today, the organization's IT personnel keep a close eye on what goes in and out of their firewalls. They have also instigated a virtual machine program for end users. They prepare the VMs and then provide them as an IT service to the users who require them.

As you can see, it is easy to face VM sprawl when users are allowed to install their own virtualization software and create their own virtual machines. This is another reason why IT should have a formal machine creation program for any user that requires it.

Figure 10-4.   Unmanaged desktop virtualization can lead to issues within the organization.

For example, using the virtual laboratory outlined in Chapter 6 would help reduce the chance of VM sprawl in your organization because you are providing VMs as an official IT service.

The third model, stateful virtual desktops, focuses on centrally managed desktops that are tied to each specific user. In this model, each user connects to his or her own particular desktop virtual machine(s). The VMs are stored in a central shared storage container, much as they are when you virtualize server software. Host servers running production hypervisors manage all of the desktop virtual machines and make sure they are highly available. This model tends to require a significant amount of storage since each VM can easily take up dozens of megabytes or more. Users rely on a remote desktop connection to connect to their VM PCs (see Figure 10-5).

The last model, stateless virtual desktops, focuses on the generation of virtual machines on an as-needed basis. Machines can either be generated when the user connects or they can be pre-generated and linked to a user when a connection request occurs. The advantage of this model is that the machines are completely volatile and built on the fly. The core desktop image is generated and then, when the user is identified during the connection, the applications they require are applied to the desktop image (see Figure 10-6). The user's data and preferences are also applied at logon. While you may think that this process is time-consuming and can cause user dissatisfaction, it is not actually the case. The ideal volatile desktop will also rely on application virtualization to profile applications only when the user actually requests them. And, because everything occurs on a back-end storage area network, applications and user profiles are provided through high-speed disk-to-disk exchanges, which are practically transparent to users, even multiple users.

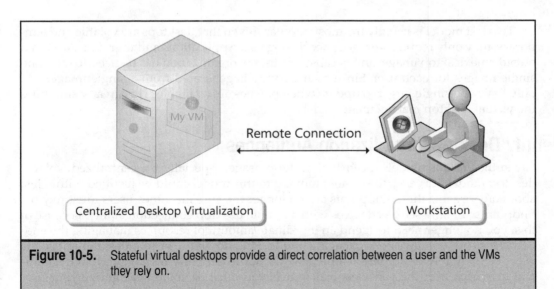

Remote Connection

Centralized Desktop Virtualization

Workstation

Figure 10-5.   Stateful virtual desktops provide a direct correlation between a user and the VMs they rely on.

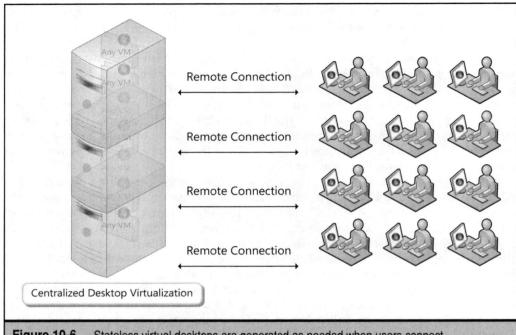

Remote Connection

Remote Connection

Remote Connection

Remote Connection

Centralized Desktop Virtualization

Figure 10-6.   Stateless virtual desktops are generated as needed when users connect.

This last model is usually the most popular. Given that desktops are volatile and temporary, they only require storage space during use. Applications and user data are stored outside the desktop image, and because of this, the organization has no need to maintain single images for each user. Since each desktop is generated from a single image, you only have one single target to update when patches are available. This greatly simplifies the virtual desktop management model.

Identify Desktop Virtualization Audiences

Given the various models for virtual desktop usage, especially the centralized, volatile desktop model, it is easy to see how moving to this model could be justified within just about any organization. Endpoints are no longer the core machines users must rely on. Endpoints are only seen as devices with a remote desktop connection ability. Because of this, you no longer need to spend an inordinate amount of resources managing the endpoint. Instead, you focus on managing and locking down the virtual desktop image the users actually rely on to perform their work. But to properly manage virtual desktops and give each user the very best experience, you must be able to categorize your user bases and assign the appropriate solution to each target user audience. There are three audience types you will need to work with:

▼ The basic productivity worker will require fewer application types. Normally, they will require nothing more than the kernel of a system constructed on the PASS model mentioned earlier. They will have intermittent usage and will be primarily text-based. They will have limited mouse usage and limited printing requirements. This desktop user type will log in at distributed times and will create a variable workload on centralized host servers. This worker type is ideal for the standard virtualized desktop.

■ The knowledge worker will require a more powerful centralized desktop because they tend to run multiple business and productivity applications at the same time. They use applications that are richer in graphics and therefore require more memory per user. Knowledge workers also tend to be logged in at the same time. If your PASS system kernel is properly designed, it should also meet the requirements for most knowledge workers. This means that you must include at least basic graphics tools along with the productivity suites within the kernel. The virtual desktop they use will require a richer graphical experience and more resources per VM.

▲ The rich desktop user will most likely run multiple computer- and graphics-intensive applications at the same time. Engineers or traders are examples of this type of user. They often require specialized engineering or trading peripherals and will often require multiple displays connected at the same time. They will also require high-end graphics resolutions, something most host servers lack. For this reason, it is often best to solve these users' requirements with blade PCs—PCs that are centrally hosted in datacenters in blade enclosures—instead of virtual desktops, though virtual desktops are improving in capability. For example, Microsoft acquired Calisto Technologies in 2008. Calisto specializes in improving the remote desktop experience for end users through 3-D acceleration. This technology will be embedded in Windows, which should improve the remote desktop connection users experience when they connect to virtual desktops. In addition, VMware is working with Teradici and Wyse to improve remote protocol support in its products. In these cases, the blade PC may no longer be required.

As you can see, each user type requires a different centralized solution. However, as pointed out earlier, centralizing the desktop is not always the best solution. Table 10-2 describes the different solutions that are available for reducing the cost of distributed desktop computing. It lists several solutions, many of which have already been discussed, but it also includes technologies such as Presentation Virtualization, which is really server-based computing, and PC Blades. It also outlines the impact each solution has on the end-user experience.

Rely on this table to determine which solution best fits your own users. Categorize them within the three core user types and then identify the solution you need to apply to

Feature	Free VM Engine	Encrypted Local VM	Advanced Local VM Engine	Presentation Virtualization	Centralized Virtual Desktops	PC Blades
Graphics	Fair	Fair	Fair	Fair	Good	Better
Video	Fair	Fair	Fair	Fair	Fair	Better
Performance	Average	Average	Average	Average	Better	Best
Redundancy	Poor	Poor	Poor	Good	Best	Good
Printing	Good	Good	Good	Fair	Good	Good
USB	Fair	Fair	Better	Fair	Fair	Best
Active Directory Integration	Good	Good	Good	Good	Good	Good
Application Compatibility	Good	Good	Best	Average	Best	Best
Management	Poor	Better	Poor	Average	Best	Best
Deployment	Poor	Good	Poor	Average	Best	Good

Table 10-2.   Comparing Distributed Versus Centralized Desktop Virtualization

their needs. To do so, you will need to properly understand the various desktop virtualization technologies and determine which will best fit the needs of both your organization and your user base.

CENTRALIZED DESKTOP VIRTUALIZATION INFRASTRUCTURES

When you run a desktop virtualization infrastructure (VDI), you need to determine which of the three supported models will best fit your organization's requirements. These three models include:

▼ **Persistent or assigned desktops**   The desktop is tied to one single user and the same desktop is provided to the user each time he or she logs on. As mentioned earlier, this model requires considerable central storage space. Use this model if you have only a few users or if storage space is not a concern in your organization.

- **Nonpersistent, volatile, or pooled desktops**   A new, generic desktop is provided to the user each time he or she logs on to the infrastructure. Applications and user profile data are provided at logon to customize the shared image to meet this user's particular requirements. This model requires considerably less storage because each user's environment is generated from one central image. All of the content that is specific to a particular user is stored in a differencing file. A database containing the user's specific settings is used to customize the image and generate custom content, such as security identifiers (SID) for the machine, machine name, and other data that must be unique in an Active Directory environment.

▲ **Persistent clone desktop**   A personalizable clone is generated the first time a user logs on; from that point on, the user relies on that clone each time he or she logs back on. This model only requires storage once the user has logged on to generate the custom desktop image.

Each model has its own benefits and each has its own drawbacks, but the volatile desktop tends to be the most popular because of its minimal storage requirements and its reduced update management overhead. However, the key to centralized desktop virtualization is the notion of a desktop broker or a software component that matches the user to a particular virtual machine—volatile or persistent—at logon. The broker makes it possible for the IT administrator to dynamically assign custom settings to each user. Without this broker, IT administrators either need to manage this assignment manually or have users connect to specific machine names or IP addresses. Without this broker, there can be no concept of volatile virtual desktops.

Several vendors provide solutions for centralized desktop virtualization, or VDI as it is commonly called. The three main providers on the market for central desktop virtualization are the same as those for server virtualization. They include VMware, Microsoft, and Citrix. VMware was the first organization to provide a VDI solution—or rather, their customers were when they started using VMware's server virtualization technologies to host desktops. After seeing the potential market for centralizing desktops, VMware created the VDI solution by basically linking its server virtualization engine with a custom desktop broker.

Citrix also created a VDI solution, the XenDesktop, by linking all of its virtualization solutions together. XenDesktop relies on the XenServer virtualization engine as well as Citrix's presentation and application virtualization solution: XenApp. It also uses Citrix's Independent Computing Architecture (ICA) client to improve the end user's remote desktop experience. In addition, XenDesktop can work with both VMware and Microsoft hypervisors which makes it a good choice no matter which hypervisor you run. For example, Microsoft does not have its own desktop broker. Therefore, it relies on the Citrix XenDesktop solution, but this time, using the Windows Server 2008 Hyper-V virtualization engine as the back-end.

As mentioned earlier, there are also other companies that offer desktop brokers and therefore desktop virtualization solutions. These include InstallFree, Quest, and Desktone.

Each solution has its own strengths. You must select carefully before you implement a virtual desktop solution.

VMware Virtual Desktop Manager

Most organizations run Windows as their desktop infrastructure. This is changing, but because of this, most VDI solutions are designed to link to and integrate with Windows technologies. This is the case with VMware's Virtual Desktop Manager (VDM). VMware VDM, which is also called VMware View, is a solution that provides virtual desktop provisioning on a one-to-one basis with users. It creates one virtual machine image per user. These VMs can either be persistent or volatile. At the time of writing, VDM was the most popular centralized virtual desktop solution, with over 20,000 customers worldwide relying on it. According to VMware, these customers included 100 percent of the Fortune 100 companies.

VDM includes the following features and components:

▼ The virtualization back-end is provided by VMware's Virtual Infrastructure (VI) with ESX Server or ESXi. If high availability is required for the virtual desktops, Virtual Infrastructure is required to provide both scalability and high availability. It also provides policy-based resource management, letting the system move virtual machines as needed to appropriate hosts to provide them with required resources.

■ Back-end management is performed through VirtualCenter, which is the same as when you run server virtualization.

■ VDM provides direct integration with Microsoft's Active Directory (AD) for account provisioning. Note that AD integration is not optional. In order to run VDI, you must have an existing AD designed with a proper structure. Note that no schema changes are required to integrate VDI with your AD.

■ VDM can rely on existing user accounts and policies to assign desktop VMs to users. If two-factor authentication is required, you can integrate VDM with RSA SecurID. Linking VDM with AD provides a single-sign-on solution, which makes VDM access by end users much simpler. They just launch the VDM client and log into AD to gain access to their own particular VM.

■ VMware's desktop broker is the Virtual Desktop Manager, which provides desktop provisioning to end users. One of its most powerful features is its ability to act as a broker to relink users to existing virtual desktops each time the user reconnects. Management of the VDM is performed through a web interface. Using this interface, administrators can assign and deploy desktops from one central location. They can also control logoff policies and provisioning rules.

■ VDM offers an option to deploy virtual desktop VMs within perimeter networks, letting remote and travelling users access their desktop VM.

■ VDM relies on a variety of common endpoints to connect to their VDM VM. These endpoints include computers running Windows operating systems—note that a special client is required; thin client devices; or browsers running on either Windows, Linux, or Macintosh operating systems.

■ Persistent desktops in VDM are generated from a common template. Users must be manually associated with a virtual desktop by an administrator through the VDM interface. This way, each user gets a dedicated desktop. Users are connected to the same desktop on each subsequent connection.

▲ Volatile desktops in VDM are also generated from a common template; however, individual isolated desktops are returned to the desktop VM pool after each use because each desktop reverts to its predetermined state for future use at logoff. If you want to retain user settings, you must store them outside of the desktop VM image.

As you can see, the overall VDM solution is made up of several moving parts (see Figure 10-7), but it can provide a powerful infrastructure for centralized virtual desktops.

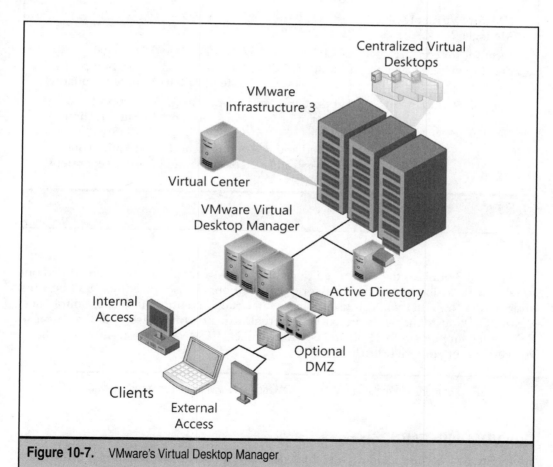

Figure 10-7.   VMware's Virtual Desktop Manager

Contents	VMware VDM Starter Kit	VMware VDM Bundle	VMware Virtual Desktop Manager
VMware Infrastructure 3 Enterprise Edition for VDM	X	X	
VMware VirtualCenter	X VirtualCenter Foundation (limited to three hosts)	X VirtualCenter Management Server	
VMware Virtual Desktop Manager 2	X	X	X
Licenses for concurrent desktop virtual machines	10 (one starter kit per customer)	100 (add-on packs of ten available)	100 (add-on packs of ten available)
Support Requirements	Support and Subscription (SnS) required and sold separately	Support and Subscription (SnS) required and sold separately	Support and Subscription (SnS) required and sold separately

Table 10-3. VMware VDM Editions and Features

Table 10-3 outlines the various editions of VDI VMware makes available. If you opt to rely on VDM for centralized desktop virtualization, choose the edition that best fits your needs. Note that you can use a starter kit, obtain an entire bundle, or simply add Virtual Desktop Manager to an existing Virtual Infrastructure. Also note that because ESX Server supports both 32-bit and 64-bit machines, VDM will let you run either x86 or x64 versions of your favorite desktop.

NOTE For more information on VMware VDM, go to www.vmware.com/products/vdi.

Run VDM with EMC Celerra

As mentioned earlier, running a virtual desktop infrastructure requires a centralized shared storage solution. By default, when you run VDM with shared storage, it generates one VM per user, eating up considerable space. However, EMC, VMware's parent company, offers a special storage engine called Celerra that offers special features, which include, among other things, the ability to vastly reduce the amount of storage required by virtual desktop images. Using the Celerra SnapSure feature allows you to generate copies of the virtual desktop images by using differential files that stem from the original disk image. Each differential file then takes up a fraction of the space required for normal images. This storage method is considerably more efficient than traditional storage methods.

Since you have to use shared storage to run VDM because it requires VMware's Virtual Infrastructure, and shared storage is a requirement to run VI, you should seriously consider using a technology such as EMC's Celerra as the storage container, or at least use a storage container that includes features similar to the SnapSure feature. Otherwise, you will end up storing multigigabyte files for each virtual desktop image. SnapSure can save considerable costs in disk space and, therefore, disk drives, yet provide you with all of the functionality required to make VDM operate correctly.

NOTE Remember that by using NetApp storage, you automatically gain access to this feature since NetApp has the ability to deduplicate live storage contents. Because of this, NetApp storage containers reduce storage costs by up to 40 percent when storing virtual machines using the same operating system.

VMware View

In September 2008, VMware announced a new vision for centralized desktop virtualization, basically transforming the traditional VDM offering into one that let users link to a single central VM wherever they are, even if they may be offline. VMware View is a portfolio of tools that work together to give users a single view of all their applications and data in a standard desktop that can be accessed from any device or location and can even be carried around offline.

VMware was well positioned to make this a reality in the following months since they were the first to deliver a VDI. VMware developed the Virtual Desktop Manager (VDM) to let administrators create desktop virtual machines (DVMs) and assign them to users through Active Directory. Despite the fact that they were first to market with VDI, VMware's product lagged behind others in some key areas. For example, Citrix's XenDesktop has the ability to create desktop virtual machines from one single read-only core VM. All other machines are managed as differential files tied to this VM. When you consider that each Desktop Virtual Machine (DVM) can easily be as large as 10GB in size, you quickly realize the benefits XenDesktop has over VDM, where each machine takes up its own space. Because of this feature, XenDesktop can easily save upwards of 50 percent or more of all disk space required to host DVMs—and that's not the only feature it has over VDM. However VMware's desktop-anywhere vision goes beyond differential files for each DVM. It also includes the ability to run the DVM offline, something that few, if any, products offer today. Currently, centralized desktop virtualization is plagued with the same failings as server-based computing such as Terminal Services: You have to be connected to access the service. To do this, VMware has brought to bear its considerable lineup of desktop virtualization tools and linked them with VDM to create one seamless

DVM experience for users. VMware View allows users to rely on any device—standard desktop or laptop running Windows or the Macintosh OS, Web browser, public computer, thin computing device, or even a mobile phone such as the iPhone—to access their DVM. In addition, users are able to carry their DVM on transportable devices, such as USB memory sticks, or run them offline on their laptops. Better yet, users are able to make offline modifications within their DVM and have them automatically synchronized with their centralized DVM once they reconnect.

VMware has been maintaining a full line of desktop virtualization products, and because of this had the ability to turn dream into reality in a relatively short time. For VMware View to work as advertised, VMware had to come up with several different innovations and link them with their existing desktop virtualization products (see Figure 10-8).

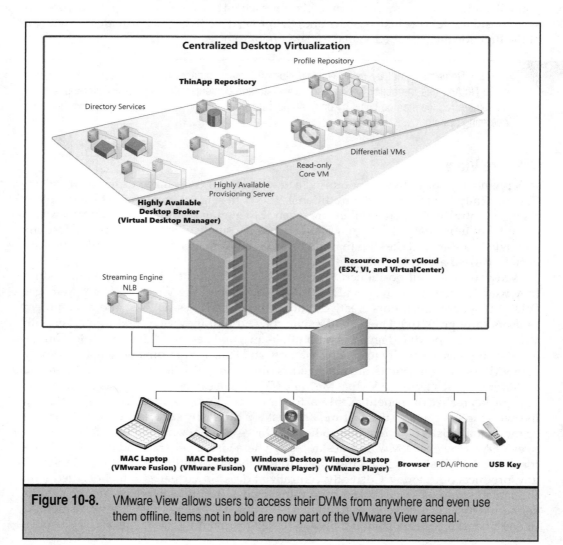

Figure 10-8.   VMware View allows users to access their DVMs from anywhere and even use them offline. Items not in bold are now part of the VMware View arsenal.

First, VMware needed the tools to support DVM access from anywhere; however, it already had several of them. VMware's Virtual Desktop Infrastructure includes the Virtual Desktop Manager, which is the DVM broker and assigns a DVM to each user. VMware Workstation is VMware's flagship desktop virtualization engine and through its Unity feature can expose applications contained within desktop virtual machines without exposing the virtual desktop itself. This provides a seamless interaction to users and makes it much easier for them to work with virtual machines. However, VMware relied on VMware Player, a free virtual machine-execution engine, to run offline DVMs on Windows desktops, through web browsers, or on Windows laptops. VMware ACE already lets users carry their DVMs on USB sticks. VMware Fusion lets you run DVMs on the Macintosh OS. So VMware was good to go at this level.

Second, VMware needed to improve DVM graphics on endpoint devices. For this, VMware has announced that it will be working with manufacturer Teradici to further develop Teradici's PC-over-IP protocol to replace the default Remote Desktop Protocol (RDP) built into Windows and improve graphics control. Once again, Citrix is one up on VMware here with its Independent Computing Architecture (ICA), a remote protocol that has vast improvements over Microsoft's RDP. Microsoft is also working to improve graphics performance in RDP.

Despite this, VMware is now well positioned to regain mastery over VDI through VMware View through the addition of several components.

▼   The ability to run a DVM on a personal digital assistant (PDA), such as the iPhone or even Windows Mobile devices. This will require a new virtual machine player or VMware's planned custom remote desktop protocol.

■   The integration of a better remote desktop protocol, which will have to be installed as a core utility within desktops and remote devices. VMware has announced that it is working with Teradici to integrate its PC-over-IP protocol to meet this need, but that is not its only improvement at this level. VMware is also working with Wyse Technology—makers of thin clients—to license Wyse's TCX-MMR software for improved remote multimedia experience and to increase multidisplay support. Both software products run on the endpoint device and, therefore, have no impact on back-end server performance while improving the end-user experience. These software products will be available for both thin clients and full-fledged PCs. Overall, VMware will provide multiprotocol support, letting users choose among the default Microsoft RDP, Teradici's PC-over-IP, the Wyse products, or even other protocols from HP and Sun.

■   The ability to run offline desktops allows users to check out a virtual desktop from the central datacenter store and run it offline to finally check it back in when they reconnect to the datacenter.

- The capability to stream DVMs to offline containers such as laptops. Also, the ability to stream virtual applications into volatile desktops. Streaming desktops and applications is like streaming videos: You only need a core amount of information—sometimes less than 10 percent—to be able to begin using the tool, saving bandwidth and supporting the application-on-demand concept. VMware now has Offline Desktop to do this. Symantec, who also offers application virtualization through its Software Virtualization Solution (SVS) Professional offering, has one of the best streaming engines on the market through its acquisition of AppStream. AppStream can stream desktops as well as applications, but Symantec is not using this component in its offering as yet.

- The ability to create differential DVMs from one central read-only DVM image and provision them as needed based on user demand. Right now, XenDesktop can prepopulate volatile DVMs in anticipation of user demand. For example, if you have 500 users logging in between 8 and 9 A.M., XenDesktop can ensure that all of the required DVMs are created beforehand to increase system response to user demands. VMware has the broker with VDM, and now uses VMware Composer as a differential engine and provisioning tool.

▲ The ability to virtualize user profiles to support volatile desktops and capture user changes. However, this can be done with basic Windows technologies, such as the roaming profile and folder redirection, so the need for a third-party tool is not pressing. Microsoft was the first to invent profile virtualization by embedding this capability in Windows, a capability that provides offline support through data caching in the local device. With desktop virtualization, profile virtualization takes on new meaning and becomes a core part of any VDI solution.

VMware shipped View within three months of making its initial announcement of the product. Having hundreds or even thousands of DVMs running from one single core image; having only one single image to update and modify when needed; letting you access this image from anywhere at any time; capturing and protecting all of your changes, online and offline; and basically tying the user to one single desktop image is the right direction for centralized desktop virtualization. View is available in two versions. Enterprise edition provides functionality similar to VDM. The Premier edition includes all of the tools that are required in a true DVM solution.

NOTE To view a video of VDM in action, go to http://blogs.vmware.com/vmtn/2008/02/bring-on-the-vd.html.

Citrix XenDesktop

As mentioned earlier, Citrix also offers a centralized desktop virtualization solution, the XenDesktop. Citrix XenDesktop is a solution that provides virtual desktop provisioning on an as-needed basis to users. By default, it relies on one single base image, very much like the combination of VMware VDI with the EMC Celerra storage area network or VMware View. All desktops are provisioned from a single image through software and will run from the core image, regardless of the shared storage container you use. This core image is not duplicated at any time. This feature alone can save up to 40 percent of storage space, a considerable savings, which often offsets the original cost of a XenDesktop solution.

XenDesktop was formed by combining the features of the XenServer server virtualization engine with those of Citrix's XenApp delivery mechanism, as well as the feature set from an acquisition, that of Ardence. Ardence provides the technology required to generate differential files from the core desktop image. This technology now allows XenDesktop to rely on a database to automatically redirect registry queries for critical PC items, such as computer name, Active Directory domain relative ID (RID), and so on. This method lets XenDesktop manage hundreds or even thousands of differential images based on one single core image.

This is a critical feature because normally, you need to customize each PC image through the System Preparation Tool (SysPrep.exe). SysPrep will automatically depersonalize a Windows PC image so that it may be reproduced as many times as required. When the PC image is opened, the SysPrep process automatically repersonalizes the image, giving it the right SID, RID, computer name, and so on. When you use the XenDesktop, you do not need to perform this task; however, you do need to create a reference computer image and prepare it according to your organizational standards. Then, instead of depersonalizing the image through SysPrep to generate a source image, you create a second, read-only copy of your golden image. This second copy then becomes the core image used by XenDesktop. It is maintained in read-only mode. User changes and customizations are captured in the differential file and either discarded when the user logs off (stateless PC image), or saved to a personal user file (stateful PC image). Differential files are block-level files that capture only the changes made to the core image.

This is one of the most impressive features of the XenDesktop. However, because XenDesktop is from Citrix and Citrix has years of experience in remote Windows computing, XenDesktop also provides improvements in terms of remote desktop delivery because it relies on Citrix's ICA protocol instead of Microsoft's RDP. ICA provides a considerable improvement, especially in terms of graphics rendering, over RDP, which makes the end-user experience richer and more lifelike. This set of technologies is called SpeedScreen in XenDesktop.

NOTE   To view the difference between the RDP and the ICA experience, see the demonstration on YouTube at www.youtube.com/watch?v=_RMTM7vaMnl.

Traditionally, XenDesktop will require a XenServer back-end, the XenDesktop—which acts as the desktop delivery controller or the desktop image provisioning engine—and the XenApp delivery server to provide remote desktop connectivity to the desktop images through the ICA protocol (see Figure 10-9). However, because XenDesktop was formed partly from the Ardence acquisition and Ardence supported VMware ESX Server first, it also supports a full VMware back-end. In addition, because of its strong partnership with Microsoft, XenDesktop has been adapted to support a Windows Server 2008 Hyper-V back-end. This means that you can use the XenDesktop solution with any of the major server virtualization engines. This is a boon for most every organization because early adopters of server virtualization will already have both Citrix Presentation Server (now named XenApp) and technologies like VMware ESX Server or Microsoft Virtual Server already in place. Since they already have a server virtualization infrastructure and they already own Citrix products, adding XenDesktop is often a low-cost solution.

XenDesktop comes in several editions, each including its own feature set. Table 10-4 outlines each of these editions and the feature set it includes. As you can see, because Citrix has a lot of experience in presentation virtualization (PresentV), many of its PresentV features are included in each edition of XenDesktop. One edition even includes Citrix EasyCall—a feature that integrates telephone communications with any application, and stems from the original Presentation Server before Citrix's acquisition of XenSource and Ardence.

XenDesktops can either be persistent or pooled. Persistent desktops retain the differential information generated by each user. The user is then connected to this particular differential file each time he or she reconnects. Pooled images are stateless images that are reset to a standard state each time a user logs off. Obviously, pooled images take up less storage space. Each image mode, persistent versus pooled, applies to a different user type. Persistent images would most likely apply to permanent users, while pooled images are best for temporary or task-based employees who do not need to retain customizations and preferences. Pooled or persistent images can either be x86 or x64 versions of the desktop OS since all of the supported virtualization engines—VMware ESX Server, Citrix XenServer, or Microsoft Hyper-V—support both 32-bit and 64-bit VMs.

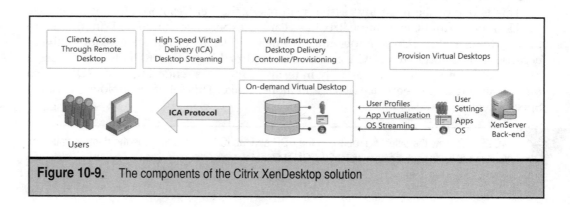

Figure 10-9. The components of the Citrix XenDesktop solution

Feature	Express (ten users)	Standard	Advanced	Enterprise	Platinum
Blade PC Support	X	X	X	X	X
Broad Hypervisor Support	X	X	X	X	X
Citrix-Ready Products	X	X	X	X	X
Desktop Appliance	X	X	X	X	X
Desktop Assignment	X	X	X	X	X
Heterogeneous Client Support	X	X	X	X	X
Instant On	X	X	X	X	X
Session Management	X	X	X	X	X
Session Reliability	X	X	X	X	X
SpeedScreen	X	X	X	X	X
Universal Printer Driver	X	X	X	X	X
Virtual Machine Infrastructure	X	X	X	X	X
High Availability/ Failover		X	X	X	X
Secure Remote Access		X	X	X	X
Desktop Image Management			X	X	X
Desktop Storage Optimization			X	X	X
On-Demand Desktop			X	X	X
On-Demand Image Provisioning			X	X	X
Integrated App Delivery				X	X
Desktop Performance Monitoring					X
Desktop Support					X
EasyCall					X
Wide Area Network Optimization					X

Table 10-4.   Citrix XenDesktop Editions and Feature Sets

Since each image is based on a central core desktop and is generated at logon, you might think that it takes some time for the image to build when a user first tries to activate it by logging on. It will indeed take some time, especially if thousands of users log on at the same time, even though the differential file is a small file. However, Citrix solves this problem through image pre-provisioning. XenDesktop allows administrators to set image generation policies that will pre-populate images *before* users begin to log on. For example, take the following scenario. Organization A has three main offices. Office A is in New York City and contains 500 users. Office B is in Salt Lake City and contains 200 users. Office C is in San Francisco and contains 400 users. Each morning, the users log on between 7:00 and 9:00 A.M.; however, because each office is in a different time zone, the load on the back-end host servers is somewhat attenuated.

By using pre-population policies, the administrators at Organization A have XenDesktop generate images ahead of time before users begin to log on. The policy generates 500 machines in New York City at 6:30 A.M. Eastern time, 200 machines at 6:30 A.M. Mountain time (two hours later), and 400 machines at 6:30 A.M. Pacific Time (one hour later). While this scenario is a bit unrealistic because no one starts work at 7:00 A.M. on the West Coast, it does illustrate the power of pre-provisioning with XenDesktop policies. And through XenDesktop's wide area network (WAN) acceleration features, all of the desktops can reside in the NYC datacenter and yet all users can have a rich virtual desktop experience.

NOTE For more information on the XenDesktop, go to www.citrix.com/english/ps2/products/product.asp?contentID=163057. For a video comparing VMware VDI with Citrix XenDesktop, go to www.youtube.com/watch?v=J_i_EpZHMLc&feature=related.

Other Technologies

As mentioned earlier, Citrix and VMware are not the only providers of centralized desktop virtualization products. InstallFree, Quest, and Desktone also offer similar products. Of the three, only InstallFree offers a technology that manages its own PC images. Quest and Desktone offer products that are really only front-ends to other virtualization technologies.

The InstallFree Desktop

InstallFree uses a custom engine that generates a mini-desktop which runs based on the resources of the local machine. This technology relies on InstallFree's application virtualization engine, but instead of generating applications that are decoupled from the operating system, these applications are encapsulated inside the mini-desktop and run as if they were a real desktop. InstallFree Virtual (IFV) desktops are controlled centrally through Active Directory, but because they are processed locally, relying on the PC's own resources, they are available both online and offline. And because they are based on the IFV application virtualization engine, they are not real virtual machines and do not require a virtualization engine on the back-end. Machines can run either x86 or x64 versions of Windows; however, in order to run an x64 version, the operating system on the host or physical desktop must be an x64 OS.

The InstallFree application virtualization engine is an executable that can be loaded on any system, whether or not you have administrative rights, because it runs in user mode on the host OS, not kernel mode. This means you can carry a virtual desktop on a portable USB memory stick and plug it into almost any PC, even a locked-down public PC. This gives you a lot of flexibility, both inside and outside the organization. Even though they are not based on a traditional virtualization engine, IFV desktop images appear and operate as traditional PC images. They can be localized, personalized, and even encrypted for content protection.

User data is stored in an encrypted file that is external to the desktop so that it can be protected at all times. Applications must be virtualized using the IFV engine and must be prepared in advance. InstallFree Desktop is the only solution that currently provides offline support for virtual desktops, but its preparation requires the full use of the Install-Free solution. More on this topic will be discussed in the following chapter as we discuss the virtualization of applications. However, if you need both online and offline access to virtual desktops, perhaps InstallFree is the solution that best meets your needs.

NOTE For more information on the InstallFree Desktop, go to www.installfree.com/pageload .aspx?page=products_InstallFree_Desktop.html.

The Desktone Desktop As A Service

Desktone is unique in that they offer virtual desktop provisioning for both enterprise and service providers, hence the name Desktop As A Service (DAAS). Enterprise providers manage their own internal virtual desktops, but do not need to have access to a full datacenter infrastructure because the entire server virtualization infrastructure is managed offsite in a datacenter owned and managed by a desktop service provider (DSP) running DAAS. This gives organizations of all sizes access to virtual desktops and can allow them to reduce their costs since they do not need to own the bits that support desktop virtualization.

DAAS relies on two key components: the Virtual-D Platform and the Desktone Access Fabric. The Access Fabric is the desktop broker that connects users with their own particular desktop. It is designed to deliver a "best-fit" desktop to each user based on policies, user entitlements, access point, and the available resources in the datacenter. This infrastructure links to your own existing Active Directory and gives you full control over the distribution and allocation of the desktops.

The back-end is completely removed from your own datacenter and is hosted in the DSP's center. This makes it easier to deploy and run virtual desktop infrastructures because you do not need to implement the server virtualization components—host servers, shared storage, and more—that are required to host the virtual desktop images. This is a novel approach and may well fit your needs if you do not want to and have not implemented server virtualization already.

According to Desktone, their solution is simpler to implement because you do not need to worry about the back-end host environment. You don't even need to know on which virtualization engine it is running. All you need to do is hook up with a DSP and begin to virtualize your desktops. At the time of this writing, Desktone had two DSP partners: IBM and HP. More will surely come in time.

If you want to run VDI but don't want the hassle of implementing the host server infrastructure, Desktone may well be the best solution for you.

NOTE   For more information on the Desktone DAAS, go to www.desktone.com.

The Quest Provision Networks Virtual Access Suite

Quest Software also offers a VDI tool through the acquisition of Provision Networks. The new Quest Virtual Access Suite (VAS) is a desktop broker that offers a VDI that is independent of the back-end server virtualization engine you run. At the time of writing, VAS supported VMware, Citrix, Microsoft, Virtual Iron, and Parallels virtualization engines, letting you use any of the engines you may already have in place. VAS is composed of four core products and features.

▼ The Virtual Access Broker, which links users with virtual desktops through links with your internal Active Directory.

■ The Access Infrastructure, which is the conduit that allows endpoints such as desktop PCs or thin clients to link with the virtual desktops through a web interface.

■ Enhanced End-User Experience and Last-Mile features, which are designed to provide rich graphical experiences for users of the virtual desktops.

▲ End-Point Computing, which is the component that links the end-user's requirements with applications and data through the web interface.

Each of these tools makes up Quest's VAS and provides a complete VDI implementation solution. Of course, you must have your own server virtualization infrastructure in place. If you need an independent VDI solution, perhaps Quest VAS is the solution for you.

NOTE   For more information on the Quest VAS, go to www.provisionnetworks.com/solutions/vas/vas.aspx.

PROFIT FROM VDI

As you can see, virtual desktop infrastructures offer much in the way of simplifying desktop management and reducing the various issues you face when working with distributed desktops. Desktops are delivered quickly and reliably to any linked location. You control which devices are linked to the VM, therefore controlling the management of data and reducing the potential loss of intellectual property. You can significantly reduce the cost of each desktop, sometimes by as much as 40 percent. You can reduce the number of images to manage, especially when you work with volatile PC images. Machines are easier to patch and update since you often only have one core image to update.

Basically, VDI transforms the desktop life cycle and reduces its components (see Figure 10-10). Traditionally, you must procure, image, secure, deploy and then monitor, maintain, back up, and eventually retire your physical desktops. With VDI, you only need to generate the original image through the creation of a reference computer, use it as the core image for all systems, personalize it (which is usually performed by the VDI engine), then monitor and update it. Images are automatically retired by the desktop broker when the user logs off.

However, using technologies such as XenDesktop and others does present a challenge in terms of PC image construction and management. Ideally, organizations will require a single PC image, as outlined earlier when discussing the PASS system construction model. Using one single image to meet each and every user's needs means that you have to devise a system that will automatically provision the image with the required applications and user data at logon. The best way to do this is to rely on application virtualization (covered in the next chapter) and user profile protection mechanisms (covered in Chapter 12). User profile data absolutely must be stored outside the PC image if it is to be protected. XenDesktop did not offer this feature at the time of writing, but Citrix obviously intends to provide it sometime in the future. Windows, however, already offers a profile protection mechanism through roaming profiles and folder redirection.

Application provisioning is more complicated since it requires the ability to provide the end user with the applications they need when they need them. Using traditional application delivery methods will not work since they take time to install and deploy. If this was the method you used, your users would be completely dissatisfied with VDI as they waited for long periods of time at login as the applications they required were attached to the desktop image. This is why VDI does not work on its own. It absolutely must be tied to application virtualization to make it work. Keep this in mind when you prepare and choose your desktop virtualization solution.

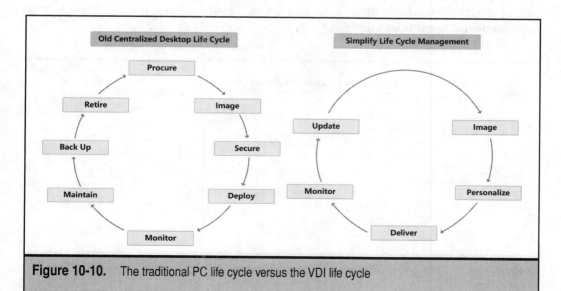

Figure 10-10.   The traditional PC life cycle versus the VDI life cycle

Major Vendor Positioning

As you have seen, there are several solutions for desktop virtualization. Once again, the three major vendors offer similar solutions, but each has something unique to offer. In addition, there are third-party solutions that sometimes offer completely different approaches to the problem. Of these, InstallFree is the most innovative because they do not use a virtualization engine on the back-end. This might be the right choice if you do not have or intend to put a server virtualization solution in place. However, organizations without server virtualization solutions will be rare and few in the coming years. Microsoft offers presentation virtualization through its Terminal Services feature. Citrix offers powerful enterprise desktop virtualization and can run on any back-end platform. VMware has the most mature solution, especially since VMware View is now available. Consider these options when you choose a solution.

Make the Desktop Virtualization Decision

Remember that there are several different solutions for desktop virtualization. When you make the decision to virtualize desktops, you should consider the business need first and then the solution you should apply to the problem (see Figure 10-11). If you need to run applications that are sharable, perhaps the best solution is simply to implement presentation virtualization, something many organizations already have in place. If you want to secure and centralize data, choose a virtual desktop infrastructure. If your users need to have offline access to virtual desktops, choose a secure and encrypted solution to have the VM run on their own desktop.

Remember, however, that VDI and desktop virtualization often does not work on its own and requires additional components, components that are covered in future chapters. VDI is a powerful solution that reduces desktop management costs and is definitely part of the dynamic datacenter. Once again, you'll find that you'll learn more as you implement and use this solution.

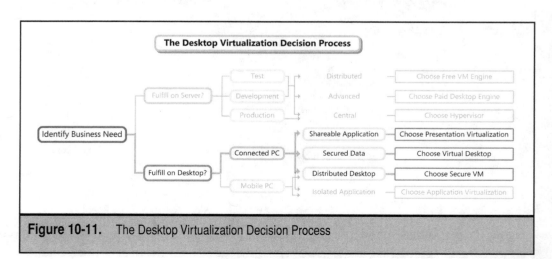

Figure 10-11. The Desktop Virtualization Decision Process

CHAPTER 11

Work with Application Virtualization

One of the most demanding aspects of distributed systems management is software asset management—the science of tagging, packaging, deploying, and maintaining software assets in your organization. Depending on your organization's size, you may have from a dozen to several hundred applications in operation in your network. Packaging and testing each of these applications to ensure they will properly cohabitate with others on the same target system is one of the biggest tasks administrators face. What's worse, this task must be repeated each time you change operating systems, making it one of the most onerous tasks in IT today.

Traditionally, organizations manage endpoints through layered approaches, building first the operating system, and then applying core operating system utilities, such as disk defragmentation, antispam and antivirus tools, and any other core component that must be on every system in the organization. Once the core OS is ready, applications are deployed, also in layers. The first application layer deals with applications everyone in the organization requires—tools such as Microsoft Office, graphics viewers, database engines, and more. The second layer deals with specialized applications, which relate to the particular function a user performs within the organization: graphic designers require advanced graphics tools, application developers require application construction tools, finance users require custom money management tools, and so on. Since these user functions are not widespread throughout the organization, this second layer is deployed only to specific groups of machines. Finally, the last application layer is deployed on an ad hoc basis as different users require highly specific tools. This is the structure of the Point of Access for Secure Services (PASS) system construction model outlined in Chapter 10.

Applications must be categorized in this way to avoid conflicts and reduce application management and support overhead. But today, thanks to virtualization technologies, there is a better way.

APPLICATION MANAGEMENT ISSUES

The basic structure of Windows is also the cause of many of the woes administrators face with applications. Windows serves as the foundation for application operation. Features such as application information exchange, application interaction, printing, graphical display, communications, and more are all embedded into the core operating system. Application developers do not need to program these features into their applications, only learn to call on them when required. However, developers often learn that the core components they call upon, the Dynamic Linked Libraries (DLL) within Windows, are subject to change on a regular basis. Sometimes these changes will make their calls no longer work. To protect the operation of the application, the developer tends to integrate the Windows DLL into the installation of the application, sometimes replacing newer components on the target machine. The replaced DLL will work for their application, but will no longer work for others, causing their applications to break.

DLL conflicts are the bane of all system administrators and are commonly known as DLL Hell. DLLs are at the heart of all executables. These conflicts arise when the application manufacturers decide to include shared components within their application.

Because of this, application administrators have learned that the best way to manage applications is to examine each of the components they install and compare them to all of the other components on a system to avoid and proactively repair conflicts. But to reduce this application management overhead, administrators categorize applications and make sure as few as possible can coexist on one system at a time.

Because of this, organizations must manage several application categories: newly released commercial applications, legacy commercial applications, and updated or new custom applications—applications that are developed in-house, legacy custom applications, and custom commercial applications (for manufacturing). Legacy applications are subject to DLL Hell the most, and new applications are subject to other potential conflict types. All must be managed.

Traditional Application Management Solutions

DLL Hell has caused administrators and developers alike to come up with a variety of methods for solving the application management headache. First, they have taken the time to identify and integrate applications into a life cycle. Then, they rely on this life cycle to work with the Windows Installer service—a service Microsoft has integrated into Windows to help standardize application installations. Another solution is to install applications on servers and present them to users through server-based computing or presentation virtualization. However, each approach has its own issues and none is a perfect solution.

Rely on the Application Life Cycle

All applications, no matter their category, have a life cycle, and organizations must manage the applications throughout their life cycle (see Figure 11-1). The life cycle includes four phases. The first deals with application acquisition or, if the application is built in-house, application requirements and the need for the application in the first place.

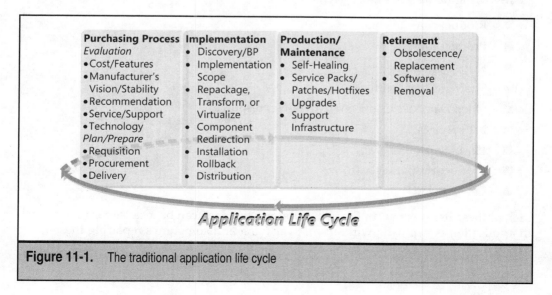

Figure 11-1.   The traditional application life cycle

The second deals with implementation. This is where most of the proactive work against DLL Hell is performed as the application is prepared for deployment. The third deals with application maintenance, and the last deals with application retirement. Unfortunately, this last activity is rarely performed, as organizations do not remove obsolete applications from systems—everyone has the "you never know what removing an application might destabilize" attitude—and prefers to reimage systems on a regular basis.

Work with Windows Installer

To help organizations properly manage applications throughout their life cycle and also to help standardize application installations in Windows, Microsoft developed the Windows Installer service (WIS). WIS is a tool that supports the installation of software through the use of a consistency database. Each product has its own consistency database. This database is used to provide comprehensive application installation support features. Features such as self-healing, application installation monitoring, application installation rollback on failure, and more are all part of the WIS feature set. However, understanding and working with WIS is an art in and of itself.

NOTE For comprehensive information on the Windows Installer service and its inner workings, download the free white paper titled Working with Windows Installer from www.reso-net.com/articles .asp?m=8#p.

To properly manage Windows Installer, system administrators need to package applications in the MSI format. To do that, they can rely on commercial tools such as Altiris Wise Package Studio or InstallShield AdminStudio from Acresso Software. WIS is designed to remove DLL conflicts from application installations, but it does not solve all problems because other conflicts continue to exist. This is why application conflict detection is still necessary, even with MSI packages. Conflict detection should cover the following items (see Figure 11-2):

- ▼ Product components
- ■ Product files
- ■ Registry entries
- ■ Shortcuts and INI files
- ■ Open Database Connectivity (ODBC) resources
- ■ NT services
- ■ File extensions
- ■ Product properties
- ▲ OS kernel drivers

Each of these items is part of the WIS standard, but each can be a cause for issues when an application is deployed without first verifying and sometimes repairing these items within the MSI you create to automate application deployment.

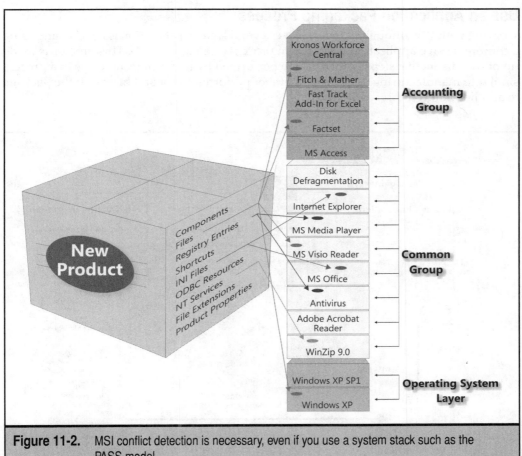

Figure 11-2. MSI conflict detection is necessary, even if you use a system stack such as the PASS model.

Even though Microsoft has improved WIS throughout the various releases of Windows, it still has some issues. For example, if you are thinking of moving to Windows Vista, you will need to work with Windows Installer 4.5. Vista relies on the Restart Manager to stop and restart the applications when installations require it. In addition, Windows Installer is integrated with User Account Control, the applications are automatically installed with elevated privileges, and they are stored in Windows' HKEY_Local_Machine registry hive, the same as using ALLUSERS=1 property through the WIS command interface: msiexec.exe. In addition, applications integrated with WIS 4.5 must be digitally signed if you are to support application patching in standard user mode. And, because of the new Windows Resource Protection feature in Windows Vista, Windows Installer will skip the installation of system files if they are contained within a package and then log an entry into the log file before continuing the installation.

Use an Application Packaging Process

Working with WIS, though it does resolve several legacy installation issues, means using a comprehensive application preparation process (see Figure 11-3). This process is made up of five distinctive steps, which can be performed by teams of technicians in a process similar to manufacturing. Each team member performs a task and hands off the package to another through this workflow.

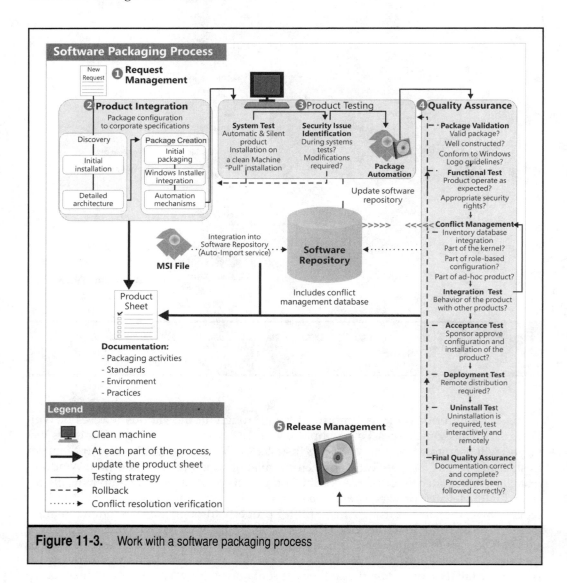

Figure 11-3. Work with a software packaging process

Step one centers on request management. If your organization is focused on application management issue reduction, this step will include a rationalization strategy to ensure that only applications that are absolutely required are introduced into the system.

Step two prepares product integration and begins the application analysis process. What are the application requirements? Does it integrate with others? What is its installation process? These are all questions that this step aims to answer before the package is created and is ready to move on to the next stage.

Step three tests the initial package to ensure that it works properly and has been integrated with your organization's security and other standards. It finishes off with the automation of the package.

Step four performs quality assurance (QA) on the package, testing both remote and interactive installations, identifying if conflicts remain and if the package can be removed without issues remaining on the target system.

Once the package has passed through QA, it moves on to release management and then it is ready for deployment. The package is fully documented and is integrated with the software repository in your network. It is then deployed to all target systems.

As you can see, while WIS does help protect systems, preparing MSI packages is a comprehensive task that requires planning and forethought.

Work with Presentation Virtualization

When packages are prepared in MSI format, they are often deployed through traditional electronic software distribution (ESD) systems to all target machines. For example, to deploy Microsoft Office, organizations often send out more than 500 megabytes (MB) of data through unicast communications to hundreds of distributed PCs. Then, once the Office installation is on each of these distributed nodes, these organizations have to manage its update and maintenance throughout its life cycle.

Such deployments can cause a lot of issues. First, the bandwidth required for the deployment is massive, as is the time window required to actually perform the deployment. Then, since many organizations have granted their users local administrative rights, the application they deployed in a pristine state is often modified beyond recognition, causing more issues. Also, local disk drives fail and systems need to be reimaged. Service packs need to be deployed to maintain Office, and these service packs are sometimes even larger than the original deployment.

Because of these issues, many organizations have moved to server-based computing, or presentation virtualization (PresentV). PresentV relies on server-based installations that are shared among multiple users. This strategy provides many benefits.

▼ Because the software is installed on a server, there are only a few locations where conflicts can arise. This reduces the conflict management overhead.

■ There are also only a few locations to update and maintain.

■ But, you still need to use MSIs as much as possible to maintain the WIS advantage. However, these applications must be installed in shared mode.

▲ And, if you rely on the built-in PresentV features of Windows Server, especially Windows Server 2008 (WS08), there are no additional commercial systems required to make PresentV work. WS08 has the ability to publish server-based applications on a one-by-one basis, making the experience completely transparent to end users.

Windows relies on the Remote Desktop Protocol (RDP) to provide access to these remote applications. Prior to WS08, Microsoft's Terminal Services provided users with access to a complete remote desktop, which could be confusing. Because of this, many organizations opted to implement Citrix's remote application solution, then called Presentation Server. Presentation Server provided one-to-one access to applications, making them look as if they were actually installed on the desktop. Citrix has since updated the name of Presentation Server to XenApp; however, not all customers have opted to upgrade to this version.

With WS08, Microsoft has integrated the same or similar features to publish only applications. However, even with this improvement, there are still issues with server-based computing.

▼ Mobile users do not have access to centralized applications when they are on the road.

■ Server-based computing only works for connected systems. Disconnected systems do not have access to remote applications.

▲ Server-based computing requires massive server configurations and large server farms to make the applications highly available.

Because applications are shared and multiple users access them remotely, the servers that host them must have massive processing power, a configuration that is normally reserved for host servers running hypervisors.

As you can see, traditional application management, whether it is on distributed systems or on remote servers, can still cause a lot of issues, especially if it isn't done right.

REDESIGN APPLICATION MANAGEMENT

Fortunately, with the introduction of virtualization technologies, there is now a better way to manage applications, even distributed applications: application virtualization (AppV). Application virtualization transforms the traditional application management process by removing all possibility of application conflicts as well as transforming the delivery mechanism by turning it into a pull rather than a push mechanism. With the proper AppV technology, your users will request applications when they need to use them and you will no longer need to deploy the bits beforehand. These are only two of the major advantages AppV provides.

Work with a Virtualization Layer

While application virtualization was introduced several years ago, it hasn't yet become mainstream. Organizations continue to concentrate on traditional software management and installation procedures, building software packages for WIS and relying on ESD systems to deploy these packages to endpoints. But today, as virtualization becomes a core aspect of datacenter management strategies around the world, application virtualization is also taking its place at center stage as systems administrators realize the powerful benefits it brings to distributed systems management.

That's because AppV provides the ability to maintain a pristine operating system, despite the fact that the OS runs a multitude of software packages. This is definitely a boon to all organizations and administrators everywhere are beginning to bank on this feature to considerably reduce application management and support costs.

Basically, application virtualization creates a protective layer around the operating system to safeguard it against any changes that could be made by actually installing an application. The core concept of AppV is that instead of capturing a software installation, such as when packaging installations for the Windows Installer service, AppV captures the *running state* of an application. It is this running state that is then "installed" on the target system, but since it is a running state and not an actual installation, no changes are made to the operating system, except, of course, for the new files that reside on it.

The application virtualization layer translates this running state into instructions the operating system and other applications can understand and interact with, keeping the core OS pristine at all times and containing application components in such a way that they can never cause conflicts with other applications. Traditional application installations penetrate the operating system and change its configuration, but AppV protects the operating system from any modifications (see Figure 11-4).

AppV completely isolates applications from both the operating system and from other applications by protecting the OS from file system and registry changes. Yet the application will continue to interact normally with the OS and other applications. Because of this, AppV allows different versions of applications to coexist with each other on the same system without issue. AppV fully supports the ability to run notoriously conflicting applications, such as Microsoft Access 97, Access XP, Access 2003, and Access 2007, on the same system, at the same time and then even lets you cut and paste contents from one to the other, proving that each one can continue to interact properly with the other.

Another powerful advantage of AppV is that it can be both a stand-alone solution—working on its own on individual systems—or it can be integrated into both traditional (push installations) and streaming (pull installations) software delivery solutions. When used with traditional ESD systems, AppV delivers the fully configured application to the endpoint. But when it is used in conjunction with a streaming system, only the bits that are required to run the base application functionality will be delivered at first—usually less than 10 percent of the application—and the remainder of the application components will be delivered on demand as users work with more of the application's functions and features. Better yet, only the applications the end user actually works with will be delivered. If the user does not require an application during a session, no bits are delivered.

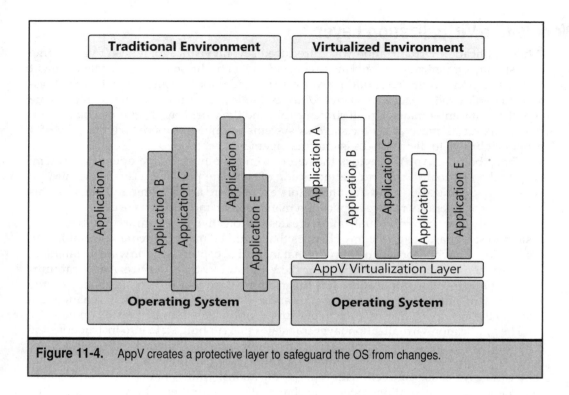

Figure 11-4.   AppV creates a protective layer to safeguard the OS from changes.

However, in order to create a complete systems management strategy, organizations should consider the use of all three elements in their IT infrastructure.

▼   AppV helps resolve all of the most common issues related to application usage and management while maintaining the integrity of endpoint systems.

■   Streaming systems help deploy applications and updates to endpoints on a just-in-time and just-enough basis.

▲   ESD helps maintain and manage the more traditional components of your IT infrastructure—core desktop utilities and services, server-based deployments, and, if the option is available in the tool you choose to use, operating system deployments and updates.

ESD is used for core OS and utility updates, streaming is used for application delivery, and AppV is used to protect all systems at all times. This makes for a powerful combination.

The Components of AppV

There are several products on the market that can help make the application management pain go away once and for all because AppV packages are independent of the underlying operating system. The process is simple. Begin by preparing an application for virtualization. To do so, you capture the running state of the application and store it in an AppV package. This package contains all of the files, processes, and settings required to run the application. Each application is captured into a specific package that will then be deployed to a target system. Next, you make the package available to the endpoints, either through traditional ESD systems or through streaming technologies. Because of their reduced overhead, streaming systems are preferred since they only provide the application's shortcut to the system and bits are deployed only when the user clicks the shortcut.

Since the AppV packages are captured in their running state, users or administrators can reset them to their original state in the event that an untoward incident occurs. When it is time to retire the application, simply delete it from the system. Now that is a much simpler application life cycle.

When you select your AppV solution, you should look for several features, including:

▼ Application isolation or sandboxing
■ Windows version independence
■ Agent versus agentless operation
■ Activation or nonactivation support
■ Streaming delivery mechanisms
■ Endpoint AppV cache control
■ Active Directory integration
■ License control
■ Production project-based packaging
▲ Software as a Service (SAAS) support

Each of these provides extensive functionality that reduces the overall application management life cycle and removes many of its headaches.

The AppV System Stack

Chapter 10 outlined how traditional desktops are constructed through the PASS model. However, because AppV provides protection for the operating system and because AppV can work with streaming technologies to provide applications on demand, organizations moving to application virtualization will want to redesign the PASS model and move to a thin system kernel (see Figure 11-5). The core of the system construction model, the kernel, is now reduced in size and only includes the following items:

▼ The core operating system and its required updates.
■ Core utilities, such as antivirus, antispyware, firewalls, management agents, and virtualization agents if they are required.
▲ From then on, you virtualize everything else.

The application layers are transformed into three layers. The PASS system kernel and the generalized application layer (GAL) meet the needs of the average or generic user. Role-based applications and the commercial software are added on top of the new thin kernel to meet the requirements of the special IT roles, and finally, the ad hoc layer responds to highly specialized IT requirements. With this system stack, the kernel or the core OS stays pristine at all times; basically, it stays the way you built it.

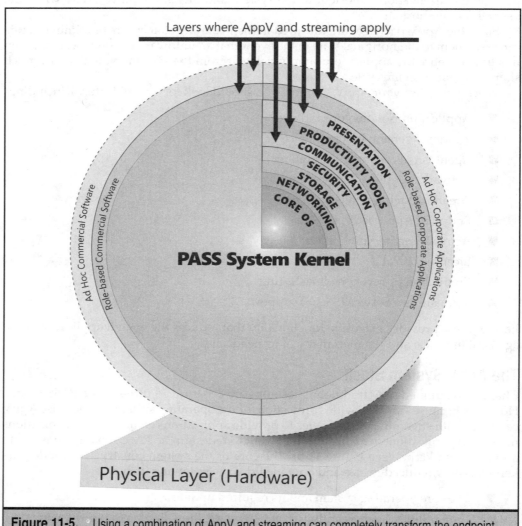

Figure 11-5.   Using a combination of AppV and streaming can completely transform the endpoint construction model.

Windows Version Independence

Besides transforming the system construction model, AppV reduces the application packaging effort because of the way it works. Each AppV system can support multiple versions of Windows. This means that when you package an application for AppV, you never need to package it again.

Because the AppV engine manages all transactions between the application and the OS, it has the ability to translate these instructions into the format required by a specific target OS. Some AppV products will go as far back as Windows NT and allow you to run an AppV package from NT through Windows 2000, XP, and Vista.

This feature alone is worth its weight in gold. Traditionally, application packagers must revisit the application each time a new OS is released and their organization has selected to deploy it. This activity is the single most expensive application management activity organizations face when choosing to upgrade desktop operating systems and is one of the major reasons why Windows Vista has not seen the expected rate of adoption.

But, because of Windows OS independence, AppV packages will simply run on Vista even if they were originally created for Windows XP. The same will apply when Microsoft releases Windows 7. You will, of course, have to wait until the AppV engine you rely on has been upgraded to work with Windows 7, but you should not have to revisit each AppV package.

This makes it much, much easier to upgrade operating systems and greatly reduces the cost of new OS deployments.

Agent Versus Agentless AppV

AppV engines come in two flavors. The first is agent-based, requiring a predeployed agent on the target system to run the virtualized applications and to communicate with the central AppV repository. The second is agentless, or rather, the agent is either embedded within the virtualized application or the agent is carried with the application. Both have their advantages and drawbacks.

Agent-based AppV means that the agent must be available before the virtualized applications can run. This means that the agent must be deployed through a standard electronic software distribution tool, installed with the core OS, or, in some cases, deployed through the streaming engine. In the latter case, the streaming engine itself requires a local agent, which must also be predeployed. In a way, agent-based AppV is a protection mechanism because the applications you virtualize will not run unless the agent is available. Remember that an application that is virtualized will run on any version of Windows and on any system. If your AppV engine is agent-based, your applications are protected, since a malicious user wanting to walk away with your applications would somehow also need to obtain and have the ability to install the agent before being able to use them.

Deploying agents is not a difficult task since the thin PASS kernel will usually require other agents and utilities within the core OS image, such as:

▼ **Inventory agent** to keep track of all systems.

■ **ESD agent to support software deployment** for example, the Active Directory deployment agent is the Group Policy client that is already part of Windows.

- ■ **Patch deployment agent** once again, the Windows patching agent is the Windows Update Client, which is also part of Windows.

- ■ **Antivirus and antimalware** once again, the antimalware agent in Windows is Windows Defender.

- ▲ **Search engine** in Windows, this would be Windows Search or a third-party tool.

But even if your core system requires an agent, or a series of agents, managing these utilities is still much, much simpler than managing traditional applications.

Agentless AppV (where the agent is embedded into the virtualized application) means that the virtualized application transports the engine with it and can run as-is on any Windows platform. The advantage is that you do not need to worry about pre-deploying agents. These AppV applications are completely transportable and will run on any system with nothing more than standard user rights. This includes your own locked-down systems, public systems, kiosk computers, and more. Users can transport their entire application environment—for example, Microsoft Office, along with their documents—on a Universal Serial Bus (USB) key. They can activate their applications on any computer simply by plugging in the USB key and launching the application.

This is a powerful model; but on the other hand, you do need to worry about application security. Agentless AppV applications are completely transportable. This means that any user can copy an agentless AppV application and take it to any system to run it. Additional means must be taken to protect these applications if you don't want your licenses spread everywhere. This means that you must embed licenses and license protection mechanisms within the packaged application to ensure that they only run in your environment.

Local Repository Management

Each AppV technology, whether agent-based or agentless, relies on a local cache to run the application. When the application is activated, the application's bits are made available locally to run the application. This local repository is a temporary container for the application. It can be volatile, that is, the cache is cleared as soon as the user logs off. It can be temporary, that is, the cache is available on a timed basis. For example, if your team is working on a project for three months, you give them a three-month-long cache of Microsoft Project. After the three-month period, the cache is automatically cleared and the application is no longer available. The cache can also be set to semipermanent, which means that it will not expire until you manually modify it. This latter mode is useful for mobile computers which need access to the application whether they are connected or disconnected.

Using cache controls allows you to make the applications as persistent as you need them to be. And, because the application is not actually deployed to the target system, when it comes time to update the application, simply update the central repository. The next time the application is launched, the system will verify with the central repository to see if any changes were made and, if so, it will automatically update the local cache, updating the application at the same time.

Applications can be also be precached and then activated as needed. The applications do not get installed or alter the operating system; you can even use XCopy to place the bits on the target system since no "installation" is required, yet tasks process locally on the host computer as if the applications were installed.

Active Directory Integration

Most AppV technologies will integrate directly with Active Directory, allowing you to assign AppV applications through security group assignments. Create a group, attach it to an application assignment in the AppV management tool, and then simply assign applications by placing user accounts within the group.

While traditional applications must be assigned to computers—otherwise the installations will always occur each time a user logs in—this rule does not apply to AppV applications. Since the AppV application is not deployed in the traditional sense, you can assign it to users. AppV applications are only deployed when the user activates them by double-clicking the application's shortcut. When the user's account is added to an Active Directory (AD) group linked to the application, the shortcut is automatically displayed on the desktop. Then, to determine how many licenses are assigned for the application, all you need to do is find out how many users are in the application's group.

To assign applications according to the application layers in the thin PASS model, you can use a flowchart decision process (see Figure 11-6). If an application is contained within the global application layer (GAL), it is assigned to all users. If it is in the role-based layer, it is assigned to specific groups whose role corresponds to the grouping; if it is an ad hoc application, it is assigned to individual users.

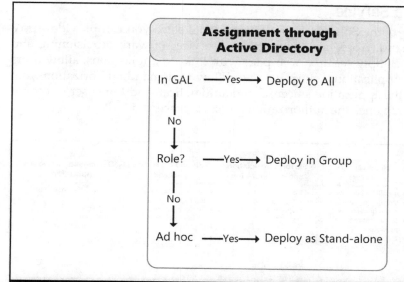

Figure 11-6. Assigning AppV applications through Active Directory security groups

AppV Software Packaging

Packaging is also completely different. In the traditional packaging process, you must always return to a pristine operating system each time you start a new project. But with AppV, since the application isn't really installed on the system and you only capture the running state, you do not need to be as strict with the environment. The virtual application packaging process isolates the software because all system components are virtualized. Applications are packaged in a special format that "sandboxes" applications to provide complete isolation from the system.

And then, once the applications are packaged, they are placed in a core software repository from which they are pulled to endpoints by end users. If you have multiple sites, you simply replicate this repository as needed to wherever it is required. For example, in a Windows environment, you could use the Distributed File System Replication (DFSR) engine, which is a delta compression replication engine that will replicate only changes from one location to another.

NOTE For more information on DFSR, look up *Microsoft Windows Server 2008: The Complete Reference* by Ruest and Ruest (McGraw-Hill, 2008).

AppV packaging, however, must still be structured and must include quality control (see Figure 11-7). You'll note a major difference in the process compared to traditional packaging: There is no more need to perform conflict detection since AppV isolates all applications. This is a great benefit and, coupled with the fact that you no longer need to update packages each time you change operating systems, is a great time-saver.

Run Software as a Service

Finally, AppV supports the Software as a Service model since you can provide AppV applications on demand. AppV also supports self-service software provisioning and on-demand delivery. Simply set up a web page with links to applications, allow users to request their own applications, integrate a workflow to demand authorization from managers to pay for the application's license, and automatically add the user's account in the application group once the authorization has been processed.

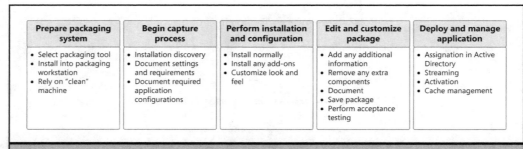

Prepare packaging system	Begin capture process	Perform installation and configuration	Edit and customize package	Deploy and manage application
• Select packaging tool • Install into packaging workstation • Rely on "clean" machine	• Installation discovery • Document settings and requirements • Document required application configurations	• Install normally • Install any add-ons • Customize look and feel	• Add any additional information • Remove any extra components • Document • Save package • Perform acceptance testing	• Assignation in Active Directory • Streaming • Activation • Cache management

Figure 11-7. The AppV packaging process

In addition, applications are completely transportable. You can deliver them through network shares, even using offline files in Windows to cache them locally on endpoints. You can deliver them on USB keys or read-only media, such as CDs or DVDs. You can also deliver them through web pages using WebDAV, the Hypertext Transfer Protocol (HTTP), or the File Transfer Protocol (FTP). Because of this, traditional system management tools are definitely optional when it comes to AppV.

In addition, there are tools on the market that let you convert all of your applications from the Windows Installer MSI format to AppV. If you have taken the time to create MSIs for all of the software you manage, this might be the best way for you to move to AppV.

NOTE   One tool, InstallShield AdminStudio, will convert MSI files in a batch process overnight and target two formats: Citrix XenApp or VMware ThinApp. More formats are in the works. Learn more at www.Accresso.com.

Application Streaming: A New Distribution Strategy

As mentioned earlier, AppV engines also include a new software delivery mechanism as well as abstracting software from the operating system. AppV packages are captured in a special structure that transforms application packages into 4-kilobyte (Kb) segments, turning them into streamable components—components that can be divided into several different categories, depending on the engine you use.

▼   Most engines support the startup block, or the components that are required to launch the application and allow the user to begin working with it. In many cases, these components form less than 10 percent of the entire application. For example, with Microsoft Word, this would be enough code to let the user begin typing in a new or existing document.

■   Some engines support a second block type, predictive blocks. As users throughout the organization continue to work with a streamed application, the streaming server analyzes usage data to determine which application blocks are most commonly requested. These blocks are then identified as predictive blocks and are set to automatic streaming to endpoints for anyone who has activated the application. When users who haven't used the features contained in the predictive blocks begin to work with them, the blocks are already on the system and provide even better response levels. Predictive blocks usually make up less than 10 percent of the application and begin streaming as soon as the startup block download is complete.

▲   All engines support the final block type, on-demand blocks. These blocks are provided to end users on an on-demand basis, mostly because the features they contain are rarely used and do not warrant precaching on endpoints.

The experience is completely transparent to end users. In most cases, the streaming engine displays an icon in the system tray at the lower-right corner of the screen. You can, if you want, have the streaming agent display streaming events to end users; however, hiding these events provides a better end-user experience.

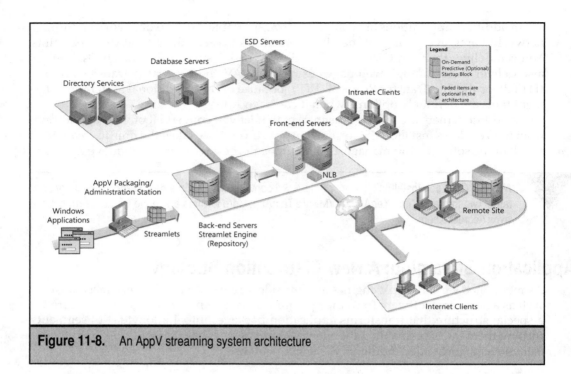

Figure 11-8. An AppV streaming system architecture

The applications are packaged in streams; this way, only a few bits are required for the application to start. For example, Microsoft Office is more than 500MB, but through the streaming process, users can run Word with only 9MB, and this startup block is usually streamed to the desktop in less than ten seconds.

As mentioned earlier, streamed applications are cached locally, so all users have access to them as long as their profile or Active Directory access rights allow it. Mobile users have disconnected permissions and can travel with the application. The streaming process does not require a complex infrastructure; it can often be as simple as a file server; or if you have a complete streaming engine, it is a server much like a media server. Because of this, infrastructures can be made highly available through the use of technologies like the Network Load Balancing (NLB) service, which presents a single address to endpoints but runs multiple servers to provide service continuity (see Figure 11-8). Databases that are required to contain management data can also be made highly available through Windows Failover Clustering Services.

The Application Streaming System

Application streaming systems provide a host of features to organizations.

▼ The first is on-demand deployment. By using the streaming console—a standard web interface accessed through any browser—to identify which users can access which applications, you automatically make the application's shortcut available on the endpoint. That's because the streaming agent will provision authorized applications on any endpoint the user accesses. Then, when the user launches the application, it will automatically be streamed to the endpoint and ready to use in seconds. During the streaming process, the application's streaming shortcut is replaced with the actual shortcut, again through a process that is completely transparent to the user.

■ The second is remote access. When applications are assigned to users, the administrator can determine if it will be cached locally. If yes, the application becomes available offline. If not, the application is re-streamed each time the user accesses it.

▲ The third is license control. The streaming agent automatically reports application usage in real time to the server on an ongoing basis. Because of this, any streamed application provides usage data on a constant basis. The result is constant licensing compliance and considerable reduction in licensing costs, sometimes up to 50 percent, because you can easily and quickly reharvest any unused license. As you can see, dynamic license management offers a compelling business case for itself.

These key features are provided alongside the other considerable features AppV offers. For example, endpoint hard disk usage is considerably reduced since only portions of each application reside on the disk. Application distribution can now be done either on-line or offline. Application assignment can be performed through group memberships in Active Directory or any other Lightweight Directory Access Protocol (LDAP) directory; just place the user in a group and assign the application to the group instead of individual users. And the entire system can easily be made redundant since it relies on standard HTTP protocols and works much like a web server.

BENEFITS OF APPV FOR THE ORGANIZATION

Application virtualization is one of the most compelling technologies available to data-centers of any size today. Whether you're in an organization that has 20 or 20,000 users, you'll profit from AppV. Once it is in place, your streaming infrastructure can scale to meet any needs your organization faces. Even in the case of mergers or acquisitions, you can easily update your streaming system to integrate any number of new clients, whether they are centralized or distributed.

Because applications are cached locally, users always have access to them, whether they are connected or not. If you need to update the application, simply create an update package and it will automatically update the next time the user accesses the application. Keep in mind that the streaming engine will not replace the whole application the way a traditionally installed application would be replaced; instead, it will only replace the bits that have changed, further reducing the demand on bandwidth.

In addition, application virtualization and streaming provides complete flexibility—flexibility that traditional systems management tools do not offer. Consider these key points:

▼ **Manageability**   Your systems are manageable from any point in the organization since the management interface is a web interface and only requires a web browser for access.

■ **Security**   All applications are completely secure since you require both the streaming and the virtualization agents—either on the system or within the AppV package—to operate. In addition, you can rely on technologies such as Active Directory Software Restriction Policies to digitally sign each application and ensure that only authorized applications run in your network infrastructure.

■ **Resiliency**   Each of the components of your streaming system can easily be made redundant, providing the utmost in resiliency.

■ **Flexibility**   You can dynamically manage licenses and easily reharvest unused licenses to redistribute them as needed. Imagine trying to do this with traditionally deployed applications.

■ **Disaster recovery**   Since application bits are pulled by end-user systems, users can rely on any computer in your network and immediately have access to the applications they use. In the event of a disaster, users can even access their applications through the Internet and work on remote systems. In addition, AppV is ideal for virtual desktop infrastructures (VDIs), since it provides the ability to build systems dynamically based on a user's needs.

■ **Portability**   Applications do not need to reside on a particular workstation. They can be cached or not, as you determine. Since less than 10 percent of the application is required to operate, users can be provisioned in minutes, if not seconds, on any system.

▲ **Optimization**   You can finally optimize application license usage in your organization because you are always aware of who is using what in real time.

End users also benefit because they have the very best application experience. Applications are updated without their knowledge, and because each application is virtualized, they will never face an application conflict issue ever again. If something untoward happens with the application, simply reset it to its original virtualized state and it is ready to go once again.

CHAPTER 12

Work with AppV

Application virtualization (AppV) offers many benefits and may warrant immediate adoption, but it requires redeployment of all the applications. This means replacing the applications that are already running—uninstalling the application and then redeploying it as a virtual application—but uninstalling may leave the operating system in a potentially unstable state. The ideal time to do this is when deploying a brand-new, "clean" computer in an operating system migration or in a move to virtual desktop infrastructure (VDI).

You should start with baby steps and focus on the most problematic applications in your network to start, and then move to all applications in time. It's guaranteed you would never go back to the "old" application installation model. But first, you must select which AppV solution to work with.

COMPARE APPLICATION VIRTUALIZATION PRODUCTS

There are several different types of application virtualization engines. Table 12-1 outlines several of the different products available on the market. Note that each of the three major virtualization vendors—Citrix, Microsoft, and VMware—offer AppV products.

Manufacturer	Web Site	Description
Ceedo	www.ceedo.com/ products/ceedo-enterprise.html	Comes in three editions. The Enterprise Edition enables multiple applications to be virtualized together to create a virtual work environment. The Personal Edition enables you to create a portable virtual desktop comprised of Windows applications, carry it with you on a USB, portable hard drive, iPod, or any other portable storage gadget and run it on any PC without installation. The Mobile Edition provides seamless interaction between the PC and the mobile phone, and enables service providers to easily extend their services into the PC/Web platform by launching a full application suite on any PC from a mobile phone or a Subscriber Identity Module (SIM) equipped USB drive.

Table 12-1.   Application Virtualization Technologies and Vendors

Manufacturer	Web Site	Description
Citrix XenApp	www.citrix.com/English/ ps2/products/product .asp?contentID=186	Combines presentation and application virtualization into one product. Supports application streaming to desktops or servers running server-based computing services. Comes in several editions (see Table 12-3 later in this chapter).
Endeavors Technologies Application Jukebox	www.endeavors .com/live/ showscreen.php?site_ id=23&screentype= folder&screenid=710	AppV and streaming system for Windows. Comes in three editions: Enterprise, Software as a Service (SAAS), or Lite. The SAAS Edition, in particular, allows Internet service providers (ISPs) to provide applications on demand. The Lite Edition is free and is used to let organizations test out AppV and streaming on a single server.
InstallFree Bridge	www.installfree .com/pageload .aspx?page=products_ InstallFree_Bridge.html	Clientless platform that deploys InstallFree's Virtual (IFV) applications to the host PC seamlessly and transparently to the end user, allowing virtual applications to function as if they were installed on the host computer while protecting the OS from any change.
LANDesk Application Virtualization	www.landesk.com/ SolutionServices/ product.aspx?id=776	LANDesk provides application virtualization by combining its deployment technologies with VMware's ThinApp AppV engine.
Microsoft Application Virtualization (MS App-V)	www.microsoft.com/ systemcenter/softgrid/ msappvirt45/default .mspx	Formerly known as SoftGrid Application Virtualization, MS App-V lets you control virtual applications and stream them to endpoints. Endpoints can be PCs, virtual desktops, or servers running presentation virtualization.

Table 12-1.   Application Virtualization Technologies and Vendors (*continued*)

Manufacturer	Web Site	Description
Symantec Software Virtualization Solution (SVS) Professional	www.symantec.com/ business/products/ overview.jsp?pcid=pcat_ infrastruct_op&pvid=sv_ sol_pro_1	Places applications and data into managed units called Virtual Software Packages. Can instantly activate, deactivate, or reset applications and avoid conflicts between applications without altering the base Windows installation. Application streaming provides the on-demand delivery mechanism.
Trigence AE	www.trigence.com/ products/index.html	Runs on Windows or Linux. Encapsulates applications at the OS level, creating application capsules.
VMware ThinApp	http://vmware.com/ products/thinapp	Formerly known as Thinstall Application Virtualization Suite, ThinApp lets you package and run applications without installation. ThinApp applications execute on locked-down PCs in standard user mode.
Xenocode Virtual Application Studio	www.xenocode.com/ Products/	Allows Windows, .NET, and Java-based applications to be deployed in compact, preconfigured virtual executables that run instantly via Web, USB keys, or existing desktop management infrastructures.

Table 12-1. Application Virtualization Technologies and Vendors (*continued*)

Because of this, it may make the most sense to select the same vendor for all aspects of your datacenter virtualization project.

As you can see, there are several potential AppV providers. The one you choose will depend on how you implement your virtual infrastructure and whether you are ready to move to a VDI infrastructure. No matter which solution you choose, however, application virtualization will pay for itself in a very short time because it makes applications independent of the underlying operating system. Whether you use real or virtual desktops, a protected desktop is always a less expensive desktop. To facilitate your decision, Table 12-2 compares the offerings from the most important AppV vendors according to

Feature	Symantec SVS Pro	Citrix XenApp	Microsoft App-V	VMware ThinApp	InstallFree Bridge
Application isolation, or "sandboxing"	x	X	X	X	X
Windows version independence	X	X	X	X	X
Agent/agentless	X	X	X		x
Activation/no activation	X			X	x
Cache control – Timing/duration	X	X	X		x
Streaming	X	X	X	x	x
Software as a Service	X	X	X	X	X
Active Directory integration	X	X	X	X	X
License control	X	X	X	x	X
Production project-based packaging	X	X			X
MSI conversion to AppV	X	X	x		
Thin kernel	X	X	X	X	X
Global application layer	X	X	X	X	X
Support for role-based/ad hoc applications	X	X	X	X	X

Table 12-2.   Potential AppV Solutions

the AppV feature set. Within this table, a large "X" means that the tool fully supports the feature, while a small "x" means that the feature is not completely supported by the tool. Omissions mean that the feature is not available within the product.

As you can see, each major product supports most of the AppV feature set.

NOTE   For an up-to-date comparison matrix of several of these vendors, see The application virtualization solutions Overview and Feature Matrix by Ruben Spruijt at www.virtuall.nl/articles/ applicationanddesktopdelivery/ApplicationVirtualizationSolutionsOverviewandFeatureMatrix.pdf.

Citrix XenApp

While it is focused on application virtualization and streaming, Citrix XenApp blurs the line between application and presentation virtualization because it stems from Citrix's former Presentation Server. In order to support AppV, Citrix added significant features to the Presentation Server engine. The resultant AppV engine, XenApp, is available in three editions (see Table 12-3). Each edition builds on the other to provide a complete set of features. XenApp, like XenServer, is also integrated into the XenDesktop offering.

NOTE For more information on XenApp, see www.citrix.com/English/ps2/products/product .asp?contentID=186. To test drive XenApp, download the XenApp virtual appliance at www.mycitrix .com. You must register first.

InstallFree Bridge

InstallFree Bridge operates on the same principle as the InstallFree Desktop and uses the local PC resources to run applications. Applications are also optimized for streaming, though no streaming engine is available with the product. Applications are simply placed on a file share for users to access. Application access is supported through Active Directory integration.

Feature	Advanced	Enterprise	Platinum
Server-side application virtualization	X	X	X
Application-based load management	X	X	X
SpeedScreen progressive display	X	X	X
Client-side application virtualization		X	X
Application performance monitoring		X	X
System monitoring and analysis		X	X
Application performance monitoring			X
Universal Secure Sockets Layer (SSL) virtual private network (VPN) with SmartAccess			X
Single-sign-on			X
Application password policy control			X
SmartAuditor session recording			X
Wide area network (WAN) optimization			X
EasyCall click-to-call technology			X

Table 12-3.   The Different XenApp Edition Feature Sets

InstallFree requires an agent, but its agent is also virtualized and will run on any Windows platform using standard user access rights. This means that InstallFree AppV applications are completely transportable. Just launch the agent on any machine and you can run any virtualized application.

In addition, the agent is the tool that runs the InstallFree packaging process. Because of this, you can package any application on any workstation without impacting the workstation and all through standard user rights.

In addition, InstallFree has a built-in mechanism for application integration. To get two virtualized applications to work together, simply place them in the same folder. When they are launched, each application will automatically be aware of the other. This makes InstallFree a powerful AppV offering.

Microsoft Application Virtualization

Microsoft entered the AppV fray when they acquired SoftGrid. They later took the time to rewrite the SoftGrid code to release Application Virtualization. MS App-V provides three different deployment scenarios. You can deploy it through the System Center Application Virtualization Management Server to provide a complete set of features for AppV and streaming. This solution requires Active Directory (AD) and SQL Server to operate. You can also use a lighter-weight System Center Application Virtualization Streaming Server, which does not require AD integration but still provides AppV and streaming capabilities. Smaller shops can deploy the stand-alone version of Microsoft Application Virtualization. This provides AppV features, but no streaming.

Application Virtualization is only available in 32-bit client versions, but Microsoft is working on a 64-bit version. MS App-V works with both desktop and server-based or Terminal Services applications. It is available only through the Microsoft Desktop Optimization Pack (MDOP) for Software Assurance and is not available to clients who do not own Software Assurance.

MS App-V includes the ability to support dynamic virtualization, which lets you package middleware applications in such a way that they are available to multiple virtualized application packages. For example, one single virtualized .NET Framework package can support multiple .NET applications once they are virtualized.

Symantec SVS Pro

Software Virtualization Solution was the first to market with an AppV feature set when it was owned by Altiris. Later, when Symantec acquired Altiris, it also acquired AppStream and combined the two feature sets to create SVS Pro. SVS uses a filter driver to virtualize packages. Packages are created as archives (.vsa) and then compressed into deliverable units using a common compression format, such as WinZip. For this reason, virtual packages (.vsp) are viewable through the WinZip utility. VSPs are deployed to endpoints and, once deployed, can be activated or deactivated. If issues arise, VSPs can be reset to their original state, resetting the application so that it runs properly.

Through the AppStream component, SVS Pro can support the utmost in streaming. In fact, this component offers the best streaming feature set of any AppV tool. AppStream can even stream virtualized desktops if required. And because it supports all three streaming block types—startup, predictive, and on demand—AppStream can ensure that all systems are populated according to the policies you set. This provides the very best in user experience.

Because of the powerful feature set included in the Altiris product line, integrating SVS Pro with the Altiris ESD solution can create a comprehensive management set for any distributed desktop environment.

VMware ThinApp

VMware significantly enhanced ThinApp once they acquired it from ThinStall in late 2007. Its claim to fame is the ability to run without an agent because the runtime agent is included within the package itself. This makes applications completely transportable; however, this requires you to implement special procedures to protect applications from theft.

ThinApp applications run on both 32-bit and 64-bit versions of Windows. ThinApp does not include a distribution mechanism, but ThinApp applications are optimized for streaming when they are built. This means organizations must rely on traditional deployment tools, such as ESD systems or Active Directory deployment. Deployment systems can also be as simple as a file share or a deployment web page.

To update an application, all you need to do is replace the original application, wherever it may sit. ThinApp includes a feature called AppSync. AppSync will automatically update deployed applications on target workstations. In order to do so, you must add the AppSync Web site in the application's .ini file. Also, .ini files must be named exactly the same for each version of the application; otherwise, the application will not be updated. This procedure is undocumented in the ThinApp documentation. For example, in order to update WinZip 10.0 to 12.2, you would ensure that the WinZip 10.0 .ini file pointed to the appropriate web page. Then, when you create the WinZip 12.2 package, you name its .ini file exactly the same as the one you used for version 10.0. The application will automatically update the next time the user launches it.

ThinApp also includes Application Links, which link virtualized applications together. For example, you can virtualize Microsoft Office and Adobe Acrobat separately, but still get them to integrate with each other once virtualized. ThinApp applications work on any version of Windows, from Windows NT to Windows Vista.

NOTE   If you make applications available on a file share, you can still control who sees what by using Access-Based Enumeration (ABE) in Windows. ABE will only display the files users have access to. Control access rights through Access Control Lists linked to AD security groups, and you will get a similar effect to streaming. Learn more about ABE at www.microsoft.com/windowsserver2003/techinfo/overview/abe.mspx.

Major Vendor Positioning

As you can see, vendors take different approaches to AppV, but the result is extremely similar. However, each vendor has something to offer.

▼ Microsoft offers Application Virtualization through Microsoft Desktop Optimization Pack (MDOP), which limits its availability. Because of this, you may have to choose another solution if you do not have Software Assurance, even if you have an all-Microsoft shop.

■ Citrix offers XenApp, which is an update of Presentation Server and combines the best of AppV with presentation virtualization (PresentV).

■ VMware Thinstall and InstallFree Bridge are both agentless, which makes applications transportable, but presents licensing challenges.

▲ Symantec leads the pack with SVS Pro because of its comprehensive streaming features.

Consider this positioning and evaluate each feature set before you make a decision on which platform to select.

Use the AppV Decision Process

Like the other two mainstream virtualization processes, making a decision for AppV is based on the actual business need you face (see Figure 12-1).

However, in this case, the decision addresses the needs of mobile PCs. If a complete desktop is required, opt for a secure virtual machine; if you only need to access applications, virtualize them. Desktop PCs are not included in this decision tree because all applications should be virtualized within the organization.

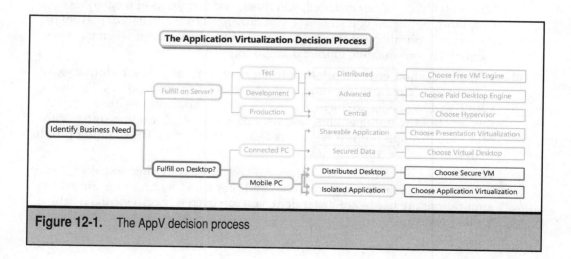

Figure 12-1. The AppV decision process

KEY POINTS ON APPV

Organizations everywhere spend inordinate amounts of resources managing application installation packages and making sure these applications always work in their network. What's worse, application packaging or repackaging is one of the biggest barriers to OS migrations because organizations do not want to face massive application preparation efforts.

To reduce the application management effort, most organizations have designed system images that include entire application sets. These organizations manage anywhere from tens to hundreds of system images, updating each and every one on a regular basis. While this makes it simple to reimage a system, it is cumbersome, time-consuming, and requires a lot of administrative overhead just to make it work.

Now you can have one or two single system images, since all the image requires is the core OS and base utilities. Everything else is streamed from central locations. In fact, you can reimage a system and have the end user up and running in minutes once the system is rebooted, because streaming only sends the bits the user needs at any one time. Isn't this a better desktop management model?

Consider the following and then decide if you're ready to reap the benefits of AppV streaming:

▼ Virtualize applications wherever possible to deal with application conflicts once and for all. Perform "spot" virtualizations, repackaging the most problematic applications you own to reap immediate benefits from application virtualization. Virtualizing applications will also render them OS-version-independent and let them run on any OS. This will remove one of the most significant barriers to OS migrations.

■ By streaming applications, you simplify application access and reduce the strain application distribution has on your network. Take, for example, Microsoft Office: When installed, you must send hundreds of megabytes to endpoints, but when you stream it, you only need to send 10 to 20 percent of the entire application set to your endpoints. Bits are only sent when users need them, not in one massive unicast distribution.

■ With application virtualization, you can now concentrate on a simpler way to build PCs. Create a core image with base utilities and updates. Ensure your SVS Pro agents are included in this image. Applications are assigned through the streaming engine, and user data and configuration settings are protected through built-in Windows features combining the roaming profile with folder redirection.

■ With AppV, you can now build one single reference computer and always keep it "clean" as applications are captured and prepared for streaming. Since few applications are hardware-dependent, you can even rely on a virtual machine for this system.

▲   Complete endpoint management means using point technologies where they fit best. Rely on your ESD system to manage the core OS, its updates, and the base utilities it includes. Rely on AppV to protect applications and package them only once for multiple target operating systems. Rely on streaming to provision end-user applications. Rely on your directory service to manage application groupings and end-user data. Use these integrated technologies to put an end once and for all to the application management nightmare and move to a 21st-century dynamic datacenter.

To implement this strategy, rely on the Ten Commandments of AppV:

1.   Learn how application virtualization can revolutionize the application life cycle.
2.   Determine which product best fits your needs.
3.   Experiment with the tool to understand its ins and outs.
4.   Categorize your applications and use application sponsors.
5.   Rationalize all applications.
6.   Use a standard system construction model and a standard system stack.
7.   Move to the application virtualization model.
8.   Remember that packaging best practices still apply.
9.   Rely on application streaming for delivery.
10.   Learn to manage the local cache.

With these commandments in mind, look to a completely new application life cycle (see Figure 12-2), one that replaces the traditional application management approaches.

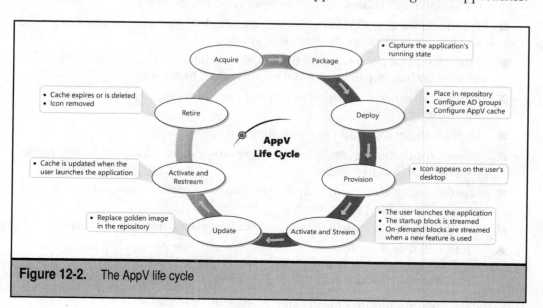

Figure 12-2.   The AppV life cycle

In the new life cycle, you begin by capturing an application's running state once the application has been approved for integration into your application portfolio. Then, you place it in the repository and configure the AD groups and the caching mode for the application. This is much simpler than traditional deployments. The shortcut icon appears on users' desktops when they log in. The application is streamed when activated.

If updates are required, apply them to the software repository. The next time the application is launched, it is automatically updated in the local cache. When it is time to retire the application, simply wipe the local cache and remove it from the repository. This is a powerful new application management model.

INTEGRATE APPLICATION, PROFILE, AND DESKTOP VIRTUALIZATION

Desktop virtualization offers the promise of centralized simplicity. Application virtualization offers the promise of applications on demand. Profile virtualization offers the promise of data protection at all times. Combining all three lets you create a completely new approach to desktop management. All three can now apply throughout the system construction model and continue to protect it at all times. In fact, this allows you to concentrate on the key components of any endpoint and protect them as follows:

▼   Use standard system construction practices to build the core OS. Rely on models such as the PASS system kernel to do so.

■   Install core utilities into the system—for example, the agents required to run the software components, including both AppV and streaming, as well as protection mechanisms, such as antivirus and antimalware.

■   Transform the core OS into an image to be deployed to all systems or deployed as a read-only desktop virtualization image.

■   From that point on, rely on traditional ESD technologies to manage installed utilities and update them as required, as well as to manage core OS updates.

■   Package all other applications as virtual applications and prepare them for streaming.

■   Deposit all packages into the streaming repository.

■   Stream applications globally, either in groups or on an ad hoc basis, and make them available at user login.

■   Use the streaming system to update all streamed applications and to manage application caching parameters.

■   Use the streaming system to manage and harvest all application licenses.

▲   Protect all user data through Windows' built-in user personality protection capabilities, such as roaming profiles and folder redirection, which can also cache user data locally in much the same way as the streaming system.

This strategy greatly simplifies the desktop management model.

Assign Applications on Demand

When you work with distributed systems, you need to manage components at several different levels. First, you need to manage and update the OS itself. Then, you need to manage and update any core utilities or drivers that have been deployed in support of the physical technologies your organization has selected. These two levels of management are often best controlled by ESD systems since these systems are designed to offer support for physical device control and reimaging. ESD systems are also best suited to the management of the agents you need to deploy for both AppV and streaming management.

In addition, the AppV and streaming datacenter will support new desktop management models.

▼   In an AppV and streaming datacenter, there is little or no need for presentation virtualization or the operation of applications on centralized servers that share access to the application for multiple users. Technologies such as Windows Terminal Services require the client to be physically connected to operate. In addition, they require massive servers that include multiple processors and heaps of memory to support application sharing. With a streaming system, you no longer need this application management model since streamed applications are cached locally and remain available when users are disconnected. In addition, the streaming server is nothing but a glorified file or web server, requiring fewer resources than Terminal Services servers.

■   By virtualizing desktops as well as applications, you can gain the best of all worlds. A desktop that relies on AppV, streaming, and a user information protection strategy becomes entirely volatile. This means that you do not need to assign specific desktops to end users. Each time a user connects to a virtual desktop, it is built to suit on-the-fly by generating the standard desktop, assigning the user's applications as required, and deploying the user's data as needed. Since the virtual desktop image, the virtualized applications, and the end-user data are all centralized on a storage area network (SAN) back-end, system construction is extremely fast—no network transmissions are required, and all data is located on the same disk sets.

▲   For end users that require high graphics capabilities, you can rely on centralized blade PCs—physical systems that are located in the datacenter and assigned to specific users. Blade PCs include hardware acceleration for graphics, providing the very best centralized desktop experience. Once again, since all data and applications are centralized, access to these systems is extremely fast and provides the very best experience for graphics-intensive users, such as engineers or graphic artists.

Each model provides a fast and efficient way to support both distributed and centralized PCs.

Use a Volatile Desktop VM

The next level is the productivity application layer. This level includes and addresses all of the virtualized and streamed applications that you manage and provide to your users, both internally and externally. The final level is the data level and is designed to protect end-user data and configuration options at all times. Designing your distributed systems management infrastructures in this manner lets you create a modern datacenter that will go a long way towards reducing traditional systems management headaches.

This simple process gives you the ability to manage all of your systems and provides you with an effective management model. In fact, all of your endpoints are transformed into a sort of "bull's eye target" that is made of three key layers (see Figure 12-3).

- ▼ The first layer consists of the OS itself.
- ■ The second layer is the application caching layer, where all virtualized applications reside.
- ▲ The third layer is the user data and configuration layer.

All three layers are completely protected at all times. For IT administrators, this means that you can reimage any PC at any time with little or no consequence. For users, it means that they can rely on any PC in the organization—physical or virtual—to work with both their own data and their own applications.

This new construction model can be applied to both physical computer instances and virtual desktops, letting you rely on a new "volatile" system construction strategy. But to do so, you need to put new elements in place in your datacenter.

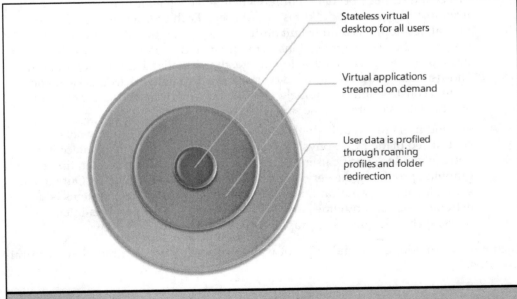

Stateless virtual desktop for all users

Virtual applications streamed on demand

User data is profiled through roaming profiles and folder redirection

Figure 12-3. The new "bull's eye" endpoint system stack

Virtualize User Profiles

While many AppV vendors are trying to put together special features that will protect user data at all times, you can begin to do this immediately through the built-in features of Windows. User data is stored within the user profile in Windows. This profile makes up the personality of each user's environment.

Personality protection is probably the most important aspect of operating system management; not, of course, from the technician's point of view, but rather, from the end user's point of view. After all, while we, as IT professionals, view a computer as a system we need to build and maintain; end users view it as a necessary evil they need to work with to perform their job functions. And personalities—the collection of data, favorites, desktop settings, application customizations, and more—are the most important aspect of this system for them.

That's because users perceive their computer's personality as part of their workspace, and many of them will spend considerable time optimizing it for the work they do. For many users, losing printer settings, e-mail configurations, Microsoft Word templates, or even the placement of shortcuts on their desktop can compromise their comfort level and effectiveness with any system. This disorientation decreases productivity and increases the help desk workload because it leads to unnecessary end-user support calls and training.

Therefore, preserving the personal computing environment of each user is a critical step in mitigating the productivity impact of any OS management strategy.

Define Your Personality Protection Policy

In order to define your protection policy, you first need to understand personalities or profiles and how they work. A profile is generated the first time a user logs on to a system. Basically, the first time the user logs on, the contents of the default user profile are copied and personalized for the user. The system automatically resets the security parameters of these contents so that the user has exclusive access to them. This is one reason why it is so important to properly manage the contents of the default user profile when you work with different operating systems. By creating one single default user view, you standardize how end users access and interact with the computer systems you deploy to them. Of course, they will make this profile evolve, but you can at least ensure that certain key elements remain common in all profiles.

Users can log on through a domain, relying on an Active Directory (AD) authentication, or through the local system, relying on the local security accounts manager (SAM) database that can be found on every Windows system. Each first-time logon will create a profile. This means that technicians who log on to a system for repair purposes will automatically generate a profile, as will any other user logging on for other purposes.

Most local logons are volatile because few organizations run their network without a central authentication database such as AD provides. This means that in most cases, you can discard any local profiles from your protection strategy—that is, unless you have custom systems that operate in a workgroup only. Many organizations use such systems to monitor and maintain systems connected to a demilitarized zone (DMZ), such as those found in a perimeter network. You can evaluate the opportunity to protect such local profiles versus having administrators and technicians re-create them when these machines are upgraded. If your default user profile is properly created, the value of protecting any local profile will be minimal.

Therefore, your protection policy should concentrate on profiles that are generated through domain logins. If your network offers a single PC to a principal user, you'll have it relatively easy, since all you will need to do is identify the principal user's profile on a system, protect it, and discard all other profiles. If your network uses shared computers, it will be slightly more difficult. Domain login profiles can also be protected by other means, such as roaming profiles—profiles that are stored on the network and download-ed to each PC as the user logs on—or folder redirection policies—Group Policy objects (GPOs) that move the contents of local folders found in the profile to network locations. Your analysis will need to take these factors into account if you want a protection policy that will meet the needs of every user in your network.

Some organizations, especially those that must operate 24/7, will also have generic accounts in their network. Generic accounts are shared accounts that allow operators to share a machine without needing to log on or off at the end of their shift. There are two types of generic production accounts. The first deals with 24/7 operations and is re-quired to run a machine without the need to log on or off. Operators share the password to this account and can thus change shifts without closing the session.

The second type is for environments that have a high personnel turnover. A good example of this is on naval vessels. Since officers and staff change almost every time the ship docks and crews are rotated, some organizations choose to use generic role-based ac-counts instead of named accounts. For example, a first officer would use the First Officer account instead of one named after him- or herself. In this situation, the password may or may not be shared. It depends on the amount of effort the administrative staff is willing to undertake at each crew change. They can either reset the passwords of each generic ac-count or not, as they want. Obviously, a policy that would require either named accounts that could be renamed each time a crew member changes, or password changes at each crew change, would be much more secure than one where passwords are shared.

Choosing the Profiles to Protect

Because of the various types of profiles in a network, you need to have the means to de-termine which profiles to protect. The best way to do this is to use a flowchart that identi-fies which profiles to protect and under which circumstances (see Figure 12-4). Keep in mind the reasons why you would or would not protect a given personality.

Your decision flow should include the following guidelines:

▼ Local profiles are only protected if they are situated on special machines that are not part of the domain and cannot be replaced by a custom default profile.

■ Domain profiles are protected if they have been used recently and on a constant basis.

■ Only profiles with actual content are protected (based on profile size).

■ Only active profiles are protected.

▲ If your machines have principal users, their domain profiles are protected at all times.

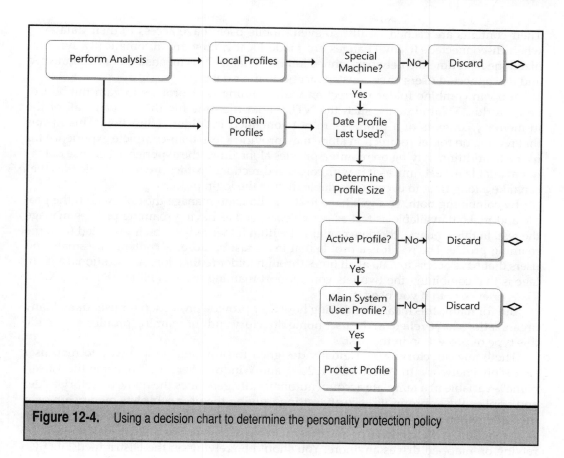

Figure 12-4.   Using a decision chart to determine the personality protection policy

There are, of course, other considerations, but these decisions should form the main crux of your personality protection policy.

Create the Personality Protection Strategy

Now that you know which profiles to protect—mostly domain profiles—you can move to the creation of your profile protection strategy. Microsoft has put in a lot of effort to make personality protection an everyday process. That's right—the entire User folder structure has been designed to provide support for one thing: folder redirection and general profile protection.

Folder redirection is an aspect of Group Policy that will automatically redirect user folders to central locations. When coupled with offline folder caching, folder redirection can provide the best of all worlds for users, whether they are roaming or not. Folders are located on network shares where they can be backed up and made available at all times.

Their contents are cached locally, so even mobile users have access to their data even when disconnected. If any changes are made locally, they are automatically synchronized the next time the network connection is available. This means that both connected and disconnected users have constant access to their data.

You can combine folder redirection with roaming user profiles to gain the best of both worlds. Volatile items, such the NTUser.dat file—the file that contains all of the in-memory contents of a profile—are not contained in folder redirection. This means that relying on folder redirection alone may provide a less-than-complete experience for users. In addition, relying on roaming profiles alone limits the experience because data is not available in real time as it is with folder redirection. Profiles are monolithic files that can take a long time to become available during the login process.

By combining both, you will have folder redirection manage the data within the profile and make it available as fast as possible, as well as having roaming profiles manage the rest. In this scenario, the data contained within folder redirection is excluded from the roaming profile. The result is a profile that loads fast because its contents are small, and users that have access to data at all times through folder redirection. An additional advantage is that combining the two lets you support roaming users in either Windows XP or Vista, or even both if you need it.

But for many, this means rethinking how they provide protection for user data. Many organizations have relied on the user home directory and/or roaming profiles to provide this type of protection in the past.

The home directory was originally designed to provide a simple way to map user shares on a network. In Windows NT, 2000, and Windows Server 2003, using the %username% variable in a template account automatically generates the home directory folder and applies the appropriate security settings, giving the user complete ownership over the folder when you create a new account. When the user logs on, this folder is automatically mapped to the H: drive or any other letter you assign. But today, you shouldn't be relying on mapped drives anymore. You should be relying on the Distributed File System (DFS), especially DFS namespaces.

DFS namespaces use universal naming convention (UNC) shares to map resources for users. But instead of using the \\servername\sharename approach, DFS namespaces use \\domainname\sharename and each namespace is mapped to an appropriate target in each site of your organization's network. DFS replication keeps the content of these target shares synchronized over the WAN.

NOTE Find more information on DFS at www.microsoft.com/windowsserver2003/technologies/storage/dfs/default.mspx.

Since Windows 2000, Microsoft has focused on the use of the My Documents folder as the home of all user documents. This folder is part of the security strategy for all Windows editions beyond Windows 2000, even though it has been renamed Documents in

Windows Vista. This folder is stored within a user's profile and is automatically protected from all other users (except, of course, administrators when appropriate access rights are assigned).

Folder Redirection in Windows XP

In Windows XP, folder redirection can manage four critical folders and assign network shares for each. These include:

- ▼ Application Data, which stores all application-specific settings.

- ■ Desktop, which includes everything users store on the desktop.

- ■ My Documents, which is the user's data storage folder. Storing the My Pictures subfolder on the network is optional.

- ▲ Start Menu, which includes all of a user's personal shortcuts.

When redirection is activated through Group Policy, the system creates a special folder based on the user's name (just like in the older home directory process) and applies the appropriate security settings. Each of the folders mentioned is created within the user's parent folder. Data in these folders is redirected from the desktop PC to the appropriate network folders and because of this, can also be made available offline for clients such as mobile users. When users are disconnected, data is stored locally; when they reconnect, it is automatically synchronized with the network folders.

But the user profile includes much more than these four main folders. In fact, highly volatile information, such as Local Data and Favorites, is not protected. Because of this, you can't rely on Windows XP's folder redirection alone to properly protect a system's personality.

NOTE For users that roam to remote offices, you can combine folder redirection with DFS namespaces and replicate the contents of their folders to DFS target shares in remote locations. Make sure you are running Windows Server 2003 R2 or later to take advantage of the new delta compression replication engine in DFS replication.

Folder Redirection in Windows Vista

All of this changes with Windows Vista because it finally provides a mechanism for true folder redirection and personality protection. This is evidenced in the settings available for folder redirection in a Vista Group Policy object (GPO). As you can see, it includes redirection for much more than XP ever did (see Figure 12-5).

This makes folder redirection an excellent choice for long-term personality protection since it is completely transparent to the user. While they think they are using the Documents folder located on their PC, they are actually using a folder that is located on the network. This way, you can ensure that all user data is protected at all times.

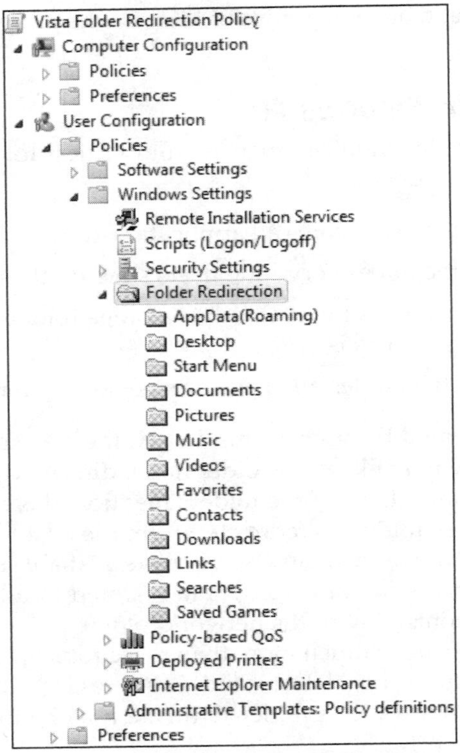

Figure 12-5.   Vista's Folder Redirection GPO

Using a folder redirection strategy rather than a home directory simplifies the user data management process and lets you take advantage of the advanced features of a Windows network. For example, even though data is stored on the network, it will be cached locally through offline files. Redirected folders are automatically cached through client-side caching when they are activated through a GPO. Data in these folders can also be encrypted through the Encrypted File System (EFS). In fact, all offline files can be encrypted.

Vista lets you redirect ten different folders. When you combine the redirection of these folders with roaming profiles, you offer the best roaming experience to users with a lower impact on network traffic than with roaming profiles alone (see Table 12-4).

Vista folder redirection policies include more settings than for XP. For example, you can automatically delete older or unused user profiles from your PCs (see Figure 12-6).

Folder to Redirect	Comments
AppData (Roaming)	This folder contains all roaming application data. Redirecting this folder will also support Windows XP clients with limitations.
Desktop	Users should not store data or any other items on their desktops; they should rely on the Quick Launch menu instead. This reduces the size of the folder to redirect. Include this in your communications to them.
	Redirecting this folder will also support Windows XP clients.
Start Menu	The contents of the Start menu are redirected. If you use application virtualization, users will always have access to their applications on any PC, even if they are not installed.
	Redirecting this folder will also support Windows XP clients.
Documents	This contains all user data. Make sure your storage policy and quotas support today's large file sizes and give users enough room to breathe.
	Redirecting this folder will also support Windows XP clients.
	Applying this policy to pre-Vista operating systems will automatically configure Pictures, Music, and Videos to follow Documents even if they are not configured.
Pictures	Determine if your organization wants to protect this folder. If you do, use the Follow The Documents Folder option or rely on the setting in Documents.
	Redirecting this folder will also support Windows XP clients.
Music	Determine if your organization wants to protect this folder. If you do, use the Follow The Documents Folder option or rely on the setting in Documents. Using this option will also support Windows XP clients.
Videos	Determine if your organization wants to protect this folder. If you do, use the Follow The Documents Folder option or rely on the setting in Documents. Using this option will also support Windows XP clients.
Favorites	Only applies to Vista.
Contacts	Only applies to Vista. If you are using Microsoft Outlook, this Contacts folder is not necessary.

Table 12-4.   Recommended Settings for Combining Vista Folder Redirection with Roaming Profiles

Folder to Redirect	Comments
Downloads	Only applies to Vista. You will need to determine if your organization wants to protect downloads users obtain from the Internet.
Links	Only applies to Vista.
Searches	Only applies to Vista.
Saved Games	Only applies to Vista. The contents of this folder are small and apply mostly to the games included in Vista. Your organization will need to determine if you want to spend network bandwidth and storage space on this content.

Table 12-4. Recommended Settings for Combining Vista Folder Redirection with Roaming Profiles (*continued*)

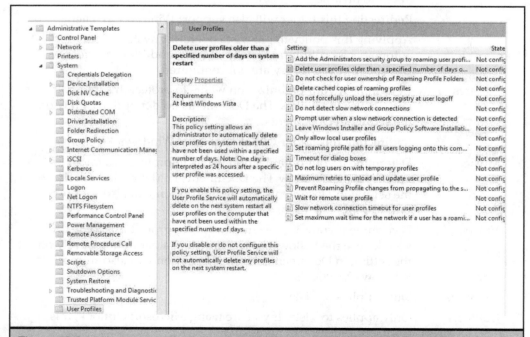

Figure 12-6. Windows Vista lets you control the behavior of user profiles on each PC.

In addition, the settings you can use for personality protection are much more granular than in any previous version of Windows. Music, Pictures, and Video can all be set to automatically follow the policy you set for the Documents folder.

You can also use the same policy to manage folder redirection for both Windows XP and Windows Vista (see Figure 12-7). This provides powerful system management capabilities and lets you set one single policy for both operating systems.

Enable Folder Redirection with Roaming Profiles

There are special considerations when enabling folder redirection. First, you need to ensure that each user is redirected to the appropriate server. It wouldn't do to have a user in New York redirected to a server in Los Angeles. To do this, you must create special administrative groups that can be used to regroup users and ensure that each user is assigned to the appropriate server; you most likely already have security groups you can use for this. You must also ensure that offline settings are appropriately configured to guarantee that users are working with the latest version of their offline files.

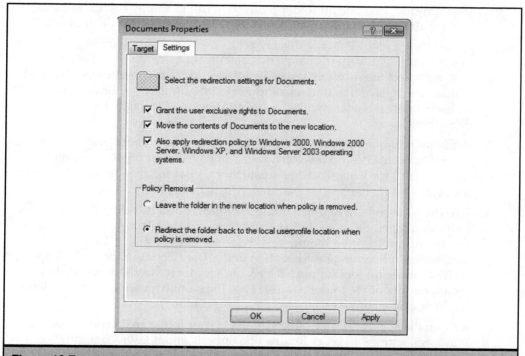

Figure 12-7.   Folder redirection in Vista offers several more choices than in Windows XP, but lets you set one policy for both Vista and XP.

CAUTION Make sure you assign appropriate amounts of storage to each user for folder redirection. There is no point in making this effort if you limit disk space access to something that is unacceptable.

Redirecting folders through user groupings is, in fact, similar to creating regional, or rather, geographically based user groups. Since each server is a physical location, you will need to create a user group for each one. Begin by enumerating the location of each file server that will host user folders and then name each global group accordingly. Once the groups are created, you can begin the redirection process. Using groups allows you to limit the number of GPOs required for the folder redirection implementation.

Use the following procedure to prepare your folder redirection with a roaming profiles strategy. Make sure you are running Windows Server 2003 Service Pack 1 (SP1), R2 or Windows Server 2008 as your server OS. Also, make sure all GPO settings are prepared and modified from a Vista PC with SP1 to gain access to the most complete settings.

1. Begin by creating the shares that will support redirection and roaming. You will need a minimum of two shares: one for the user profiles (for example, User_Profiles) and one for folder redirection (for example, Folder_Redir). If you are already using XP roaming profiles, use this share for the profiles.

2. Because Vista and XP do not display much user information during logon and logoff, you might want to change this default behavior. Apply a GPO to all PCs and select the Administrative Templates | System | Verbose Vs Normal Status Messages option under Computer Configuration | Policies. This will let users know what is happening during logon, and it might also be useful for debugging issues.

3. Verify that roaming profiles have been set up in user account properties in AD. If you use both XP and Vista, each user will have two profiles—version 1 for XP and version 2 for Vista. To differentiate them, Vista tacks on the .v2 extension to the profile folder names (for example, JDoe.v2).

4. To reduce the content of the roaming user profile and therefore limit network traffic and logon times, exclude key folders from the roaming profile contents. Use the Administrative Templates | System | User Profiles | Exclude Directories In Roaming Profile option under User Configuration | Policies. List each of the ten folders supported by Vista's folder redirection (see Table 12-4 for a reminder of the folder names). Type the name as it appears in Windows Explorer and separate each name with a semicolon (;).

5. Rely on the suggestions in Table 12-4 to set your folder redirection policy. Use Windows Settings | Folder Redirection options under User Configuration | Policies to do this. Change the property of each folder. Redirect them to your folder redirection share. Here are a couple of caveats:

   ■ When you set the folder properties for folders that are supported by both Windows XP and Vista, use the Also Allow Redirection Policy option under the Settings tab (see Figure 12-8).

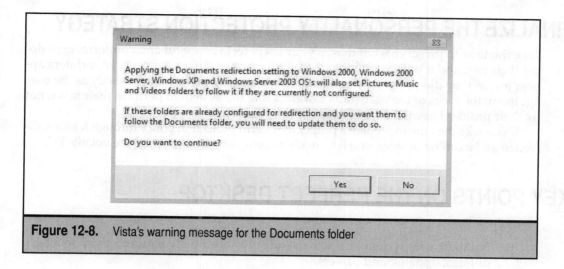

Figure 12-8.   Vista's warning message for the Documents folder

- When redirecting AppData (Roaming), you will get a compatibility warning message (see Figure 12-9). This is because older Windows operating systems do not support the full functionality of Vista in terms of folder redirection.

- When redirecting the Documents folder, you will also get a warning message. In this case, it tells you that by selecting to support older operating systems, you automatically change the behavior of the Pictures, Music, and Video folders; they will be protected by default and set to Follow The Documents Folder. If you do not want to protect them, set the policy explicitly for each folder.

Test the strategy in the lab before deploying it to production. To make sure you have it right, have expert users sign off on it through acceptance testing to make sure they are happy with its operation.

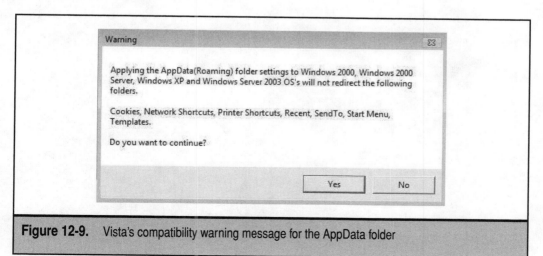

Figure 12-9.   Vista's compatibility warning message for the AppData folder

FINALIZE THE PERSONALITY PROTECTION STRATEGY

Take the time to preserve what makes your users feel successful and comfortable in doing their jobs and it will pay dividends. When mapped drives are restored, printers appear just as they did previously and data, shortcuts, and favorites are exactly as the user left them; the focus of the user shifts toward using the system to perform their tasks, not fix their profile. They will, therefore, be more productive.

If you take the time to prepare a proper long-term protection policy through folder redirection and roaming profiles, you'll be ready to provide full support for the volatile PC.

KEY POINTS ON THE PERFECT DESKTOP

Keep the following in mind when you set up your volatile PC strategy:

▼ Build the core system image to include only absolutely required components, utilities, updates, and drivers.

■ Virtualize all applications and provide them through a streaming engine to increase the speed of their availability.

▲ Virtualize all profiles and protect them outside of the PC image. Make sure the profiles are redirected to long-term shared file folders. Use DFS to simplify shared folder access.

This way, all of your centralized desktop virtualization images can be completely volatile and built on-the-fly as users log in. This will save inordinate amounts of disk space and will work to complement the delta-based differential VM files created by technologies such as XenDesktop or VMware View.

This is the only strategy to use when you want to move to virtual desktops and create a dynamic desktop datacenter strategy.

PART III

Consolidate the Benefits

CHAPTER 13

Secure Your Virtual Infrastructure

ecurity is a pervasive issue because it involves almost everything within your network. The object of security is to protect information. Determining the value of the information you need to protect will help you determine which level of security you need to apply to it.

While protecting traditional networks is nothing new, protecting virtual infrastructures presents challenges that you may never have faced before. First, you need to understand which types of challenges will arise in the resource pool, the grouping of your host servers. Second you need to learn if unknown or unforeseen challenges will arise in the infrastructure you create to run your virtual workloads. This division of the infrastructure into physical and virtual machines demands new approaches and a serious reflection on security practices.

However, traditional security approaches still apply even if you have two different infrastructures to protect. To protect each of these infrastructures, you must put in place a layered protection system that will provide the ability to perform the following activities:

▼ Identify people as they enter each infrastructure.

■ Identify appropriate clearance levels for people who work within each environment and provide them with appropriate access rights once identified.

■ Identify that the person modifying the data is the person who is authorized to modify the data (irrevocability or nonrepudiation).

■ Guarantee the confidentiality of information once it is stored within your infrastructures.

■ Guarantee the availability of information in your infrastructures.

■ Ensure the integrity of the data stored within your infrastructures.

■ Monitor the activities within each infrastructure.

■ Audit security events within the network and securely store historical auditing data.

▲ Put in place the appropriate administrative activities to ensure that the network is secure at all times and at all levels.

For each of these activities, there are various scopes of interaction.

▼ **Local**   People interact with systems at the local level; these systems must be protected, whether or not they are attached to a network.

■ **Intranet**   People interact with remote systems. These systems must also be protected at all times, whether they are located on the local area network (LAN) or the wide area network (WAN).

■ **Internet**   Systems that are deemed public must also be protected from attacks of all types. These are in a worse situation because they are exposed outside the boundaries of the internal network.

▲ **Extranet**   These systems are often deemed internal, but are exposed to partners, suppliers, and/or clients. The major difference between extranet and Internet systems is authentication—while there may be identification on an Internet system, authentication is *always* required to access an extranet environment.

Whatever its scope, security is an activity (like all IT activities) that relies on three key elements: *people, PCs,* and *processes*.

▼ **People** are the executors of the security process. They are also its main users.

■ **PCs** represent technology. They include a series of tools and components that support the security process.

▲ **Processes** are made up of workflow patterns, procedures, and standards for the application of security.

The integration of these three elements will help you design a security policy that is applicable to your entire organization.

THE CASTLE DEFENSE SYSTEM

The best way to define a security policy is to use a model. The model we have relied on for more than a decade is the Castle Defense System (CDS). In medieval times, people needed to protect themselves and their belongings through the design of a defense system that was primarily based on cumulative barriers to entry, or as we would say today, defense in depth. Your virtual environment should be protected the same way as you protect your physical network environment. A castle is used because it is an illustration that is familiar to almost everyone, from users to technicians as well as management.

NOTE   For more information on the Castle Defense System and how you apply it to virtual workloads, see *Microsoft Windows Server 2008: The Complete Reference* by Ruest and Ruest (McGraw-Hill, 2008).

An IT defense system should be designed in the same way as a CDS. Just like the CDS, the IT defense system requires layers of protection. In fact, five layers of protection seem appropriate. Starting from the inside, you'll find:

▼ **Layer 1: Critical Information**   The heart of the system is the information you seek to protect. This is the information *vault*.

■ **Layer 2: Physical Protection**   Security measures should always begin with a level of physical protection for information systems. This compares to the *castle* itself.

■ **Layer 3: Operating System Hardening**   Once the physical defenses have been put in place, you need to "harden" each computer's operating system in order to limit the potential attack surface as much as possible. This is the *courtyard*.

■ **Layer 4: Information Access**   When you give access to your data, you'll need to ensure that everyone is authenticated, authorized, and audited. These are the *castle walls* and the doors you open within them.

▲   **Layer 5: External Access**   The final layer of protection deals with the outside world. It includes the perimeter network and all of its defenses. It is your castle *moat*.

This is the Castle Defense System (see Figure 13-1). In order to become a complete security policy, it must be supplemented by two elements: people and processes. These two elements surround the CDS and complete the security policy picture it represents.

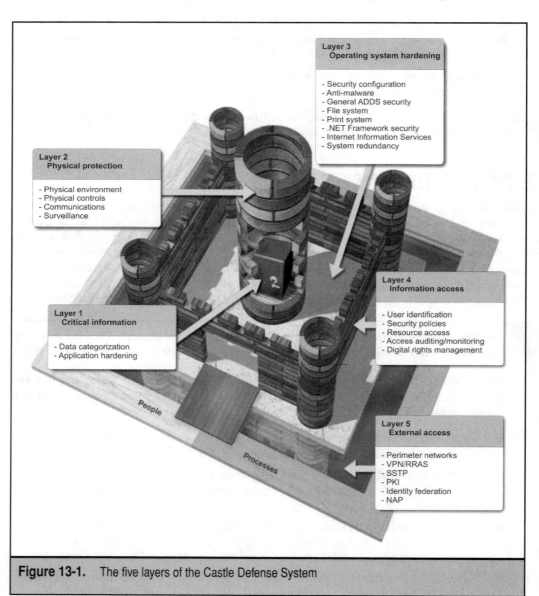

Figure 13-1.   The five layers of the Castle Defense System

Resource Pools Versus Virtual Service Offerings

The challenge is to identify how security must differ when running virtual infrastructures. Virtual Service Offerings (VSOs) will run all of the networked services your end users interact with. Therefore, the traditional security measures you undertake when building and designing these services still apply. The fact that users interact with virtual machines instead of physical machines does not change the need for tight security at all levels in this infrastructure.

What does change is how you secure resource pools. By their very nature, resource pools are not designed to interact with users. They are nothing more than host servers that run a virtualization engine. Because of this, they will be dealt with by administrators and technicians only. An end user running Microsoft Outlook will never have any interaction with the resource pool itself. Instead, the end user will interact with a number of different virtual machines running Active Directory, Microsoft Exchange, and perhaps a collaboration engine such as Microsoft Office SharePoint Server. Since these machines are all virtual, there is no direct interaction between users and host servers (see Figure 13-2).

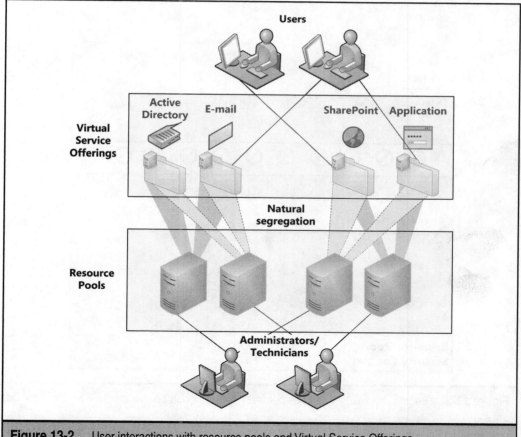

Figure 13-2.   User interactions with resource pools and Virtual Service Offerings

Because of this, you should consider creating segregated security contexts for both the resource pool and the Virtual Service Offerings (see Figure 13-3). By segregating security contexts, you are assured that there can be no seepage from one environment to another. For example, if you use two completely different security contexts, an end user from the VSO environment will not have any access to the resource pool.

The security context segregation is often facilitated by the very technologies you use to run your network services. For example, many organizations rely on Windows to run their user productivity infrastructure within the virtual workloads. If this is the case for you and you have decided to work with either Citrix XenServer or VMware Virtual Infrastructure (ESX or ESXi Server), the segregation will occur naturally since

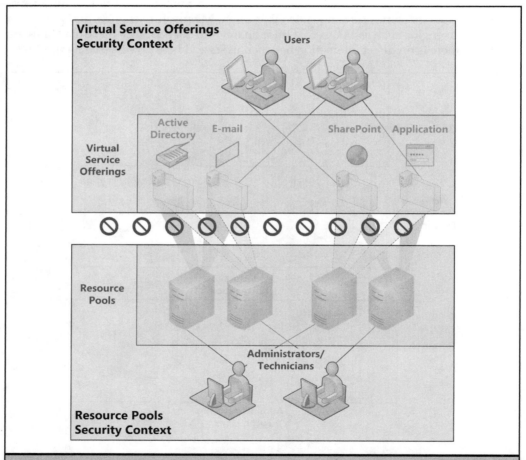

Figure 13-3. Segregated security contexts between resource pools and Virtual Service Offerings

both hypervisors run on a modified Linux infrastructure. However, you will need to make sure that you do not put in place any of the technologies that support the integration of security contexts between Windows and Linux. For example, you could create a Kerberos realm between Active Directory and a Linux security context. This would let you use single-sign-on between the two networks. But since your aim is to protect the host servers from end-user access, you would consciously make sure that these technologies are not linked together in this way.

If you use Linux to deliver your Virtual Service Offerings and you use either the Citrix or the VMware hypervisor, you'll be in a similar situation as if you were using Windows for VSOs and Hyper-V as the hypervisor. In this case, both environments use the same technologies to provide security contexts. Because of this, you need to consciously create separate security contexts to protect host server access. For example, in Windows, you would create an Active Directory (AD) forest for your production users and another for your resource pool. These two forests would not be linked together and would be kept separate at all times. Also, while your AD forest for production will most likely have a complex organizational unit (OU) structure, the forest you create for the resource pool should really be a utility forest and, as such, should rely on the most basic of OU structures.

Secure Resource Pools

Because you will be using segregated security contexts, you need to take a two-pronged approach to the design of your CDS. As mentioned earlier, the CDS for VSOs should really be similar to the standard defense mechanisms that you have used to date and, therefore, does not need to be covered in as much depth here.

Instead, you need to focus on creating a Castle Defense System for the resource pool itself since this is a new activity for you and your team. This pool must include strict protection strategies because it is so easy to walk away with an entire virtual machine. Anyone with an iPod and access to the virtual machines (VMs) can easily copy them and take them away.

As such, the CDS for resource pools will require particular attention to the levels identified in Table 13-1.

Resource pools are a new concept in IT and, therefore, need a particular attention to detail when it comes to the implementation of their security settings. You need to make sure you understand the scope of protection you need to apply to this infrastructure (see Figure 13-4). This scope will address only the host servers in the datacenter (blade or rack-mounted servers preferably), all-in-one box servers in remote offices, the machines used to control the host servers, and the machines used as consoles to access the host server management interfaces. The last set of machines can be virtual machines, running management server VMs in redundant configurations, and using virtual desktops tied to the resource pool security environment to connect to the management interfaces.

Layer	Contents	Contents
Layer 1: Critical information	Data categorization	Pay special attention to the files that make up virtual machines, their storage containers, and how people can access them, especially offline copies.
	Application hardening	Secure the database installations required to support the server virtualization engine or hypervisor you run.
Layer 2: Physical protection	Physical environment	Make sure datacenters have sufficient power and cooling resources.
		Remote offices should rely on server-in-a-box concept.
	Physical controls	Pay special attention to physical access to servers.
		All servers, especially remote servers, should be under lock and key.
	Communications	Make sure all resource pool administrators and technicians understand their responsibilities in terms of security practices.
	Surveillance	If possible have sign-in and sign-out sheets for administrators and technicians physically entering the datacenter.
Layer 3: OS hardening	Security configuration	Pay special attention to the server virtualization engine installation on each host server according to the manufacturer's best practices.
	File system	Secure the shared storage file system to protect VSOs.
	Print system	Not applicable because only administrators have access to this network and they can print from their workstations.

Table 13-1.   Applying the CDS to Resource Pools

Layer	Contents	Contents
	Web server	Implement tight Web server security if you need to rely on software virtualization engines such as Microsoft Virtual Server or VMware Server to add life to 32-bit hardware.
	System redundancy	Rely on the principles in Chapter 15 to ensure business continuity of host servers.
Layer 4: Information access	User identification	Create named accounts for each administrator or technician that has access to the resource pool.
	Security policies	Assign proper policies to the resource pool.
	Resource access	Only administrative accounts are required in this network. Use a proper delegation of administration strategy.
	Access auditing/ monitoring	Turn on auditing and logging to track all changes.
	Digital rights management	Not applicable since this infrastructure is not used to produce documentation.
Layer 5: External access	Perimeter networks	There is no perimeter network in the resource pool, but you should still properly configure the virtual LANs (VLANs) that control access to host servers.
	Virtual Private Networks (VPNs)	Rely on VPN connections for all remote administration.
	Routing and Remote Access (RRAS)	Implement a remote access authentication service for administrators working remotely.
	Secure Sockets Layer (SSL)	Ensure that all remote communications as well as internal intraserver communications are encrypted.

Table 13-1.   Applying the CDS to Resource Pools (*continued*)

Layer	Contents	Contents
	Public Key Infrastructures (PKIs)	Either purchase trusted server certificates for your servers or implement Active Directory Certificate Services (ADCS) in support of an internal server certificate deployment to support encrypted communications with host servers.
	Identity federation	Not applicable since there is no need for federation in this infrastructure.
	Network Access Protection (NAP)	Implement NAP if possible to ensure that all machines that link to the resource pool have approved health status.

Table 13-1. Applying the CDS to Resource Pools (*continued*)

Secure Virtual Service Offerings

Your Virtual Service Offerings will also require the application of the CDS. But in this case, you need to focus on all of the security elements you normally find in a production network. As such, the items identified in Table 13-2 are provided for your review only

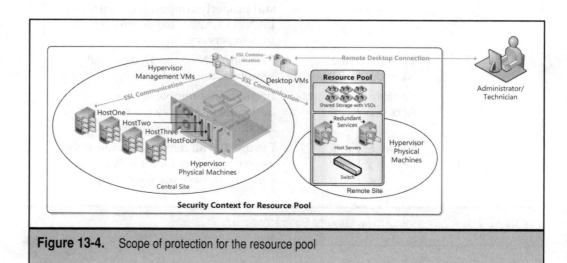

Figure 13-4. Scope of protection for the resource pool

because covering the full implementation of security settings for a production network is beyond the scope of this book. However, you can rely on this table as a type of checklist that identifies how the security of your production network should be addressed.

Layer	Contents	Contents
Layer 1: Critical information	Data categorization	Categorize the information that makes your organization run to identify the different levels of protection you need to apply to them.
	Application hardening	Make sure your vendors and your internal developers create secure code, and rely on best practices to harden each application.
Layer 2: Physical protection	Physical environment	There is little physical access to virtual machines except to the files that make it up.
		Protection for these files is addressed in the resource pool CDS, as is the security of the physical environment where host servers reside.
	Physical controls	Not applicable since this is applied at the resource pool level.
	Communications	Make sure all users, including administrators, understand their responsibilities in terms of security practices. However, end users do not need to know if the machines they interact with are virtual or physical. This information is privileged and should be available to administrators and technicians only. Both should be briefed on the privacy of this information.
	Surveillance	Be as vigilant as possible and control USB device access on physical desktops within the production network.

Table 13-2.   Applying the CDS to Virtual Service Offerings

Layer	Contents	Contents
Layer 3: OS hardening	Security configuration	Pay special attention to the following: Service hardening.
		Security configuration settings for virtual servers.
		Limited role installations on each virtual machine with only required components for the service it delivers. You might even consider creating more single-purpose machines to avoid having to secure multiple roles on the same VM.
		If you are running Windows Server, consider the following as well:
		BitLocker Drive Encryption for servers playing critical roles.
		User Account Control (UAC) for all administrators and all users.
		Device Control to ensure that unauthorized USB disk drives cannot be connected to any access point, including any physical PC on the network.
		BitLocker Drive Encryption for highly secure notebooks.
		Wireless networking security.
	Antimalware	Implement proper antimalware engine along with proper antivirus technologies.
	General directory security	Implement tight permissions management.
		Implement multiple password policies to require highly complex passwords and perhaps smart cards for administrators.
		Tighten delegation of authority settings on your servers.
		Implement read-only domain controllers in remote offices if using Windows.

Table 13-2.   Applying the CDS to Virtual Service Offerings (*continued*)

Layer	Contents	Contents
		Implement software restriction policies to ensure that no malicious code is allowed to run in the production domain.
	File system	Secure the file system to protect VSOs.
		Implement access-based enumeration to further protect information.
		Rely on digitally signed Windows Installer Packages for all third-party or custom product installations.
	Print system	Implement a full security strategy for all printers.
	.NET Framework security (Windows)	Applicable to any machine that has an application role or any machine that includes PowerShell (in most cases, this will be every Windows server in the VSO network).
	Web services	Implement tight Web server security on all Web servers.
	System redundancy	Rely on the principles in Chapter 15 to ensure business continuity of key VSO servers.
Layer 4: Information access	User identification	Rely on smart card or two-factor authentication for administrators in highly secure environments.
		Highly secure environments will use two-factor authentication for all users.
		Otherwise, use complex passwords for all users.
	Security policies	Assign proper policies for the VSO network.
	Resource access	Tightly control all resource access.
		Implement Encrypting File System (EFS) for mobile users.

Table 13-2.   Applying the CDS to Virtual Service Offerings (*continued*)

Layer	Contents	Contents
		Rely on lightweight directories such as Active Directory Lightweight Directory Services (ADLDS) for custom application resource access.
	Role-based access control	Implement in every application as much as possible.
	Access auditing/ monitoring	Turn on auditing as well as directory auditing to track all changes.
	Digital rights management (DRM)	If using Windows, rely on AD Rights Management Services (ADRMS) to apply DRM to all documentation that is copyrighted or sensitive in any other fashion.
Layer 5: External access	Perimeter networks	Configure server firewalls with control access to all servers, especially those in the perimeter network.
		Apply the built-in firewall to XP and Vista PCs and mobile workstations.
	Virtual Private Networks	Rely on VPN connections for all remote access.
	Routing and Remote Access	Implement a remote access authentication service for users working remotely.
	Secure Sockets Layer	Ensure that all remote communications as well as internal intraserver communications are encrypted.
	Public Key Infrastructures	If using Windows, implement Active Directory Certificate Services (ADCS) in support of smart card deployment and software restrictions. If not, use a third-party certification engine.
	Identity federation	If using Windows, rely on AD Federation Services (ADFS) for extranet access if it is required.
	Network Access Protection	Implement NAP to ensure that all machines that link to the VSO network have approved health status.

Table 13-2.   Applying the CDS to Virtual Service Offerings (*continued*)

Virtual Service Offerings require more in terms of security settings than resource pools because they are designed to interact with end users and, therefore, have more services built into the infrastructure. The scope of protection for VSOs will depend on the size of your organization. Certain security technologies are reserved for resource pools, as some are reserved for Virtual Service Offerings. For example, there is little need to run digital rights management within the resource pool since this infrastructure is not a productivity network. Keep this in mind when you review the security settings of the services your virtual machines offer to your users.

APPLY THE CASTLE DEFENSE SYSTEM TO THE RESOURCE POOL

To address the security of the resource pool, all you need to do is follow the guidelines in Table 13-1. Address each of the layers of the Castle Defense System one by one and make sure the resource pool is as secure as it can be. Security practices will differ based on the hypervisor you have elected to run. They will also differ based on the level of virtualization you have achieved. For example, if you only work with server virtualization, you will only need to secure the environment and the VMs that make it up. If you have elected to work with desktop virtualization, you will need to secure the core virtual machine because you should be working with read-only desktop VMs that are volatile and can be assigned to any user. If you are working with application virtualization, then depending on whether you are using agent-based or agentless application virtualization (AppV), you will need to consider how you secure and protect your virtual applications.

Considerations for each are discussed in the following sections.

Layer 1: Critical Information

The first place to start is with what you need to protect. In terms of resource pools, you need to protect two layers of data.

▼ The virtual disk drives that make up each virtual machine in the VSO network. This includes online and running machines, offline machines, virtual appliances (VAPs) or virtual machine templates, and any other virtual machine container.

▲ Data contained within the management database. The database engine you use to store this data will vary, depending on which hypervisor you have selected to run, but most every hypervisor management engine relies on a database to store information such as settings files, policies tied to VMs, host configuration settings, and more.

Each of these requires special attention.

Protect Virtual Disk Drives

Protecting virtual disk drives means more than protecting the .vhd or .vmdk files that make up your virtual machines. You must also protect configuration files, snapshot files, log files, and anything else that can make up a virtual machine in your network. This would also include any templates or virtual appliances you obtained in Open Virtualization Format (OVF), as well as the VAPs you create in-house, such as Windows-based VM templates. It would also include the ISO files you use to store source operating systems and other server technologies.

In most cases, your virtual machines and related files will be located in up to six different types of containers.

▼ Server VMs located in the datacenter will reside in some form of shared storage. Whether you use network attached storage (NAS) or a storage area network (SAN), the storage container's engine will provide technologies and features in support of data protection and security.

■ Server VMs located in remote sites will be in an all-in-one box server, which should be using shared storage as well. Rely on the storage infrastructure's capabilities to secure the contents.

■ Shared content, such as ISO images and source software, is usually contained within a library file share. For VMware and XenServer, this is usually a Network File System (NFS) share, but both can also work with the Common Internet File System (CIFS), which is usually found in Windows. In either case, make sure your disks are formatted in a system equivalent to New Technology File System (NTFS) and provide tight file share permissions. This container might also store offline VMs or OVF files. Be sure to provide tight protection for the folders that contain these files.

■ Unit and functional testing and development VMs may be transported in external USB disk drives. Use at least NTFS to format the drives if you run your test and development environments on Windows. You might also consider using the Encrypted File System to further protect the contents of these drives.

■ Data protection strategies involve backing up the VMs and creating VM snapshots. These should be kept centrally within the datacenter and should be hosted on shared storage to provide the highest level of security. If you back up to tape, make sure your offline vault is totally secure, as is your method of transport to the vault.

▲ Business continuity strategies for VMs involve replication from one location to another, usually from the core datacenter to a remote backup datacenter. Make sure you implement the same or similar security strategies in both datacenters.

Any time a machine is made virtual, it is made transportable. In addition, virtual machines are self-contained and will often include highly sensitive information, such as passwords and access rights. If someone is able to walk off with your VMs without your knowledge, they can take all the time in the world to decipher them and discover your most guarded secrets. Make sure your administration personnel are completely trustworthy to protect this information.

Protect Management Data

Every hypervisor management system runs on a database. VMware VirtualCenter runs on either Microsoft SQL Server or on an Oracle database. It also works with the Microsoft SQL Server 2005 Express Edition, but this engine is only supported for production environments with up to five host servers. Microsoft System Center Virtual Machine Manager also requires a database, and because it is Microsoft, the database runs in SQL Server.

The exception is Citrix XenCenter. It does not rely on a database. Instead, it stores all configuration data inside Extended Markup Language (XML) files on each host. Host configuration files are collected together when you build resource pools or pools of servers linked together in a high-availability configuration through a master/slave relationship, which resembles the traditional primary versus secondary Domain Name System (DNS) server relationship. Because each host contains a copy of all of the configuration files for the resource pool, it can act as a master whenever one of the other hosts fails.

When you run hypervisors directly through the hypervisor's management tool, for example, through Virtual Infrastructure Client in VMware or through Hyper-V Manager in Windows, you do not use a database because settings are located on the host server alone. Unlike with XenCenter, these files are not replicated from one machine to another, though you could easily do so if you want.

Centralizing management data into a database makes sense as long as you make sure this database is always highly available (see Chapter 15). However, there are two aspects you must consider from the data security point of view.

▼ You must make sure that only the appropriate people have access to the data held within the management database. In addition, secure your data at two levels. First, protect it through the same mechanisms you use for documents because databases store information in files just like documents. Second, protect it through the features of the database system used to store it.

▲ You also have to make sure that your installation of the database engine is hardened and protected. SQL Server especially has a great reputation for being wide open. Of course, Microsoft has done a lot of work to tighten the security around SQL Server in their 2005 and 2008 releases, but this is no reason why you shouldn't make sure the installation and configuration of the database engine is as tight as it can be.

Whether the data is in distributed repositories or within a central database, make sure it is protected at all times.

> ***NOTE***   For information on SQL Server security best practices, look up download.microsoft
> .com/download/8/5/e/85eea4fa-b3bb-4426-97d0-7f7151b2011c/SQL2005SecBestPract.doc.
> You can also rely on the Microsoft Baseline Security Analyzer to check your SQL Server installation
> (http://technet.microsoft.com/en-us/security/cc184924.aspx). For information on Oracle database
> security best practices, look up the Oracle security technology center at www.oracle.com/technology/
> deploy/security/index.html.

Layer 2: Physical Protection

The second layer of security lies with the physical protection of your computing systems.
Physical protection deals with a variety of issues. A physical server that is located under
a stairway in some regional office cannot be considered secure by any means, unless,
of course, it is contained within a proper system casing, such as those provided by Kell
Systems (www.kellsystems.com).

As you will imagine, this layer mostly applies to resource pools, but it also extends
to your PCs or any physical system that has the right to connect to your network, even
if they only interact with VSOs. Of course, since most organizations moving to a virtual
infrastructure are moving from a physical infrastructure, most of the elements in this
layer should already be familiar to you and you should already have most of its elements
in place.

The elements that you need to cover at the physical protection layer include:

▼   **Geographical location**   Is the physical location of your buildings within
environmentally endangered locations? Is there the possibility of floods,
avalanches, or cave-ins that may affect the buildings you do business in? Are
they near roads where accidents may affect the building?

■   **Social environment**   Are your personnel aware that physical access to any
computing equipment should be protected at all times? Are they aware that
they should never divulge passwords under any circumstance?

■   **Building security**   Are your buildings secure? Are entries guarded and are
visitors identified at all locations? Are guests escorted at all times? Are rogue
computing devices allowed within your buildings? Is the electrical input to
the building protected; does it have a backup, especially for datacenters? Is the
building's air control protected and does it include a backup system? Is there a
good fire protection plan in all buildings? Is the wiring inside and outside the
building secure? Are wireless emissions secure?

■   **Building construction**   Is the building construction safe? Are the walls
in your datacenters fireproof? Are datacenter doors firebreaks? Are floors
covered in antistatic material? If there is a generator on premises, is it in a
safe and protected location? Does the computer room protect communication
equipment as well as computer equipment? Does the building include security
cameras to assist surveillance?

- **Server security**   Are servers within locked rooms or locked cabinets in all locations? Is access to server rooms monitored and protected? Are the servers themselves physically secured? Is access to physical servers controlled? Windows Server 2008 supports the use of smart cards for administrator accounts. In highly secure environments, you should assign smart cards to all administrators. With new low-cost smart card options, especially USB smart cards, there are few reasons not to implement this policy.

- **BIOS security**   All computing devices should have some form of protection at the BIOS level. For physical host servers, this should also include power-on passwords. For all systems, BIOS settings should be password-protected and like all passwords, these passwords should be highly protected and modified on a regular basis. New desktop management interface (DMI) management tools allow for the centralization of BIOS password management.

- **Staging security**   Are all physical security policies extended to staging rooms where physical systems are installed? It doesn't do to have highly secure computer rooms when the staging facilities are wide open. Note that with built-in hypervisors, staging a host server is much less time-consuming than traditional system staging, but if you run Microsoft Hyper-V or if you still build physical PCs, you will require a staging area, which must be secured.

- **PC security**   Are workstations and mobile devices secure? Are hardware identification systems such as biometrics and smart cards used for mobile devices? Is data on the mobile device secure when the device is in transit? Are external connections from the mobile devices to the internal network secure? Do you control the connection of rogue USB devices?

- **Network security**   Are the network and its services secure? Is it possible for someone to introduce rogue Dynamic Host Configuration Protocol (DHCP) servers, for example? With Windows Server 2008, as with Windows 2000/2003, DHCP servers must be authorized to allocate addresses, but only if they are Windows-based DHCP servers. Is there a wireless network in place? Is it secure? Can rogue wireless users penetrate the network?

- ▲ **Redundancy**   Are your critical systems redundant? This should include all systems—data systems, fire protection, Internet and WAN connections, air conditioning, electrical, and so on.

All of the physical aspects of your installations must be maintained and documented. In addition, appropriate aspects of the physical protection plan must be communicated to employees at all levels. Note, however, that host server systems will not require user interaction and, therefore, can be omitted from the general end-user communication plan, but not from technicians and administrators.

Finally, physical protection must be supplemented by a surveillance program. Once again, this is a part that can be played by personnel at all levels. Each employee must be aware that they can and should participate in the surveillance of any suspicious activity or the notification of any untoward event that may compromise your information systems.

Layer 3: Operating System Hardening

The object of operating system hardening is to reduce the attack surface of your servers and PCs. To do so, you need to remove anything that is not required on a system. For host servers that run bare-metal hypervisors, this hardening process is straightforward since the hypervisor is already pared down to the bare essentials.

However, a host server infrastructure includes several different components (see Figure 13-4 again).

▼ The hypervisor, which is like a bare-metal operating system (OS) on each host

■ The console system, which in most cases runs on Windows servers

■ The desktops or remote systems administrators use to access the console through management clients

■ The database or file repositories that store configuration and policy information about the resource pool

■ The storage containers that serve as a repository for all VMs

■ The file share that stores all source and ISO files

▲ The security context you use to assign administrative roles in the resource pool

And, as mentioned previously, the structure of each of these elements will differ based on the type of hypervisor you run. But no matter which system you run, you should consider the following for each of the components that make up the resource pool infrastructure:

▼ System security configuration

■ Antimalware strategy

■ Directory service security

■ File system security

■ Print system security

■ .NET Framework security (in Windows, especially with PowerShell)

■ Web server security

▲ System redundancy

Each of these elements requires particular attention for resource pools.

System Security Configuration for Host Servers

System security configuration involves the application of security parameters during the machine staging process. When you install a machine, especially a server, you need to perform some modifications to the default installation to ensure that your machine is protected.

For VMware ESX server, the operation is relatively simple; just set Security=high during the installation and it will automatically configure the hypervisor in a secure mode. This is the default installation setting for VMware ESX. It automatically encrypts all traffic to and from the server, user names and passwords are never sent in clear text, and no FTP access is allowed to the server.

For Citrix XenServer, you must harden the host OS through standard Linux security practices. For Microsoft Hyper-V, you must first make sure you install Server Core on your hosts and then harden the installation as much as possible through standard Windows security practices. Fortunately, Windows Server 2008 already does a good job of hardening the OS on its own, especially Server Core, because it installs only the barest of components—the complete installation, including the Hyper-V role, is less than 2.6GB—and then you add the required roles and features to the server. Since it is Server Core, it does not include the .NET Framework or Internet Information Services by default and it does not include any graphical user interface components, such as Microsoft Internet Explorer or Windows Media Player.

In addition, both the Citrix XenServer and the Windows Server 2008 installations are true 64-bit operating systems, which, by default, contain additional security components. However, at 32MB, VMware's ESXi is tightly controlled even though it is a 32-bit engine.

Since Windows Hyper-V and Citrix XenServer run on more complete operating systems, you should perform two additional activities on each server.

▼   First, perform some post-installation security configuration modifications.

▲   Second, apply security templates to the server by server role. In Windows, this second portion of the system configuration process relies on the Security Configuration Wizard (SCW) to automatically apply security settings to your system based on its role. In Linux, you may have to use a third-party security configuration tool to tighten security settings.

Tighten OS security as much as possible to fully protect your host servers.

NOTE   For information on securing Hyper-V hosts, see Chapter 10 of *Microsoft Windows Server 2008: The Complete Reference* by Ruest and Ruest (McGraw-Hill, 2008). For information on securing ESX Server, see the Top 10 Recommendations for Improving VMware ESX Security at http://blogs .vmware.com/vmtn/2007/02/top_10_recommen.html.

System Security Configuration for Console Servers

Console servers mostly run on Windows Server. Ideally, you will be using Windows Server 2008 (WS08), since it is the most secure server OS Microsoft has ever released. But since this server is a Windows server, you should perform a minimal installation and add no additional roles to the server as much as possible. If you are using WS08, you will need to perform a Full Installation since the console components require the installation of graphical components.

In this case, you should prepare a security configuration with the Security Configuration Wizard and tighten any and all of the components of the server. Remove or at least disable any unused services. SCW is the best tool to secure Windows servers because it provides complete information on each of the items you choose to enable or disable, letting you understand exactly what you are doing (see Figure 13-5). In addition, you can

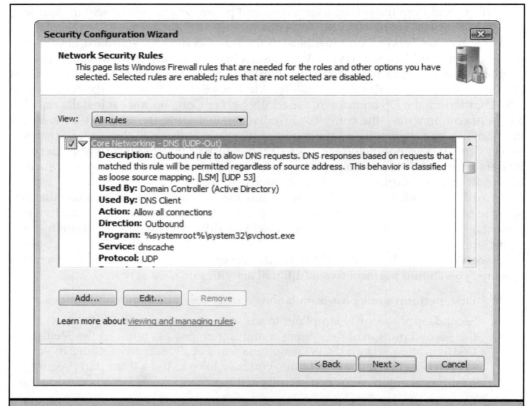

Figure 13-5. The Security Configuration Wizard provides extensive information on each security element it applies.

create templates with SCW to apply the same changes to any other console server you need to create or install.

You can run SCW in auditing mode if you are unfamiliar with it. This lets you gain a better understanding of its workings and does not make any actual changes to the system. Then, when you are more familiar with the tool, you can use it to tighten security on your Windows servers.

NOTE For more information on the Security Configuration Wizard, go to http://technet.microsoft .com/en-us/library/cc771492.aspx.

Antimalware Strategies

A lot has been said about running antimalware software, including antivirus software, on host systems. If you are running Hyper-V or XenServer, you should consider a standard

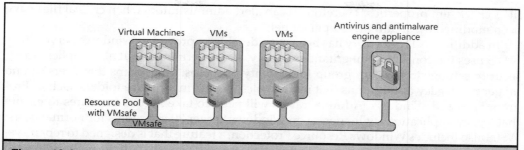

Figure 13-6.   VMware's VMsafe runs directly on the hypervisor and provides full protection for any VM.

antivirus program for Windows or Linux. No full-system OS should run without this type of protection, even if it impacts system performance.

If you are running ESX Server, you should run VMsafe. VMsafe runs directly on the ESX hypervisor and provides application programming interfaces for common antivirus and antimalware tools to run on top of it (see Figure 13-6). Because it runs on the hypervisor, you do not need to add antimalware or antivirus technologies inside the virtual machines. Any VM you place on a hypervisor using VMsafe will automatically be protected. VMsafe scans critical VM components, such as memory, CPU, network, and disk resources. It even scans internal VM processes for protection.

VMsafe provides a new way to protect VMs. For example, if you run the console systems in virtual machines on top of a hypervisor running VMsafe with a proper antivirus engine, you do not need to add the overhead of an AV engine inside the console VM. This greatly facilitates VM creation and provides ongoing protection for any VM.

NOTE   To learn more about VMsafe, go to www.vmware.com/overview/security/vmsafe.html#. Note that VMsafe was not yet available at the time of writing of this book.

The VMsafe model is proving to be so compelling that the developers of Xen virtualization components in Linux distributions are working on a similar feature. This feature should be available in future iterations for Xen-based hypervisors.

File and Print System Security

The file system is also a portion of operating system hardening that supports a secure environment. If you are running Windows, you must use NTFS. There is no doubt that despite its reported failings, NTFS is an absolute must and a pillar of the Castle Defense System. Without NTFS, there is no encryption. In Linux, you must run a secure file system.

One of the important aspects of secure file management is the ability to log all file changes and alert organizations when unauthorized changes occur. This can be done in some form with file access auditing, but for critical data files, professional help is required. This help comes in the form of a utility such as Tripwire for Servers (www.tripwire.com/products/servers). Tripwire monitors all file changes, even down to the file's checksum properties. Therefore, it can alert administrators when critical files have been modified by unauthorized personnel.

In addition, NTFS security has been considerably improved in Windows Server 2008. NTFS uses the concept of inheritance to apply access permissions. It also applies strong security settings to the User group for stability purposes. This means that users can no longer run legacy applications that modify files located in sensitive folders such as Program Files and Windows. Administrators will need to take special measures to ensure that legacy applications will operate on Windows Server 2008 systems for normal users. WS08 also includes Windows Resource Protection, a feature that is designed to repair system files and registry entries when damaged by software installations or other untoward events. More information on these features is available in the WS08 Help system.

Make sure that all file repositories are secured through the best features of the OS that supports them.

As for print systems, there is little need for print systems within the host infrastructure because all VM communications are performed through Remote Desktop Connection (RDC) and you can simply configure RDC to automatically connect the printer of your own desktop to the remote system (see Figure 13-7). This means you have one less element to secure in the host infrastructure.

Figure 13-7.   Using the Remote Desktop Connection settings, you can connect local printers to any session.

Directory Service Hardening

Because consoles run on Windows, many organizations find it easier to configure an Active Directory within the resource pool to provide centralized access control. And if you run Hyper-V, even on Server Core, you will require the implementation of an Active Directory Domain Services (ADDS) directory.

In either case, you should create what is called a utility directory. Utility directories use a simple forest structure, usually including a single root domain. Since you will not have any users interacting with this directory—only administrators and technicians—you can run utility directories in host environments because you do not need to provide protection for root-level access in the directory.

In hypervisors such as VMware ESX Server, you can rely on the utility directory to provide role-based access to console components. Simply create a series of different security groups in ADDS and assign each group to the various roles supported in Virtual-Center (see Figure 13-8). Then, tie your ADDS security groups to the roles in the console

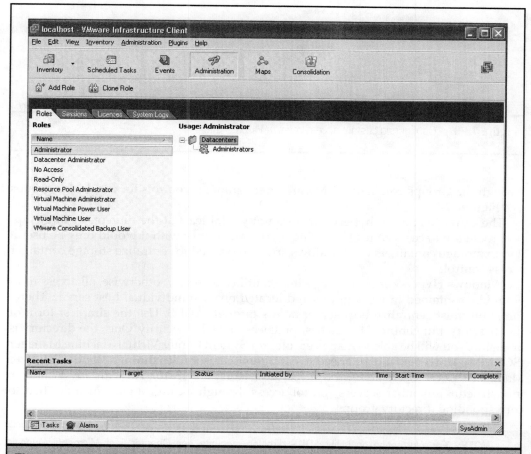

Figure 13-8.   VMware VirtualCenter offers several default access roles.

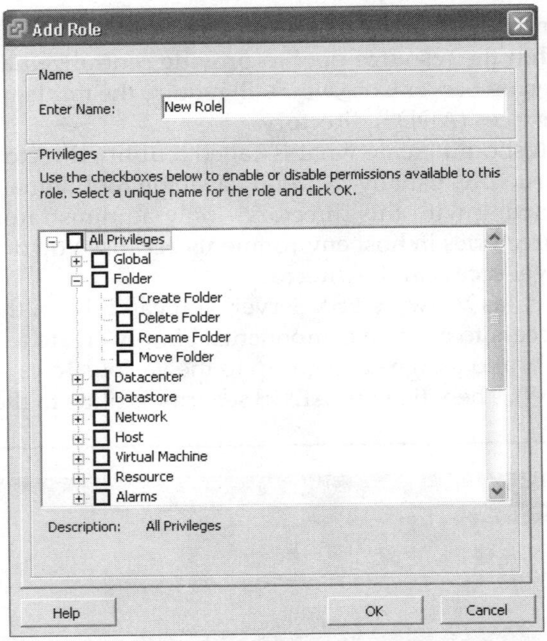

Figure 13-9.   Configuring custom access roles in VirtualCenter

through the Groups command. VMware offers granular controls for role-based groups (see Figure 13-9).

The Citrix XenServer hypervisor does not yet (at least at the time of writing) support role-based access control, so using a utility directory with it would only be useful if your storage containers ran Windows and you wanted to centralize storage container access control.

Windows Hyper-V must be run within a utility directory; otherwise, all access roles would be contained in workgroups and located on each individual host server. Therefore, you must centralize host server access through ADDS. Use the simplest form of the directory, but continue to use best practices in ADDS security. Once the directory is available, you will be able to map user roles for System Center Virtual Machine Manager (SCVMM). However, you will need to configure the user roles through Windows Server Manager's Local Users and Groups feature (see Figure 13-10). As with any Windows infrastructure, member servers control access through local groups, which are tied to corresponding directory groups.

NOTE For information on utility ADDS directory security, see Chapter 5 of *Microsoft Windows Server 2008: The Complete Reference* by Ruest and Ruest (McGraw-Hill, 2008).

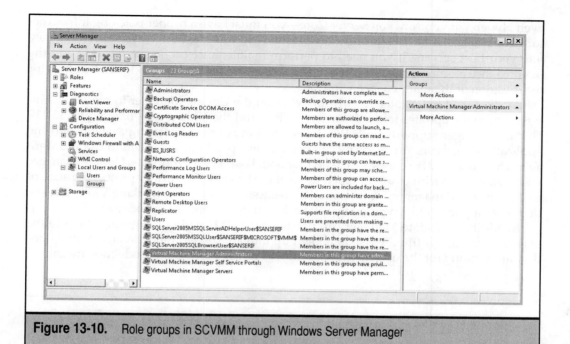

Figure 13-10. Role groups in SCVMM through Windows Server Manager

When you build your utility directory, you may consider placing this role on the same servers running your console services for several reasons.

▼ First, the console servers should be set to autostart if they are running on VMs so that you have access to infrastructure management tools as soon as your host servers are booted up. The utility directory service also needs to autostart to ensure you can log into the environment when it boots up.

■ Second, you want to limit the number of Windows servers you run in your infrastructure—at least if you are not using a Windows hypervisor—to keep the environment as secure as possible. By placing both the management and the directory role on the same servers, you minimize the number of Windows VMs you require.

▲ Third, by integrating the two services together, you will gain faster throughput for authentication since directory communications will be direct.

One drawback is that you must give local logon access to some of the more restrained roles in the management console. However, you may not even require the restrained roles in your network, so this issue may well be moot.

Final Operating System Hardening Activities

Additional activities are required for you to finalize the hardening of your operating systems. The first involves updates and patches. While hypervisors are rarely updated—yes, even Hyper-V if you run it on Server Core—you must have a proper patching infrastructure in place for them. This is one more reason why you must build system redundancy into your host servers. If you need to perform maintenance on one host server and the maintenance requires a reboot, you must be able to move your VMs off to another host for the duration of the maintenance window.

As discussed in Chapter 7, VMware relies on the Update Manager to provide its infrastructure for updates for both the hypervisor and the VMs it runs (see Figure 13-11). Update Manager supports both Windows and Linux guest operating systems and the applications they run. You begin by creating baseline patching levels within Update Manager. Then, once the baselines are created for both host servers and VMs, Update Manager will ensure the machines are updated to meet the baseline. To further protect the state of a VM, Update Manager will automatically create snapshots of the working VM before the update is applied, letting you easily roll back updates if something goes awry.

In addition, Update Manager can patch offline VMs without exposing them to the network. To do so, offline VMs are booted up into an isolated mode to ensure that once they are running for the update process, they do not interfere with production machines.

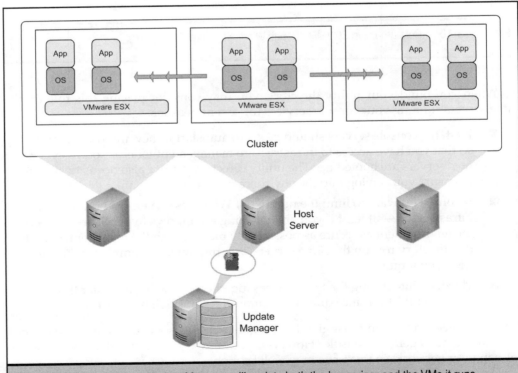

Figure 13-11. VMware Update Manager will update both the hypervisor and the VMs it runs.

However, the ability to automatically update offline machines is an essential part of any virtualization implementation, since only in this instance will you have multiple copies of a specific machine.

To protect hypervisors and the workloads they run, Update Manager will work in conjunction with VMware's Distributed Resource Scheduler (DRS) to move VM workloads to other hosts before a patch is applied to the current host. It moves the VMs back once the newly patched host is back up and running. Because it provides a critical role for VMs and hosts, Update Manager is part of every edition of VMware's Virtual Infrastructure.

Citrix XenServer includes a similar ability through its XenCenter management interface. Pool-wide patching will automatically check with the Citrix Web site to see if patches are available for XenServer and, if a patch is available, move workloads off the host with XenMotion before patching it in a method similar to VMware Update Manager. Pool-wide patching is performed through a wizard that takes you through the process step by step. However, this capability is only available for the XenServer hosts, not the VMs they run. For VM patching, you need to turn to a third-party solution.

Microsoft relies on the free Windows Server Update Services (WSUS) to patch both hosts and VMs. WSUS would also be required if you run Windows VMs on XenServer, since XenServer does not patch VMs. WSUS maintains a database of baseline patch levels for different machine types. Machines are patched on a schedule you set through the Windows Update client within each version of Windows. Microsoft also offers other products that support patching, such as System Center Essentials for small to medium firms or System Center Configuration Manager for larger shops; but WSUS is free and scales well, so it might be all you need.

WSUS also works with the Microsoft Offline Virtual Machine Servicing Tool (OVMST), which brings together a series of PowerShell scripts that work with System Center Virtual Machine Manager to launch an offline VM, create a snapshot, update it through WSUS, and then shut it down (see Figure 13-12). OVMST relies on maintenance hosts to service offline VMs. Maintenance hosts are used to avoid any impact on operational host workloads during the offline patching process.

NOTE More information on WSUS can be found at http://technet.microsoft.com/en-us/wsus/default.aspx. Find out more about the Offline VM Servicing Tool at http://technet.microsoft.com/en-us/virtualization/default.aspx.

NOTE Because XenServer runs VMs in the Microsoft virtual hard disks (VHD) format, the Microsoft Offline VM Servicing Tool can also be used with the VMs XenServer runs.

Finally, in order to complete your OS hardening procedures, you need to put in place redundant systems at all levels. System redundancy means building resilience into your host and management servers and into the services they deliver. More will be covered in Chapter 15 as you build additional resilience through high availability clusters.

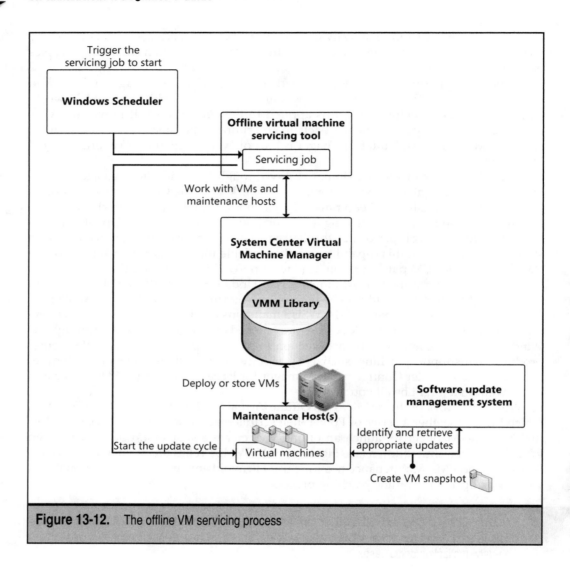

Figure 13-12. The offline VM servicing process

Layer 4: Information Access

Layer 4 deals with user identification and the attribution of permissions allowing them to operate within your network. The most important of these for an internal network is the Kerberos security protocol. A lot has been said on this protocol. It has many advantages, one of which is that it operates in both Windows and Linux. One of its best features is the fact that once it has authenticated users, the users do not need to return to the server for authorization. In Kerberos, the user caries rights and permissions within the access token that is granted by the Kerberos server. This access token is in the form of the Kerberos ticket that is granted to the user at logon. In addition, the server authenticates to the client, making sure that it is authorized to grant user access within its realm of authority. Finally, Kerberos also supports two-factor authentication. This two-factor authentication can be in the form of a smart card or a biometric device, such as a fingerprinting device.

One of the key elements of a Kerberos realm—the Kerberos equivalent of a Windows Active Directory domain—is the timestamp. Time synchronization is essential in Kerberos because the authentication server matches the time of the client's request with its own internal clock. If the time differs by more than the allotted time—set within your account policies—the Kerberos server will not authenticate the user.

Secure User Identification

User identification happens on many levels within a resource pool network. The most obvious authentication is through the ADDS utility domain you create. For this, you need to set global account policies for the utility forest and domain. In addition, authentication occurs in cross-machine scenarios. Local host machine authentication will vary, depending on the hypervisor you use. With VMware, host machine authentication is centralized through VirtualCenter and tied to the utility directory, as discussed previously. In XenServer, host machine authentication is centralized through XenCenter by replicating machine configuration from host to host. In Hyper-V, host machine authentication uses the member server structure and can be centralized through the utility directory.

Rely on the role-based authentication capabilities of your hypervisor to control which administrator and technician has access to what.

Secure Layer 4 Through Group Policy Objects

The best way to manage authentication, authorization, and auditing is through Group Policy, which is at the core of Active Directory. For example, you set auditing of access controls through a Group Policy object (GPO). You can modify the default GPOs within the utility domain, but as a best practice, it is easiest to create a new GPO and use it to tighten security on all objects in the utility domain, as well as track administrator and technician operations within the environment.

Fully document each GPO you create and use a structured change management approach for any modification, as you should for any access control structure.

The default domain policy is the account policy for the domain. Since only one policy can contain account information, this information should be defined in a single area. Be careful when working with this policy because it cannot be deactivated. If you make a mistake while editing this policy, you will affect the entire domain. This is one reason for a structured Group Policy change management strategy.

The elements that need to be covered in this account policy are outlined in Table 13-3. All of the elements outlined in this table are from the Computer Configuration | Policy | Windows Components | Security Settings branch of Group Policy. Once again, remember to document all of your GPO settings.

Section	Setting	Recommendation	Comments
Account Policies/ Password Policy	Enforce password history	24 passwords	At the rate of one password change per month, this setting remembers two years' worth of passwords.
	Maximum password age	42 days	This is approximately a month and a half.
	Minimum password age	2 days	This stops users from changing their passwords too often.
	Minimum password length	8 characters	This is the threshold where password crackers start taking longer to break passwords.
	Password must meet complexity requirements	Enabled	This ensures that passwords contain both alphabetic and numeric characters, both upper- and lowercase, as well as special symbols.
	Store passwords using reversible encryption	Disabled	Enabling this setting is the same as storing plain-text passwords. This setting should never be enabled.
Account Policies/ Account Lockout Policy	Account lockout duration	60 minutes	This setting determines how long an account is locked after several bad logon attempts.
	Account lockout threshold	3 invalid logon attempts	After three bad logon tries, the account is locked out.
	Reset account lockout counter after	60 minutes	This must be equal to or greater than the account lockout duration.
Account Policies/ Kerberos Policy	Enforce user logon restrictions	Enabled (default)	This ensures that users have the right to access either local or network resources before granting them a Kerberos ticket.

Table 13-3.   Default Domain Account Policy Elements

Section	Setting	Recommendation	Comments
	Maximum lifetime for service ticket	600 minutes (default)	This states the duration of the session ticket that is used to initiate a connection with a server. It must be renewed when it expires.
	Maximum lifetime for user ticket	10 hours (default)	This must be greater than or equal to the previous setting. It must be renewed when it expires.
	Maximum lifetime for user ticket renewal	7 days (default)	This details the duration of a user's ticket-granting ticket. The user must log on again once this ticket expires.
	Maximum tolerance for computer clock synchronization	5 minutes (default)	Kerberos uses timestamps to grant tickets. All computers within a domain are synchronized through the domain controllers.
Restricted Groups	*Domain/* Enterprise Admins	Individuals only	Select trusted individuals should be members of this group.
	Domain/ Domain Admins	Individuals only	Select trusted individuals should be members of this group.
	Domain/ Administrators	Enterprise Admins Domain Admins	This group should contain only trusted groups.

Table 13-3.   Default Domain Account Policy Elements (*continued*)

TIP   All of the settings for Kerberos policy are set at the default Windows Server settings, but setting them explicitly assists your Group Policy operators in knowing what the default setting actually is.

All of these settings are applied at the domain level to ensure that they affect every object within the domain. In fact, the account policy is a computer policy. This means that the user configuration portion of the GPO can be disabled.

TIP It is very important to ensure that you have a strong communications program to keep administrators and technicians aware of the importance of having a comprehensive account policy within your resource pool network. Also indicate to them the settings in your account policy. Finally, educate them on the protection of passwords and the need for immediate renewal of passwords they think may be compromised. This will ensure that your resource pool account policy is supported by the very people who use it.

Layer 5: External Access

Layer 5 normally focuses on the perimeter network and the protection of your internal network from outside influences. In today's connected world, it is impossible to create internal networks that are completely disconnected from the external world, even when dealing with host networks. For example, an administrator may need to perform work from home during emergencies. Because of this, you need to secure the internal resource pool network as much as possible, creating a barrier that must be crossed before anyone can enter. This barrier can take several different forms, but in the case of the resource pool network, it means the creation, or rather the continued use, of your perimeter environment. This environment is often called the demilitarized zone or DMZ.

Perimeter networks can contain any number of components, but in the case of a resource pool, they can be limited to a series of firewalls that protects your internal network, and they should not include and contain Internet servers or extranet services.

Resource pools do not have a perimeter network because they do not interact with users and do not provide any user-related services. They do, however, interact with remote administrators. For this level of interaction, you must work with either the Secure Sockets Layer or IP Security (IPSec)–based Virtual Private Network connections. You will also need a Public Key Infrastructure in support of SSL because SSL communications are validated through server certificates. You should also ensure that any remote site will use IPSec for server-to-server communications, especially when replicating virtual machine images. You may also determine that you need to implement Network Access Protection to ensure that any system that connects to the resource pool is always up-to-date in terms of security patches and antimalware protection.

Virtual Service Offerings, because of their productivity focus, have a perimeter network and therefore need protection at multiple levels. Perimeter networks for VSOs can include a host of services, but most often they include:

▼ Remote connections for mobile end users acting outside your premises

■ Federation services for partner organizations

- ■ Network Access Protection for any system that wants to connect to the network
- ▲ Public Key Infrastructures to provide protection for the applications you make available in the perimeter as well as in support of smart card deployments

The level of implementation is more comprehensive in the VSOs than it is in the resource pool since resource pools only interact with administrators.

CAUTION   Since your perimeter network will be made up of virtual machines, you should rely on the internal settings of your hypervisor to create virtual LANs, segregating the virtual machines that belong to each part of your VSO network. You might also consider placing perimeter machines on specific host servers and make sure they are never intermingled with machines from the Intranet zone.

Secure Windows Servers with the Windows Server Firewall with Advanced Security

One of the first tools you must work with within the perimeter—as with all servers in any zone of your network—is the Windows Server Firewall with Advanced Security (WSFAS). The Windows Firewall is built into every edition of Windows and is installed by default. In fact, when you install WS08, Windows Firewall is set to deny all remote access. Then, as you configure roles for your server, you modify the default firewall policy to open and control specific network ports.

The difference between the basic firewall and the WSFAS is that the latter combines a firewall with IPSec management into one tool to provide integrated secure communications management. This means that you use WSFAS to manage internal and external server communications as well as Virtual Private Network connections. WSFAS is controlled through Group Policy and can be set to apply the same rules to all systems (see Figure 13-13).

A lot more can be said on the firewall, but basically, you should rely as much as possible on the Security Configuration Wizard to help you properly configure firewall rules based on server roles. This will go a long way to protecting your management and other servers, wherever they are in your network.

Note that in most perimeter networks, WSFAS is not enough on its own. Most organizations will also include either hardware-based protection technologies or software-based stateful inspection tools. It is also good practice to implement some form of intrusion detection in the perimeter.

NOTE   For more information on the Windows Firewall, go to http://technet.microsoft.com/en-us/network/bb545423.aspx.

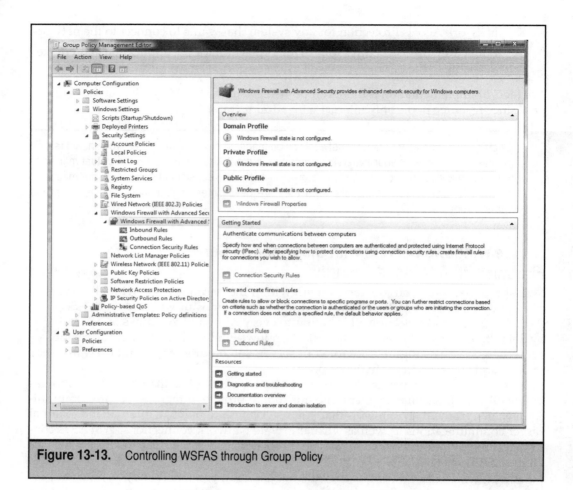

Figure 13-13.   Controlling WSFAS through Group Policy

Use the Secure Sockets Layer to Protect Communications

Communications between the administrative workstations and the host servers should always be encrypted, whether they originate inside or outside your network. In fact, to further protect your administrative communications, you should create a specific VLAN and place all of the host and administrative machines on it. This will limit the ability of any other user or service to interact with these machines.

But even then, you must encrypt all communications. When you install VMware ESX with the Security=High switch—the default setting, as mentioned earlier—it automatically generates certificates for the host servers and relies on them to encrypt all communications to and from the server. However, for communications to work properly with the Secure Sockets Layer, each machine in the communication link must trust the originator of the certificate. Since the certificates are self-signed on each host server, you have three choices.

▼ Import each of the self-signed certificates into your management machines to ensure they are trusted certificates.

■ Implement your own internal Public Key Infrastructure—which can easily be done with Windows Server AD Certificate Services—and integrate it with your utility directory. Any machine that is part of this directory will automatically trust any of the certificates you generate through it. Then you must replace the self-signed certificates with the new certificates you generate.

▲ Obtain trusted certificates from public certification authorities such as Verisign, Thawte, Entrust, or others. Use these certificates to replace the self-signed certificates on your servers. Since the public authorities are automatically trusted by most client systems and web browsers, these new certificates will be trusted without further effort. You can also look to new Subject Alternate Name (SAN) certificates. SAN certificates can include multiple names within the certificate, letting you add all of the names of your host servers into one certificate and use the same certificate on all servers. However, you must update the SAN certificate each time a new host is added.

If you are using Windows Hyper-V, you will also be able to rely on the new Secure Sockets Tunneling Protocol (SSTP). Traditionally, Virtual Private Network connections in Windows networks relied on the IPSec protocol, which provides an end-to-end connection at the networking layer. However, IPSec VPNs cannot work in every situation. For example, when you use Network Address Translation devices or even web proxy servers, your IPSec VPN connection will be blocked at the gate. In addition, IPSec VPNs are more complex to implement and require you to have some degree of control over the endpoint or client system making the connection from the external world. As you know, this is often not the case.

This is one reason why Microsoft has implemented the Secure Sockets Tunneling Protocol. SSTP relies on HTTP over the Secure Sockets Layer, or HTTPS, to create VPN connections over port 443. SSTP supports Network Access Protection as well as IPv13. When you create an SSTP VPN, the client establishes a single connection to the internal server and all traffic travels over this connection. You cannot, however, use it to create site-to-site connections.

SSTP relies on PKI certificates to create connections. The servers hosting SSTP connections must have installed certificates that include the Server Authentication or the All-Purpose Enhanced Key Usage property in order to accept SSTP connections. SSTP VPNs are part of the Network Policy and Access Services server role and must be managed through the Routing and Remote Access Services console node.

NOTE For a complete overview of SSL VPNS, see The Case for SSL Virtual Private Networks at www.reso-net.com/articles.asp?m=8#c under the Advanced PKI section.

Rely on an Internal Public Key Infrastructure

PKI implementations can be quite complex, especially if you need to use them to interact with clients and suppliers outside your internal network. The main issue at this level is one of authority: Are you who you say you are and can your certificates be trusted? When this is the case, you should rely on a third-party authority specializing in this area to vouch for you and indicate that your certificates can and should be trusted. WS08 can play a significant role in reducing PKI costs in these situations. Since it includes all of the features required to implement a PKI service through Active Directory Certificate Services (ADCS), all you need to do is acquire the root server certificate from an external source. This certificate will then be embedded into every certificate issued by your infrastructure. It will prove to your clients, partners, and suppliers that you are who you are and you won't have to implement an expensive third-party PKI solution.

But you don't need this type of certificate for the purposes of the resource pool network since you control all of the systems within the network and you don't need to prove yourself or your organization to them. ADCS supports several types of security situations. You can use them to:

▼   Secure web services, servers, and applications

■   Secure and digitally sign e-mail

■   Support Encrypting File System

■   Sign code

■   Support smart card logon

■   Support Virtual Private Networking

■   Support remote access authentication

■   Support the authentication of Active Directory Domain Services replication links over Simple Mail Transfer Protocol (SMTP)

▲   Support wireless network authentication

WS08 provides two types of certificate authorities (CA): Standalone and Enterprise. The latter provides complete integration with ADDS. The advantage of Enterprise CAs is that since their certificates are integrated with the directory, they can provide auto-enrollment and auto-renewal services. This is why the PKI service you implement in the resource pool network should be based on Enterprise CAs.

PKI best practices require high levels of physical protection for root certificate authorities. This is because the root CA is the core CA for the entire PKI hierarchy. If it becomes corrupted for some reason, your entire Public Key Infrastructure will be corrupted. Therefore, it is important to remove the root CA from operation once its certificates have been issued. Since you will remove this server from operation, it makes sense to create it as a stand-alone CA within a virtual machine (removing an enterprise CA from the network will cause errors in ADDS).

CAUTION   Root CAs should be removed from operation for their protection. This is why the ideal configuration for root CAs should be in virtual machines. Taking a virtual machine offline is much easier than a physical machine. In addition, the virtual machine can be placed in a suspended state indefinitely, making it easier and quicker to bring back online when it is needed.

PKI best practices also require several levels of hierarchy. In fact, in PKI environments that must interact with the public, it makes sense to protect the first two levels of the infrastructure and remove both from the network. But in an internal PKI environment, especially one that will mostly be used for secure communications in the resource pool, two levels are sufficient. Subordinate CAs should be enterprise CAs so that they can be integrated with ADDS. In order to add further protection to the subordinate CA, do not install it on a domain controller. This will reduce the number of services running on the server.

Even if your PKI environment will be internal, you should still focus on a proper PKI design. This means implementing a seven-step process.

1. Review WS08 PKI information and familiarize yourself with key concepts. An excellent place to start is online at http://technet2.microsoft.com/ windowsserver2008/en/library/532ac164-da33-4369-bef0-8f019d5a18b81033 .mspx?mfr=true.

2. Define your certificate requirements. Identify all the uses for resource pool certificates, list them, and define how they should be attributed.

3. Create your PKI architecture. How many levels of certificate authorities will you require? How will you manage offline CAs? How many CAs are required?

4. Create or modify the certificate types you require. Determine if you need to use templates. Templates are the preferred certificate attribution method.

5. Configure certificate duration. Duration affects the entire infrastructure. Root CAs should have certificates that last longer than subordinate CAs.

6. Identify how you will manage and distribute certificate revocation lists as well as which ADCS roles you want to include in your infrastructure. This can include Web Enrollment and Online Responders in addition to CAs.

7. Identify your operations plan for the certificate infrastructure in your organization. Who will manage certificates? Who can provide them to users? If smart cards are in use, how are they attributed?

The result should provide the architecture you intend to use (see Figure 13-14).

Consider each step before deploying ADCS. This is not a place where you can make many mistakes. Thoroughly test every element of your ADCS architecture before proceeding to its implementation within your resource pool network. Finally, just as when you created your security policy to define how you secure your environment, you will need to create a certification policy and communicate it to your administrative personnel.

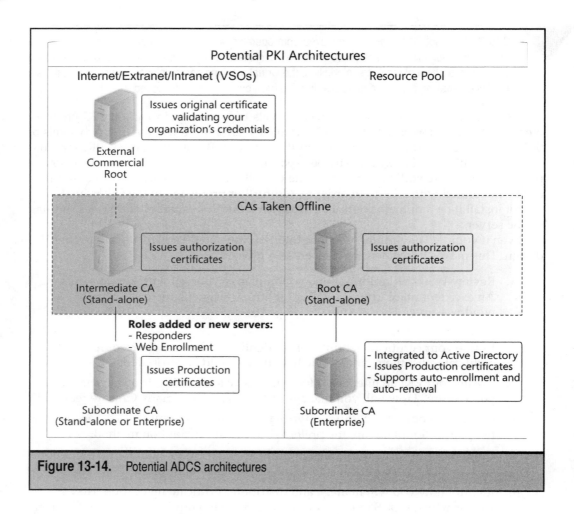

Figure 13-14. Potential ADCS architectures

NOTE For more information on PKI and the world of trust it supports, go to www.reso-net.com/ articles.asp?m=8#c. For information on implementing and working with ADCS, see Chapter 16 in *MCTS Self-Paced Training Kit (Exam 70-640): Configuring Windows Server 2008 Active Directory* by Holme, Ruest, and Ruest (Microsoft Press, 2008).

COMPLETE THE RESOURCE POOL SECURITY POLICY

The Castle Defense System provides a structured approach to the design of a security policy. But it cannot stand alone to defend your critical resources. It must be supplemented by a defense plan, a plan that includes both reactive and proactive defense measures. This means additional defenses at several levels, especially in terms of system resilience.

There are also ongoing operations that must take place at regular intervals to ensure that your defense system is constantly monitored and that your reaction plans work properly. Simulations are good practice. You will see how you respond and also if your response plan is adequate. You do not want to find yourself in a situation where the only response is unplugging a system, especially a host system with multiple VMs running on top of it.

One of the keys to a solid response plan is ensuring that everyone in the organization knows and understands their role in the plan. Resource pools bring considerable change to your network, especially in terms of the types of services they run. It is important that these changes be fully understood by your administrative staff. It is also important that you identify each new role within your operations as well as the modifications you must bring to existing roles. Finally, to support your security policy to its fullest, you need to limit the delegated rights you assign to administrators and operators within your network.

CHAPTER 14

Protect Your Virtual Infrastructure

Even though you have done your best to ensure the security of your servers and services, disasters can always happen, and servers, both host and virtual, can always go down. This is why it is important to prepare for system recovery. No system is perfect, but the more protection levels you apply to your systems, the less chance you have of losing data and experiencing downtime. Therefore, you need to implement data protection strategies to supplement your security strategies.

Recovering systems is never an easy task. The best way to avoid having to recover systems is by using a multilayered protection strategy. But if you do get to the stage where a recovery operation is required, you must have a detailed strategy to follow. Like every other operation in the virtual infrastructure, recoveries must be planned. Your recovery strategy must begin with an understanding of the hypervisor's built-in capabilities for the protection of virtual machine states. Once you're familiar with the tools the hypervisor offers to help you protect systems, you can outline or adjust your protection strategy.

DEVELOP YOUR SYSTEM PROTECTION STRATEGIES

System protection in a virtual infrastructure must focus on several key elements.

▼ There is little need to back up host servers since they are redundant, and in most cases, you can easily re-create a host server through the integrated hypervisors now available.

■ You must also protect the management database and the management virtual machines (VMs) for your resource pool. The management database especially must be protected if you want to ensure that your resource pool continues to operate properly. As for the management VMs, you would use normal VM protection measures.

■ You can easily protect virtual machines through the snapshot capability of each hypervisor. You can create up to 512 snapshots per VM. A snapshot is a capture of the current state of a VM, a state you can return to at any time. This state captures all of the operating system settings and configuration, the application state, and all of the data contained within the VM at the time. For most hypervisors, snapshots are usually stored within the resource pool's library store. In some cases, for example VMware, the snapshots are stored in the virtual machine folder.

■ You can back up the files that make up a virtual machine, capturing all of its content and therefore protecting all of the data contained within it.

▲ You can back up the contents inside a virtual machine, just as you would normally back up any physical machine.

There is a lot of discussion on the market concerning the last two points. A lot of people tend to use the last strategy, backing up the contents of each VM and using traditional recovery strategies for their VMs. However, the very fact that machines are now virtual and are stored on shared storage containers should make you rethink this strategy.

If you can back up the entire VM and mount its virtual disk drives offline, you can easily restore any content from within those disk drives. This process is easier and simpler to work with.

However, before you look at how you will protect a system, you need to ensure that your system recovery and protection strategies are sound.

Use Standard System Recovery Strategies

Every organization, large and small, must rely on a standard system recovery strategy to protect their machines. In a virtual infrastructure, this means using the same strategy for both resource pools and the virtual machines they run. Standard recovery strategies should be based on the following activities:

▼ A service interruption is detected. This interruption can be in either the resource pool or a VM. If it is in a VM, the impact is contained to the VM only; but in the resource pool, the impact can affect any number of VMs offering services in the productivity network; therefore, reaction must be even more prompt.

■ The interruption must be investigated and categorized. The best way to do this is to rely on a standard troubleshooting strategy.

■ The level of risk must be evaluated. This level of risk will determine the required level of response. For example, if a host running 20 VMs fails and there is no replacement host, response must be immediate. If the trouble is with a noncritical VM, the response can take more time.

■ The recovery plan for this level of risk is put into action. Standard recovery plans should already be in place for the most common situations. These standard recovery plans should also include a "Plan B" in case the main recovery strategy does not work for some reason.

■ You perform the recovery. Focus on core recovery activities to get the service back up and running as fast as possible. Once the basic recovery is complete, you should fully test the results of the recovery actions to ensure that everything is back to normal.

■ Secondary recovery actions can be performed once the core activities and testing are complete; for example, broken VMs that were taken offline are repaired, or users are notified that their files are back online.

▲ Once complete, the incident should be documented and procedures are updated, if required.

It is important to detail the actual recovery plan for each type of situation. This is one reason why risk evaluation is so important. You may not have time to document recovery processes for every single disaster situation, but if you have taken the time to evaluate risks, you can ensure that recovery plans for the most critical situations are documented. In the end, you will have multiple recovery plans that will "plug into" your recovery strategy.

All of these should be based on standard operating procedures (SOP) to ensure that your staff responds in the same manner to similar situations.

In order to support this recovery plan, you'll also need:

▼   An offsite copy of the plan to protect the plan itself

■   Spare hardware components onsite for the resource pool

■   Reliable and tested system backups

■   Distanced offsite storage for rotated backup media, such as tape

▲   Available resources—systems, components, personnel—to perform systems recovery

In addition, you need to have either failsafe servers or a hot site—a separate site that mirrors your production site and that can take over in the case of a disaster—in support of your recovery plan. Hot sites can either be under your full control or hosted by external service providers, depending on the resources you have available to you. More on this will be discussed in Chapter 15. As you will see, with resource pools, this secondary site is easy to set up.

Use Standard Troubleshooting Techniques

A core element of the system recovery process is a sound troubleshooting strategy. This is the strategy your operations staff should use to identify the type of disaster they are facing. It is essential that this strategy be clear. It should also be a standard within your organization because this strategy is so critical to the recovery process. For example, if the issue you are facing is wrongly identified, the recovery strategy applied to it may cause an even worse disaster. You should apply this strategy to both resource pools and Virtual Service Offerings.

In general, help requests and problem reports should be dealt with through an organized/scientific approach that treats system errors as always being causal; that is, problems don't just happen—they are deviations from a norm that have distinct, identifiable causes. The troubleshooting technician's job is to logically deduce causes of problems based on his or her knowledge of how the system works. The best way to do this is to use a standard procedure.

For example, your technicians could rely on the following procedure to troubleshoot system issues:

1. Once the issue is discovered, document appropriate information, such as the time, the date, the affected machine, and any appropriate user information.

2. Document all of the relevant information concerning the problem. Refer to your baseline system operation information if necessary.

3. Create an itemized problem description. Answer these questions:

   ■   Is the problem reliably reproducible or random?

   ■   Is it related to the time of day?

- Is the problem user-specific?
- Is it platform-specific?
- Is it version-specific?
- Is it related to hard disk free space?
- Is it network traffic-related?
- What is it not?

4. Research similar occurrences in your internal troubleshooting databases. Review the help system of the affected component if it is available. Also, review external troubleshooting databases, such as manufacturer knowledge bases. It is also a good idea to draw on the expertise of your coworkers.

5. Create a reasonable hypothesis based on all of the available information.

6. Test the hypothesis and document the results.

7. If the test successfully cures the problem, document and close the case. If unsuccessful, modify the hypothesis or, if necessary, create a new hypothesis. Repeat the hypothesis and test cycle until the issue is resolved.

Note that complex problems (more than one cause-effect relationship) may require several iterations of steps 2 through 7. Relying on this approach will greatly simplify issue resolution whenever untoward events occur within the resource pool or within VMs.

Categorize Issues for Resource Pools and VSOs

One of the important aspects of troubleshooting is problem classification. It is often helpful to categorize errors according to the circumstances surrounding the occurrence. Table 14-1 includes a sample list of problem classes.

As you can see, your troubleshooting procedure is not only used in disasters. It can be used in all troubleshooting situations. But for disasters, the key to the troubleshooting and recovery strategy is the quality of your backups—data, operating system, and components. This is why the backup strategy is one of the most important elements of your system resiliency plan.

Hypervisor Manufacturer Offerings

Backup strategies will differ based on the hypervisor you run. Each hypervisor uses a completely different approach. In addition, approaches will differ based on the number of host servers you run and their configuration.

VMware Consolidated Backup

VMware offers a Consolidated Backup tool, which, like the Update Manager, is available in all editions of the Virtual Infrastructure because it is such a critical component of the infrastructure. Consolidated Backup relies on a centralized proxy server to perform and

Problem Classes	Key Characteristics
Resource Pools Only	
Peripherals	Keyboard, video display, hardware components, drivers
Network	Adapter configuration, traffic, cabling, transmission devices
Resource Pools and Virtual Service Offerings	
Installation	Procedure, media, hardware/software requirements, network errors
Bootstrap	Missing files, hardware failures, boot menu
Security	File encryption, access rights, permissions
Service Startup	Dependent services, configuration
Application	Application-specific errors
Logon	User accounts, validating server, registry configuration, network access
Virtual Service Offerings Only	
User Configuration	Redirected folders, user profiles, group memberships
Procedural	User education, control

Table 14-1. Sample Problem Classifications

run all backup operations of both the resource pool database (if it is contained within a VM) and the VMs it runs (see Figure 14-1). The key to its operation is that backups are performed through the storage container, not through the local area network (LAN), which is what traditional backup strategies do. Because it provides an open application programming interface, Consolidated Backup will integrate with your existing backup tool to provide centralized VM backups.

Consolidated Backup can stream to tape or disk by relying on snapshots of the VMs you run, whether they are online or offline. Note however that it will stream to disk first when you perform a full image backup. When a backup job is triggered, Consolidated Backup captures the snapshot and mounts it to perform the backup, leaving the running VM on its original host and having minimal effect on its operation. Once the backup operation is complete, the snapshot is dismounted and discarded.

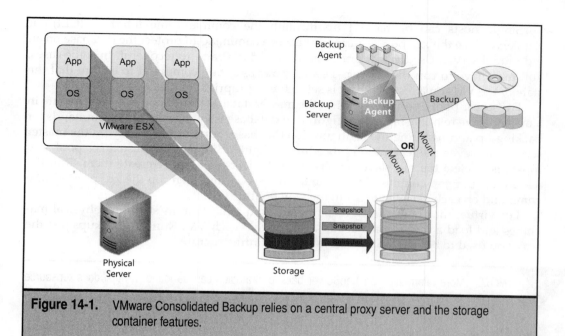

Figure 14-1. VMware Consolidated Backup relies on a central proxy server and the storage container features.

Consolidated Backup also supports file-level or incremental backups as well as full image backups of the entire VM. Note that incremental backups are provided by the third-party backup tool you use with Consolidated Backup. Consolidated Backup supports any type of storage—storage accessed through Internet Small Computer Systems Interface (iSCSI), network attached storage (NAS), storage area networks (SAN), or even direct attached storage (DAS).

NOTE For a list of compatible backup software for VMware, go to www.vmware.com/pdf/vi35_backup_guide.pdf.

Citrix XenServer

Citrix does not offer any special tool for either host or VM backups. Instead, Citrix recommends that hosts be kept as simple as possible in their structure. If a host fails, just reinstall it since no data is lost. However, because each host server stores a local copy of the configuration database, it is important to protect this database at all times because if you lose local data, you stand a chance of losing entire VMs. The protection strategies you will use for each of these databases will depend on the number of hosts you run.

Single hosts can be backed up through the command-line interface (CLI) for XenServer. Use the `xe pool-dump-database` command to protect the database on an individual server. Use the `xe pool-restore-database` to recover it. In some cases, you may have to run the `xe vm-reset-powerstate` command to ensure that the state of the VMs on a restored host is set to the appropriate mode.

For server pools, you must protect the master database since pooled hosts operate in a master-slave relationship for configuration databases. You use the same commands for backing up and restoring the configuration database, but you run it only on the master server. However, the restoration procedure is slightly different. Because it is a pool, you must also delete the old slave servers from the lost pool and re-create them. Run the `xe host-forget` command to delete the old slaves and then run the `xe pool-join` command on each new slave to join the new pool.

For virtual machines, Citrix recommends you treat them as standard physical machines and load a traditional backup agent within each VM. Run VM backups just the way you used to before you moved to a virtual infrastructure.

NOTE More information on XenServer backup strategies can be found at http://docs.xensource .com/XenServer/4.0.1/installation/apbs04.html.

Microsoft Hyper-V

Since Hyper-V is a standard role that runs on Windows Server 2008, backup of both VMs—at least Windows VMs—and host servers is similar to the standard backup practices you run within any Windows network. The key to any backup in Windows Server, since version 2003, is the Volume Shadow Copy Service (VSS). VSS can take a snapshot of any running machine and then rely on this snapshot to perform the backup. VSS works with several backup providers, including Windows Server Backup (WSB), the new tool in Windows Server 2008; Microsoft's System Center Data Protection Manager (DPM), a streaming backup engine; and most third-party backup tools that work with Windows Server.

Basically, VSS acts like an orchestra conductor. It is the central actor that controls a volume shadow copy operation. To do so, it must communicate with all of the other actors in the process. The process works as follows (see Figure 14-2):

1. A registered requestor—an application that is designed to work with the Volume Shadow Copy Service, for example, Hyper-V—begins a VSS session and requests the creation of a volume shadow copy.

2. VSS sends a request to all registered writers—applications that are designed to understand VSS requests—to freeze all input and output (I/O) activity on the requested volume.

3. The targeted registered writer indicates to VSS when this is done.

4. Once it receives confirmation that the freeze is active, VSS notifies the storage provider to perform its vendor-specific shadow copy of the volume.

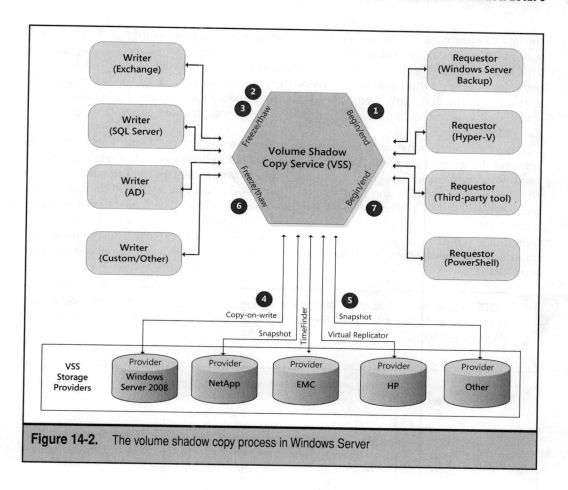

Figure 14-2.   The volume shadow copy process in Windows Server

5. When the shadow copy is complete, the storage provider confirms to VSS that it is finished.

6. VSS notifies the targeted registered writer that it can thaw I/O activity on the frozen volume and continue normal operations.

7. Finally, the VSS indicates to the original requestor whether the operation was a success or a failure.

This process occurs extremely fast. In fact, if registered writers are designed properly, the process is completely transparent to users.

Another important factor in the VSS process is related to the way storage technologies actually create the shadow copy. If they created an entire copy of a volume, they would require significant physical space. This can become cost-prohibitive. This is why most storage providers prefer to use a single-instance store approach. They do not actually create a complete copy of the disk, but rather focus on the changes to the volume since the last shadow copy. Microsoft's provider uses a copy-out process for this: Every time a disk block is to be overwritten, it is moved to a reserved area before the write operation. This is a significant technical challenge that can lead to overworked disk heads. Other providers use a method that never overwrites the same area: All of the information is appended to the disk. This method leads to lower costs in disk space and is much easier on the disk heads. This is the method used by most hypervisors to generate snapshots of the VMs they run.

As you can see, when a backup operation is requested, Hyper-V initiates a VSS process and the backup is run off the copy. Copies can either be discarded or retained as you need. Retaining copies is a good idea since it allows you to rely on the Previous Versions client to restore lost files and folders (see Figure 14-3). You can even rely on this tool to recover lost VMs on a Hyper-V host. Previous Versions is a feature of the properties of a file in Windows. Simply right-click the object—file or folder—view its properties, and then move to the Previous Versions tab to recover the content you lost. This is a powerful feature of this operating system and one that Hyper-V simply inherits since it runs on top of the OS.

NOTE For more information on the backup strategies for Windows Server 2008 (WS08), see Chapter 11 of *Microsoft Windows Server 2008: The Complete Reference* by Ruest and Ruest (McGraw-Hill, 2008).

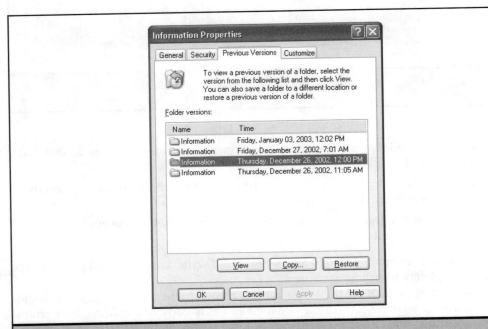

Figure 14-3. Using the Previous Versions client to restore lost data

With System Center Data Protection Manager, Microsoft offers a streaming backup engine that will capture remote VSS images and store them centrally, allowing administrators to centrally manage all snapshots. The user's Previous Versions clients are automatically redirected to the central VSS repository, which makes it simpler to support. DPM streams all backups to a central disk system and can then store them on tape for offline storage. This is a must for most organizations since Windows Server Backup, the tool integrated with WS08, no longer supports tape as a backup medium.

Data Protection Strategies for Hyper-V Resource Pools

Backing up Hyper-V host servers means backing up two different types of objects.

▼ **Operating system**   The partition that makes up drive C: and runs the Hyper-V role.

▲ **Data partitions**   The data drive that contains the Virtual Service Offerings. This should be some form of shared or replicated storage.

Hyper-V servers are the simplest kind of server in your Windows network because they only run one major role: virtualization. If you set up your infrastructure right, backing up these machines will be relatively easy. Ideally, each and every drive that makes up the server will be hosted within the shared storage infrastructure. This provides several levels of defense against data or system loss.

▼ Each partition can either rely on the Volume Shadow Copy Service or the internal snapshot tool provided with the storage unit to provide a first line of defense.

■ The second line of defense is provided by the volume shadow copy of the virtual machines located on the data drive.

■ A third line of defense is provided through replication of the files that make up each of the Virtual Service Offerings (VSOs).

■ A fourth line of defense is provided through failover clustering.

▲ The last line of defense is provided through backups of the disks that make up each host system.

CAUTION   You will need to add another disk partition to each host server in order to perform backups through Windows Server Backup. WSB does not support backup to tape. Our recommendation: Obtain a third-party backup tool, since you will want comprehensive backup support for the host servers. Good examples are Symantec BackupExec (www.symantec.com/backupexec/index.jsp) or CommVault Galaxy (http://commvault.com/products/data_protection.asp).

Set up your schedules to protect systems on an ongoing basis. You should perform full backups once a week and then follow with differential backups every day. Differential backups take up more space than incremental backups, but they are easier to recover from because they include all of the changes since the full backup. In a recovery situation, you only need the most recent full backup and the most recent differential to restore the system. This is faster than using incremental backups because you need to add each incremental until the point of failure to restore a system.

If you do decide to perform host system backups from Windows Server Backup, use the following command line. It performs a full system backup once a day at 6:00 P.M. to a disk partition.

```
wbadmin enable backup addtarget:DiskID schedule:18:00 user:Username password:Password
```

Where *DiskID* is the ID number of the disk to back up to; use the DISKPART, then List Disk commands to identify the disk ID. *Username* and *Password* should belong to a service account with local administration rights on the host server.

NOTE When you use WSB, destination drives should be reserved exclusively for backup purposes because all other data will be erased.

Data Protection Strategies for Virtual Service Offerings

Backing up your Virtual Service Offerings will mean backing up several types of information: user data, corporate data, databases, documents, system state information for your servers, and Active Directory data. As mentioned, you can use either the built-in backup tool or a third-party backup tool to perform these backups. Whichever one you use, make sure that you will use a standard backup strategy, creating backup sets of specific data types—for example, creating only user data backups in one backup set and only system data in another. This will simplify the restoration process.

Data backups are rather straightforward; select the data drive and back it up. Remember that in most cases, whether you use Windows or a shared storage provider, the backup tool will automatically create a snapshot before backing up the data and then create the backup set from snapshot data. This avoids issues with open files. Snapshot tools have special application programming interfaces (APIs) that enable them to work with databases such as Active Directory, SQL Server, and Exchange Server, making the snapshots valid even for databases.

Basically, you should back up data and operating systems on a daily basis. Perform a full backup once a week and then rely on differentials. You need to support your backup strategy with both a remote storage solution and offsite media storage. Remember that you will need a third-party backup tool if you want to back up to tape on Windows Server 2008 machines. You will need to ensure that you have a safe offline storage space for media. You should rotate offsite media on a regular basis. For example, every second complete backup should be stored offsite in a controlled environment.

A common schedule relies on a four-week retention strategy. This means that you retain backup media for a period of four weeks. If you keep every second copy offsite, you are always only a week away from complete disaster. In addition, your archiving schedule will outline which copies you should keep offsite on a permanent basis.

Rely on Replication for Backups

If you are using a replication engine to replicate all of your running VSOs to a remote site, you may not need to focus on internal machine backups, since you already have off-site copies of all of your virtual machines. In the event of data loss, you can rely on your hypervisor engine to mount virtual disk drives in an offline mode, letting you recover any data file you need from the mounted virtual hard drive.

VMware supports offline disk mounting with the Virtual Disk Manager and the DiskMount utilities. Both are found within the VMware Virtual Disk Development Kit at www.vmware.com/support/developer/vddk/VDDK-1.0-Relnotes.html. Use the Virtual Disk Manager to clone, create, relocate, rename, grow, shrink, or defragment offline virtual machine disk (VMDK) files. Use the DiskMount utility to mount an offline disk in Windows or Linux and view its contents as if it were another disk attached to your system. You can then recover the necessary files from within the offline disk file.

Microsoft and Citrix can both rely on the Microsoft VHDMount tool, which is a Windows utility that mounts offline virtual hard disk (VHD) files and lets you view their contents as a separate disk drive from within your system. Find this utility within the Virtual Server 2005 R2 download at www.microsoft.com/windowsserversystem/virtualserver. The utility is contained within the download and must be extracted from it to use it on its own.

NOTE Follow these instructions from Chris Wolf, one of our technical reviewers, to extract VHDMount without installing Virtual Server: http://myitforum.com/cs2/blogs/rcrumbaker/archive/2007/06/13/vhd-mount.aspx.

Using this strategy would greatly simplify your VSO backup and restore strategies. Make sure, however, that the replication tool you use is virtual machine–aware and understands the makeup of VMs to ensure proper data replication. More on this is covered in Chapter 15.

Select a Third-Party Backup Tool

In many cases, organizations will opt to rely on a third-party backup tool to protect their environments. VMware recommends the use of a third-party tool; Citrix absolutely requires a third-party tool; and Microsoft's new Windows Server Backup is not an enterprise-class backup tool. Because of this, you will most likely find yourself in a situation where you need a third-party tool, if you don't already have one.

One of the most important aspects of the selection of a third-party backup tool is its awareness of the components that make a hypervisor operate. Many backup tools are not designed to interact properly with the hypervisor you run and, therefore, will not understand the make-up of virtual machine files. When you choose a backup tool, make sure it is hypervisor-aware.

A number of third-party backup solutions on the market are specifically designed for hypervisors. They all meet specific criteria, which must include:

▼ Being aware of the inner workings of the hypervisor

■ Being able to protect centralized management database data

■ Being integrated with the snapshot service of your storage provider, triggering a snapshot before launching a backup operation

■ Being able to work with either Windows or Linux virtual machines, depending on the infrastructure you run in your VSOs

■ Enabling complete host system recovery from a simple process

▲ Enabling complete virtual machine recovery from a simple process

Meeting these basic criteria is essential. There are other criteria, of course, such as integrating with massive storage products that are supported by your hypervisor engine, including special drivers for SQL Server, Exchange, Active Directory, Oracle, and so on; but the ones listed here are the core requirements for an intelligent, third-party backup solution.

NOTE One good way to proceed is to rely on your hypervisor vendor's recommendation for the very best backup tool selection. Each manufacturer lists third-party tools that work with their engines. For VMware, go to wwwa.vmware.com/partnercatalog/catalog and select ISV System Infrastructure and the Backup and Availability Software subcategory. For Citrix, go to www.citrix.com/English/partners/partnertop.asp?ntref=hp_nav_US. For Microsoft, go to www.windowsservercatalog.com and look for Infrastructure Solutions, then the Hyper-V subcategory.

COMPLETE THE RECOVERY STRATEGY

Protecting data within the virtual infrastructure means adapting traditional approaches to the new requirements created by the segregation of the resource pool and the Virtual Service Offerings. Securing these environments also requires adapting your methods. Overall, you'll find that because you now have two infrastructures, you'll have to adapt other management methods as well. This, along with system redundancy strategies, is the topic of the next chapter.

Be prepared. Securing, protecting, and managing virtual infrastructures is different than working with physical infrastructures alone. If your organization is large enough, you may be able to dedicate resources to each infrastructure; but if not, you'll have to train yourself and your colleagues to wear different hats and respond in different manners when issues arise.

CHAPTER 15

Prepare for Business Continuity

Virtualization transforms the way organizations run their datacenter. Server virtualization transforms productivity workloads into malleable engines that can be run when needed and scaled based on business requirements. Desktop virtualization lets you create volatile or stateless desktop operating system images that can greatly simplify management and reduce the pains of distributed desktop administration. Application virtualization finally gives you the ability to defeat DLL Hell once and for all and provide users with an application-on-demand model. Profile virtualization lets your users use any desktop anywhere within your organization.

All of these levels of virtualization finally let you build the dynamic datacenter—a datacenter that can adjust itself dynamically to business fluctuations. But this datacenter does not build itself on its own. So far, you've seen how all of the different levels of virtualization can impact your datacenter; but in order to run virtualization and make the best of it, you have two items left to cover: business continuity and management practices.

Business continuity focuses on making sure that your services are always available at all times, wherever you are and wherever you need them. To support this new IT model, management practices must be updated and must be supported by the appropriate toolset. These management changes are covered in Chapter 16.

BUSINESS CONTINUITY ESSENTIALS

System redundancy relies on the implementation of methods and measures that ensure that if a component fails, its function will immediately be taken over by another or, at the very least, the procedure to put the component back online is well documented and well known by system operators. Some of the most common administrator headaches are network security and disaster recovery. It's not surprising. We've all faced disasters, such as 9/11 and Hurricane Katrina, and we all know just how damaging these events can be to businesses of any size. In fact, a vast majority of businesses that do not have a business continuity plan in place and face a major disaster often go under since they cannot recover from such catastrophic events. These issues are at the very core of any network design. No matter what you do, you must ensure that your systems are protected at all times.

Once again, the Castle Defense System can help. Layer 1 helps you identify risk levels because it helps you determine the value of an information asset. Risk is determined by identifying value (the importance of an asset) and multiplying it by the risk factor that is associated with it. The formula looks like this:

```
Risk = asset value * risk factor
```

For example, an asset that is valued at $1 million with a risk factor of 0.2 has a risk value of $200,000. This means that you can invest up to $200,000 to protect this asset and reduce its risk factor.

While these calculations can be esoteric in nature, what remains important is to invest the most in the protection of your most valued assets. This is one reason why it is so important to know what you have. Figure 15-1 is a good reminder of this principle.

Chapter 3 introduced the concept of a virtual infrastructure architecture (see Figure 15-2). This architecture focused on the seven layers of virtualization and how you protect them.

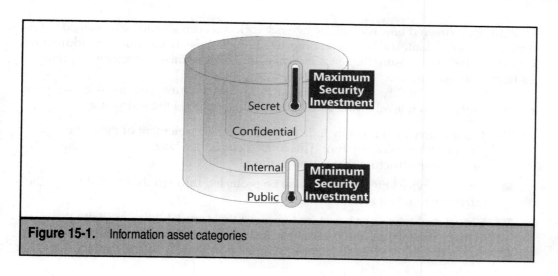

Figure 15-1.   Information asset categories

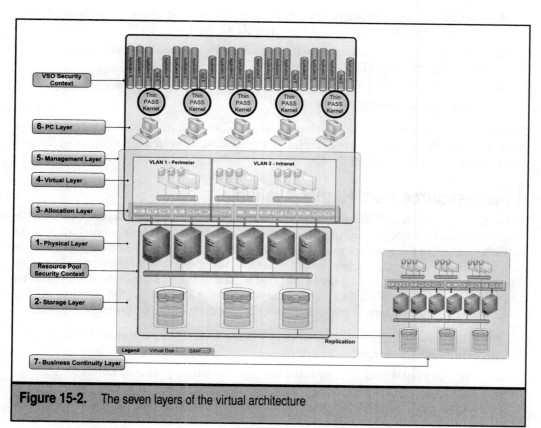

Figure 15-2.   The seven layers of the virtual architecture

In addition, it covered how each of the two networks you run should be contained within different security contexts. Now you need to complete this architecture and address the elements which will ensure that each critical component of this architecture is protected and available at all times.

To ensure availability of each piece of the infrastructure, you must address the requirements of each level of the architecture. This includes the following:

▼ The resource pool must include protection for each element of the server virtualization infrastructure. This must focus on the host servers and the storage infrastructure that supports them.

■ Virtual Service Offerings must also be protected through the capabilities of the infrastructure you run for them.

■ Virtual desktops must be set up to protect their availability, especially the ability of users to reconnect to their desktops whenever they need to.

■ Application repositories must be made highly available to ensure that applications run all the time.

■ Profile storage containers must also be available at all times and protected through backups, as discussed in Chapter 14.

■ The allocation and management layers must be updated to include new ways of doing things in IT.

▲ The entire infrastructure must be protected through offsite replication and other business continuity practices.

Protecting each resource and ensuring its availability will allow you to complete the entire virtualization architecture and run IT in response to your organization's business imperatives.

Make the Resource Pool Highly Available

By focusing on physical protection, or protection of the resource pool, Layer 2 of the Castle Defense System also helps you plan for system redundancy. But host servers are not the only component in the resource pool. As outlined in Chapter 14, the resource pool contains several different elements, each of which must include some level of protection to ensure it is running and available at all times and that system outages or maintenance windows cannot leave you out in the cold when you need to access a feature of the resource pool.

This means that you must provide protection for each of the following elements:

▼ **Host servers**   These servers must be made redundant, whether they are centralized or in remote locations.

■ **Storage containers**   These must not become single points of failure.

■ **Management database**   This database contains critical operational information and must be available at all times.

- **Management virtual machines (VMs)**   These machines provide access to the management database and control the resource pool hosts. For this reason, they must be made redundant.

- **Management desktop virtual machines (DVMs)**   The virtual desktops that operators use to access the management infrastructure must be protected at all times.

- **Resource pool Active Directory**   This directory must have built-in redundancy to become highly available.

- ▲ **Additional servers**   Any additional server you include in the infrastructure must be made highly available. For example, if they are required, you may have to run licensing servers to support your implementation. Also, if they are in use, the certificate servers you run in support of encrypted communications must be protected. The same would go for any other infrastructure element you maintain for the resource pool—Network Access Protection, Virtual Private Network, Update Services, and so on.

Protecting the resource pool means protecting each of these elements (see Figure 15-3).

Create Highly Available Host Servers

As you know, for your resource pool to work and your Virtual Service Offerings to remain available at all times, you must integrate high-availability concepts and components in each host server. Begin with the construction of the server itself. Random Arrays of Inexpensive Disks (RAID) and teamed network cards, for example, provide direct hardware-level protection for a host system. However, the ideal host system includes an integrated hypervisor and will not require local disk drives; if you must run a host operating system, run it from shared storage, not local disks.

It is also important to include uninterrupted power supply (UPS) systems; these can either be individual USB–connected UPS devices (for regional servers), or centralized power management infrastructures that protect entire computer rooms (usually at central sites).

Resource pools also need redundancy. Each one of the physical servers playing host to a Virtual Service Offering (VSO) must have some form of redundancy built in. If a host server is running 10 to 15 VSOs, it must be able to fail over these VSOs to another physical host in the event of a failure at the hardware level. This means the physical hosts must be clustered—sharing the VSO workload so that VSOs are available to users at all times. This is one reason why it is so important to host VSOs on shared storage. Because they are hosted on a storage structure that each host server has access to, VSOs can be moved from host to host with little impact on users. This provides site-level redundancy. This also means that you must have more than one host to support virtual workload failover. Remember the golden rule: If you perform a physical consolidation of 20 servers, you will not have a 20-to-1 consolidation ratio; rather, you will have a 10-to-1 consolidation ratio since you must have two hosts to support high availability of the 20 virtual servers (see Figure 15-4).

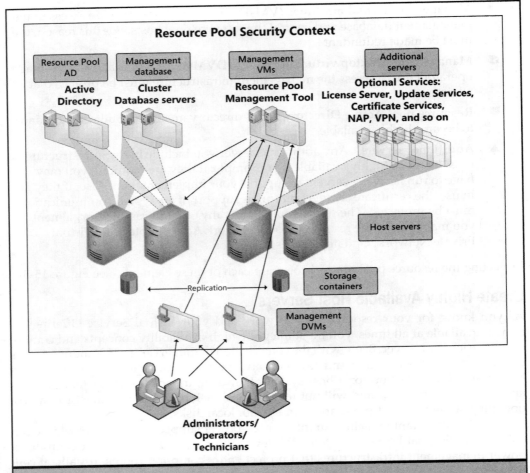

Figure 15-3. Protecting the resource pool

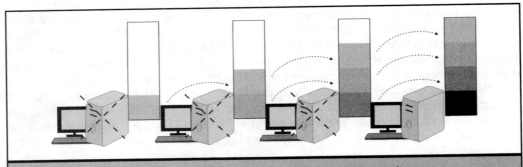

Figure 15-4. To provide site-level redundancy, you must always have spare hosts.

VMware relies on the Virtual Machine File System (VMFS) and the High Availability feature to provide this level of availability. Citrix XenServer relies on the resource pool concept along with shared storage. Microsoft, because Hyper-V runs on Windows, relies on the Windows Server Failover Clustering feature along with, of course, shared storage.

Site-level redundancy is also necessary at the regional level if you choose to host virtual workloads in remote locations to provide better service availability. This is why the ideal regional server will be an all-in-one box that includes at least two physical host servers, shared storage, and wide area network connectivity. By including two host servers, you can make sure the regional VSOs this infrastructure hosts will always be available (see Figure 15-5).

Protect Storage Containers

When you build for high availability, you must ensure that no single component can become a point of failure. This means that each and every component must have some redundancy built into it. For example, you can't place all of your virtual workloads into a single shared storage container, because if it fails, you'll have even more problems than with a single host server failure because all of your virtual machines will fail.

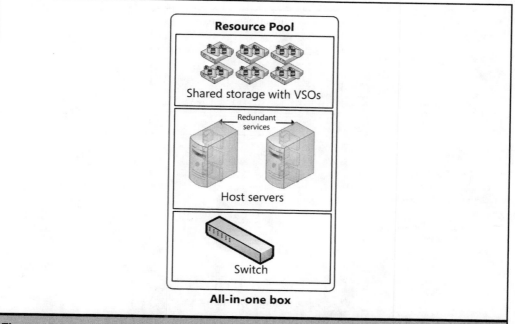

Figure 15-5. Use all-in-one boxes to provide regional site-level redundancy.

Storage containers will also include RAID configurations to provide a first level of defense against failure. They also contain several features that let you snapshot contents so that you can protect them through backups. In addition, many storage containers, especially storage area networks (SANs), will include the ability to replicate contents from one SAN structure to another.

Several host systems can take advantage of this replication engine while running within the same site. VMware provides this feature through Storage VMotion, a tool that will automatically move the contents of a VM from one storage container to another without failure (see Figure 15-6). Of course, you must structure the SAN according to VMware's guidelines for Storage VMotion to work. This solution is a site-level solution only.

NOTE VMware publishes information on how to configure SANs with its technology through the VMware SAN System Design and Deployment Guide at www.vmware.com/pdf/vi3_san_design_deploy.pdf.

Microsoft can use multisite failover clustering to do the same thing with its Hyper-V engine. Windows Server 2008 supports the ability to create a cluster that does not rely on shared storage, but can actually rely on direct attached storage (DAS). This cluster will

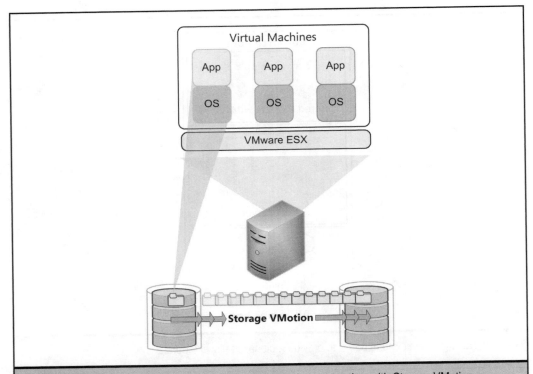

Figure 15-6. VMware can move a VM from one container to another with Storage VMotion.

provide failover for the virtual machines it runs—not, of course, through live migration, but through the Quick Migration feature, which pauses the machine, transfers it, and then restarts it. This failover will not rely on a shared disk infrastructure, but will require data replication through a third-party engine between each of the hosts in the cluster. Cluster data is stored on a File Share Witness to ensure that each host is aware of the status of others. This is a majority-node-set cluster structure in Windows. This cluster structure is designed to provide multisite failover, running a cluster node in different sites, but there is no reason why you cannot use this structure to provide single-site failover as well as storage container protection at the same time (see Figure 15-7).

NOTE For more information on multisite clustering with Windows Server 2008, go to www.microsoft .com/windowsserver2008/en/us/clustering-multisite.aspx. For a step-by-step guide on clustering Hyper-V, go to http://technet.microsoft.com/en-us/library/cc732181.aspx.

Citrix XenServer relies on third-party products to provide this type of protection. Citrix partners Steel Eye (www.steeleye.com), LeftHand Networks (www.lefthandnetworks .com), and others such as Marathon Technologies (www.marathon.com) provide tools that protect both data and the host in either a single or multiple sites.

Other storage vendors, such as NetApp, provide replication capabilities for network attached storage (NAS) as well as SANs. NetApp relies on the same strategy as VMware for systems management. VMware always relies on VirtualCenter for management of their virtual infrastructure, adding functionality to the tool as you grow. NetApp does the same, adding functionality to its storage management engine as you grow without differentiating between NAS or SAN offerings. This greatly simplifies the use of their products.

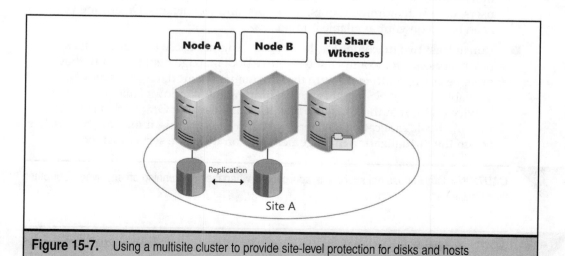

Figure 15-7. Using a multisite cluster to provide site-level protection for disks and hosts

Protect the Management VMs and DVMs

As discussed in Chapter 14, the resource pool is not only made up of physical machines. In fact, it often contains several virtual machines. These machines can play any number of roles.

▼ Run the virtualization management software.

■ Run a desktop operating system (OS) to support administrative access to the resource pool management VMs.

■ Run the Active Directory, which synchronizes security groups with the roles you assign in the resource pool.

■ Run the database engine (local, SQL Server, or Oracle), which contains management data.

▲ Possibly run additional roles, such as certificate services, Network Access Protection, Virtual Private Network, and so on.

While it is possible to run many of these roles on the same VM, it makes sense to use at least two VMs and possibly even more than that to ensure the high availability of the services that make the resource pool run. Use these guidelines to create a highly available resource pool infrastructure:

▼ As a best practice, run at least two machines for Active Directory. Keep these machines separate from other roles. These machines should also run the Domain Name Service (DNS) role since Active Directory requires DNS to operate. While it is possible to run multiple services on a domain controller, it is not recommended since this is a highly secure role. It may be okay to run more than one service on these servers since they do not interact with end users, only with administrators, operators, and technicians. Determine your need based on your available budget.

■ Run at least two machines for the database engine. These machines can run other services—for example, the resource pool management tool—but they must be clustered to make sure that the management database is highly available. For SQL Server, this means running the Windows Failover Cluster Service (WFCS) in the VMs that host the database. For Oracle, this means running Real Application Clusters (RAC). Because of this, it may not be possible to run the virtualization management tool on the same server instances.

CAUTION Oracle does not support its applications when they are running on any hypervisor other than Oracle VM.

NOTE XenServer does not require this server role since it uses a master/slave configuration repository on each host server.

- If you separate the host management tool from the database, run at least two instances of this service on two different VMs. Set the VMs to autostart when the host server boots to ensure you have immediate access to host management when the resource pool is running.

> **NOTE** As a best practice, you should set each of the VMs that is part of the resource pool administration infrastructure to autostart. This way, you have immediate access to all of the tools that support resource pool operations.

- Run desktop VMs with the management client to connect to the resource pool management VMs. As a best practice, it is always best to access management tools through a desktop rather than through a server. Make these desktop VMs part of the resource pool Active Directory (AD). Using DVMs will let administrators, operators, and technicians connect to the resource pool from their production desktops or any other connected system. They launch the virtual desktop, log into the resource pool AD, and access the management tool through a completely separate security context, protecting the infrastructure from their production network.

- Run additional services from other VMs. Services such as Certificate Services will require at least two VMs: one that is offline—the root certificate authority (CA)—and one that is online—the issuing CA. These machines, especially the offline machine, should not be domain controllers. Virtual Private Network (VPN), Network Access Protection (NAP), and Update Services could be cohosted on the same servers. You do not want them to be cohosted on the management VMs because VPN servers are often the point of entry into a network from outside your zone of influence. If someone compromises the VPN server and it is cohosted on the management server, this could compromise your resource pool.

Many of these services, except the obvious Windows services, can run on Linux as well as Windows. However, remember that the Windows Server Enterprise Edition license grants you the right to run up to four free instances of Windows in virtual machines. If you do this right, you can run the entire infrastructure in fewer than eight VMs, keeping your Windows licensing costs down.

Building redundancy in your systems is valuable only if you know it works. It's not enough to be prepared; you need to know that your preparation has value. To do so, you'll need to test and retest every single redundancy level you implement in your resource pool. Too many organizations have made the fatal error of putting high-availability technologies in place without testing them, only to find out that they didn't work when they needed them. This is not a myth. It actually happens. Don't let it happen to you. Test all your systems and document your procedures. In fact, this is another excellent opportunity for you to write standard operating procedures.

Protect Your Virtual Service Offerings

Building a redundant network to support the resource pool is part of the high-availability structure you need to put in place. You also have to make sure that the services you offer within your productivity network are highly available. While some think that you don't need to worry about this if you have the right virtual infrastructure in place, it is still good practice to do so.

Take, for example, an Exchange server running in a VM. This server is running as a stand-alone service. Since it is in a VM, it will be made highly available because the resource pool is highly available. If the host server running the VM fails, the VM will automatically be moved to another host through High Availability (HA) features. There will, however, be a minor interruption in service because HA is not like live migration; since there is a failure at the hardware level, all of the VMs running on this host will also fail before the hypervisor's HA feature detects the host failure. Once the host failure is detected, the machines are moved and restarted.

But what happens if the failure is in the VM, not on the host? In this case, hypervisor technologies offer a lot of features that are not available on physical machines. For example, you can restart the Exchange VM from a snapshot or from an older offline copy, but this would mean losing some data. Your e-mail users won't be too happy about that.

The answer is to cluster within the virtualization layer. If you're running Windows, you can run either Failover Clustering or Network Load Balancing (NLB) on the virtual machines. If you're running Linux, you'll want to implement enterprise clustering to make the workloads highly available. Then, if a service fails for any reason—host server failure, VM failure, and so on—it will automatically fail over to another VM in your network and won't cause a service interruption for your end users.

Consider High Availability for Different Services

Clustering is not the only form of high availability you can run. Many services include built-in reliability features. Consider the following:

▼ **Directory services**   Resiliency here is created through the distribution of directory servers throughout your network. It is also based on multimaster replication systems and the creation of an appropriate replication topology.

■ **DNS**   DNS is often married to a directory service. By integrating DNS with the directory service, you ensure that your network name resolution service will always function because it has the same resiliency as the directory service. This feature is provided through DNS replication.

■ **DHCP**   Your address allocation infrastructure also has resilience built in because of the way you structured it with redundant scopes. In addition, if you place your Dynamic Host Configuration Protocol (DHCP) servers in different sites, you have a solution that would continue to work in the event of a disaster.

- **File shares** Your file shares can be made resilient through various features of the operating system you run on them. For example, Windows includes the Distributed File System (DFS), which can copy file share contents from one site to another, making them resilient. DFS also supports automatic failover—i.e., if the service fails in one site, it automatically fails over user connections to the other site. DFS can also be protected through failover clusters.

▲ **Volume snapshots** Your shared files, shared databases, Exchange stores, and other shared information repositories are also protected through the snapshot feature, either in your OS or your storage container. For example, in Windows, the Volume Shadow Copy Service can take system snapshots on a regular basis and even allow end users to recover files themselves.

These are only a few examples of built-in resiliency features. But despite the fact that several of your systems are resilient, there remain areas that could have significant impact on your operations if they failed.

Remember, one of the main reasons for hacker attacks is Distributed Denial of Service or DDoS. This type of attack can succeed for two reasons. First, the server hosting the service is not protected, and second, the service is hosted by a *single* server, i.e., there is no failover service. Chapter 14 showed you how to protect your systems through the Castle Defense System. Now you need to add additional resiliency to the VSO network.

Cluster Services for Virtual Service Offerings

While many services include their own built-in resiliency, others must rely on the resilient features of the OS they run on. As mentioned earlier, for Windows, this is Failover Clustering and NLB. To determine which to use when, keep the following in mind:

▼ When protecting stateless systems or systems that provide read-only services, rely on Network Load Balancing.

▲ When protecting stateful systems or systems that provide read-write services, rely on Failover Clustering.

It's a simple formula: Systems that do not persist data rely on NLB. These systems are usually front-end systems. Systems that persist data rely on Failover Clustering. These systems are usually back-end systems.

NLB clusters do not need any particular hardware since they rely on network interface cards to work. Failover clusters, however, rely on either Small Computer System Interface (SCSI) emulation or Internet Small Computer System Interface (iSCSI) connectors. Failover Clustering also works with Fibre Channel, but there is no Fibre Channel emulation in the virtualization layer, at least not yet. In Windows Server 2008, you can create either 2-node or up to 16-node clusters with Failover Clustering. NLB supports up to 32 nodes in a cluster.

You'll find that clustering in VSOs will be more comprehensive than in resource pools because there is more to protect. Table 15-1 outlines the features and supported services for each clustering mode for VSOs in Windows Server 2008 (WS08).

Clustering Service	Network Load Balancing	Failover Clusters
WS08 edition	Web Standard Enterprise Datacenter	Enterprise Datacenter
Number of nodes	Up to 32	Up to 16
Resources	Minimum of two network adapters	SCSI or iSCSI disk connectors Minimum of two network adapters
Server Role	Application Servers (stateless) Dedicated Web Servers Collaboration Servers (front-end) Terminal Servers (front-end)	Application Servers (stateful) File and Print Servers Collaboration Servers (storage) Network Infrastructure Servers
Application	Web Farms Internet Security and Acceleration Server (ISA) Virtual Private Network (VPN) Servers Streaming Media Servers Unified Communications Servers	SQL Servers Exchange Servers Message Queuing Servers File Servers Print Servers

Table 15-1.   WS08 Clustering Services

As you can see, NLB and failover clusters are rather complementary. In fact, it is *not* recommended to activate both services on the same server; that is, a failover cluster should not also be a member of an NLB cluster. In addition, NLB clusters are designed to support more static connections. This means that they are not designed to provide the same type of failover as a server cluster. In the latter, if a user is editing a file and the server stops responding, the failover component will automatically be activated and the user will continue to perform his or her work without being aware of the failure (there may be a slight delay in response time). This is because the server cluster is designed to provide a mirrored system to the user. But an NLB cluster will not provide the same type of user experience. Its main purpose is to redirect demand to available resources. As such, these resources must be static in nature, since NLB does not include any capability for mirroring information deposits.

Both clustering services offer the ability to support four service-offering requirements.

▼ **Availability**   By providing service offerings through a cluster, it is possible to ensure that they are available during the time periods the organization has decreed they should be.

■ **Reliability**   With a cluster, it is possible to ensure that users can depend on the service offering, because if a component fails, it is automatically replaced by another working component.

■ **Scalability**   With a cluster, it is possible to increase the number of servers providing the service offering without affecting the service being delivered to users.

▲ **Maintenance**   A cluster allows IT personnel to upgrade, modify, apply service packs, and otherwise maintain cluster components individually without affecting the service level of service offerings delivered by the cluster.

An advantage that failover clusters have over NLB clusters is the ability to share data. Failover cluster resources must be tied to the same data storage resource, ensuring the transparency of the failover process.

Clusters do have disadvantages. They are more complex to stage and manage than stand-alone servers, and services that are assigned to clusters must be cluster-aware in order to take advantage of the clustering feature.

CAUTION   Remember that if you create a highly available configuration for a Virtual Service Offering, you must ensure that anti-affinity rules have been applied to the VMs within the resource pool. Anti-affinity rules will ensure that the virtual machines that make up a highly available service will not reside on the same host and will be distributed among available hosts. After all, if the two nodes of an Exchange cluster run on the same host and that host fails, both nodes will fail and all your efforts towards creating a highly available Exchange service will have been for naught.

Windows VSO Cluster Compatibility List

If you're running Windows services within your VSO, as most organizations do, you'll want to know how to protect each service you run in the productivity network. Even in Microsoft's own product offering, there are some particularities in terms of clustering compatibility. Cluster compatibility can fall into one of four categories:

▼ **WSFC-aware** is a product or internal WS08 service that can take full advantage of the cluster service. It can communicate with the cluster application programming interface (API) to receive status and notification from the server cluster. It can react to cluster events.

■ **WSFC-independent** (or unaware) is a product or internal WS08 service that is not aware of the presence of the cluster but that can be installed on a cluster and will behave the same way as if it were on a single server. It responds only to the most basic cluster events.

- ■ **WFSC-incompatible** is a product or internal WS08 service that does not behave well in the context of a cluster and should not be installed on a server cluster.

- ▲ **NLB-compatible** lists products that are well suited to NLB clusters. NLB and WSFC are often incompatible with each other.

Table 15-2 categorizes Microsoft's Windows Server System and WS08 functions in terms of cluster compatibility.

Product or Service	WSFC-Aware	WSFC-Independent	WSFC-Incompatible	NLB-Compatible	Comment
Active Directory Domain Services (ADDS)		X			Not recommended; availability is provided through multimaster replication.
Active Directory Lightweight Directory Services (ADLDS)		X			Not recommended; availability is provided through ADLDS replication.
BizTalk Server	X	X		X	BizTalk state server and message box are cluster-aware. Messaging and processing servers are cluster-independent. All other services should use a Network Load Balancing cluster. BizTalk can also take advantage of a clustered SQL Server back-end.
COM +		X			Component load balancing clusters preferred.
Commerce Server			X		Component load balancing clusters preferred.
DFS	X				Stand-alone DFS namespaces only.

Table 15-2.　Windows VSO Cluster Compatibility List

Product or Service	WSFC-Aware	WSFC-Independent	WSFC-Incompatible	NLB-Compatible	Comment
					Domain DFS namespaces use redundancy provided by ADDS. Also supports DFS replication.
DHCP-WINS	X				Fully compliant.
Distributed Transaction Coordinator	X				Fully compliant.
DNS		X			Redundancy provided by ADDS when integrated with the directory.
Exchange 2000 and later	X			X	Fully compliant.
					In Exchange 2007, different server roles can take advantage of different modes.
File Server	X				Fully compliant.
Generic Application		X			Supports non-cluster–aware applications through custom integration.
Generic Script		X			Supports non-cluster–aware scripts through custom integration
Generic Service		X			Supports cluster-independent services through custom integration.
Hyper-V	X				While not run in a VSO, the Hyper-V role is most definitely cluster-aware.
IIS		X		X	NLB clusters are preferred.
ISA Server			X	X	NLB clusters are preferred.

Table 15-2.   Windows VSO Cluster Compatibility List (*continued*)

Product or Service	WSFC-Aware	WSFC-Independent	WSFC-Incompatible	NLB-Compatible	Comment
Internet Storage Name Service (iSNS) Server	X				Fully compliant.
Microsoft Identity Lifecycle Manager	X				Fully compliant.
Microsoft Message Queuing	X				Fully compliant.
Network File System	X				The Windows NFS engine is completely cluster-aware.
Office Live Communications Server (LCS)			X	X	LCS is incompatible with WFSC. Use an NLB cluster for front-end servers. Use a WFSC for SQL Server back-ends.
Office Project Server	X				Only the SQL Server portion.
Office SharePoint Portal Server			X	X	Only the SQL Server portion. The IIS portion should use NLB.
Other Server		X			WSFC supports cluster-independent server roles through custom integration.
Print Server	X				Fully compliant.
SQL Server 2000 and later	X				Fully compliant.
System Center Configuration Manager	X				SQL Server back-ends can be clustered under special conditions.
System Center Operations Manager			X		Not supported.
Terminal Services Session Broker	X				Fully compliant. Also used to support virtual machine connections.

Table 15-2. Windows VSO Cluster Compatibility List (*continued*)

Product or Service	WSFC-Aware	WSFC-Independent	WSFC-Incompatible	NLB-Compatible	Comment
Windows Deployment Services			X		Not supported.
Windows Server Update Services				X	Front-end servers can be load-balanced; however, WSUS only updates systems once a month and may not require a highly available infrastructure.
Windows SharePoint Services			X	X	Only the SQL Server portion. The IIS portion should use NLB.
Windows Streaming Media			X	X	NLB clusters are preferred.

Table 15-2.   Windows VSO Cluster Compatibility List (*continued*)

The information in Table 15-2 is subject to change as each of the products evolves, but it serves as a good starting point in determining how you can configure high availability for your services.

NOTE   As server virtualization evolves, Microsoft server product teams are refining the supported high availability strategies for their particular product. For example, Exchange 2007 is now only supported when high availability is applied at the guest OS level and not at the host level. For more on this policy see: http://technet.microsoft.com/en-us/library/cc794548.aspx.

Make Virtual Desktops Highly Available

Chapter 10 outlined how centralized desktop virtualization worked and how it fit into your server virtualization infrastructure. The major difference between the resource pool for server virtualization and the resource pool for desktop virtualization is that for the first time, security boundaries are crossed. This is due to how desktop virtualization actually works. The process works like this (see Figure 15-8):

1. The user turns on his or her point-of-access device. This can be a workstation, personal computer at home, thin client device, or even a public browser. Then, the user goes to the virtual desktop infrastructure (VDI) interface and logs on.

2. The production Active Directory verifies the user's credentials and, if they are valid, logs them on.

3. Together, the Active Directory and the desktop broker assign the desktop virtual machine to be used.

4. The provisioning engine assigns the desktop virtual machine (DVM) to a host within the server virtualization infrastructure.

5. The login process begins, and the virtualized application icons appear on the user's desktop. The user's remote profile is also loaded.

6. Once the user has finished work and logs off of the session, the DVM is discarded because the core DVM image is read-only.

7. The DVM then goes back to the pool, and all changed information in the user profile is saved in the user profile store.

This process is relatively simple, but it requires thought and preparation to set up and work properly.

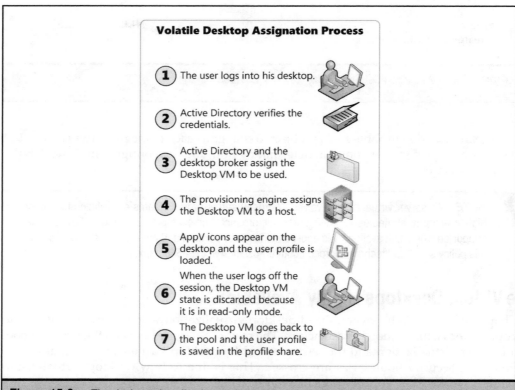

Figure 15-8. The desktop virtualization assignment process

However, the DVM assignment process outlines a few key items that are different from the server virtualization infrastructure.

▼ First, in step four of the DVM assignment process, there is an operation that crosses security boundaries. This is because the desktop broker sends a signal to the provisioning engine to assign the DVM to a host server. In this particular operation, the provisioning engine, which is contained within the production Active Directory, must interact with the resource pool because it needs access rights to assign the DVM to a host server. This interaction is usually performed by embedding the credentials required for the operation within the command that is sent. For this reason, the link between the provisioning server and the resource pool must be encrypted.

■ Second, this operation requires several supporting components, including a repository for AppV applications, a repository for user profiles, a streaming engine for AppV applications, the DHCP to assign volatile Internet Protocol (IP) addresses to DVMs, Active Directory, DNS, and much more. Each of these components must be rendered highly available to support DVM assignments.

▲ Many of the items required to make the DVM assignment process operate should already be in place in most Windows networks.

This means that the DVM architecture must be a mix of resource pool and Virtual Service Offering components (see Figure 15-9). You must keep in mind that any interactions between the VSO and the resource pool infrastructures must always be highly secured and protected.

Protect DVM Assignment Infrastructure Components

While your server virtualization infrastructure is already well protected, several components of the desktop virtualization infrastructure have not been addressed yet. These include the following items:

▼ The production Active Directory

■ The production DNS

■ The DHCP service

■ The file-sharing stores that contain application virtualization (AppV) applications and profiles

■ The AppV streaming engine

■ The virtual desktop infrastructure components, such as the desktop broker and the provisioning server

■ The virtual desktops themselves

▲ Optionally, file share replication and abstraction engines

Each component requires discussion. Both AppV and profile protection mechanisms are discussed later, but the other components must be addressed here.

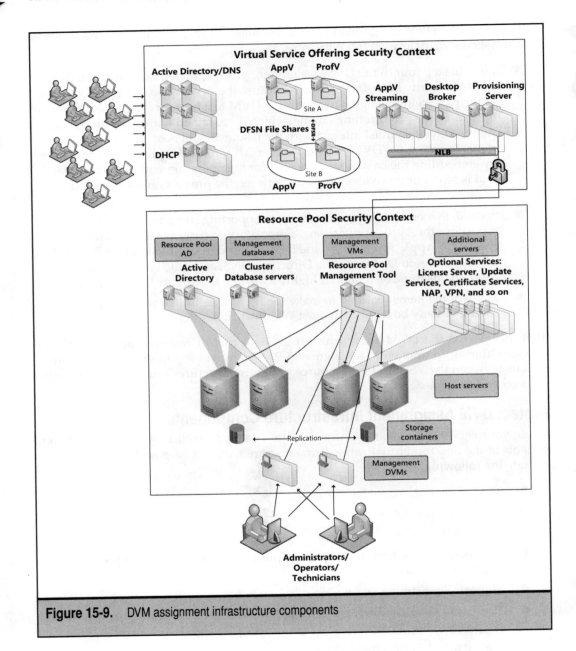

Figure 15-9. DVM assignment infrastructure components

The production Active Directory is used for several items. It links user accounts with assigned desktops, provides the desktops with security identifiers, applies Group Policy to the desktops and to users, and assigns AppV applications to users. Group Policy especially is the core engine that will control roaming user profiles and folder redirection settings, making profile virtualization work along with desktop virtualization.

Basically, any production Active Directory (AD) must have at least two domain controllers for each domain it contains. Normally, production ADs run in a multidomain forest, protecting the root of the forest from end-user interaction. This means a minimum of four domain controllers and possibly more. AD structures focus on both the logical (structure of the organizational units within each domain) and the physical (structure of the sites contained within the forest to control replication). Make sure your AD structures are sound and ready for prime time.

NOTE   For a discussion on production Active Directory structures, download the free Chapter 3 from Windows Server 2003, Best Practices for Enterprise Deployments at www.reso-net.com/livre .asp?p=main&b=winsvr&m=12. This chapter covers each aspect of a production Active Directory structure.

DNS is also a key component of the DVM infrastructure for several reasons. DNS is at the core of the operation of the production Active Directory. As such, it should normally be integrated directly with the directory. The best way to do this is to marry the DNS role with each and every domain controller in your network. DNS is also critical for the operation of the DVMs. Since each DVM is volatile, it will be assigned a volatile IP address. This address must be registered in DNS for the DVM to work properly. Using a Windows DNS server integrated with AD and with the Windows DHCP service will ensure the proper operation of the DVMs.

DHCP is also a requirement. A DHCP server is used to assign volatile or dynamic IP addresses to machines as the machines start up within a production environment. In addition, the Windows DHCP server will automatically interact with the Windows DNS service to ensure that each machine is properly registered. Modern Windows operating systems will manage their own registration within DNS once they receive the IP address from the DHCP server. To make a DHCP infrastructure resilient, you must have at least two DHCP servers in the production network and each DHCP server must be configured to support 50 percent of the addresses within this network.

The VDI components must also be highly available. The high-availability solution will vary, depending on the VDI engine you use. In some cases, both the desktop broker and the provisioning server can be made highly available by installing more than one copy of the service and running them against a load balancer. The load balancer you use will greatly depend on the VDI product you use; but basically, the process uses an IP address translation scheme, which redirects Transmission Control Protocol/Internet Protocol (TCP/IP) requests to available servers. This is similar to the Network Load Balancing service discussed earlier, and while some products will run with NLB, others require third-party load balancing appliances to run.

In other cases, the VDI components will include their own capability for high availability. For example, Citrix XenDesktop provides built-in high availability for each of its components. A XenDesktop farm consists of multiple Desktop Delivery Controllers (DDCs), which include a DDC master and multiple DDC member servers. If a DDC master becomes unavailable, a DDC member will automatically be promoted as the new master. In addition, a pooled virtual desktop environment will use Provisioning Server to boot DVMs through the Pre-boot Execution Environment (PXE) capabilities of network interface cards. For high availability, Provisioning Server will ensure that PXE boot requests from DVMs are handled in a transparent manner by load-balancing requests across multiple servers.

DVMs must also be protected to ensure that they are always available. For a DVM to work properly, it must communicate with the desktop broker. DVMs discover desktop brokers through the link to Active Directory. If multiple desktop broker servers are available, the DVM will pick one at random, making it highly available.

Finally, the last component is the protection of the file shares that host both virtual applications and user profile contents. Virtual application shares can be read-only since user systems only read the contents to run the applications. Profile shares, on the other hand, must be read and write. Windows Server includes a powerful tool called the Distributed File System (DFS). DFS is made up of two components. The first is the DFS namespace (DFSN). A DFS namespace is used to create one single namespace for file shares with multiple targets. DFS namespaces use the Universal Naming Convention (UNC) file sharing format, but instead of using a \\servername\sharename format, they use a \\domainname\sharename format. The namespace uses one single name, but multiple targets. This allows it to be available in multiple sites. Using multiple file share targets makes your file shares redundant. DFS namespaces integrate with Active Directory to make sure users always find the appropriate target wherever they are.

For DFS namespaces to work properly, they must contain the same items. This is why the second DFS component, DFS replication (DFSR), must be used in conjunction with the namespace. DFSR is a delta compression replication engine that will replicate only the changes made to a file at the byte level and compress them before sending them over WAN links. In addition, DFSR can control the amount of bandwidth used for replication, letting you control exactly how replication will run in your network. Using DFSNs with DFSR will make sure your applications are always available locally in remote sites and your users will always find their profiles, wherever they are in your network.

NOTE For more complete instructions on building and configuring each of these Windows Server components in support of VDI high availability, see *Microsoft Windows Server 2008: The Complete Reference* by Ruest and Ruest (McGraw-Hill, 2008).

Making sure each of these items is highly available will ensure that your users will always find their centralized desktops, wherever your users are and whenever they need them.

Make Virtual Applications Highly Available

As discussed in Chapter 11, application virtualization brings major changes to the way you work with applications. Several components are required to make AppV work, many of which have already been made highly available through the VDI you prepared.

▼   Active Directory is used to assign AppV applications to end users.

■   File shares are used as the AppV repository. They should be running with DFS, should you require the repository in more than one site.

- Streaming servers should be used to make the applications available within the virtual desktops you run.

- Management servers allow you to assign applications and link them to AD security groups.

- Database servers are used to store AppV assignment information.

▲ AppV packaging and administration stations are used to create the AppV packages and administer the AppV infrastructure. These machines can simply be volatile DVMs with AppV components.

The major difference between the AppV infrastructure and the VDI infrastructure is that the AppV infrastructure does not need to interact with the resource pool at any level because virtualized applications are end-user applications—at least for now—and do not run on servers. Even if they did, you would most likely assign AppV server tools to the production network rather than to the resource pool network.

Of all of the components required to make AppV work (see Figure 15-10), Active Directory, file shares, and the NLB components that make the streaming servers highly available have already been dealt with. The database servers should run the same Failover Clustering service as the database engines for the resource pool. However, these database servers are located within the production network, not the resource pool, and may support other infrastructure management databases, such as the ones required for Update Services, inventory, or the traditional Electronic Software Distribution (ESD) engine you use to manage utilities and components that cannot be virtualized.

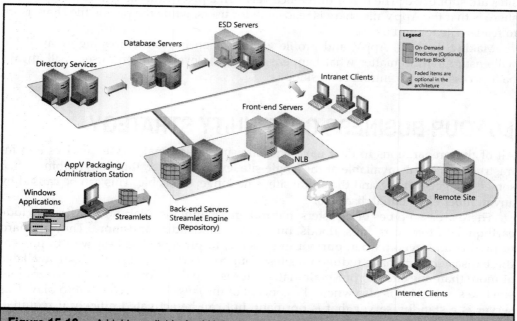

Figure 15-10.   A highly available AppV infrastructure

The packaging workstations, if prepared properly, can simply be volatile desktop VMs and because of this, will be made highly available through the components of your VDI.

Make Profiles Highly Available

As seen in Chapter 11, profile virtualization is supported through a mixture of roaming profiles and folder redirection. Roaming profiles are assigned in Active Directory since they are an attribute of the user's account. However, roaming profiles alone are monolithic and can take a long time to load. By removing contents from the roaming profile and assigning them to redirected folders—both of which are done through Group Policy settings—you can ensure that the roaming profile remains small and loads fast.

Contents such as the user's documents, which are made available through folder redirection, are then available on demand. Redirected folders are network file shares and, because of this, do not need to download contents into the volatile desktop as the user logs in. When a user opens a redirected document, the document is opened from the file share and automatically cached within the desktop machine. Once it is cached locally, access is even faster. If changes are made offline for some reason, the Synchronization Manager in Windows will automatically synch the contents from the local cache to the network.

Components that support profile virtualization have already been addressed through both the VDI and the AppV infrastructures. Active Directory is already highly available and the file shares should be running DFSN and DFSR, especially if remote sites are supported. The major difference between a profile file share and an AppV file share is that the AppV file share is read-only for users, while the profile file share is set to read-write for end users.

Making the VDI, AppV, and profile virtualization infrastructures highly available will ensure that no matter what happens at the site level, your end users will always have access to their centralized desktop.

BUILD YOUR BUSINESS CONTINUITY STRATEGY

All of the preparations to date have had one single aim: make your services and infrastructures highly available at the single site level. However, this does nothing when something goes wrong and the entire site is no longer available. This can be caused by any number of potential disasters.

There are two types of disasters: natural and manmade. Natural disasters include earthquakes, tornados, fires, floods, hurricanes, landslides, and more. They are hard to predict and even harder, but not impossible, to prevent. The best way to prevent these disasters is to have redundant sites: Your core servers and services are available at more than one site. If your main datacenter is impaired for any reason, your other site takes over. This is also where the concept of the *failsafe server* comes into play. This server is a standby server that is dormant, but can be activated quickly if required.

In the dynamic datacenter, this means providing redundant resource pool servers and saving copies of each of the VSOs you run in production.

There are also manmade disasters: terrorist attacks, power failures, application failures, hardware failures, security attacks, and internal sabotage. These attacks are also hard to predict. Some require the same type of protection as for natural disasters. Others, such as application and hardware failures and security attacks, can be avoided through the Castle Defense System.

To determine the level of service protection you need to apply, you can use a service categorization that is similar to the Layer 1 categorization for data.

▼ **Mission-critical systems**   These are systems that require the most protection because interruption of service is unacceptable.

■ **Mission-support systems**   These require less protection than mission-critical systems, but interruptions should be minimized as much as possible.

■ **Business-critical systems**   These are systems where short service interruptions can be acceptable.

▲ **Extraneous systems**   These are deemed noncritical and can have longer-lasting interruptions.

What most people seldom realize is that the basic network infrastructure for your network is, in many cases, part of the mission-critical level because if it does not work, nothing works.

Because VMs are nothing but a set of files on a server somewhere, you can ensure a better business continuity management (BCM) practice. As seen earlier, a local BCM is ensured through high-availability measures. For example, all host servers are connected to a shared storage. If a host server has an outage, the high availability automatically shifts the load to another node in the cluster, but you must have spare nodes in each cluster. To protect against site-level disasters, you must implement a multisite BCM. And because virtual machines are nothing but a set of files on a server, you'll find that the multisite BCM is much easier to implement than ever before.

Provide Multisite Redundancy

Site-level redundancy is no longer sufficient for organizations. Too many organizations literally lose everything when disaster strikes. You don't want all of your eggs in the same basket. Fortunately, the advent of virtualization makes it much easier to provide multisite redundancy. First, you need to build a second datacenter, if it isn't already available. This secondary datacenter does not need to host the same resources as your production environment (see Figure 15-11). It just needs a modicum of resources—just enough, in fact, to help you get back on your feet in the case of an emergency. This means it requires a few host servers attached to shared storage. It also needs central power protection devices and WAN connectivity.

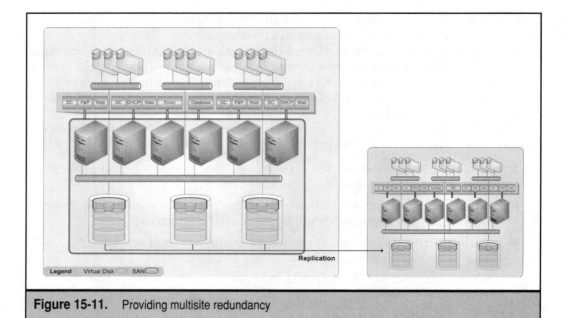

Figure 15-11.   Providing multisite redundancy

This secondary site could even be hosted by an Internet service provider (ISP). Several are available on the market. Using an ISP might be the best choice for small and medium businesses, because setting up a secondary datacenter for the purpose of business continuity management is a complex and sometimes expensive venture.

NOTE   Several ISPs offer this service, for example SunGard (www.availability.sungard.com), Sunrad (www.sanrad.com/products/overview.aspx), and INetU (www.inetu.net/innovative-support/virtualization.php). Choose your provider carefully and look to their privacy agreements to ensure that your data is secure when hosted outside your organization.

Adjust Your Service Level Agreements

Service level agreements (SLAs) for disaster recovery are not the same as those for normal production. When a disaster occurs, you will need to begin with essential services only. In addition, when you are in a disaster recovery situation, it should not last forever, but only for the time you need to get back on your feet. Because of this, the host server resources you need in the disaster recovery site are not the same as those in your production datacenter.

You can rely on a formula to help you determine just how many physical resources your disaster recovery center will require. The formula looks like this:

```
Production Resources/Recovery Time=Disaster Recovery Resources
```

For example, if you are running your infrastructure on 15 physical hosts and you expect your recovery time to be three hours, you can run the disaster recovery center with five physical hosts. The lower the recovery time, the more resources you will need to populate your recovery center.

Balance the number of physical resources in your recovery center with the need to reload critical services. In the event of a disaster, your recovery will require essential services first—for example, Active Directory Domain Services and DNS—then load secondary services, DHCP, file and print servers, and so on. Using a graduated approach for the reloading of services for users will let you bring everything back online in stages and will reduce the overhead cost of the secondary datacenter.

Business Continuity Management Through Replication

Remote business continuity for resource pools is provided through data replication technologies that will replicate the contents of your storage containers from one location to another. You can rely on the storage container's own replication engine or you may use a third-party engine. The advantage of using a third-party replication engine is that it often includes the components you need to redirect the services your end users are accessing to the remote site in the event of a disaster. This simplifies the disaster recovery process.

Each resource pool vendor relies on a different solution for multisite resiliency. For example, Microsoft can rely on the multisite Failover Cluster mentioned earlier to make Hyper-V multisite-resilient (see Figure 15-12). This solution relies on the built-in features of Windows Server 2008, but also requires a third-party replication engine to maintain storage contents that are identical between the sites. Note that for this solution to work, you must have the exact same resources available in both the production and the remote sites. This negates any cost-effectiveness for this solution.

NOTE For a list of supported replication partners for Hyper-V Failover Clustering, go to www .microsoft.com/windowsserver2008/en/us/clustering-multisite.aspx.

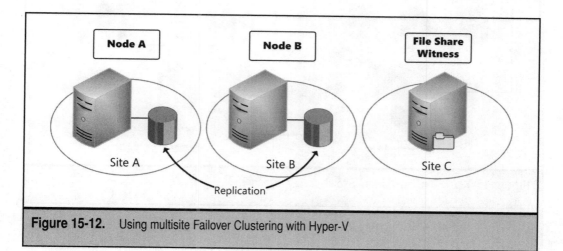

Figure 15-12. Using multisite Failover Clustering with Hyper-V

Citrix relies on third-party products for business continuity. Basically, you must obtain a replication engine for a XenServer resource pool. The engine will include the capability to perform continuous data protection (CDP) through replication, as well as the ability to redirect all users to a remote site in the event of a failure. Redirection is mostly performed through changes in the DNS entries for each of the services users rely on.

VMware relies on Site Recovery Manager (SRM) as well as integrated SAN capabilities or replication engines to provide multisite redundancy. Site Recovery Manager is a component of the VMware virtual infrastructure that helps you build, manage, and execute disaster recovery plans. SRM ensures that recoveries will be reliable by enabling nondisruptive testing. It also eliminates manual recovery steps through automation, and provides centralized management of recovery plans (see Figure 15-13).

SRM provides a simple integrated interface that is, once again, an extension of the capabilities of VMware Virtual Center (see Figure 15-14). This greatly simplifies the administration of the tool since you always work with the same interface.

SRM fully supports the datacenter replication model discussed earlier. Recovery or secondary sites do not need to have the same or identical resources as the production or primary site. For example, if your production site relies on a SAN using Fibre Channel and the very best high-speed drives, your recovery datacenter can easily run iSCSI on

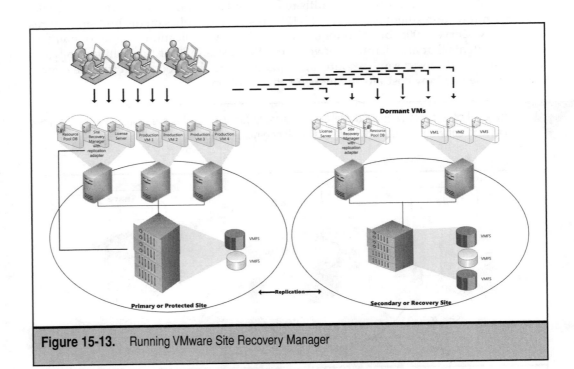

Figure 15-13. Running VMware Site Recovery Manager

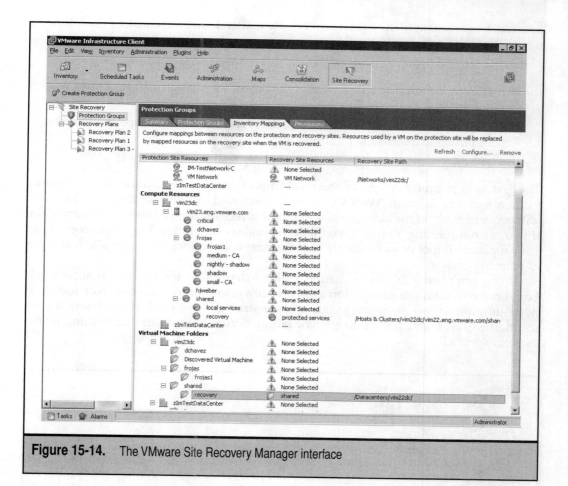

Figure 15-14. The VMware Site Recovery Manager interface

Serial ATA (SATA) drives. This means that the recovery site is much cheaper to put in place than the production site. Rely on the formula outlined earlier to determine just which kinds of technologies you will want to put in place in the recovery site.

NOTE For more information on VMware Site Recovery Manager, go to www.vmware.com/products/srm.

Choose the Proper Replication Tool

The replication tool you select must be able to fully understand the make-up of your virtual machines and virtualization engine to work properly. Several SAN-based replication tools are only capable of replication and nothing else. Since replication occurs at the byte level, the content of the data doesn't really matter. However, consider the following when you select your replication engine:

▼ The engine must be officially supported by the virtualization vendor.

■ The engine must be able to work with any of the storage infrastructures you put in place: DAS, NAS, or SAN.

■ The engine must support automatic failover of resources, properly redirecting end users to the remote location.

▲ The engine must support isolated recovery testing (see Figure 15-15).

The last item is probably one of the most important since replication alone does not make a recovery solution. With VMware, as discussed earlier, Site Recovery Manager will perform many of the key activities required to recover from a site-based disaster. But if you are not running VMware, you'll need similar capabilities. These will come from your replication tool or a combination of your replication tool and the built-in features of your hypervisor.

If you can't test a failover situation without disrupting your production network, you'll have to take the production network down to perform the test. Not testing is not a solution. If you do not test your failover strategies, you will never know if your solution works. Don't wait until a major failure occurs to find out that nothing works as you expected!

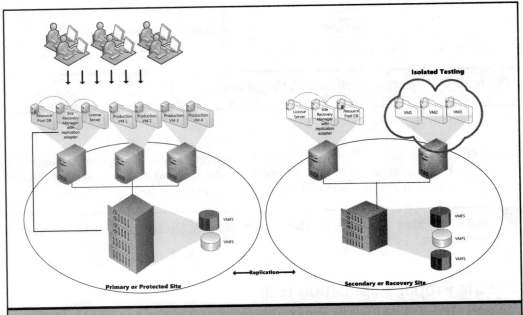

Figure 15-15.   Performing isolated recovery testing

Also, while previous physical networks relied on replication technologies to provide availability of a service, you no longer need to be concerned about this in a resource pool. For example, several replication vendors have made small fortunes protecting Microsoft Exchange through replication engines. In the past, you would implement a replication engine to ensure that should the Exchange server in one location go down, another duplicate Exchange server would spring back up elsewhere. With resource pools, you do not need to worry about this because if you replicate the VM running Exchange and the VM can be brought back up elsewhere, that's all you need. Don't replicate inside the VMs—only focus on replicating the resource pool contents and your solution will be adequate.

Finally, remember that replication is not a backup solution; it is a BCM solution. But if you have the proper BCM solution in place, it may act as an additional level of protection for virtual machine contents.

Prepare for Site-Based Disasters

When planning for your remote business continuity management site, keep the following items in mind. In BCM situations, you must:

- ▼ Begin with critical services first: domain controllers, DNS, DHCP
- ■ Then launch critical applications: business applications, e-mail services, and so on
- ▲ Run in reduced service level agreement mode—not all services are required in the BCM situation

Because of this, you can start with just enough hardware to get core VMs going and to keep your business running. If the BCM situation lasts longer, provision more host servers and launch additional virtual workloads. If you use integrated hypervisors, they will be easy to add to the BCM resource pool.

Use the following rule of thumb: Start with 25 percent of your production hardware capacity. Identify all of your critical applications. Assign a priority to each of these applications. Then run continuous tests to ensure that all critical applications will load with this BCM configuration. Adjust your configuration as necessary. Finally, make sure you document your BCM strategy completely and that all administrators and technicians are aware of it. Disasters don't only happen to machines; they happen to people as well. Making sure your entire team knows what to do in a disaster situation will go a long way towards protecting your bases when the worst happens.

CHAPTER 16

Update Your Management Structure

Last, but not least, you'll have to review your management practices. This means looking to new administrative and technical roles your staff will play in the resource pool infrastructure. It also means working with new policy-based workloads or workloads that dynamically boot up when required in support of business processes. Resource pool management will also force you to look at new ways to do things in branch offices. In addition, they will move you to create a new division of responsibilities between resource pools and production networks.

To make sure you have full control over the two infrastructures you run, you'll need to make sure you have the right management tools in place. Will you use the same tools for each infrastructure, or will you segregate the two? These questions will help you complete the reflection you must undertake to move to a completely virtual infrastructure.

LOOK TO NEW ADMINISTRATIVE ROLES

Managing two infrastructures, physical and virtual, changes the way IT needs to work within the datacenter. This is evident in the tools you use to manage your resource pool. For example, in VMware VirtualCenter, the Administration tab includes default resource pool roles (see Figure 16-1). While you don't need to rely on each of these roles, some additional roles are required. Table 16-1 outlines some of the new or changed roles you will find in a datacenter that virtualizes servers, desktops, and applications and maps them to the appropriate infrastructure.

The roles outlined in Table 16-1 cover both networks. For example, the server virtualization roles all reside in the resource pool only, but the desktop and application virtualization roles all reside within the productivity or virtual network.

Remember that these roles do not need to have a specific body attached to them. Larger organizations will probably have personnel to fill each role, but smaller and medium-sized organizations will probably rely on a few people to fill all of the roles. In the latter case, personnel will have to wear multiple hats to make sure everything gets done.

MOVE TO POLICY-BASED WORKLOADS

One of the biggest impacts virtualization has on IT operations is the ability to create policy-based workloads. In a virtual infrastructure, physical servers are nothing but resources that are pooled together to create a whole, much like the network infrastructure. Productivity service offerings—the offerings that interact with the users—are running in virtual machines only. Because these services are all offered at the virtual layer, they become much more malleable than ever before.

While no organization could afford to have multiple physical servers that just sit there waiting for a business need, every organization can afford to do this with virtual machines. Let's say you have a pressing need for temporary services in support of a seasonal business fluctuation. In yesterday's IT world, you would have to plan for this workload fluctuation well ahead of time to ensure you could run the additional services

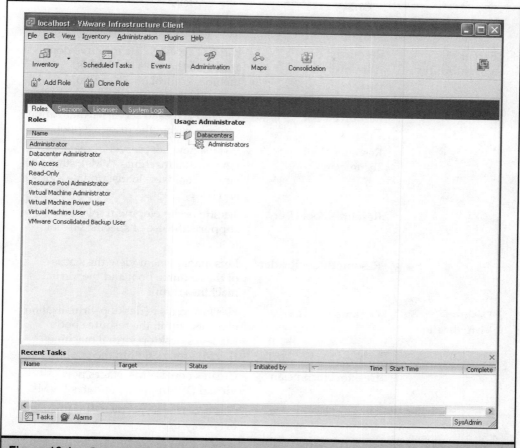

Figure 16-1. Default administrative roles within VMware VirtualCenter

you require for it. But today, you can simply create workloads on-the-fly, adding them to your infrastructure as needed—provided, of course, you have the required host servers to run them.

This ability to create machines when needed, run them, and then remove them is part of the automation that is required in the virtual datacenter. Each VM has a life cycle, as discussed in Chapter 9, and this life cycle includes steps that might not have been addressed or were not required in the past. Machines are created as needed and run on one host or another based on the policies and priorities you set for the machine. While it is much easier to create VMs on-the-fly, it is also easy to let them linger when not in use. Several VMs are often "at rest" waiting for someone to use them but still consuming space and resources. This is one reason why it is often better to create time-based machines that will automatically be returned to the VM pool when their purpose has been completed.

Virtualization Type	Role	Description
Server Virtualization	Resource Pool Administrator	Has full access to the resource pool and all of the tools it contains. Includes control of the desktop virtualization infrastructure as well.
	Resource Pool Operator	Has full access to server virtualization controls within the resource pool.
	Resource Pool Technician	Installs new host servers, creates new virtual machines (VMs), stages new virtual workloads, updates VMs and hosts.
	Resource Pool User	Testing or development role that supports the use of specific virtual machines.
	Resource Pool Reader	Lets management view the status of the resource pool and the virtual machines it runs.
Desktop Virtualization	Desktop Operator	Has full access to desktop virtualization controls within the resource pool. Manages desktop virtual machine (DVM) groups within the pool.
	Desktop Technician	Creates new DVMs, stages new virtual DVM images, updates DVMs.
	Desktop User	Has access to a specific DVM for everyday use.
Application Virtualization	Subject Matter Expert	Application owner that provides support for specific applications within the productivity network. Responsible for quality assurance of virtual application packages.
	Application Operator	Manages application allocation and access rights. Controls the streaming engine and manages the application repository.
	Application Packager	Prepares applications for virtualization through the use of the application virtualization (AppV) packaging tool.

Table 16-1. New IT Roles in Virtual Infrastructures

As you can see, policies are at the heart of the automation of processes within a virtual infrastructure. But you can take this one step further to create policies that affect host servers as much as virtual machines. In this scenario, Virtual Service Offerings (VSOs) are powered on and off on an as-needed basis, and resource pools are powered up based on VSO workloads (see Figure 16-2). For example, a payroll application only requires extensive resources when it runs the payroll payload. Depending on your pay schedule, this can be every two weeks or twice a month. For the rest of the time, the payroll machine is "at rest" and can be parked on a host server along with other virtual machines. In parked mode, the machine still runs, but does not draw upon extensive resources.

You can even extend this feature to all of your workloads. For example, a large datacenter can populate services as needed. There is no reason to run ten Exchange Servers at night when no one is using them. You can, however, run two of these machines at night and then set policies that wake up the others and their corresponding hosts when they are needed—for example, at peak times, such as early in the morning and after lunch.

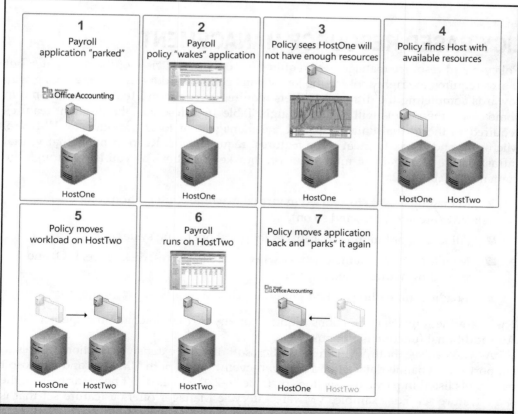

Figure 16-2.   Policy-based workloads at work

Running policy-based workloads changes the datacenter paradigm and provides even greater support for greening the datacenter. If host servers can be at rest and run only when required, it will have a positive impact on the datacenter's power and cooling bottom line. But to control this new dynamic datacenter, you must have the right toolset.

NOTE Vendor Cassatt already offers automated power efficiency software; see their power saving calculator at www.cassatt.com/tools/powersavecalc.php.

NOTE Microsoft has updated its Windows Server product licensing. Before, each license was tied to the physical server, that is, the host where the VM was running. Now, licenses are tied to a datacenter or a pool of host servers. This means that you can use policy-based workload management without having to worry about reassigning licenses each time a VM moves from one host to another.

POLICY-BASED RESOURCE MANAGEMENT

Policy-based resource management requires not only a new view of the datacenter, but it also requires the right tool for the job. Virtualization vendors have come a long way towards completing the different toolsets required to run the virtual datacenter, but in some cases, these tools will not be enough. Table 16-2 describes the different features required in the virtual datacenter and the management tools provided by VMware, Microsoft, and Citrix to meet these features' requirements. Keep in mind that virtual infrastructure management must focus on four key functions as you look through the contents of Table 16-2:

▼ Managing drivers to be used in virtual machines (integration components, VMware additions, and so on).

■ Allocating or building VM spaces for guest operating systems.

■ Monitoring VM characteristics (RAM, processor cores, disk space, I/O) and providing alarms when needed.

▲ Loading, unloading and backing up each VM.

These are the four basic functions required of any virtual machine management tool. Any additional function is a bonus.

As you can see, both VMware and Microsoft offer an extensive selection of tools to support the dynamic datacenter. However, even though both VMware and Microsoft have tools listed in particular sections of Table 16-2, the tools don't necessarily have the same feature set. For example, VMware Lifecycle Manager offers a feature set that is more comprehensive than Virtual Machine Manager when it comes to VM provisioning automation. Another example is with VMware's Distributed Power Management compared to Microsoft's Operation Manager when it comes to host power management.

Feature	VMware	Microsoft	Citrix
VM/Host Management	VirtualCenter	Hyper-V Console System Center (SC) Virtual Machine Manager	XenCenter
VM Provisioning	Lifecycle Manager	SC Virtual Machine Manager	XenCenter or third-party
VM Automation	Infrastructure Toolkit for Windows (PowerShell) VMware Infrastructure Perl Toolkit	Windows PowerShell (in Windows Server 2008)	Third-party
Live VM Migration	VMotion	Quick Migration Live Migration to come in WS08 R2	XenMotion
Site-Level High Availability: VMs	High Availability	Failover Clustering	Resource Pool
Site-Level High Availability: Storage	Storage VMotion	Windows Server Simple SAN	Third-party
Backup	Consolidated Backup	Windows Server Backup SC Data Protection Manager Volume Shadow Copy	Third-party
VM Placement Management	Distributed Resource Scheduler	SC Operations Manager with SC Virtual Machine Manager	XenCenter
Security	VMsafe	Windows Server Integration	XenAccess (in development)
Patching and Updates	Update Manager	Window Server Update Services SC Configuration Manager	XenCenter for hosts Windows Server Update Services (WSUS) for VMs
Host Power Management	Distributed Power Management	SC Operations Manager at host level	Third-party
Wide Area Network (WAN) business continuity management (BCM)	Site Recovery Manager	Failover Clustering Geoclusters	Third-party

Table 16-2.   Recommended Functions for Virtualization Management

Another major difference is that VMware offers its entire toolset within VirtualCenter, adding functionality as you move forward with additional features. VirtualCenter supports seven different key functions—basic virtual machine and host management, provisioning, migration, resource management, system monitoring, security, and access control—and also provides an application programming interface (API) for third-party integration with the tool (see Figure 16-3).

To facilitate the acquisition of all of the tools you require to maintain the dynamic VMware datacenter, VMware offers two software bundles along with the Virtual Infrastructure editions. The VMware IT Service Delivery bundle includes VMware Lifecycle Manager, Lab Manager, and Stage Manager, letting you control VM life cycles through automated policies. The VMware Management and Automation bundle includes everything from the previous bundle as well as Site Recovery Manager.

Citrix's XenCenter is similar to VirtualCenter in that it provides a single interface for operation and management of the resources for both hosts and virtual machines (see Figure 16-4). Host servers can be managed individually, as with the Express and Standard Editions, or through resource pools with the more advanced editions. The interface provides all basic management functionality in one tool.

Microsoft's toolset relies mostly on System Center tools, which all have the same look and feel, but which are all separate tools. However, for single machine and pool management, Microsoft relies on the Hyper-V Manager, which is available either as a

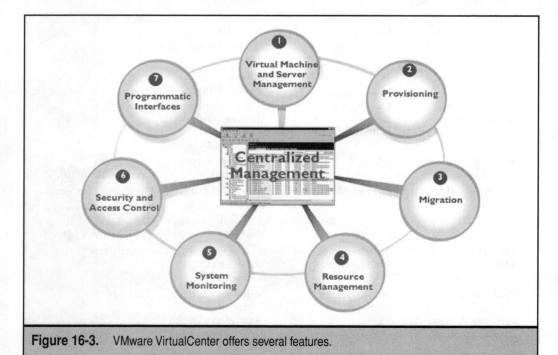

Figure 16-3. VMware VirtualCenter offers several features.

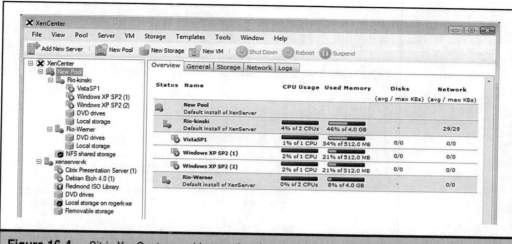

Figure 16-4. Citrix XenCenter provides one interface for XenServer management.

stand-alone tool (see Figure 16-5) or as an add-in to the Windows Server 2008 Server Manager (see Figure 16-6). The latter is often preferable if you do not have access to System Center tools because it brings together all of the server management features in one single interface. Note, however, that Server Manager cannot be installed on a workstation because it is an integral part of Windows Server. Because of this, many organizations tend to install Terminal Services in application mode on their servers and use it to publish Server Manager as a remote application through the Terminal Services RemoteApp feature. This gives administrators the same experience as with a locally installed tool.

Server Manager cannot manage remote machines and can, therefore, only be used on full installations of Windows Server 2008 (WS08). If you install the Hyper-V role on Server Core—as you should to reduce host operation overhead—you will not be able to rely on Server Manager and will have to fall back on the individual interfaces for Failover Cluster and Hyper-V management. Both of these are available through the Remote Server Administration Tools (RSAT), which are available for both x86 and x64 versions of Windows. RSAT can be installed only on Windows Server 2008 or Windows Vista with Service Pack 1.

NOTE RSAT for x86 can be found at www.microsoft.com/downloads/details.aspx?FamilyID= 9ff6e897-23ce-4a36-b7fc-d52065de9960&displaylang=en and RSAT for x64 can be found at www .microsoft.com/downloads/details.aspx?FamilyId=D647A60B-63FD-4AC5-9243-BD3C497D2BC5& displaylang=en. Both are documented in Microsoft Knowledge Base article number 941314. Validation of Genuine Windows is required to obtain the download.

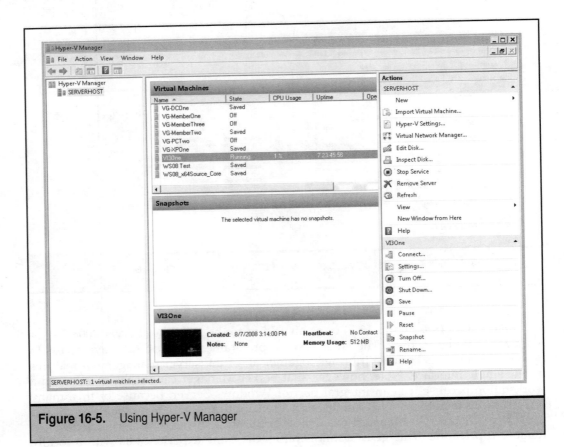

Figure 16-5. Using Hyper-V Manager

But when you run virtual infrastructures, everything but the simplest infrastructures requires the base functions found in VMware's VirtualCenter. In order to achieve this level of functionality, you need Microsoft's System Center tools. Smaller shops can rely on System Center Essentials along with System Center Virtual Machine Manager (SCVMM) Workgroup Edition. Workgroup Edition supports up to five host servers.

Larger shops require the entire System Center toolkit, which is available through a special bundle—the Server Management Suite Enterprise (SMSE)—which includes four tools:

▼ System Center Configuration Manager (formerly Systems Management Server), which can provision machines, either hosts or VMs, as well as manage their configuration and maintain configuration compliance.

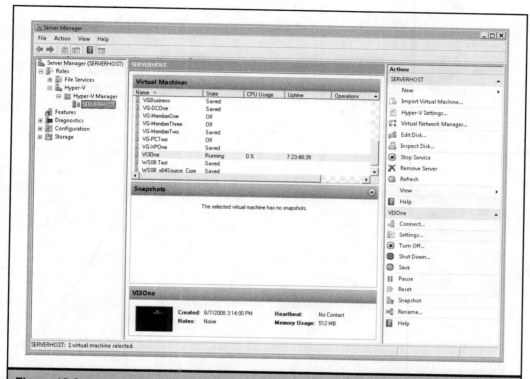

Figure 16-6. Using WS08 Server Manager to manage Hyper-V

- System Center Operations Manager (SCOM), possibly Microsoft's best tool, is designed to monitor the health and performance of host servers, VMs, and the applications within the VMs. SCOM relies on management packs to support any server workload or application. Third-party vendors such as nWorks (www.nworks.com) even offer management packs for VMware ESX Server, letting you manage mixed environments through one single tool.

- System Center Data Protection Manager, which is a continuous protection tool that can be used to centralize all backup and recovery operations.

▲ System Center Virtual Machine Manager, which manages host and VM operations.

This bundle simplifies management, and while each of the tools offers the same interface (see Figure 16-7), they are separate and independent tools.

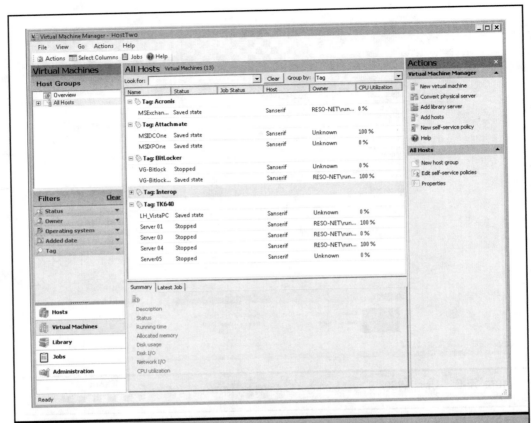

Figure 16-7. System Center tools such as Virtual Machine Manager all rely on the same interface.

LOOK TO THIRD-PARTY MANAGEMENT TOOLS

While each vendor offers powerful management tools for their hypervisors, and some will even manage their competitors' hypervisors, you might find that some features and functions are simply not covered by this toolset and that third-party tools are required. Table 16-3 provides a sample list of some of the most innovative third-party tools to date. Others will surely follow in their footsteps as virtualization becomes mainstream.

As you can see, third-party tools try to address needs that have not been addressed by the big three yet. VM optimization, multivendor life cycle management, host server provisioning, and, especially, control over virtual machine sprawl are all functions you will eventually need in your environment. For these reasons, obtaining a third-party tool might be the best strategy for many.

Vendor Product	Description
Akorri (www.akorri.com)	BalancePoint: Agentless tool focused on system monitoring, utilization optimization, and performance improvements of hosts and VMs. Supports Citrix, Microsoft, and VMware.
CiRBA (www.cirba.com)	Data Center Intelligence: Policy-based management tool that dynamically reassigns VM workloads in the datacenter. Excellent virtualization assessment tool. Constantly captures and analyzes technical, business, and resource constraints to manage workloads and ensure they have the appropriate resources available.
DynamicOps for Citrix, Microsoft, VMware, and Solaris (www.dynamicops.com)	Virtual Resource Manager: Life cycle management tool that includes a self-service portal, controls VMs through policies, tracks resource usage, and provides extensive reporting. Supports scalability through federation. Supports multivendor virtualization deployments for Citrix, Microsoft, and VMware.
Embotics (www.embotics.com)	V-Commander: Policy-based VM management product. Supports full automation of VM life cycles. Supports multivendor virtualization environments running Citrix, Microsoft, or VMware.
	V-Scout: *Free* agentless tool that links with up to two VMware VirtualCenter servers to provide VM information in real time.
Fortisphere (www.fortisphere.com)	Virtual Essentials: A suite of policy-based virtualization management solutions that provides visibility, control, and automation around the inventory, configuration, and policy-based management of virtual machines.
	Virtual Insight: An operational management product that enables enterprises to automate the process of identifying, tagging, tracking, and reporting on all virtual machines as they move throughout preproduction and production environments. Provides vision into all virtual machines, centralized or distributed.

Table 16-3.   Sample Third-Party Management Tools

Vendor Product	Description
	Virtual Foresight: A policy-based management product that delivers out-of-the box best practices for enforcing operational and IT security policies in virtual environments. It ensures policy enforcement throughout the life cycle of a virtual machine, regardless of location or state.
Scalent (www.scalent.com)	Virtualization: Acts as the pre-boot environment for hypervisors, taking physical machines from a dead, bare-metal, powered-off state to installed, operating, connected VMware ESX or Xen. Focused on host server repurposing.
VEEAM (www.veeam.com)	Backup: A backup and data replication tool that is designed to protect VMs in VMware ESX.
	Reporter Enterprise: A data collection and reporting tool for entire VMware infrastructures.
	Monitor: A monitoring, capacity planning, and troubleshooting tool for VMware infrastructure management.
Vizioncore (www.vizioncore.com)	vRanger Pro: A backup and recovery solution for virtualized environments. Can schedule regular image-level backups of virtual or physical machines while the machine is still running. Supports VMware.
	vConverter: Physical-to-virtual (P2V) engine that uses a cloning method executed at the block level as opposed to the file level. Can create images of both physical and virtual machines that can be sent and archived at a remote site. Can add on a P2V-DR module that can extend the disaster recovery strategy to cover the physical machines.
	vReplicator: Host-level software-based replication solution for VMware infrastructure to leverage virtualization to support High Availability (HA) and BCM strategies.
	vCharter Pro: Monitoring tool that provides a single view into multiple layers of virtual environments.

Table 16-3. Sample Third-Party Management Tools (*continued*)

Vendor Product	Description
	vOptimizer: An optimization solution that reduces a virtual machine's virtual hard drive to the smallest size possible while optimizing Windows guest operating system for speed and performance. Comes in two editions: Desktop and Network.
	vEssentials: Management bundle for VMware Infrastructure that includes vRanger Pro, vReplicator, and vCharter Pro.
	VDR for SMB: Bundles VMware Virtual Infrastructure Starter Edition with vEssentials. Provides complete BCM for small to medium businesses.

Table 16-3. Sample Third-Party Management Tools (*continued*)

UPDATE YOUR MANAGEMENT PRACTICES

Virtual machine management and resource pool administration bring many changes to the modern datacenter. Because of this, you need to update your management practices. In small shops, IT personnel will have to learn to wear new hats and be especially careful not to traverse security boundaries when they perform their activities. In larger shops, you'll want to create specific positions for resource pool versus Virtual Service Offering management and keep them separated.

The ideal dynamic datacenter is one where resource pools are bundled resources that are only available for hosting services. Virtual machines offer all other services as much as possible. This duality is now a fact and is the way datacenters will run and operate moving forward. Make sure you carefully examine your current practices and be prepared to update them as you transform your datacenter into a dynamic environment.

Afterword

Y ou now have a good understanding of how virtualization can transform your datacenter. Now you need to look at your adoption path. According to IDC, organizations that have made the move most often use a three-tiered approach (see Figure 1). First, they focus on capital expenditures and aim for physical consolidation. Next, they move to operational changes and focus on the implementation of high availability and disaster recovery. Finally, they begin to view the strategic advantages virtualization offers and truly begin to transform their datacenters into the dynamic systems they should be.

Begin with your short-term needs. Most often, organizations have problematic applications that can immediately profit from being virtualized. Then, once your infrastructure is stable, look to the long term. You should aim for 100 percent virtualization, but keep the following caveats in mind:

▼ Virtualize applications unless the application owner or vendor can provide a cost justification for not doing so.

■ Aim for 60 to 70 percent utilization ratios on your host servers.

■ Keep host server farms or resource pools to a maximum of eight servers or fewer to maintain manageability. VMware supports 32 machines in a farm, while Microsoft Hyper-V and Citrix XenServer will support 16. However, creating farms with the maximum number of nodes tends to make them unwieldy.

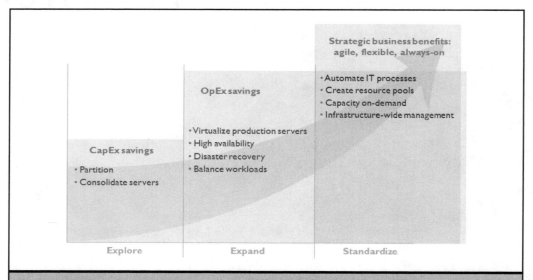

Figure 1. Potential adoption paths (Source: IDC, *Virtualization 2.0: The Next Phase in Customer Adoption*, Nov. 2006)

■ Design for Virtual Service Offering high availability. You want to ensure your machines, at least the machines that offer production services, are available at all times.

■ Match processor types in each server farm to support live migration capabilities, and start a new server farm each time a processor type changes. Though this is changing, it is still a good practice for now.

■ Make sure you perform cost accounting for each virtual machine (VM) running on a host—it's easy to lose track of VM costs because they are so easy to create and deploy.

▲ Use a specific VM allocation process, both administrative and technical, to ensure that only required VMs make it into your network.

These practices are good strategies. Keep them in mind as you move forward with your project.

CALCULATE YOUR RETURN ON INVESTMENT

Finally, you'll want to perform a project post-mortem in which you will calculate your return on investment (ROI). You'll find that hard dollars are easy to come up with, but the soft dollars are much harder to locate. Keep the following questions in mind when calculating your ROI:

▼ How much do you value the time you save in preparing a virtual versus a physical server?

■ How much do you value the preparation of standard testing and development environments?

■ How much do you value the flexibility a virtual infrastructure gives you to meet changing business needs?

▲ How much do you value the reduced time to market for all of your core applications?

Time is money, but it is hard to quantify. Table 1 outlines some of the potential cost savings you will benefit from when you move to virtualization.

Virtualization will also change the metrics in your IT department (see Figure 2). You can reduce capital expenditures by up to 50 percent. Response times will decrease, sometimes by up to 90 percent. Operating expenses, especially power and cooling costs, will be greatly reduced. And recovery times will also benefit from this move.

This is only the beginning. By the time you move to a virtual infrastructure, dozens of new firms will have appeared and hundreds of new products will be available. The future is now, and in terms of IT, it means virtualization of everything that moves in the datacenter.

Category	Potential Savings
Power savings	$300 to $600 per virtualized server
Cooling savings	Up to $400 per virtualized server
Hardware savings	From $2,500 to $$$ per virtualized server
License savings (Microsoft)	75 percent of Enterprise license per virtualized server
License savings (open-source)	Nil, except for support costs
Processor power savings when using AMD	Between 15 to 65 percent per processor
Power rebates (selected utility firms)	Up to 50 percent total cost of the project
Government rebates (federal, provincial, and state)	Variable reduction rates (income tax, rebates, and more)
Space savings	90-plus percent space reduction (based on an average of ten VMs per physical host)

Table 1.   Potential and Real Cost Savings

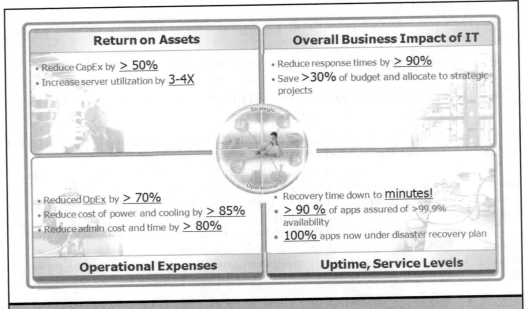

Figure 2.   Potential returns from virtualization

INDEX

B

C

E

F

G

H

S

T

W

X